Also by Jeffrey Alford and Naomi Duguid

Seductions of Rice: A Cookbook

Flatbreads and Flavors: A Baker's Atlas

HOT SOUR SALTY SWEET

HOT SOUR SALTY SWEET

A Culinary Journey Through Southeast Asia

Jeffrey Alford and Naomi Duguid

Studio photographs by Richard Jung
Location photographs by Jeffrey Alford and Naomi Duguid

ARTISAN
NEW YORK

Food styling by Sandra Cook
Prop styling by Sara Slavin

Published by Artisan
A Division of Workman Publishing, Inc.
708 Broadway
New York, New York 10003
www.workman.com

Library of Congress Cataloging-in-Publication Data
Alford, Jeffrey.
Hot, sour, salty, sweet : a culinary journey through Southeast Asia /
Jeffrey Alford & Naomi Duguid.
p. cm.
ISBN 1-57965-114-3
1. Cookery, Southeast Asian. 2. Mekong River Region.
I. Duguid, Naomi. II. Title.
TX724.4S68 A44 2000
641.5'0959—dc21 00-022092

Printed at Arnoldo Mondadori Editore, Verona, Italy

10 9 8 7 6 5 4 3 2 1

Book Design by Level

To Dom and Tashi, with love and thanks for being such great traveling companions

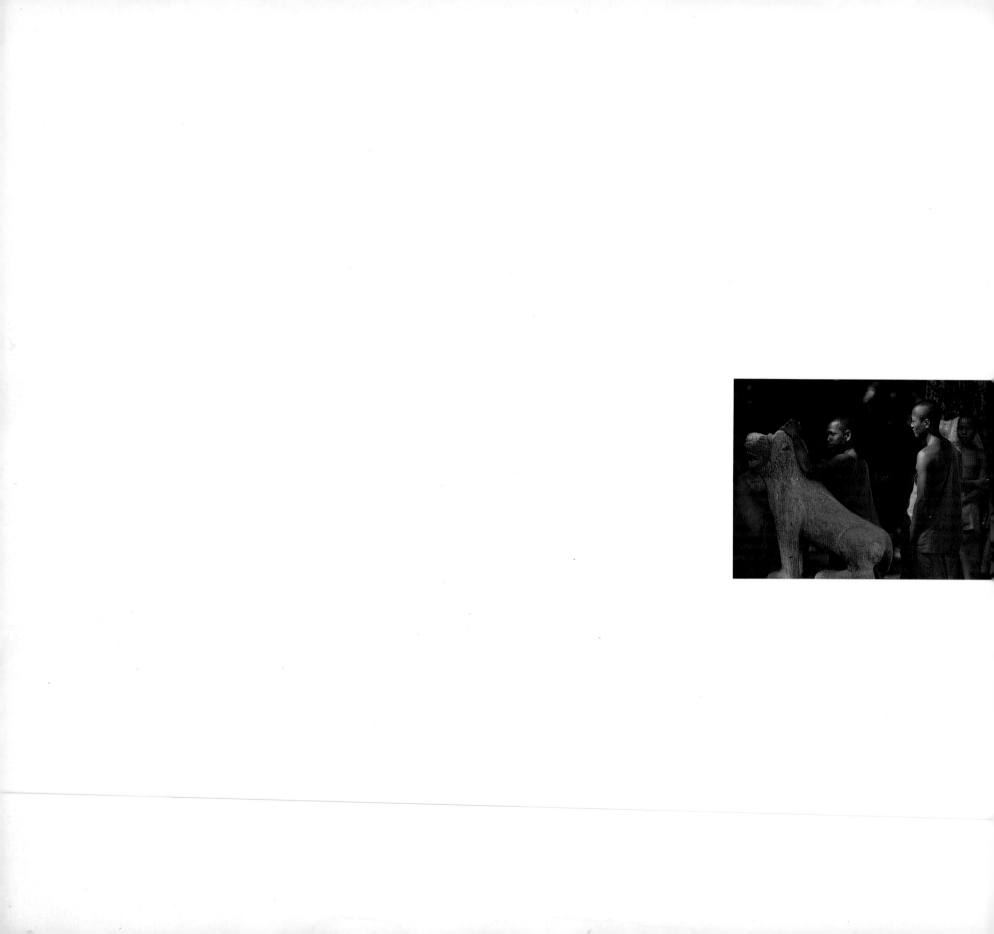

PREFACE: We first started traveling (and eating) in Southeast Asia years ago, in the seventies. For a long time, because of the war in Vietnam and changes brought about by the war, we could travel only in Thailand and for short stays in Burma. In the mid-1980s, travel restrictions in China loosened up, and parts of China's Yunnan Province became open to outsiders. In the late 1980s, restrictions on travel to Laos, Vietnam, and Cambodia also loosened; we first went to Laos in 1989, and to Vietnam a few months later. By the mid-1990s, we were able to travel by land from mountainous northern Vietnam into China, and from China into remote northern Laos, crossing land borders that had been closed to outsiders for decades.

The more we traveled, the more we became aware of close relationships within the region in terms of food and culture. Our culinary map of Southeast Asia slowly changed, no longer grouping Thailand together with Malaysia and Indonesia, as is traditionally done, but seeing it as a close cousin to parts of southwest China (Yunnan) and to the Shan State in Burma, as well as to Laos, Cambodia, and Vietnam. Just as we think of the Mediterranean as having a common palate, we began to see mainland Southeast Asia in the same way. That uniquely wonderful food, the food we'd originally been introduced to in Thailand, we came to realize, was unique to an entire region, not to just one country.

In 1997, confident that Southeast Asia would continue to open its doors, we eagerly began work on this cookbook. Our goal was to eat our way from village to village, town to town, sometimes returning to places where we'd been before, sometimes crossing borders into regions new to us. Would there, we wondered, be fish sauce in southern Yunnan? Would cooks in Cambodia brown their garlic the way Thais do, and would they rub grilled meats with black pepper and ground coriander root? If there were indeed a shared palate throughout the region, what would be its essential characteristics? In the Mediterranean, there is a common approach to food, but Moroccan and Greek are hardly close cousins. In mainland Southeast Asia, what would be the similarities among the cuisines, and the differences?

When we first began, eating and traveling, taking photographs, we felt as if we were working on a giant jigsaw puzzle, tracking ingredients, methods, dishes, names, and so on. But as time went by, we found ourselves gravitating toward the Mekong river, as if the river were a well-worn trail through the forest. The Mekong (Mae Khong, or River Khong, in Thai) flows south through China from its source in Tibet, draws the border between Burma and Laos, and then between Laos and Thailand. It flows on down through Cambodia before reaching its massive delta in the southern part of Vietnam. Along the way, tributaries flow into it, swelling it with water from distant hills.

The Mekong watershed doesn't define the food and cooking of Southeast Asia, but, like the Mediterranean Sea, the Mekong and its tributaries are an integral part of the region's food. They carry and deposit fertile soil for dry-season gardens. They irrigate rice fields and support an abundant fish and plant life. They help transport goods and people, and at times are the only roads around. And in the heat of the day, the river is always there for a cool swim. . . .

The Mekong became our thread, our compass. Whenever possible, we tried to travel down the river, from Huay Xai in Laos to Luang Prabang, from Cantho to Tra Vinh, getting lost in the massive Delta's tangle of waterways. When river travel wasn't possible, we took small nearby roads. Always we searched for key locations along the river to settle into, places that had been important historically, or places simply too beautiful, or too interesting, to pass by.

And just as the river became our road, village life became our point of reference. Traveling in Southeast Asia, we have always been happier eating in small towns and villages than in big cities. It seems that it should be the opposite, because in the city there is so much more food to choose from, and so many more ingredients for cooks to cook with. Bangkok, Ho Chi Minh City, and Kunming are all incredible places to eat, places where we have enjoyed some of the best meals we've ever had. But give us a choice, and we will almost always choose to eat, and to spend time, in smaller towns and villages.

Perhaps it is because we are foreigners and have so much to learn. In a village, we can see how rice grows and how it is harvested. We can watch as noodles are made by hand, first by pounding soaked rice into a paste, then by pushing the paste through a sieve into boiling water. We can observe how a household fish pond works, and how river fish are fermented to make *padek* and *prahok*. A family pig is fattened with scraps and leftovers from the kitchen, paper-thin slices of beef are set out in the hot sun to dry, and cracklings are made from scratch in a huge wok full of hot oil, set over a charcoal fire in the backyard. In villages we feel we see the foundations of the cuisine, the building blocks. They are more visible, more accessible.

It is also true that our home is in Toronto, a big North American city, and for us, time spent in rural areas in Southeast Asia is very different from our life in the city. The pace of life, the sounds and smells, the daily rhythms, the night sky, the sense of scale: Everything is different. Whenever we settle into a small town or village having come directly from home, it takes us time to find our feet, to get acclimated, to adjust our expectations for what each individual day will bring. Time genuinely slows down, and it affects everything. It affects our feelings about the food we eat, and how the food tastes.

So, our initial goal of eating our way through Southeast Asia evolved into the somewhat specific goal of exploring the food of the Mekong region by eating our way along the river, from Yunnan to Vietnam. Like students in a life drawing course, instead of drawing the entire model, we found ourselves drawing only an arm, an elbow, a hand.

Hot, Sour, Salty, Sweet: A Culinary Journey Through Southeast Asia is, as a result, a cookbook, a photo essay, a journey down a river, and an introduction to one of the world's great culinary regions. It is also, because so much of the research and travel and recipe work was done with our two sons, Dominic and Tashi, a family tale, a diary. Food and life, we rationalize to ourselves, reflect forever in each other.

OVERLEAF: VIETNAMESE GREEN PAPAYA SALAD *(page 75) and* QUICK AND TASTY YUNNANESE POTATOES *(page 162).*

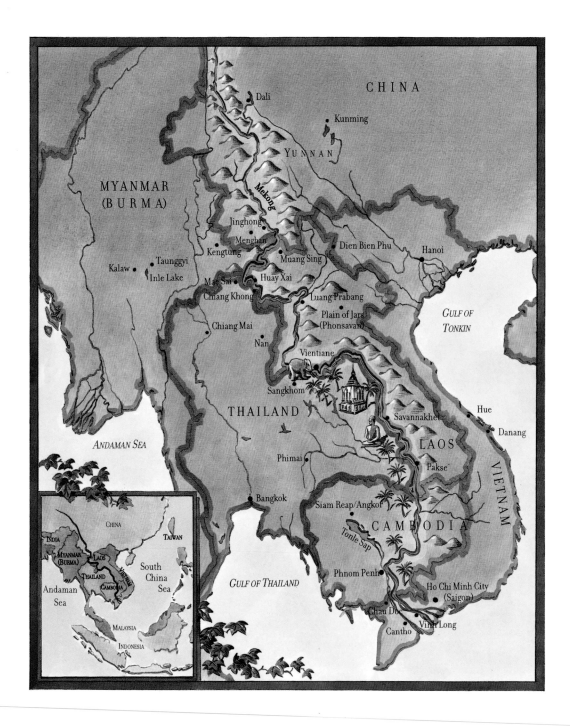

THE RIVER: The Mekong river begins as a tiny thread up on the Tibetan plateau (maps don't always agree about exactly where it rises) and then starts heading south. About fifty miles away, on either side, lie two other major Asian rivers—the Yangtze to the east and the Salween to the west—each separated from the Mekong by a steep ridge of mountains, as if a giant's fingers had raked furrows in the hard rock for the rivers to follow. If you follow the course of the Yangtze, suddenly in northern Yunnan it makes a sharp bend, a huge bend, changes its mind it seems, and heads eastward, toward the South China Sea.

The Mekong and Salween keep heading south, rushing through their gorges toward Southeast Asia, flowing past tangled bamboo and dense jungle. They rise with the snow melt and the monsoon rains, then fall during dry season (November to April), leaving wide steep banks of sand and clay. The Salween soon heads into northern Burma; the Mekong continues to cut south through Yunnan, all the way to its southern tip. There the river valley is wider; there are villages up some of the side valleys, the surrounding hills are less craggy, and the climate is semitropical. The hills are terraced, growing rice and soybeans, tea farther up, and, near the high ridges, corn and root vegetables. On and over the ridges of hills that border the river live mostly tribal peoples: Shan, Akha, Wa, Mien, Hmong.

As the Mekong leaves China, the right bank of the river is Burma (the Shan State), and soon the left bank is Laos. In colonial times, this was also the border between the British and French colonial empires. Another hundred and twenty miles, and the river reaches the Golden Triangle near the ancient Thai town of Chiang Saen, where Burma, Laos, and Thailand meet. Nearby, the Kok River flows in from northern Thailand, bringing news of Chiang Rai and Tathon. There's some river traffic on this stretch: A small boat full of fragrant apples from China is checked by Thai customs officials before being unloaded; little ferryboats take locals and tourists back and forth between Thailand and Laos; and cargo traffic from Huai Xai (Laos) heads down the river to central Laos.

For a short distance south of the Golden Triangle, the right bank is Thailand and the left Laos, but soon the river turns sharply east, leaving Thailand, and becomes wholly Lao. The Mekong is the central artery of Laos. It flows east through the forested mountains and grows as it's joined by the Nam Ou and Nam Beng rivers flowing in from the north. At last it reaches the royal capital, Luang Prabang, with its gold-spired temples, then turns due south again. By now the river is wide, navigable by flat-bottomed cargo boats except in the driest part of the dry season.

About a hundred and fifty miles south of Luang Prabang, it again turns hard left, east, and once more its right bank is Thailand. Here the landscape is scrubby and sometimes bone-dry, for Issaan ("northeast Thailand") has poorer soil and less reliable rains than the north. On the left bank lies Vientiane, the capital of Laos and another of the historic city-kingdoms, along with Chiang Mai, Chiang Saen, Luang Prabang, Nan, Phayao, Chiang Rai, and Xieng Khuang, that once shared control of the central Mekong region. On either side of the river, children swim in the shallows, while women rinse off vegetables, fishermen tend their small wooden craft or mend nets, and, up on the sloping riverbanks, rows of leafy vegetables are carefully watered by hand every morning and evening. Another sixty miles east, and the river curves in a large bend to the right, south, heading past That Panom in Thailand and the Lao towns of Tha Khaek, Savannakhet, and, finally, Pakse, with its nearby Khmer ruins of Wat Phu. Then it takes a sharp jog east, away from Thailand. Soon after dropping over the Kone Falls, the river leaves Laos for Cambodia.

By now it's very wide, especially in rainy season, home to fresh-water dolphins, as well as many fish. In flood, it deposits the silt that makes Khmer rice fields productive, and it flows up into the Tonle Sap, the large fish-laden lake near the ruins of Angkor Wat. The Mekong is sluggish here, the landscape fairly flat, so the temples and the golden palace roof by the river in Phnom Penh are visible from far away. There's the occasional steep-sided hill standing out from the flat alluvial landscape.

After Phnom Penh, it's just a short distance through fertile farmland to the border with Vietnam. Here, for the first time, there's a lot of life on and near the river, with towns like Chau Doc, Cantho, Sadec, Tra Vinh, and Vinh Long. But the Mekong is no longer a single river; it has split into two giant branches, each of them full-river–sized, that slowly flow, swollen with water and silt, through the rich, level lands of the Delta. Thousands of tiny channels and canals and water byways criss-cross the Delta and it's easy to be lost, for the flow of water is imperceptible—no way is clearly "downstream." You have to ask a passing boatman, or pull over to a house and ask directions. There are fruit trees and mangrove swamps, slender arched footbridges over small canals, Khmer Buddhist temples and Cham mosques, Catholic churches, and Vietnamese and Chinese Buddhist temples, and wooden houses on stilts, and houseboats, and small boats that are home to whole families, and floating fish farms. Everywhere there are boats moving through the water: huge oceangoing cargo ships and tiny craft each rowed by a single man or woman standing up, big old ferryboats, and long narrow boats with powerful noisy motors transporting goods and people up and down and across the waterways.

Finally, near the sea, the land is less fertile, and the mosquitoes larger. Here the river has split into many more branches; it's known as the River of the Nine Dragons, Song Cuu Long, all of them flowing into the sea. Here cargo ships and fishing boats head out onto the open ocean. From here, for many years, boatloads of refugees set out to chance their luck as they fled war, political uncertainty, and economic hardship. The silt in the river water stains the ocean as they meet, soil from Tibet, from Sichuan and Yunnan provinces, from the Shan State, Laos, Thailand, Cambodia, and Vietnam.

LEFT: *Starting in early spring in Yunnan, tea leaves are picked by hand from the bushes that grow in rows like a series of tidily trimmed hedges.* RIGHT: *Boats become market stalls at the many floating markets in the Mekong region.*

THE PEOPLE: The people of Southeast Asia, like their food, are a complicated mix. Southeast Asia is one of the oldest inhabited regions in the world, and over a very long time, a great many different peoples have settled, conquered, and trickled into the region.

In Yunnan Province in China, the majority population is **Han Chinese**, though over a third of the total population is made up of people who are referred to in China as "minority peoples." Officially, the Chinese government recognizes twenty-four different minority populations living in Yunnan Province; anthropologists say there are many more. These peoples—among them, the **Dai, Akha, Hmong, Lahu, Lisu,** and **Bai**—are an important part of the history and social fabric of the province, and of Southeast Asia in general. Groups of many of them have moved south into Burma, Laos, Thailand, and Vietnam, establishing villages both in river valleys and in the hills. There is also a significant Chinese Muslim population in Yunnan, the **Hui**, who are descendants of the powerful armies of Kublai Khan that swept through the province in 1253.

In Laos, in the Shan State, and in Thailand, one very large group stands out, and that is the **Tai** (sometimes referred to as **Tai-Lao**). The Tai were originally river valley people, rice cultivators (organized rice cultivation in the region perhaps began with the Tai), with strong and complex social and political structures. As a people, they may have originated in southern China or northern Vietnam. At some point in prehistory, groups of Tai moved into many parts of Southeast Asia, particularly along river valleys. Over time, as they moved into present-day Laos and Thailand, the Tai displaced and assimilated the previous peoples, the Mon-Khmer, who had hunted and farmed in the hills and valleys. The Tai established *meuang*, or agricultural townships. Some of these *meuang*, such as Chiang Mai, Luang Prabang, and Kengtung, became powerful principalities or kingdoms, like city-states.

Today, different branches of the Tai ethnographic family are found from the Red River Valley in northern Vietnam to the Brahmaputra Valley in northern Assam, along river valleys in Yunnan and Guangxi provinces in China, in Laos, and throughout northern, northeastern, and central Thailand. They include the **Lao** of Laos and northeast Thailand, the **Shan** (also known as **Tai Yai**, or greater Tai), the **Tai Koen** (whose capital Kengtung lies in the Shan State), the **Tai Lu** of southern Yunnan (known also as **Dai**), the **Thai** of central Thailand, the **Tai Yuan** of the Chiang Mai region, the **Phuan** in Xieng Khuang in eastern Laos, the **Tai Dam** (black Tai), who originated around Dien Bien Phu in Vietnam, and more.

All these groups speak different but related languages. Some use fish sauce, others salt. Some eat mostly jasmine rice; others, sticky rice. Most are Hinayana Buddhists, with a strong underpinning of animism, a belief in river and tree spirits. Their cultural similarities give the different cuisines in the region a strong underlying coherence.

The **Khmer** were one of the original or early peoples in Southeast Asia. They came into the region more than two thousand years ago, before the arrival of the Tai-Lao. The Khmer lived in the hills and river valleys along the Mekong and its tributaries, from the southern part of present-day Laos to the area around present-day Phnom Penh and downstream along the Mekong to the Delta, as well as west into present-day Thailand.

By the ninth century, the Khmer city-states in the region had taken shape as a Khmer kingdom known as Kambujadesa, the origin of both "Cambodia" and "Kampuchea." It was centered at Angkor Wat, to the north of the Tonle Sap (Great Lake). Khmer civilization was complex and quite Indian-influenced: Khmer written and spoken language drew on Sanskrit and Pali, and the Khmer were first Hindu, then later Buddhist.

Over the following five centuries, the Khmer built cities and temples, both Hindu and Buddhist, throughout the region, from western Thailand to southern Vietnam. The ruins of an impressive Khmer city, Meuang Singh (Lion City), still stand near Kanchanaburi in western Thailand. Other Khmer ruins in the region date from the tenth to the thirteenth century, from Wat Phu in southern Laos to Phi Mai in northeast Thailand (Issaan) to the extraordinary remains at Angkor Wat and elsewhere in Cambodia. The Khmer also controlled all of what is now southern Vietnam, from Ho Chi Minh City south to the Delta, from the ninth to the seventeenth century, when they formally ceded it to the Vietnamese.

In the Mekong Delta, the Vietnamese are the majority population, but there are also large numbers of **Khmer** and **Cham**. The former are the descendants of the Khmer, for centuries the dominant population in the area, though some are more recent arrivals, fleeing the political instability and economic uncertainties of neighboring Cambodia. There are still very active Khmer temples in many towns in the Delta. The **Cham** are the Muslim descendants of the Indo-Malay people of Champa, the wealthy trading empire in the center of Vietnam, that was defeated by the Vietnamese in the fifteenth century. Cham people settled on both sides of the present Vietnamese-Cambodian border and also in the Cambodian province of Kampong Cham. Their villages are very distinctive, each built around a mosque, and alive with small herds of sheep and goats rather than the pigs found in non-Muslim villages.

The **Vietnamese** people originated in what is now northern Vietnam. They were ruled for almost a thousand years (until 938 of the modern era) by the Chinese, then became a tributary state of China. In the thirteenth century, the Vietnamese twice repelled invading Mongols led by Kublai Khan. In 1428, Le Loi, celebrated as a Vietnamese national hero, defeated the Chinese for the last time. He also defeated the Champa Empire, opening the way for Vietnamese expansion south. By 1802, with some help from the French, the Vietnamese controlled all of present-day Vietnam, which the Nguyen kings ruled from their capital in Hue.

The Vietnamese were historically Mahayana Buddhists, like the Chinese. Other religions also have large numbers of followers here, including Christianity (brought in by foreign missionaries over the centuries) and Cao Dai, a Vietnamese religion founded in the 1800s that is a distinctive synthesis of a number of religious systems.

Vietnamese culture and culinary influence in Southeast Asia extend beyond the borders of Vietnam. Because Vietnam was part of the colonial French empire and then a major player in the post-colonial wars in the region, from 1949 to 1975, there are sizeable Vietnamese communities in Cambodia, Laos, and northeast Thailand.

Vietnamese   *Shan*   *Hmong*   *Karen*

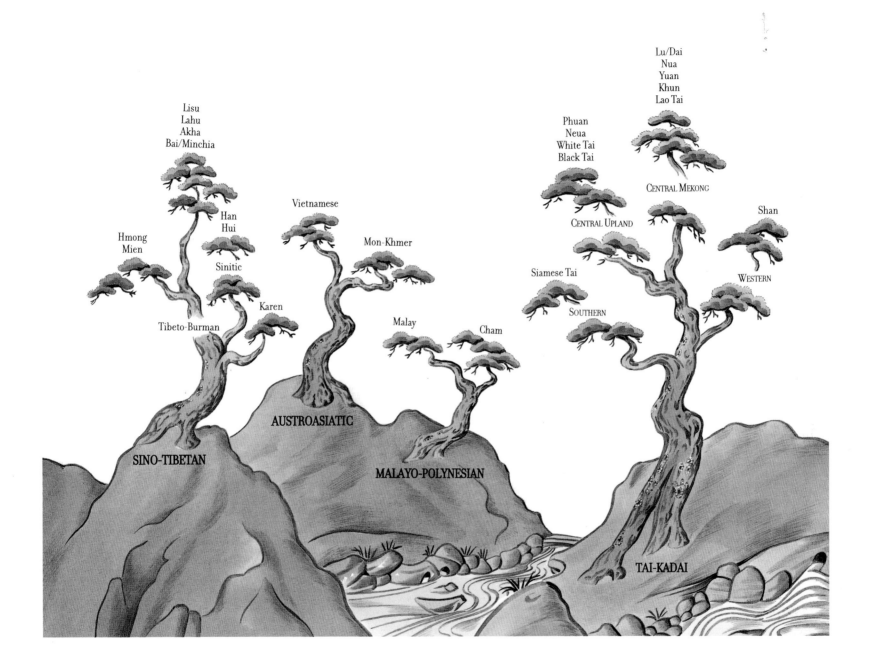

THE FOOD: The foods of the Mekong region are as different, one cuisine from another, as Lebanese food is from Italian food, but just as we think of the Mediterranean as having a common palate, the same can be said for this part of Southeast Asia.

Here a good cook is constantly balancing and contrasting different tastes and textures. The basic palate is hot, sour, salty, sweet, and, sometimes, bitter. If you order a green papaya salad from a street vendor in Thailand, the last thing the vendor will do before serving the salad is to give you a small spoonful of the salad, asking for your opinion. If you'd like it hotter, more chiles will be added; if you want it saltier, more fish sauce; more sour, lime juice will be added; sweeter, more palm sugar.

And while this balancing act takes place in an individual dish like a green papaya salad, it also shapes a meal, determining what dishes should be served alongside others. One dish will be particularly hot, another leaning toward sour, another, salty. Dishes from different parts of the region can be served at the same meal, for they are all culinary cousins.

Texture and color are also critical in creating balance and contrast. Cool, fresh raw vegetables and herbs are used in abundance, essential not only for their taste but also for their texture and color. Fresh herb plates, lettuce, and leafy green vegetables are put out on the table to be used for wrapping, garnishing, and embellishing. A hot red curry will be served simply with rice, but alongside there will be a small plate of cucumber slices, and perhaps a small wedge of lime, there to be squeezed over the curry. Contrast and balance.

And, as in the Mediterranean, in the Mekong region there is a shared approach to food as well as a common palate. People are wildly eclectic in their tastes, proudly unrestrained. When you walk through a large open-air market, like Bangkok's Weekend Market, or Thai Binh Market in Ho Chi Minh City, the diversity of the prepared foods for sale is mind-boggling, from the simple to the elaborate, from the plain to the exotic. There is little fear of food, there are few food rules, and there is virtually no hierarchy when it comes to food. Children are welcome in any restaurant, no matter how young they are or how in the way they might be. Food is for fun, for joy.

REGION BY REGION **Yunnanese** cooking is a distinctive regional Chinese cuisine, far from the culinary traditions of Beijing, Shanghai, and Guangzhou. It uses locally available foodstuffs and is strongly influenced by the culinary traditions of the non-Chinese cultures living in the area.

Hot chiles (dried and fresh), star anise, salty ham, and preserved cabbage are common ingredients and flavorings. Surprisingly little soy sauce is used; instead, salt is more important, used on its own or in combination with soy sauce. Easy stir-fries, leafy greens simply dressed, and lightly flavored soups are classic elements in Yunnanese home-style food. Condiments include Chinese pepper-salt (a blend of Sichuan pepper and salt; see page 309), chile pepper paste (*la jiang*; see page 27), and a dipping sauce for meat of dark vinegar and soy sauce. Though chiles, especially dried red chiles, are often used for flavor and heat, in general, Yunnanese Chinese food is not as chile-hot as the food of Sichuan or Hunan.

The minority peoples in Yunnan (see above) are primarily rice eaters, whose traditional meat is pork, grilled over an open fire or minced and flavored with hot chiles. In the southern tip of Yunnan, in the area known as Xishuanbanna, the majority culture is Dai, the large branch of the Tai ethnographic family also known as Tai Lu. Dai cuisine is very like northern Thai or Lao cooking in its use of grilled vegetables and flavorings. The staple rice is sticky rice, though jasmine rice is also eaten, and fish is an important food year-round. The Dai use salt for seasoning, not fish sauce.

Another thread in Yunnanese culinary tradition is Hui (Chinese Muslim). Because pork is forbidden in Hui households, the main meats used in cooking are sheep, goat, beef, and water buffalo. Hui cooks are famous in the region for their pickles and preserves, often made quite hot with dried red chiles. In a Hui restaurant, it is easy to be transported by smell and taste to Central Asia. Like the Uighur people in the Xinjiang region of western China, Hui cooks make tandoor-baked flatbreads as well as hand-cut wheat-flour noodles, accompanied by soupy dishes of stewed lamb or beef.

In Burma's **Shan State**, and in Shan households in Thailand, food looks much like northern Thai food, but when you begin to smell and taste, it's quite different. Salt, rather than fish sauce, is the staple seasoning. There is also a delicious seasoning base that is made with *tua nao*, dried fermented soybeans. It gives a wonderful nutty back-taste and depth to everyday dishes. The flavor balance is recognizably related to the Dai and the Lao; there is less sweet and more bitter and sour than in Thai cooking. Burmese influence is apparent in the occasional use of turmeric (see Chiang Mai Curry Noodles, page 134). The principal rice for Shan people is jasmine rice, not the sticky rice of northern Thais, although sticky rice is used to make sweets.

Like their northern Thai and Lao neighbors, the Shan have a large repertoire of easy, tasty, salsa-like dishes that depend on a flavor base of grilled garlic, shallots, and peppers (see, for example, Grilled Chile Salsa, Shan-Style, page 45). They call them *nam prik*, moist spicy dishes to eat with rice, closely related to the Lao dishes known as *jaew*. The Shan also use a distinctive slow-cooking method to produce a class of dishes known as *oop*, in which flavors blend as the ingredients cook in a tightly covered pot over low heat (see, for example, The Best Eggplant Dish Ever, page 159).

Until the nineteenth century, **northern Thailand** was made up of a number of separate sovereign kingdoms, the most powerful being centered in Chiang Mai. (The others included Nan, Chiang Rai, Phayao, and Chiang Saen.) The written and spoken language in the north was different from that of central Thailand. Over the last hundred and fifty years, as the northern kingdoms have been absorbed into Thailand, these regional differences have become less apparent, though northerners still speak their dialect and are proud of their distinctive culture and history.

Geography and history have significantly influenced the food and cooking of northern Thailand. The north is mountainous and has a more extreme climate than the central plains: Winters are much cooler (occasionally there's a mild frost in the high mountains) and in the dry season and rainy season, temperatures are higher than in Bangkok. Coconuts do not thrive here and relatively little fish is eaten. Because of its strategic location, bordered by Burma and Laos, and just down-river from China, northern Thailand is a culinary crossroads, where Shan and northern Thai and Lao cultures mix together in a distinctive cosmopolitan blend.

Northern Thai cuisine relies on beef and water buffalo, as well as pork (see, for example, Spicy Northern Sausage, page 256, and Northern Rice Noodle Stew, page 140). Flavors tend to the hot and sour, far from the sweet coconut-milk richness of Bangkok food. Rendered pork fat is the traditional cooking oil, and pork cracklings a much-loved snack for scooping up spicy salsas and dips. Sticky rice is the staple rice, though jasmine rice is now widely available. Like the Lao and the Shan, northern Thais have a repertoire of salsas that start with a base of grilled garlic, shallots, and chiles and proceed creatively from there.

In **northeast Thailand (Issaan)**, there is much more of a grassroots feel to the food. Most people are Lao and share a spoken language and a culinary approach with the lowland people of Laos. The land and climate of Issaan are by far the most unrewarding in Thailand. Drought has forever been a problem, as have relatively poor soil. Ingredients that can be gathered from the wild, like bamboo shoots, mushrooms, and various roots and leaves, are important to people who cannot rely on good crops. Fish from the Mekong and its tributaries is also an important staple, eaten fresh or dried, or salted and fermented to produce fish sauce and fish paste.

Northeastern cooking is direct and forceful. It's often chile-hot and always inventive. From spiced beef jerky to skewers of grilled chicken to fish rubbed with a paste of coriander root and black pepper

Fish fresh-caught from rivers, lakes, and village ponds are grilled, curried, fried, steamed, or sun-dried for longer storage, or packed in salt and fermented to make fish sauce.

Pumpkins and squash are eaten in curries and soups and are a standard part of the Steamed Vegetable Plate *(page 69) of the Shan, Lao, and northern Thai tables.*

and then roasted in a banana leaf, to eat Issaan food is to taste the rural roots of the cuisine. What comes through strongly is a sense of cooks being forced by adversity into ingenious solutions. Who else would think to roast raw rice with aromatics, then grind it to make a condiment powder? (See Aromatic Roasted Rice Powder, page 309.) Issaan food has long been our favorite food in the Thai repertoire: We love the grilled meats and sticky rice, the jerkys and *laab* and the strong earthy salsas. It's all *saep*—delicious!

In **Lao** villages and towns, the food resembles that of Issaan, but with some pronounced regional differences north to south. *Sin khouai*, or water buffalo meat, is common, and so, surprisingly to us, are turkeys. In the remote and mountainous areas, there are more tribal people than there are in lowland Lao; the rural markets are full of leaves and roots and shoots gathered in the wild, and hunters sell small animals and birds that they have snared or shot in the jungle. In every market, large or small, there are also river frogs, eels, fresh-caught fish, a wide variety of leaves and herbs, and piles of river weed for sale, all gathered locally. It's a reminder of how large, wild, and relatively unpopulated Laos is: fewer than five million people in a country half the size of Thailand (with nearly sixty million people).

In many ways, Laos feels the way Issaan and north Thailand must have felt before about 1950. Older people from Thailand, traveling to Laos, frequently remark that Lao food markets remind them of Thailand forty or fifty years ago, "the old ways."

The most distinctive regional cuisine in Laos is centered in Luang Prabang. Here flavors tend decidedly toward bitter, especially in simmered dishes such as *oaw' moo* (see Luang Prabang Pork Stew with Bitter Greens, page 245). Farther south, in Vientiane, the cuisine is more like that of Issaan, with grilled fish and chicken, stacks of sausages, thick spicy salsas, and marinated dried meats. In both regions, leaf-wrapped snacks, called *miang*, are a favorite street food (see Green-Wrapped Flavor Bundles, page 269). Some Vietnamese presence is visible in the food in major towns: Market vendors include

people selling Vietnamese noodle soups (known as *foe* in Vientiane), grilled pork balls (*nem nuong*; see page 252), Saigon Subs (page 287), and crispy Vietnamese crepes (*banh xeo*; see page 280).

One of the best reasons to travel to Laos is to taste Lao sticky rice. It's less polished than the Thai sticky rice that's commercially available, and hence has more of a grain taste. It is the daily staple, especially in villages and small towns.

Khmer (or **Cambodian**) home-style cooking, like all food and cooking in Southeast Asia, is based on dishes to eat with rice—not sticky rice, but aromatic jasmine rice. Rice noodles are an important staple, and so is fish. Fresh fish is grilled or curried or stir-fried, and, like the people of Thailand, Laos, and Vietnam, Khmers use fish sauce (*tuk traey* in Khmer) and fermented fish paste (*prahok*) to season and flavor their food. Though Khmer cuisine has no strong vegetarian tradition (unlike Vietnamese and Chinese), meat and fish are eaten only in moderation, with plenty of herbs and cooked and fresh vegetables, and always as an accompaniment to rice or noodles.

Tastes tend to be milder than in Issaan cooking, with less fiery heat. There's less sweet in the flavor balance than in southern Vietnamese food and more sour and acid citrus flavors. In the markets, the heaps of thinly sliced lemongrass, with women busy slicing more as you pass by, and the stacks of galangal and ginger for sale are surprising at first sight, and give a vivid idea of what a large role these distinctive flavors play in the cuisine. As in Thailand, galangal flavors most curry pastes; ginger is often used as a vegetable in stir-fries, huge handfuls of it, rather than just as a flavoring (see Khmer Stir-fried Ginger and Beef, page 219). Curry pastes are made fresh, pounded and ground in a stone mortar; they often have a distinctively strong lemongrass note. Curries are simmered or steamed and are rich with coconut milk (for example, Khmer Chicken *Samla'* with Coconut Milk, page 204). It's all very tropical and aromatic compared to northern Thailand or Yunnan.

French colonial rule, from the 1880s until the 1950s, had a lasting impact on Cambodian food, as it did on Vietnamese, at least in the cities and towns. In the cities, French-style bread is still sold in the mornings and is also used to make sandwiches (see Mekong Subs, page 284); butter found its way into some dishes; and meat eating, especially of beef or water buffalo, increased among those who could afford it. Coffee, cultivated in Cambodia, Laos, and Vietnam, is common in the cities.

In **Vietnam's Mekong Delta** region and in nearby Ho Chi Minh City (formerly Saigon), as in the rest of Vietnam, the standard eating implements are chopsticks (south of China, everywhere else in the Mekong region, people eat either with their hands or with a spoon and fork, except when eating noodles). Noodles and noodle soups are common, and the regional version of noodle soup is called *hu tieu*, very like the Khmer name for noodle soup, *ktieu*. The local version of *xoi*, a breakfast of sticky rice steamed with mung beans or nuts, is lush with coconut milk and adorned with fresh herbs and strong flavors (see page 98), whereas in northern Vietnam, it's a very simple steamed rice with beans or peanuts. Mekong river fish, freshly caught or from one of the many fish farms that operate from floating platforms in the river, are on sale at every market. Snake is popular, and so, at some times of year, are snails.

Fresh herbs and greens in the form of a salad plate and garnishes are important flavorings and ingredients at almost every meal. Local specialties include sour soup, a close cousin of the Thai *tom yum*, and a class of slow-cooked sweet and salty dishes known as *ko tieu* (see Slow-Cooked Sweet and Spicy Fish, page 191). The Vietnamese genius for combining fresh and cooked ingredients is evident in fresh rice paper–wrapped rolls (see Rice Paper Roll-ups with Shrimp and Herbs, page 177, and Vietnamese Grilled Pork Balls, page 252).

In this tropical climate with its abundant supply of water, the fruit is fabulous, abundant, and varied. There are lichees and longans and mangoes and rambutans, flavorful avocados, and exotic-looking bright pink fruits known in English as "dragon's eye." The Delta, Cantho in particular, is also known for its sweet snacks.

Buddhism is the dominant religion of the Mekong region, though there are also Muslims, Christians, animists, and followers of Cao Dai. Huge coils of incense burn as an offering at a temple in Cholon, the Chinese district of Ho Chi Minh City.

DISHES FOR EVERY OCCASION

In the morning markets all through Southeast Asia, people head off to noodle stalls for a warming bowl of MORNING MARKET NOODLES *(page 138).*

SAUCES, CHILE PASTES, AND SALSAS

Maybe it has to do with eating quantities of rice and noodles every day, maybe it's just regional genius: Whatever the explanation, the dipping sauces, chile pastes, and cooked salsas that bring intense flavor and life to every meal are at the heart of the regional cuisines of Southeast Asia.

The simple Thai-Lao bird chile and fish sauce combo, Thai Fish Sauce with Hot Chiles (page 33), is a table staple, there to be drizzled on bite by bite. It's chile-hot, pungent and salty, and oh so good.

In southern Vietnam, everyone sitting down to a meal, whether it's a simple bowl of noodles or a multidish feast, takes pleasure in adding extra flavor and customizing each mouthful with tart-salt-sweet sauces like Vietnamese Must-Have Dipping Sauce (*nuoc cham*, page 28) and Vietnamese Peanut Sauce (*nuoc leo*, page 28). They can be spooned over a dish of rice or noodles or used as a dipping sauce for spring rolls or grilled meats. In Thailand, another succulent sauce, Tamarind Sauce with Coconut Milk (page 26), makes a wonderful topping for noodles.

In the Index, you'll find other dipping sauces; recipes for them appear as part of the recipe for the specific dish each traditionally accompanies.

On most tables in southern Yunnan, there is a small bowl or jar of Yunnanese Chile Pepper Paste (page 27), available to add chile heat to a bowl of noodles or whatever else you're eating. It's made from dried red chiles and is a wonderful kitchen staple.

At least one of a class of dishes we call "Mekong salsas" appears at most rice meals throughout the Tai part of Southeast Asia, from southern Yunnan all the way to southern Laos. In Lao they're known as *jaew*, in northern Thai as *nam prik*, and in the Dai area of southern Yunnan as *nam mi*.

Mekong salsas make great appetizers or between-meal snacks as well as being good side dishes at any meal, complements to foods of all kinds. They're thick sauces made of cooked and pureed ingredients. Some are mild-tasting, others have more chile heat. Rich Lao Salsa (page 39) or Issaan Salsa with Anchovies (page 38) can make a wonderful addition to a multidish rice-based meal, its thick chile heat a good foil for a rich pumpkin soup or a mild, slightly sweet coconut milk curry.

Grilled Tomato Salsa (page 44) can be drizzled over aromatic jasmine rice or scooped up with Thai-Lao Crispy Rice Crackers (page 106). It is one of several salsas from the northern part of the Mekong region that are seasoned with salt, not with fish sauce, making them a great option for vegetarians wanting to embark on exploring traditional foods from the region.

In Yunnan, homemade or market-bought chile pastes and pickles are popular condiments (see Yunnanese Chile Pepper Paste, *page 27).*

FRESH CHILE-GARLIC PASTE
[THAILAND, VIETNAM]

There's nothing like fresh hot chiles, combined with garlic and lime juice, to bring out the taste of grilled or roasted meat or to hot up a bowl of noodle soup. If you have fresh chiles on hand, try this quick condiment paste. The commercial alternative, called Sriracha sauce, is bright orange and hot-tasting; it's made in Thailand and is widely available in East Asian groceries.

Serve in a small condiment dish, to accompany Vietnamese beef balls (see Vietnamese Beef Ball Soup, page 62) or other grilled, boiled, or roasted meats (see Index), or as a topping for noodle soups.

4 bird or serrano chiles, minced
2 cloves garlic, coarsely chopped
⅛ teaspoon salt
1 tablespoon fresh lime juice

Pound the chiles, garlic, and salt together in a mortar to make a paste. Stir in the lime juice.

MAKES *about 3 tablespoons paste*

TAMARIND SAUCE WITH COCONUT MILK
[*lon dao jiao* — THAILAND]

"This is a simple dish that you should know how to make," Oie (an old friend from northern Thailand) told me as she took me into her Bangkok kitchen. And sure enough, as Oie cooked and I took notes, it did seem pretty simple. Cook the coconut milk, add the *dao jiao* (fermented soybean paste), add the tamarind, and it's done: a coconut-milk curry with half the fuss. And it was delicious.

But then, of course, months later, I'm home, in the kitchen, reading through my notes and working on the recipe, and somehow it's not nearly as simple as Oie made it look. My timing is off, I'm straining tamarind when I should already be putting it in, and so on and so forth. And all the while I'm remembering how easy Oie made it look. "A simple dish . . . ," she'd said.

Well, now we've made *lon* a lot, and it is simple, as simple as Oie said. But it's a recipe that always reminds us of how even simple dishes can seem difficult the first time through, or the second time through. It reminds us of how important practice and familiarity are in cooking.

Serve this with a platter of fresh vegetables, as well as with rice if you wish. Use the vegetables to scoop up the sauce.

RIGHT: *Dai women in southern Yunnan wear sarongs and fitted cotton blouses, the traditional clothing of Lao and Thai women.* LEFT: *Bicycles as beasts of burden.*

1½ cups canned or fresh coconut milk (see page 315)

3 medium shallots, 2 minced and 1 thinly sliced

⅓ cup fermented soybean paste (*dao jiao*)

1 heaping tablespoon tamarind pulp,
   dissolved in ¼ cup warm water

2 Thai dried red chiles

¼ to ⅓ cup ground pork

2 to 3 tablespoons sugar

Salt (optional)

OPTIONAL ACCOMPANIMENTS

½ small Savoy cabbage, cut into wedges

1 small European cucumber, sliced

1 to 2 green mangoes, peeled and sliced

Heat the coconut milk to a boil in a small pot, then simmer until the oil separates, about 5 minutes.

Meanwhile, place the minced shallots in a mortar and pound to a paste. Add the soybean paste and pound until smooth. Pass the tamarind through a strainer to produce smooth tamarind liquid; discard the solids and set the liquid aside.

Add the shallot paste to the coconut milk, together with the chiles and pork. Cook until the pork has completely changed color, stirring to break up any lumps. Add the sliced shallot, then stir in the tamarind water and 2 tablespoons of the sugar. Taste and add salt or more sugar if you wish. The flavors should be strong and punchy. Bring to a boil briefly, then stir and transfer to a bowl. Serve with a serving spoon; the sauce will be quite liquid.

MAKES *about 2 cups sauce*

NOTE: *We also love* lon *poured over thin rice vermicelli. Prepare the noodles by soaking, then briefly boiling them. Place a coil of noodles in each bowl and spoon the sauce over generously. Accompany with cucumber slices.*

YUNNANESE CHILE PEPPER PASTE
[*la jiang* — YUNNAN]

Chile paste is such a great pantry staple. There are many kinds sold bottled in Chinese grocery stores. Some are really pretty good. But dried red chiles are so easily available and chile paste so easy to make that we usually manage to keep a batch of homemade paste handy, stored in a glass jar in the refrigerator. This recipe has a distinctive Yunnanese taste from the cumin seeds and the dark vinegar.

1 cup Thai dried red chiles

1 cup boiling water

1½ teaspoons salt

1 teaspoon sugar

1½ tablespoons peanut oil

1½ teaspoons cumin seeds, roughly crushed in a mortar

⅓ cup minced shallots

1½ teaspoons black rice vinegar, or substitute cider vinegar

Rinse the chiles and place them in a medium bowl. Pour the boiling water over and stir to wet all the chiles. Place a lid or small plate just slightly smaller than the diameter of the bowl on the chiles to keep them immersed. Let soak for at least 20 minutes or as long as 2 hours.

Transfer the chiles and soaking water to a food processor or blender and puree. Add the salt and sugar and process briefly to blend. Transfer back to the bowl and set aside.

Place a wok or heavy skillet over medium-high heat. When it is hot, add the oil and swirl it around, then add the crushed cumin seeds and cook about 30 seconds, stirring to prevent scorching. Toss in the shallots and cook over medium heat, stirring frequently, until softened and translucent, about 4 minutes. Add the pureed chile mixture (be careful of spattering as it hits the hot pan) and bring to a boil, then cook, stirring frequently, for about 5 minutes, until the sauce thickens slightly. Remove from the heat and stir in the vinegar.

Transfer to a clean bowl to cool, then store in a sterile, well-sealed glass container in the refrigerator.

MAKES *about 1 cup sauce*

VIETNAMESE MUST-HAVE TABLE SAUCE

[*nuoc cham* — VIETNAM]

Nuoc cham is the basic Vietnamese sauce that goes on the table at almost every meal. It brings out the flavors of the food and sparks the appetite. Everyone has a favorite version: This one includes a little vinegar, which gives it a fresh sharp edge. Even if the amount of sugar seems high to you when you make it for the first time, try it this way at least once before you start making adjustments.

¼ cup fresh lime juice

¼ cup Vietnamese or Thai fish sauce

¼ cup water

2 teaspoons rice or cider vinegar

1 tablespoon sugar

1 small clove garlic, minced

1 bird chile, minced

Several shreds of carrot (optional)

Combine all the ingredients in a bowl and stir to dissolve the sugar completely. Serve in one or more small condiment bowls. Store in a tightly sealed glass container in the refrigerator for up to 3 days (after that, the garlic starts to taste tired).

MAKES *just over ¾ cup sauce*

VIETNAMESE PEANUT SAUCE

[*nuoc leo* — VIETNAM]

Nuoc leo may read like a close cousin of satay sauce, but it's very distinctively Vietnamese. It's a little chunky and salty, and reddish brown in color. Rich with peanuts and ground pork, sour with tomato, and salty with fermented soybean sauce, it makes a great dip for cucumber slices and other raw vegetables, for Rice Paper Roll-ups with Shrimp and Herbs (page 177), Grilled Lemongrass Beef (page 225), or Vietnamese Grilled Pork Balls (*nem nuong*, page 252).

¼ cup Dry-Roasted Peanuts (page 308)

Scant 2 tablespoons tamarind pulp, dissolved in 2 tablespoons warm water, or substitute scant 2 tablespoons tomato paste

2 teaspoons peanut oil

4 cloves garlic, minced

3 tablespoons ground pork

3 tablespoons fermented soybean paste (*tuong* in Vietnamese; *dao jiao* in Thai)

About 1 cup water

1½ teaspoons sugar

1 to 2 bird chiles, minced

Generous squeeze of fresh lime juice (optional)

Place the peanuts in a food processor or large mortar and process or pound to a coarse powder; set aside. If using tamarind, press it through a sieve; reserve the liquid and discard the solids.

Heat the oil in a wok or skillet over high heat. Add the garlic and stir-fry until it is starting to change color, about 15 seconds. Toss in the pork and use your spatula to break it up into small pieces. Once it all has changed color, add the soybean paste and the tamarind or tomato paste and stir to blend. Stir in ½ cup of the water, then stir in most of the ground peanuts, reserving about 1 tablespoon for garnish. Stir in the sugar and chiles. Add up to ½ cup more water, until you have the desired texture: a thick liquid, pourable but not watery.

Serve in small individual condiment bowls or in one medium bowl with a spoon so guests can drizzle sauce onto their food or onto their plates. Serve warm or at room temperature, squeezing on the optional lime juice and sprinkling on the reserved ground peanuts just before serving.

The sauce will keep well-sealed in the refrigerator for 3 days or in the freezer for 1 month. Reheat it in a small pan and simmer briefly before placing in a serving bowl.

MAKES *about 2 cups sauce*

VEGETARIAN *NUOC CHAM*
[VIETNAM]

One of the hardest things to work around when cooking vegetarian food in Vietnam is the loss of fish sauce for flavoring and for sauces. I learned this rich-tasting sauce, a vegetarian substitute for *nuoc cham*, from Vui, a boatwoman in Cantho. She and her friend Hanh invited me to dinner several times. Since Vui was fasting (eating no meat or fish) that month, much of what they made was from the extensive Vietnamese vegetarian repertoire.

This sauce in no way tries to replicate *nuoc cham* (page 28). Instead, it's a distinctive and delicious dipping sauce in its own right, with no hint of deprivation. It's particularly good drizzled over stir-fried or parboiled green vegetables, used as a flavoring for jasmine rice or for rice noodles.

3 tablespoons soy sauce
1 tablespoon rice wine or cooking sherry
1 teaspoon finely chopped garlic
1 teaspoon finely chopped lemongrass
⅛ teaspoon ground cinnamon
1 bird chile, minced
1 teaspoon peanut oil
1 teaspoon sugar
½ teaspoon salt

In a small bowl, combine the soy sauce and wine or sherry. Place the garlic and lemongrass in a mortar and pound to reduce to a paste, then add to the sauce. Stir in the cinnamon and bird chile, then add the oil, sugar, and salt. Stir well and taste. Store for up to 3 days in a well-sealed container in the refrigerator.

MAKES *about ⅓ cup sauce*

NOTE: *If you wish to make a larger recipe, enough for 6 to 8 people with some left over, multiply the first 5 ingredients by 4; the chile, cinnamon, sugar, and salt should be increased less than proportionately. Start by doubling them, then, once you've blended all the ingredients, adjust the balance of flavors as you please.*

YUNNAN: Yunnan is big, in all ways big. Roughly the size of California and with a population of thirty-five million people, it is China's sixth largest province.

In the west, there are snow-capped Himalayan peaks, and in the south there are tropical forests and lush vegetation. Over half of all the plant species found in China are found in Yunnan. One third of the population is not Chinese. There are the Zhuang, Achang, Mien, Hmong, Hani, Jingpo, Wa, Minchia, Dai, Benglong, Bulang, Yi, Tibetan, Lisu, Nu, Dulong, Naxi, Pumi, Lahu, Jinuo, Menggu—altogether, forty to fifty different non-Han populations live in the province.

With its high mountains, huge valleys, and raging rivers, Yunnan feels as if the great Himalaya here decided to stretch its long limbs, to get comfortable, to move sideways instead of always thrusting upward. Seldom is the elevation less than a mile, yet always, in every direction, there is a view of higher mountains. Like Mexico, Yunnan straddles the Tropic of Cancer; in December you can still be happily in short sleeves.

Traveling in Yunnan is different from traveling in the rest of Southeast Asia. Not only are distances long and the terrain rugged, it's China, and China has its own way of doing things. We'd been to Yunnan many times, but on a recent visit we wanted to spend as much time along the Mekong (which in China is called the Lancang) as we could. We first headed to Dali, an ancient but thriving town that was once the center of Nan Chao Kingdom. Dali has long been popular among travelers to China. We figured we'd have a chance of finagling affordable transport along the Mekong, along a route of our own design. And we were right, more or less.

A local taxi driver agreed to make the trip along our route in a total of three days (we had wanted five). He demanded twice as much money as we were prepared to spend, and he got it, being the only one in town willing to make the trip. And, being Chinese, he insisted on staying at night in Chinese towns, a point he also succeeded in winning.

But our drive through mountainous Yunnan was worth every *yuan* and every compromise. Over and over again, we would slowly traverse our way up a valley wall, back and forth from hairpin turn to hairpin turn (Chinese road builders are masters of building roads on steep inclines). When we would get to the top, we'd look back into the giant valley we were leaving, and then ahead to that we were heading into. Beautiful terraced hillsides were planted in rice, in tea, in rapeseed. The rice and rape grew at lower levels, near the valley floor, the tea higher up the mountainsides. At dawn on our third day, we drove through a region where all the rape was in flower; in every direction were beautiful yellow fields, a brilliant blue sky, and walls and houses of rich red earth and stone.

Driving through Yunnan was a revelation, like discovering the missing piece of a jigsaw puzzle we'd sworn we'd never find. In three days we traversed the Autonomous Regions of the Lahu, Lisu, and Bai peoples. Over the past hundred years, many of these tribal peoples have migrated in small numbers into remote corners of the mountains of northern Thailand, Laos, and Vietnam. Here in Yunnan, we met them for the first time living as a dominant culture.

And each night our driver would somehow find the one and only Chinese town. Oh well.

On the third day of our trip south through Yunnan, we traveled through terraced landscapes brilliant with the yellow of rapeseed oil plants in bloom.

THAI FISH SAUCE WITH HOT CHILES

[*prik nam pla* — THAILAND, LAOS]

This common Thai chile sauce is our everyday condiment, almost as important in our house as salt. It keeps forever and brings to the table a reliable hit of salt and chile heat. It's not mild and subtle, like the Vietnamese *nuoc cham* (page 28), but brassy and forward and altogether unapologetic. Drizzle a little on fried rice or plain rice, or Thai or Lao food, or whatever you please, mouthful by mouthful.

We keep our *prik nam pla* in a plastic container in the refrigerator, topping it up with extra fish sauce as it runs low. Eventually the chiles too run low, and also lose their punch. Then it's time to top up the chiles (and then the sauce is *very* hot).

When handling bird chiles, you may want to wear rubber gloves to protect your skin. When you chop them, by hand or in the processor, you may find yourself coughing and sneezing as the capsaicin from the cut chiles hits the air. Don't worry, it passes soon. And this simple sauce is worth the effort.

½ cup bird chiles, stems removed

1 cup Thai fish sauce

Place the chiles in a food processor and pulse to finely chop (stop before they are a mush). Or, wearing rubber gloves to protect your hands, use a cleaver or sharp knife to mince the chiles on a cutting board.

Transfer the minced chiles (with their seeds) to a glass or plastic container and add the fish sauce. Cover and store in the refrigerator. The sauce will keep indefinitely, losing chile heat over time; top it up with extra chiles or fish sauce when it runs low. Serve in small individual condiment bowls.

MAKES *just over 1 cup sauce*

Women making jiao-zi *(dumplings) on a small street in Kunming chat with passersby.*

KUNMING: Kunming, the capital city of Yunnan, is changing fast. Traffic jams now mean cars, not bicycles. The main streets are lined with multistory concrete buildings. Women wear short skirts and high heels, and taxi drivers have attitude. Department stores, which a decade ago were cold cavernous dimly lit Soviet-style halls selling an indescribably bleak assortment of Chinese Spam, local cigarettes, and white sorghum whiskeys, are now almost cheerful places to shop.

Present-day Kunming reminds us of Taipei, Taiwan, twenty years ago. There is a facade of modernity, there is even modern life, but just behind it, behind the tall concrete buildings, there is still the old China. We stay in the Camellia Hotel, just down (and down-market) from the Kunming Hotel, and every morning we get up, cross the street, and walk into the dazzling local produce market, which winds around in a wonderful complex tangle. There is so much good food: Muslim food, Minchia food, Dai food, hot pickles, and steaming *jiao-zi*.

For lunch, we dine at the nearby cooking school, not because the food is particularly good, but because we can watch the cooking teachers and their students, the confident and the less than confident, cooking their way furiously through order after order.

For dinner, it's as easy as breakfast and lunch. We just disappear behind the concrete buildings. . . .

On market day in Dali, the main street—from one city gate to the other—is filled with stalls and shoppers, and the action spills down side streets and out beyond the city walls.

THAI ROASTED CHILE PASTE

[*nam prik pao* — THAILAND, LAOS]

Nam prik pao is commonly available in Southeast Asian groceries, but as with many condiments and flavor pastes, the homemade has a more immediate and fresher flavor. *Nam prik pao* (*pao* means roasted) is used to add a roasted depth of flavor, as well as chile heat, to fried rice or soups. You can also serve it as a table sauce or salsa (see Note below).

¾ cup Thai dried red chiles
Generous ½ cup shallots, unpeeled
Scant ½ cup garlic cloves, unpeeled
¼ cup peanut or vegetable oil
1 teaspoon Thai fish sauce, or substitute scant
   ½ teaspoon salt for a vegetarian version

Place a large heavy skillet over medium-low heat, add the chiles, and dry-roast them, moving them around with a spatula as necessary to prevent burning, for 4 to 5 minutes; they'll darken and become brittle. Remove from the heat and set aside to cool.

Meantime, slice the unpeeled shallots lengthwise in half, or quarters if they're very large. Place a second heavy skillet over medium heat, add the shallots and garlic cloves, and dry-roast until well browned on one side; then turn them over and dry-roast on the other side. When they're well softened and roasted, 5 to 8 minutes, remove from the heat and set aside. *Alternatively*, you can also use a charcoal or gas grill to roast the chiles, shallots, and garlic; in village Thailand, grilling is usually done over a small wood fire.

Break off the chile stems and discard them, then break up the chiles (they'll break easily) and place in a food processor or large mortar. Some recipes call for discarding the chile seeds, but it seems a pity to waste their heat and flavor, so we suggest you keep them. Peel the shallots and garlic, coarsely chop, and toss into the processor or mortar. Process or pound to a smooth paste (the chile seeds will still be whole). You may have to scrape down the sides of the bowl or mortar several times as you work. Processing is very quick; using a mortar is more traditional and will take about 10 minutes or more, depending on the type of mortar and your energy.

Place a heavy skillet over medium heat. Add the oil, and when it is hot, add the paste. Stir gently with a wooden spatula as the paste heats in the oil and absorbs it. After 4 to 5 minutes, it will have darkened slightly and will give off a wonderful slightly sweet roasted chile aroma. Remove from the heat, stir in the fish sauce, and let cool to room temperature.

Transfer to a glass jar and store, well sealed, in the refrigerator.

MAKES *just over ½ cup paste*

NOTE: *To serve the paste as a table sauce, you may wish to add more fish sauce or salt and a generous squeeze of fresh lime juice and a little sugar.*

SHAN CHILE PASTE

[SHAN STATE, NORTHERN THAILAND]

The Shan and the Tai Koen use something called *tua nao*, flat sun-dried disks made from fermented soybeans, as a basic flavor base. The disks are crumbled and fried or added as a flavoring to dishes, rather as fish sauce is in other parts of the region. The disks are also the principal ingredient in a spicy flavor powder that is used as a condiment and seasoning by the Shan and Tai Koen.

Because *tua nao* are unavailable here, we substitute fermented soybean paste (Thai, *dao jiao*; Vietnamese, *tuong*), a simple bottled combination of stewed fermented soybeans, salt, and flour sold at Chinese and Southeast Asian stores. (See Glossary for more information.) It's wet, not dry like *tua nao*, so consequently this is a flavor paste rather than a dry powder.

Use this paste as a condiment, salty and chile-hot for rice or noodle dishes or grilled meat, or as a flavoring ingredient in cooked dishes. It can also be used in place of fish sauce–based chile pastes, especially when you are converting a traditional Southeast Asian dish into a purely vegetarian dish.

3 tablespoons fermented soybean paste (see Headnote)
5 Thai dried red chiles
1 tablespoon minced ginger
Pinch of salt
2 tablespoons Dry-Roasted Peanuts (page 308)
1 tablespoon Dry-Roasted Sesame Seeds (page 308)

Place the soybean paste in a small heavy nonreactive skillet and heat, stirring occasionally, over medium heat for 5 minutes to concentrate the paste. Set aside.

In a small heavy skillet, dry-roast the chiles until softened and puffed, about 1 minute. Stem and finely chop and place in a mortar. Add the ginger and pound the two to a paste with the pinch of salt. Add the peanuts and sesame seeds and pound to create a rough paste. Add the soybean paste and pound and stir to blend. Transfer to a nonreactive container and store in the refrigerator.

MAKES *a scant ½ cup paste*

NOTE: *Shan flavor paste makes a good topping for leftover sticky rice. We were told in Mae Sai (see page 92) to shape leftover sticky rice into a flat cake 2 to 3 inches across, spread on some Shan Chile Paste, and then fry in hot oil for breakfast.*

ISSAAN SALSA WITH ANCHOVIES

[*jaew issaan* — LAOS, NORTHEAST THAILAND]

This classic Lao sauce is sometimes called *jaew pa* (*pa* is fish, and it's traditionally made with salted river fish, for which we substitute anchovies) and sometimes *jaew issaan* because Thais know it as a dish from northeast Thailand (Issaan). It's simple and very good, a great introduction to the regional salsa tradition. It makes a tasty condiment for grills and for sticky rice; the lemony flavor of galangal is addictive. The sauce is hot but not burningly so. The tomatoes can be omitted; we prefer to include them if we have some on hand.

4 medium to large cloves garlic, unpeeled

1 tablespoon chopped galangal

2 tablespoons sliced shallots (2 medium)

Pinch of salt

½ stalk lemongrass, trimmed and minced

1 Thai dried red chile

2 tablespoons finely chopped anchovy fillets (approximately 8)

2 tablespoons fresh lime juice

1 fresh or frozen wild lime leaf, torn into small pieces

2 to 3 cherry tomatoes (optional)

Place the garlic in a small heavy skillet over medium-high heat and cook, stirring occasionally with a wooden spoon, until the skins are well browned in several places, about 8 minutes. Transfer the garlic to a cutting board and add the galangal and shallots to the skillet. Cook for 3 to 5 minutes, until the shallots start to turn golden and the galangal begins to scorch. Coarsely chop the shallots and transfer with the galangal to a mortar or food processor. Peel the garlic, coarsely chop, and add to the mortar or processor.

Pound or process the garlic, galangal, and shallots to a paste with the pinch of salt. Add the lemongrass and reduce to a coarse paste. Set aside.

Heat a small heavy skillet over medium-high heat, add the dried chile, and dry-roast for about 45 seconds, just until starting to puff; do not let it scorch. Remove and finely chop, discarding any tough stem but retaining the seeds. Transfer to the mortar or processor and pound or process with the other ingredients. Add the chopped anchovies and pound or blend into the paste. Transfer the paste to a bowl and stir in the lime juice and lime leaf.

Heat a small skillet over medium-high heat, add the tomatoes, and cook until slightly scorched in several places, about 2 minutes. Coarsely chop into about 6 pieces each, then stir into the paste and serve. Leftover paste can be stored in a jar in the refrigerator for 3 to 4 days.

MAKES *about ⅔ cup sauce*

RICH LAO SALSA

[*jaew bong* — LAOS]

This is an adaptation of a classic salsa from Luang Prabang, the old royal capital of Laos. It is a beautiful, dark red-brown color with a smooth paste texture. It is eaten with sticky rice or as a side with cooked vegetables (such as Steamed Vegetable Plate, page 69; just scoop them through it), or served with mild dishes like Silky Coconut-Pumpkin Soup (page 51). Traditional versions include small chewy bits of dried water buffalo skin and are hotter than this version. Flavors are rich from the grilled shallots and garlic, spiked with citrusy, gingery galangal. The sauce is hot but not fiery; for the traditional amount of heat, increase the number of chiles to 10.

6 medium or 9 small shallots, unpeeled

1½ cups garlic cloves (from 3 to 4 heads), unpeeled

6 (or up to 10) Thai dried red chiles

1½ tablespoons chopped galangal

Several pinches of salt

2 teaspoons Thai fish sauce, or more to taste

2 to 3 tablespoons warm water

½ cup coarsely chopped fresh coriander

Heat a cast-iron skillet over medium-high heat. Place the shallots and garlic in the skillet and dry-roast until browned and blackened on all sides, about 5 minutes. Remove from the skillet and set aside to cool slightly.

Meanwhile, place the skillet over medium heat, add the dried chiles, and dry-roast, turning and moving them frequently, until they start to give off an aroma; they should not blacken or burn—just heat gently until they are dried out and brittle. *Alternatively*, you can roast the shallots, garlic, and chiles over a charcoal or gas grill.

Transfer the chiles to a mortar and pound them to a powder (discard any tough stems). Add the galangal and a pinch of salt and pound to a paste. Transfer the mixture to a small bowl and set aside. *Alternatively*, place the chiles and galangal in a blender or food processor and chop them as fine as possible.

Slide the peels off the shallots and garlic and discard. Coarsely chop the shallots, place them in the mortar with a pinch of salt, and pound to a smooth paste. Add the paste to the mixture in the small bowl, then place the garlic cloves and a pinch of salt in the mortar and pound to a smooth paste. Add all the pounded ingredients to the mortar and pound together. *Alternatively*, add the shallots and garlic to the food processor with a pinch of salt and process. Add the fish sauce and 2 tablespoons of the warm water and pound or stir to blend well. The paste should be very moist and smooth; add a little more warm water if you wish. Taste for salt and add a little more salt or fish sauce if you wish. Stir in half the coriander.

Transfer the sauce to a small bowl. Sprinkle the remaining coriander over the top. Serve at room temperature. Store leftovers in a sealed contained in the refrigerator for several weeks.

MAKES *just over 1 cup thick sauce*

FISH HEADS AND FAT: It wasn't one of my all-time favorite meals, but it was certainly one of the most memorable. I was in Dali, in central Yunnan, in April 1984. Dali, the center of the old Nanchao Kingdom, is home to the Minchia people, also called Bai. Bai women traditionally wear a distinctive tunic made from a heavy navy-blue-and-white cotton cloth, but at that time, like other "minority peoples" in China, they were dressed in the same drab proletarian green and blue Mao jackets and pants seen all across the country. Minority dress was forbidden, as was minority religious expression (though this was very soon to begin to change).

One day I noticed a group of elderly women dressed in the traditional Bai clothing walking through town. A few minutes later, I noticed another group, and then another, and another. So I got up and followed them all the way out of town.

About a mile outside Dali, everyone came together in a large dry riverbed, several hundred women altogether. As the small groups arrived they would find an unspoken-for spot in the riverbed and settle in, putting down picnic baskets and taking out the contents; each woman had several long strands of glass beads, as well as little wooden mallets and metal jingles. Then each group stood up in a semicircle and started to keep a rhythm with their mallets and jingles, and the women began to chant. I became part of the group that I'd walked out with, and even though I was the only man among several hundred women at the riverbed, they made it clear that I was a welcome participant. (All around the river, though, there were Chinese soldiers and police from the Public Security Bureau, looking on and looking none too happy.) The women told me to sit down, and so I did.

Round about noon, my group took a break from chanting and we had lunch. On my plate, I was given a large fish head and a three-inch-square chunk of fat, same as everyone else. And we had tea.

Soon they began chanting again, all afternoon long and into the evening. And then it was over, and everyone walked back home.

Bai women in the Dali area come to market to buy and sell not only vegetables and eggs and livestock, but also jewelry, old and new.

LEFT: *Chinese brushwork and calligraphy is an art, often demonstrated on the street on market day.* RIGHT: *Potatoes simply fried with chiles and other flavorings make a warming winter dish (see* QUICK AND TASTY YUNNANESE POTATOES, *page 162).*

GRILLED TOMATO SALSA

[*nam mi he man* — DAI AREA OF SOUTHERN YUNNAN]

This close cousin of the grilled tomato salsas of northern Thailand was one of our favorite dishes at the Dai guest house in Menghan (see page 60). Just before each meal, Mae or her mother would light a small fire and then grill garlic and tomatoes over it until they were blackened, softened, and warm inside. Then she'd mash the juicy tomatoes and the garlic in the mortar with simple flavorings, transfer the salsa to a small bowl, and bring it to the table, a little runny, still a little warm from the fire, and alive with fresh flavor.

Serve this as a salsa for dipping sticky rice or chips or pork cracklings, or to accompany a jasmine rice meal.

4 cloves garlic, unpeeled

3 medium juicy tomatoes

1 to 2 serrano or bird chiles, minced (optional)

½ teaspoon salt, or to taste

½ cup chopped coriander

Heat a charcoal or gas grill. Place the garlic and tomatoes on a fine-mesh rack on the grill and grill until well blackened in spots on one side, then use tongs to turn them. Continue to cook, turning the tomatoes as necessary to expose all sides to the heat, until the garlic and tomatoes are well scorched and softened, 8 to 10 minutes. *Alternatively,* heat a heavy skillet over high heat. Place the garlic and tomatoes in the skillet and lower the heat to medium-high. As soon as the garlic and tomatoes blacken on one side, use tongs to turn them and cook, until well scorched and softened, 8 to 10 minutes.

Peel the garlic, chop or mash, and place in a food processor. Coarsely chop the tomatoes, saving the juice, and add the tomatoes and juice to the processor. Add the chiles, if using, and pulse several times to blend; do not process to a puree. Transfer to a bowl and stir in the salt. Store refrigerated no more than 2 days.

Stir in the coriander just before serving.

MAKES *1½ cups salsa*

SALSA WITH POPPY SEEDS

[NORTHERN THAILAND AND LAOS, CENTRAL YUNNAN]

Buy a large package of poppy seeds, as you will find this easy salsa-paste a pleasure to have on the table, either as a condiment for rice and simple rice meals or to accompany grilled meats. It is a little salty, and, depending on the heat of the chiles you use, slightly chile-hot.

6 to 8 medium to large cloves garlic, unpeeled

3 medium to mild long green chiles (such as Cubanelles, Hungarian wax, or Anaheim)

2 tablespoons poppy seeds

¼ teaspoon salt, or to taste

1 cup packed coriander leaves and stems

Heat a heavy skillet over medium-high heat. Place the garlic cloves and the chiles in it and dry-roast, turning to expose all sides to the heat and pressing down on the chiles against the hot surface, until the garlic has softened and browned well and the chiles have softened and blistered, about 5 minutes. Remove from the heat. When they are cool enough to handle, peel the garlic cloves, coarsely chop, and set aside. Cut off and discard the chile stems, slice the chiles open lengthwise, and pull out and discard the membranes and, if you wish, the seeds. Coarsely chop and set aside.

If using a large mortar, place the poppy seeds in it and pound until pulverized. Add the garlic and pound to a paste, then add the chiles and salt and pound to a coarse paste. Add the coriander and pound until well incorporated into the paste.

If using a spice grinder (or coffee grinder) and food processor, place the poppy seeds in the grinder and reduce to a powder. Transfer to the processor, add the remaining ingredients, and process to a paste; you may have to stop the machine several times to push the ingredients down the sides of the processor bowl.

Turn out into a small bowl and serve.

MAKES *½ cup dense sauce*

GRILLED TOMATO SALSA *is pictured on page 43, along with* THAI-LAO CRISPY RICE CRACKERS *(page 106).*

GRILLED CHILE SALSA, SHAN STYLE

[*nam prik num tai yai* — SHAN STATE, NORTHERN THAILAND]

The Tai people use grilling as a flavoring technique, perhaps nowhere more brilliantly than in their salsas. The Lao season their salsas with fish sauce or fish paste, while the Shan and the Dai use salt, as we do in this Shan version of the north Thai classic, *nam prik num.*

Prik num are long pale green chiles, usually mild to medium-hot, that resemble the banana chiles we can buy in North America. In this sauce, fresh chiles, shallots, tomatoes, and garlic are thoroughly softened and blackened on a grill or in a hot dry skillet, then chopped and seasoned. The salsa has a wonderful taste of the grill and is medium-hot. If you want a milder taste, substitute Hungarian wax chiles or Cubanelles for some or all of the banana chiles.

Serve the salsa in a bowl from which guests can help themselves, as a dip for sticky rice, or raw vegetables, or crackers or pork cracklings. Place a plate of sliced cucumbers, lettuce leaves, and other greens on the table so guests can use them to scoop up the sauce. The salsa also makes a good sauce for jasmine rice or noodles.

4 to 5 banana chiles (about ¼ pound)

¼ pound shallots, cut in half, quartered if very large

6 to 8 cloves garlic, halved if large

½ pound cherry tomatoes

2 to 3 tablespoons coriander leaves, coarsely torn

2 teaspoons salt, or to taste

2 tablespoons fresh lime juice

Heat a charcoal or gas grill. Place the chiles, shallots, garlic, and tomatoes on a fine-mesh rack on the grill and grill until well blackened in spots on one side, then turn with tongs and repeat on the other side, turning the tomatoes as necessary to expose all sides to the heat.

Alternatively, heat two heavy skillets over high heat (if you have only one skillet, the vegetables will have to be cooked in sequence; with two, you can get everything cooked at the same time). Place the chiles, shallots, and garlic cloves in one skillet and place the tomatoes in the other. Lower the heat to medium-high under both skillets. Press down gently on the chiles to expose them to the heat; then, as one side blackens, use tongs or a wooden spatula to turn them. Similarly, turn the shallots and garlic as they blacken on one side to cook the other side. Use tongs to turn the tomatoes, exposing all sides to the heat.

Remove the vegetables from the grill or skillets when they seem well scorched and softened, about 8 to 10 minutes. Place on a cutting board to cool slightly. Slice off and discard the stem end of the chiles, slice the chiles lengthwise in half, and discard the seeds (unless you want a very hot salsa). Chop well, then transfer to a medium bowl. Finely chop the remaining vegetables and transfer, together with the juices from the tomatoes, to the bowl. Add the coriander, salt, and lime juice and stir to blend. The sauce will be chunky and a little bit soupy in texture. (The ingredients can be chopped together in a food processor, but the sauce is more traditional and more interesting with a hand-chopped texture.)

If you have time, let the sauce stand for 30 minutes before serving to allow the flavors to blend and mellow. Store in a covered nonreactive container in the refrigerator. The salsa will keep for 4 to 5 days. Bring back to room temperature before serving.

MAKES *about 1½ cups sauce*

NOTE: *The Shan have a whole repertoire of grilled chile salsas, building on the ingredients in this one. For example, you could grill mushrooms or eggplant, then chop and add to this, adjusting the seasonings as necessary.*

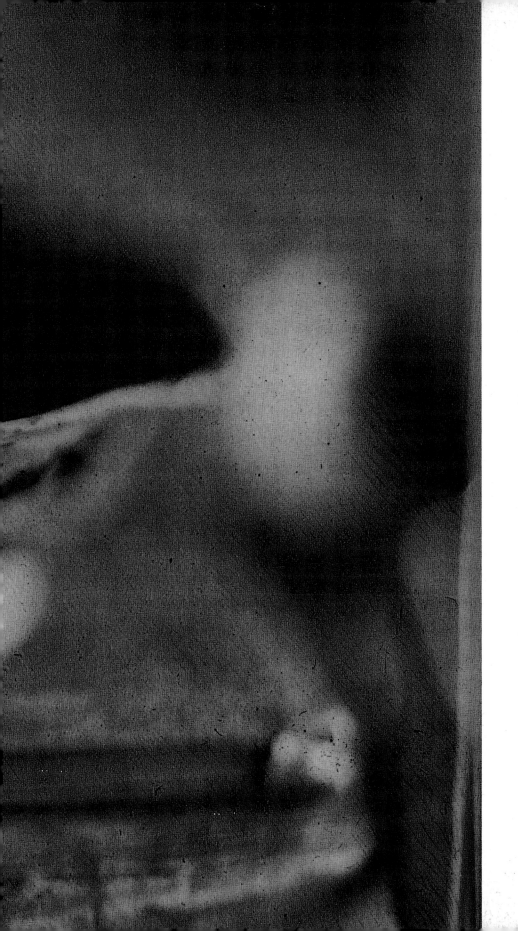

SIMPLE SOUPS

Soup is an essential part of most meals in Southeast Asian cuisines, often served as a contrast to strong-tasting dishes. The soups in this chapter do not include noodle or rice soups, which tend to be meal-in-one dishes and appear in the Noodles and Rice chapters respectively (see Index). Instead, here is a sampling of the soups that can be served as part of a family meal. Some are mild, others, especially the sour soups for which the region is famous, are more assertive tasting. All mean comfort food to the people for whom they are daily fare.

Soup as a flavorful liquid to accompany a meal begins with a light broth, chicken- or pork- or vegetable-based. The goal here is not intensity of flavor but rather a pleasingly mild-tasting liquid. Chicken Soup with Greens (page 56) and Plain of Jars Vegetable Soup (page 53) are both in this category, ideal companions for rice and spicy dishes.

Clear soups with stronger flavorings are also part of the regional repertoire. We have included both a Thai and a Lao *tom yum* here, delicious hot-and-sour clear broths (see Shrimp in Hot Lime Leaf Broth, page 53, and Lao Hot and Sour Soup with Fish, page 57). *Tom yum* is never drunk in vast quantity but instead is eaten like a hot Thai curry, sipped in small spoonfuls throughout the meal.

Thicker, more robust soups, such as slow-simmered Hearty Chicken Soup with Onions and Garlic (page 59), Silky Coconut-Pumpkin Soup (page 51), and Home-Style Pork Soup with Vegetables (page 51), are closer to the European idea of soup as a full-flavored dish or course on its own. These are rich in substance and flavor and can be served as part of a Southeast Asian or a Western meal, or as the soup half of a meal of bread and soup.

OPPOSITE, BELOW: *Soups and curries, hot and ready to carry home from a prepared food market in Vientiane.* LEFT: *Sometimes a hunter, like this young Akha man near the Lao-Yunnan border, will bring his weapon with him to the market.*

BASIC SOUTHEAST ASIAN BROTH

Ask a home cook in Southeast Asia how she makes broth, and she's apt to give an easy wave of the hand: "Some meat and bones [or chicken or oxtail]," she'll begin, and then she'll list aromatics. The details may vary: slices of ginger, or maybe not; cloves of garlic; perhaps, if she's Lao, whole coriander plants, including the root; probably some peppercorns (or, in Yunnan, Sichuan peppercorns); perhaps, if she's Khmer, a stalk or two of smashed lemongrass; and in Vietnam, with beef, she'll add a stick of cinnamon and some star anise.

Broths are a way of making good use of meat, bones, and scraps, extracting all their flavor. Generally, the more meat used, the more flavor. When making pork or beef broth, especially if using bones, you will have to skim off foam as it rises to the surface in the first 10 to 15 minutes of cooking. The broth should be gently simmered once it has come to the boil, because continuous vigorous boiling would make it cloudy. Broths and stocks made from bones generally need a long period (2 hours or more) of simmering, while those made from pieces of meat usually will be flavorful enough in less than an hour. Except for the richly flavored beef soups of Vietnam, soup broth in Southeast Asia is usually light-tasting, used for clear soups or added to a stew or stir-fry during cooking.

Having a supply of clear soup broth in your freezer and rice and noodles in your pantry is a guarantee that you'll always have food to put on the table: Heat the broth to a boil, season it, toss in some chopped vegetables or sliced meat if you wish, and pour it over rice or noodles for a hearty meal-in-one.

We usually improvise our broths, depending on what we have on hand, but here is a general recipe to give some guidance.

1 whole chicken or 3 to 4 pounds chicken necks and wings (or 1 chicken carcass)
Water to cover
4 cloves garlic, peeled
2 to 3 shallots, halved, or 2 scallions trimmed and cut into 2-inch lengths (optional)
About 10 black peppercorns or Sichuan peppercorns (optional)
3 thick slices ginger (optional)
2 whole coriander plants, including roots, well washed (optional)
Salt and/or Thai or Vietnamese fish sauce to taste

Rinse the chicken well. Place in a large heavy pot and add cold water to cover. Bring to a boil, then reduce to a simmer, skimming off and discarding any foam that comes to the surface. Add all the remaining ingredients except the salt and/or fish sauce, stir well to wet them, and simmer, half-covered, for about 40 minutes. (If you are using a chicken carcass, simmer the broth for about 2 hours.)

Place a sieve over a large bowl, pour the broth through it, and set aside meat for another purpose; discard the remaining solids. Let the broth cool completely, then pour it into one or more containers. Cover and refrigerate. After several hours, a layer of fat will have solidified on the surface; skim it off and set aside for another purpose if desired. You can use the broth immediately, or refrigerate it for up to 3 days, or freeze for up to 3 months. You can season it after skimming off the fat or instead wait, as we do, and season it with salt and/or fish sauce just before you use it.

If using the stock to make a clear broth, warm it slightly, then strain through a colander lined with a double layer of cheesecloth before proceeding with the recipe.

MAKES *6 to 9 cups broth*

HOME-STYLE PORK SOUP WITH VEGETABLES

[*rouding fanqie tang* — DALI AREA, YUNNAN]

The Bai people, who live in and around Dali in the Erhai Lake region of Yunnan, raise pigs and chickens and grow rice, soybeans, and vegetables on the sloping shores of the lake. This warming soup is almost a stew, loaded with greens and a little tomato, as well as chunks of meat. Serve it with rice or with bread as a hearty peasant soup, or as part of a rice meal, with grilled fish and a spicy salsa.

2 to 3 tablespoons minced pork fat or vegetable oil
2 tablespoons minced garlic
1-inch piece ginger, peeled and sliced
1 pound boneless pork (shoulder, butt, or loin), trimmed
    of most fat and cut into 1-inch chunks
6 cups water
2 Thai dried red chiles
1 teaspoon salt, or to taste
7 to 10 scallions, trimmed and cut into 1-inch lengths (2 cups)
1 medium tomato, coarsely chopped
1 cup packed coriander leaves, coarsely chopped

If using pork fat, place a large heavy pot over medium-high heat and toss in the fat; when it melts, raise the heat to high. If using oil, place the pot over high heat and add the oil. Toss in the minced garlic and cook briefly until starting to brown, then add the ginger slices and meat and cook, turning the pork frequently, until all surfaces of the meat have changed color, about 5 minutes. Add the water and dried chiles and bring to a boil, then reduce the heat and simmer, half-covered, for 30 minutes.

Add the salt, scallions, tomato, and half the coriander leaves and simmer for another 10 minutes. (*The soup can be prepared to this point and set aside for up to 2 hours, then reheated just before serving. Add a little water if you wish the soup to be more liquid.*) Taste and adjust the seasonings if necessary.

To serve, bring the soup almost to a boil and toss in the remaining coriander leaves. Stir briefly, then serve.

SERVES *4 as a main dish with rice or 6 as part of a rice meal*

SILKY COCONUT-PUMPKIN SOUP

[*keng bouad mak fak kham* — THAILAND, LAOS]

Serve this lush, smooth soup as part of an Asian or Western meal.

Large wedges of pumpkin with a pale gray-green skin are sold in Southeast Asian groceries and in Caribbean produce markets. Pick out the pumpkin with the reddest flesh. You can also use an orange "pie pumpkin."

3 to 4 shallots, unpeeled
1½ pounds pumpkin (untrimmed), or butternut squash
    or 1¼ pounds peeled pumpkin
2 cups canned or fresh coconut milk (see page 315)
2 cups mild pork or chicken broth
1 cup loosely packed coriander leaves
½ teaspoon salt
2 tablespoons Thai fish sauce, or to taste
Generous grindings of black pepper
¼ cup minced scallion greens (optional)

In a heavy skillet, or on a charcoal or gas grill, dry-roast or grill the shallots, turning occasionally until softened and blackened. Peel, cut the shallots lengthwise in half, and set aside.

Peel the pumpkin and clean off any seeds. Cut into small ½-inch cubes. You should have 4½ to 5 cups cubed pumpkin.

Place the coconut milk, broth, pumpkin cubes, shallots, and coriander leaves in a large pot and bring to a boil. Add the salt and simmer over medium heat until the pumpkin is tender, about 10 minutes. Stir in the fish sauce and cook for another 2 to 3 minutes. Taste for salt and add a little more fish sauce if you wish. (*The soup can be served immediately, but has even more flavor if left to stand for up to an hour. Reheat just before serving.*)

Serve from a large soup bowl or in individual bowls. Grind black pepper over generously, and, if you wish, garnish with a sprinkling of minced scallion greens. Leftovers freeze very well.

SERVES *4 to 6 as part of a rice meal*

SHRIMP IN HOT LIME LEAF BROTH

[*tom yum gung* — THAILAND]

Like the other sour soups in the region, *tom yum gung* sparks the appetite. Serve it with a mild or slightly sweet dish such as Chicken and Potato Curry (page 203) or Stir-fried Yunnan Ham (page 239) and a simple cooked vegetable such as Classic Mixed Vegetable Stir-fry (page 151) or Yunnan Greens (page 151).

3 cups mild chicken broth
2 stalks lemongrass, trimmed, smashed flat with the side
  of a cleaver, and cut into 1½-inch lengths
3 fresh or frozen wild lime leaves
3 bird chiles, stemmed and cut lengthwise in half
¼ pound oyster mushrooms, cleaned and coarsely chopped
½ pound medium or small shrimp, peeled and deveined
3 tablespoons fresh lime juice
2 tablespoons Thai fish sauce, or more to taste
Salt, if needed

Place the broth in a medium pot with the lemongrass and bring to a boil. Add the lime leaves and chiles, bring the broth back to a boil, and let cook for 5 minutes. Add the mushrooms, return to a vigorous boil, and add the shrimp. Cook for 1 minute, or until the shrimp have turned pink.

Remove from the heat and stir in the lime juice and fish sauce. Taste and adjust the seasonings with fish sauce or salt if you wish. Serve in small individual bowls to accompany jasmine rice, distributing the shrimp and mushroom pieces evenly among the bowls.

SERVES *4 with rice and one or more other dishes*

LEFT: *At the market in Dali, as at most markets outside the big cities, the vegetables and greens are locally grown and change with the season.*
RIGHT: SHRIMP IN HOT LIME LEAF BROTH.

PLAIN OF JARS VEGETABLE SOUP

[*gaeng jut pak* — PHONSAVAN, LAOS]

We had this quick vegetable soup every time we ate at the local restaurant down the dirt road from our guest house in Phonsavan, near the Plain of Jars in Laos. It was a truck-stop sort of place, not loaded with charm or frills, but the food was fresh and delicious and the owners good-natured. The soup came in a hot pot (see Note below), like a Chinese soup. The coals burning below the central chimney pleased our children and kept the soup at a very gentle simmer.

6 cups mild chicken or vegetable broth
1 tablespoon Thai fish sauce (optional)
2 slices ginger (unless your broth is flavored with ginger)
1 small onion, coarsely chopped
2 cups coarsely chopped Savoy cabbage (about 6 ounces)
2 cups cauliflower florets (about 6 ounces)
1 small to medium tomato, cut into 4 to 6 wedges
Salt to taste
Freshly ground white pepper (optional)

Place the broth and fish sauce, if using, in a medium pot and bring to a boil. Add the ginger slices and onion and boil, half-covered, for 5 minutes. Add the cabbage, cauliflower, and tomato, reduce the heat, and simmer until the cabbage and cauliflower are very soft, 10 to 15 minutes. Taste and add salt and white pepper if you wish.

Serve hot, in a hot pot or a heavy bowl with a lid, to accompany a rice meal; provide each guest with a small bowl for the soup. Or, serve as the soup course in a non-Asian meal.

SERVES *4 as a soup course, 6 as part of a rice meal*

NOTE: *Lightweight aluminum hot pots are available from Chinese groceries and cookware stores. They are shaped like a doughnut suspended on a hollow cylinder or chimney. The chimney is placed over a small Sterno or charcoal burner. The soup goes in the "doughnut" and is heated as the heat rises up the chimney.*

AKHA PEOPLE: The Akha are a people known in Laos as Kha and in China as Hani. Their original homeland is in Yunnan, where they still live in large numbers.

Over the last hundred and fifty years, however, many have moved to settle on the ridges and hilltops of parts of the Shan State, northern Laos, and northern Thailand. They live at elevations of over a thousand feet and are traditionally hunters as well as simple agriculturalists. Their houses are built on stilts, and their handwoven cotton fabric and the garments they make of it are works of art. In many villages, they still grow their own cotton and hemp, spin it, dye it (black or indigo blue), and weave it into beautiful fabrics for clothing (see The Fabric of It All, page 160). Akha women wear elaborate headdresses, striped cotton leggings, short flared skirts, and beautiful embroidered homespun jackets. They carry themselves confidently and often have a direct, earthy sense of humor.

The Akha have traditionally traded jungle products with lowland traders for salt and other necessities. In their cooking, they use salt rather than fish sauce, and they eat plain rather than sticky rice, except at festive or ceremonial occasions.

An important source of income in many Akha villages is the cultivation of opium poppies. Crude opium is gathered from the pods and sold to traders who come through the villages in January after the harvest. The opium is also used medicinally in the villages, and smoked by some Akha. After the poppy flowers have bloomed, they yield another more nourishing product that is not a narcotic: poppy seeds. These are eaten as a snack and used as an ingredient (see Salsa with Poppy Seeds, page 44).

Akha women wear their extraordinary headdresses and jewelry every day—to work in the fields or go to market.

CHICKEN SOUP WITH GREENS

[*canh ga* — VIETNAM]

Cellophane noodles and shredded chicken give this light-tasting chicken soup a little body and texture. Also called glass noodles or bean threads, cellophane noodles are beautiful once cooked, but they begin as dried-out strands that keep forever in your cupboard. They are made from mung beans, though it's hard to tell what they are the first time you see them. Sold in small cellophane packages in Chinese and Southeast Asian groceries, they are a nutritious household staple and need only a short soaking in warm water to soften.

2 chicken legs or 1 chicken breast (approximately 1 pound)

6 cups chicken broth

2 cups water

**2 ounces cellophane noodles, soaked in warm water
  for 20 minutes and drained**

5 to 6 stalks bok choi or Swiss chard, thoroughly washed

3 tablespoons Vietnamese or Thai fish sauce

Salt to taste

Freshly ground black pepper

Rinse the chicken, remove and discard the skin and fat, and place in a large pot. Add the broth and water and bring to a boil. Lower the heat and simmer, half-covered, skimming off any foam that rises to the surface, for 30 minutes, or until the chicken is cooked through.

Remove the chicken from the broth and let sit for a moment, until cool enough to handle. Discard the bones, shred the meat, and set aside. If you have time, chill the broth and then skim off the fat; if not, strain the broth into a saucepan through a colander lined with two layers of cheesecloth. (*The soup can be prepared ahead to this point and the chicken and broth stored separately, once cooled, in well-sealed containers in the refrigerator for up to 2 days.*)

Meanwhile, using scissors, cut the soaked noodles into 3- to 4-inch lengths; set aside. Cut off the bok choi or chard stems and set aside for another purpose. Slice the leaves lengthwise in half and cut crosswise into 1-inch slices.

When ready to serve, heat the broth to a simmer. Add the fish sauce, taste for seasonings, and add salt if you wish. Divide the shredded chicken among six soup bowls. Add the cellophane noodles and greens to the simmering broth and bring to a vigorous boil. Give the soup a good stir, then ladle the hot soup over the chicken, distributing the noodles and greens among the bowls. Grind black pepper generously over each bowl and serve at once.

SERVES *6*

NOTE: *This soup can be served Vietnamese style over cooked rice: Allow at least ½ cup cooked rice per person. Place the rice in large soup bowls, add the shredded chicken, and ladle the soup over.*

LAO HOT AND SOUR SOUP WITH FISH

[*tom yum pa* — CENTRAL LAOS]

Tom yum looks like a soup—a clear broth with a few flavorings in it—but it comes to the table as a dish to eat with rice, along with other dishes. Leaning toward sour and always made chile-hot, *tom yum* has an agreeable refreshing taste on the tongue. You can make it even if you don't have lime leaves, but they do add a wonderful aroma and flavor, as well as looking beautiful on the surface of the soup.

About 4 cups mild chicken or fish broth

1 teaspoon Thai Roasted Chile Paste (page 36) (optional)

3 stalks lemongrass

3 slices ginger

1 small onion, coarsely chopped

¼ to ⅓ pound small fish steaks (striped bass or other freshwater fish)

½ cup thickly sliced oyster or button mushrooms, or more to taste

1 medium tomato, cut into large chunks

3 fresh or frozen wild lime leaves

3 to 5 bird chiles

3 tablespoons fresh lime juice

½ to 1 tablespoon Thai fish sauce

¼ to ½ cup coriander leaves (optional)

Begin heating the broth in a medium pot; stir in the chile paste, if using, until dissolved. Trim the root and tough outer layers from the lemongrass, then smash flat with the side of a cleaver or knife. Cut into approximately 1½-inch lengths and add to broth. Smash the ginger slices with the flat side of the cleaver or knife and add to the broth together with the onion.

When the broth comes to a boil, lower the heat slightly and simmer for a few minutes. Cut the fish steaks in half if you wish, to make more pieces. Add the fish, mushrooms, and tomato to the broth and boil gently for 2 to 3 minutes. Add the lime leaves. When the fish has turned opaque, about 5 minutes in all, remove from the heat. Add the remaining ingredients except the coriander leaves and stir to mix. Taste and adjust the seasonings. If you wish more chile heat (a possibility if you omitted the chile paste), break one or two of the chiles into pieces and return to the soup. Let stand for several minutes, then add the coriander leaves if you wish and serve.

SERVES *4 as part of a rice meal*

NOTE: *Remind your guests that the lemongrass, ginger, and lime leaves are not for eating.*

BUDDHIST SOUR SOUP

[*canh chua dau hou* — MEKONG DELTA, VIETNAM]

This is a vegetarian version of a Mekong Delta classic called *canh chua* (literally, "sour soup"). Many people in Vietnam fast (eat no meat or fish) on the first and fifteenth days of each lunar month (at the new moon and full moon), while others choose a month-long period in which to fast. Therefore, even in this cuisine, which normally relies on the wonderful smoky saltiness of fish sauce, there's a strong and well-developed vegetarian tradition. Tofu and other soy products are available in even the smallest village market.

Canh is a category of Vietnamese soup that is meant to be eaten with rice. The soup comes to the table in a large bowl, as the main dish or one of several dishes in a meal, then is ladled out into individual bowls. The rice is served in a pot, then often spooned straight into the individual bowls of soup.

This soup is tart with tamarind and sweet with a little sugar. The two balance each other so that neither predominates and the soup slides easily on the tongue.

SOUP

3 blocks tofu (about 1 pound)
¼ cup tamarind pulp, dissolved in 1 cup hot water
Scant ½ pound okra (approximately 2 cups)
5 cups water
¾ cup fresh pineapple cut into ¼-inch chunks
1 stalk *bac ha* (giant taro), cut into 1½-inch lengths (optional)
3 tablespoons sugar
2 teaspoons salt
2 medium tomatoes, cut into wedges
1 teaspoon soy sauce
GARNISH AND FLAVORINGS
¼ cup peanut or vegetable oil
½ cup chopped shallots
2 to 3 cups bean sprouts, rinsed and drained
12 leaves Asian basil, coarsely torn
6 sprigs rice paddy herb (*ngo om*, optional)
2 to 4 bird or serrano chiles, minced

For the soup, place the tofu blocks on a plate, place another plate on top, and weight with a jar or 14- to 28-ounce can. Let stand for 30 minutes. Water will be pressed out of the tofu as it stands; drain it off every 15 minutes or so. Cut the tofu into ½-inch cubes and set aside.

Use your fingers to squeeze and press the tamarind to dissolve it completely and to squeeze the last of the pulp off any seeds and pith. Place a sieve over a small bowl and pour the tamarind water through. Discard any solids and set the liquid aside.

If the okra is large, cut crosswise in half and cut off any tough tips, leaving the stems on.

For the garnish, heat the oil in a small heavy skillet over medium-high heat. Add the shallots and cook until well browned, then remove from the heat and set aside.

To make the soup, place the tamarind liquid and the 5 cups water in a large nonreactive pot. Bring to a vigorous boil, then add the okra (if your okra is very fresh and tender, add it later, with the tomato wedges) and pineapple. Boil vigorously for 3 minutes, then add the *bac ha*, if using, the sugar, salt, and tomato wedges. Bring back to a boil, then add the tofu cubes and soy sauce and cook for 2 minutes. Taste and adjust the balance of seasonings if you wish.

To serve, divide the bean sprouts, torn basil leaves, and *ngo om* sprigs, if using, among large soup bowls. Ladle the soup, including the vegetables and tofu, into the bowls. Top each with a tablespoon of the reserved oil and shallots and a pinch of minced chiles. Serve immediately, with plenty of rice. Guests can place rice in their bowls of soup or onto separate plates or bowls as they wish. Place the remaining minced chiles in a small bowl on the table so guests can add extra as they choose.

SERVES *4 to 6 with rice*

HEARTY CHICKEN SOUP WITH ONIONS AND GARLIC

[*keng kai* — LAOS]

This satisfying chicken soup from Luang Prabang in Laos has great depth of flavor and has become a favorite in our house. Begin with a good organic chicken if you can. The whole coriander plants give a wonderful taste, and their slight bitterness is balanced by a sweetness from the boiled shallots, onion, and garlic. The recipe makes a large amount, but leftovers freeze well.

One 3-pound chicken, preferably organic, rinsed
3 to 4 scallions, trimmed
5 whole coriander plants, including roots, well washed,
  plus ½ cup packed chopped coriander leaves
8 black peppercorns
3 quarts water
3 tablespoons Thai fish sauce
1 teaspoon salt
1 large onion, finely chopped
8 small shallots, peeled, or 4 to 5 large shallots, peeled and
  cut lengthwise in half
1 head garlic, cloves separated, peeled, and cut lengthwise
  in half if large
Freshly ground black pepper

To prepare the broth, place the chicken, scallions, coriander plants, and peppercorns in a large pot with the water and bring to a vigorous boil. Lower the heat and cook at a gentle boil until the chicken is very tender, about 1½ hours. If the water does not completely cover the chicken, turn the chicken several times during cooking.

Remove the chicken and place on a platter. Strain the broth, discarding the solids. If you have time, place the broth in a wide bowl to cool to room temperature, then refrigerate; once the fat has congealed, skim it off.

When the chicken is cool enough to handle, remove the meat from the bones and pull apart into large shreds, discarding the skin, bones, and any sinew or fat. Set the meat aside. (*The recipe can be made 24 hours ahead to this point. Store the broth and meat separately in well-sealed containers in the refrigerator.*)

About 20 minutes before you wish to serve the soup, place the broth in a large pot, add the fish sauce and salt, and bring to a boil. Add the onion, shallots, and garlic and cook at a gentle boil until the shallots are tender, about 15 minutes. Add about 1½ cups of the reserved chicken to the soup; serve the rest on a small platter so guests can help themselves.

Serve in large bowls, garnished with black pepper and the chopped coriander leaves.

SERVES *6 generously*

MENGHAN: We didn't have a single good night's sleep in Menghan (a small village on the Mekong at the southern tip of Yunnan; see map, page 6). Sleeping on the wooden floor of the old thatched house built high up on stilts, like every Dai house in Menghan, we heard chickens and other creatures nibbling and poking around right under our heads all night long. And then there was the distillery, also beneath our room, and the smell of the fermented rice in all those old wooden barrels. The idea that it could all explode crossed our minds, which didn't help make getting to sleep any easier.

Days were great, though. Better than great. We were, we think, only the second lodgers ever to set foot in the Dai guest house. It was the first lodger, an Englishman, who'd told us how to find it. The family that ran the guest house had decided to rent out two spare little rooms, and they'd pulled him in off the street. Five days later, he'd reluctantly left town; hospitality at the Dai guest house was something pretty special.

When we first arrived, we'd barely had time to put our bags down before Dom and Tashi had disappeared with the family's two teenage girls and a couple of their friends. They went for ice cream, then for a motorbike ride (four people per motorbike), then to a temple festival, where they had grilled tofu with chile sauce, then back for another ice cream. Meanwhile, we had lunch.

We had a bowl of rice, an egg and tomato stir-fry, a grilled river fish wrapped around a ton of fresh coriander, a tempura made with an unknown-to-us tree leaf from the garden (served with its own chile sauce), and a fresh Dai salsa, spicy as could be. It was so good that by the time we were finished, we were already trying to imagine dinner.

So, like the Englishman, we moved in. They adopted us, and we adopted them. Every day the girls went to school in the morning and again in the early evening, and while they were at school, Dom and Tashi were sad and slow. But then around seven-thirty at night, long after dark, we'd hear laughs and giggles coming through the night, and then suddenly we'd see their faces, and the faces of their friends, and then off they'd all go together again into the dark night, Dom and Tashi in tow, in heaven.

"Do people in Thailand look like me?" the mother, Mae, asked us.

"Well, yes, sort of," we answered. It seemed strange, she being Dai, speaking Thai, and never having been to Thailand, which is not so far away. And how could we explain that to us she looked more Thai than people sometimes look in Thailand, and that Menghan looked more Thai than most Thai towns today. All the while we were there, we had the feeling we were seeing the Thailand of several generations past: the old wooden houses built high up on stilts, the modest but beautiful temples, the graceful walk of people who have spent little time with cars.

Perhaps, we thought, as national borders in the region continue to open, once again the Dai will come to know their cousins, the Thai, from the country to the south.

During and after the Cultural Revolution, places of worship throughout China were closed and fell into disrepair. Since the 1980s, religious expression has become freer, and this Buddhist temple in Menghan is now open once more.

VIETNAMESE BEEF BALL SOUP

[*sup bo vien* — VIETNAM]

We first ate beef ball soup from a street vendor in Saigon long ago on our first trip to Vietnam. The street vendor was young and cheerful, despite all her hard work. She carried her whole operation on a long carrying pole on her shoulder. On one end of the pole was a huge vat of broth on a charcoal heater; on the other, a basket containing bowls, spoons, and chopsticks and a stack of small stools for patrons, as well as a tray of condiments. When she saw we were looking hungry, she set it all down, put out some stools, and gestured for us to sit. We paid for our soup, as is usual, only when we handed back our empty bowls.

Since that street encounter, each time we eat beef ball soup, we savor the aromatic broth, the firm bite of the beef balls, and the memory of that bowl of soup in Saigon.

Beef balls are surprisingly quick to make; you can prepare them ahead and freeze them for later use.

1 pound boneless beef round, trimmed of all fat

1½ teaspoons tapioca or potato starch

½ teaspoon sugar

½ teaspoon baking powder

1 tablespoon fresh lime juice

¼ cup Vietnamese or Thai fish sauce

2 tablespoons plus 6 cups water

½ bird or serrano chile, seeded and minced

1½ teaspoons black peppercorns

1 stalk lemongrass, trimmed and smashed flat
  with the side of a cleaver

1 medium onion, quartered

1 to 2 tablespoons roasted sesame oil

3 tablespoons chopped scallion greens

3 tablespoons coriander leaves

Freshly ground black pepper

Fresh Chile-Garlic Paste (page 26 or store-bought) (optional)

Slice the beef across the grain into ¼-inch-thick slices. Place the tapioca or potato starch, sugar, and baking powder in a medium bowl and stir in the lime juice, a scant 2 tablespoons of the fish sauce, and the 2 tablespoons water. Pound the chile in a mortar with ¼ teaspoon of the peppercorns and add to the flavorings. Add the beef slices and stir and turn to coat them. Cover the bowl with plastic wrap and refrigerate for 6 to 24 hours.

Bring the 6 cups of water to a boil in a large saucepan. Add the remaining 1¼ teaspoons peppercorns, the lemongrass, and onion to the boiling water, reduce the heat, cover, and simmer for 20 minutes; set aside.

Meanwhile, place about half the marinated meat in a food processor and process to a smooth paste, about 1 minute. Transfer to a bowl and repeat with the remaining meat.

Put a large plate and a small dish of the roasted sesame oil beside your work space. Roll about 1 heaping tablespoon of the meat paste between your palms into a walnut-sized ball. Dab a little sesame oil on one palm, roll the ball on your palm, and place it on the plate. Repeat until you have about 40 beef balls.

Bring the broth back to a boil, then lower the heat to medium. Add half the beef balls; they will sink, then rise to the surface. Let them cook for 3 minutes after they rise. With a slotted spoon, transfer to a large plate and repeat with the remaining balls.

Add the remaining generous 2 tablespoons fish sauce to the broth, then strain the broth and discard the solids. Serve the beef balls in small bowls topped by the broth and garnished with the scallion greens, coriander, and freshly ground pepper. If you wish, serve the chile-garlic paste in a condiment dish on the side.

SERVES *6 to 8*

NOTE: *You can also cook and serve the beef balls in a beef broth, either store-bought or left over from a batch of Hearty Vietnamese Beef Noodle Soup (page 128). Or, serve the beef balls separately from the broth, as a snack, a filling for sandwiches, or a topping for noodles. Set out a little Fresh Chile-Garlic Paste to dab on them.*

SALADS

Salads are such a basic part of eating along the Mekong that they can almost be considered a staple food. They can be as simple as a wedge of parboiled cabbage and a plate of fresh cucumber slices or as elaborate as a mixed array of greens and herbs flavored with a dressing of succulent fried minced pork and a hot-sour-salty fresh dressing (see Luang Prabang Fusion Salad, page 78). Simple or elaborate, salads are an important part of almost every meal.

As taste dictates, there is the idea that something cooling (a simple raw vegetable or salad) should accompany something hot. A red-hot Thai curry, even if eaten only with rice as a light lunch, will always be served with fresh cucumber slices or two or three trimmed whole scallions. While these may look like a simple garnish, the fact that they are fresh and cooling makes the lunch complete, with something cold to enjoy alongside something hot.

When we walk into restaurant kitchens in Vietnam, Thailand, or Cambodia, we are immediately struck by the quantities of freshly washed lettuce leaves, bean sprouts, and coriander, mint, and basil leaves. In Vietnam in particular, in even the smallest restaurants, there will be a knee-high pail of water packed with bean sprouts, a visible reminder of how essential fresh vegetables are to almost every meal served. A basic salad plate with leaf lettuce, fresh herbs, sliced cucumber, and more is a necessary item on the

RIGHT: *Salad greens are trimmed and beautifully presented at the market in Siam Reap, Cambodia.* OPPOSITE: *By the time it reaches Vientiane, the Mekong is wide and calm.*

table at most Vietnamese meals (see Vietnamese Herb and Salad Plate, page 68). The greens are used to wrap other items, such as fried spring rolls, while the herbs and vegetables are used to adjust the flavorings of anything from soups to grilled meats. Among the most common simple salads on a Vietnamese salad plate is lightly vinegared shredded carrot and daikon (see Carrot and Daikon Pickled Salad, page 85), a favorite element in Mekong subs.

In traditional Chinese cooking, vegetables are almost never served raw, but in Yunnan, a bridge between the Chinese and Southeast Asian culinary worlds, raw cucumber is dressed with a cooked dressing, spicy with hot chile oil (see Spicy Cucumber Salad, page 79). It's a knockout.

Many salads in the Lao-Thai culinary region are more substantial and play a central rather than an accompanying role. We've put these in other chapters by main ingredient (for example, Turkey with Mint and Hot Chiles is in

the Poultry chapter). The Thai and Lao salads in this chapter have vegetables as a main ingredient, raw or grilled, then chopped and flavored with a dressing balanced between hot, sour, salty, and sweet. Among our favorites are *Som Tam* with Yard-long Beans (page 76) and Grilled Eggplant Salad (page 84).

VIETNAMESE HERB AND SALAD PLATE
[*xalach dia* — VIETNAM]

Xalach dia is an essential part of the Vietnamese table, especially in the south, a wonderful tradition that brings freshness and variety to every meal. The salad vegetables are used to wrap, to accompany, to enhance, or to alter the other dishes, or they are eaten simply on their own. The salad platter gives each person a chance to vary tastes and textures, mouthful by mouthful, as the various herbs and salad vegetables complement the cooked foods with fresh flavors. What's more, the salad platter brings color and beauty to the table.

Halfway around the world, in Iran, Armenia, and the Eastern Mediterranean, there's a very similar salad plate tradition, and its role in the meal is almost identical. In all cases, it makes each person a lively participant in how the meal comes together.

If the list of options looks daunting, just begin by putting out a bowl of salad greens, without dressing, and a bowl of fresh herbs, coriander sprigs, for example, or Asian basil leaves. Encourage your guests to use the greens and herbs as a freshening mouthful between bites of cooked food, as well as to wrap combinations of different foods.

SOME OR ALL OF
Asian or sweet basil leaves
Mint leaves
Coriander sprigs
Leaf lettuce (one or more kinds), separated into leaves
Small scallions, trimmed
Small lime wedges
Bird chiles, whole or minced
Cucumber slices or chunks
Bean sprouts, raw or briefly parboiled and drained
Carrot and Daikon Pickled Salad (page 85)
Pickled Bean Sprout Salad (page 85)

Set out the ingredients of your choice on one or more plates or shallow bowls to accompany any meal.

DAI MINT AND TOMATO SALAD
[SOUTHERN YUNNAN]

The Dai, like the Chinese, prefer their tomatoes a little green, just before their fullest sweet ripeness. Perhaps it's an aesthetic question: The mix of green and red is more interesting to the eye than the uniform red of ripe tomatoes. Or perhaps it's because tomatoes enter the regional cuisine as a slightly sour vegetable, rather than with sweetness and ripeness as their prime characteristic. All of which is to say that you should, as we do, use the tomatoes that please you.

This salad is simple to make and delicious. It's like a half-pounded Mexican salsa, ideal for scooping up with Thai-Lao Crispy Rice Crackers (page 106) or sticky rice or pork cracklings.

2 teaspoons minced garlic
1 teaspoon salt, or to taste
A little minced chile, such as jalapeño (optional)
1 cup tender mint leaves, coarsely torn (see Note)
2 to 3 scallions, trimmed, sliced lengthwise into ribbons, and then cut crosswise into 1-inch lengths
5 medium tomatoes, thinly sliced
1 tablespoon Hot Chile Oil (page 310 or store-bought)

Place the garlic and salt in a large mortar and pound together. Or place them in a large bowl and use the back of a flat spoon to mash them against the side of the bowl. Add the fresh chile, if using, the mint, and the scallions and continue to pound or mash to soften and blend. Add the tomatoes and gently pound or mash until broken up a little. Add the chile oil and toss well. Serve the salad mounded in a shallow bowl, with the juices poured over.

SERVES *4 as an appetizer or as part of a rice meal*

NOTE: *If your mint is at all coarse or rough, finely chop the leaves; or substitute Asian basil leaves.*

STEAMED VEGETABLE PLATE
[*nung pak* — SHAN STATE, LAOS, NORTH AND
NORTHEAST THAILAND]

The Lao, the Shan, and the northern Thai all include a plate of plain cooked vegetables on the table at almost every meal. As with the salad plate in Vietnam, the vegetables come to the table without any dressing and are eaten along with the meal. They are often accompanied by a few raw vegetables, such as cucumber or round Thai eggplants.

Like clear soup, *nung pak* provides a simple unseasoned contrast to the highly flavored dishes in the meal. But in tropical Southeast Asia, with the variety of vegetables used and all of their different tastes and textures, *nung pak* can almost be a meal in itself.

The following list is just a suggestion; use whichever vegetables you have on hand and are in season. You can serve them hot or at room temperature.

CHOOSE TWO OR THREE
½ small Savoy cabbage, cut into small wedges
About ½ pound kabocha or other sweet squash or pumpkin,
   peeled, seeded, and cut into 1½-inch cubes
¼ pound yard-long beans, trimmed and cut into 4-inch lengths,
   or green beans, trimmed
4 medium carrots, cut into 2-inch lengths
½ European cucumber, peeled and sliced
4 small round Thai eggplants, halved

To steam cabbage, squash, beans, and carrots (or other vegetables of your choice), place a steaming rack over hot water in a large pot. Place the vegetables on the rack, cover the pot, bring the water to a boil, and steam until the vegetables are just tender. (If steaming more than one vegetable, either steam each type separately, or remove each vegetable as it is cooked.) Remove the vegetables to a plate and serve hot or at room temperature, together with the cucumber and/or eggplant, or other raw vegetables.
SERVES *4 to 6 as part of a rice meal*

Padaung women, near the Burma-Thai border, wear metal rings around their necks and on their arms and legs from the time they are girls.

IN THE SHAN HILLS: We didn't know whether to go to Burma or not to go. The Mekong river forms Burma's eastern border with Laos, and the people who live in this region of the country are primarily Shan, also called Tai Yai, part of the greater Tai family. From the point of view of culture, food, and cooking, we definitely wanted to spend time in the Shan hills.

But there was this matter of the Burmese government, and of its abhorrent internal political situation. Not only has the current Rangoon regime trampled any trace of democracy and made a joke of human rights, but for over fifty years it has fought an ongoing war against the Karen, the Shan, the Kachin, the Kalaw, and others who have claims to sovereignty. By going to Burma, we knew that we would be contributing badly needed foreign exchange to the Rangoon government.

In the end, we went. We didn't like handing over money at the airport (Burma still has a system that requires converting a set amount of currency, which is not reconvertible, at the airport when you arrive.) We didn't like traveling by Rangoon rules. We didn't like a lot of things in the two weeks we were there, but we were very pleased to have gone, pleased we had made the decision to go.

Burma is living through its own version of China's Cultural Revolution. Neighbors snitch on neighbors, friends on friends. Universities are indefinitely suspended. Passports are unobtainable. No one would speak with us if someone else was around, but whenever we were safely in private, as on a long taxi ride, or a hike in the mountains, people would open up. Everyone is scared, and they have no idea that people outside Burma support them.

We flew up to Taunggyi, in the southern Shan State, where Naomi had been twenty years earlier. On her first visit, it was like stepping back a century in time. As a result of the government policies from 1965 to the early 1980s, there were no modern vehicles, no public telephones, very little electricity, and what manufactured goods existed were smuggled in from Thailand. The country had little or no formal international trade and was so hands-off internationally that it had not even joined the nonaligned nations movement.

The Taunggyi of today is utterly different. It is noisy, modern, and totally Chinese in character. We felt entirely at home, because it looked, smelled, and sounded like dozens of other no-name small concrete cities we have spent nights in while traveling in China. There were Chinese trucks, Chinese manufactured goods, Chinese workers, and Chinese food in the restaurants on the main streets. It hit us like a rock, unexpected as a flash of lightning. China had become an ally, a big ally, and as a result, no amount of Western embargo or sanctions on Burma was going to be effective.

Burma's war on itself will rage on.

The situation in Burma has created many refugees—like this young Karen woman—who have sought asylum in Thailand, mostly in border areas.

SIMPLE CUCUMBER SALAD

[*huanggua liangban* — CHINA]

According to Chinese tradition, cucumber is cooling and, even in the summer, should be balanced with something warming. Here the warmth, medicinal and culinary, comes from a little minced ginger.

1 medium European cucumber (about ½ pound)
1 tablespoon black rice vinegar
2 teaspoons white rice or white wine vinegar
Pinch of sugar
¼ teaspoon salt, or to taste
¼ teaspoon minced ginger

Cut strips of peel lengthwise off the cucumber, leaving alternating strips on. Cut the cucumber lengthwise into quarters and scrape off and discard the seeds. Gently smash flat each length with the side of a cleaver, then cut lengthwise in half and crosswise into approximately 1-inch lengths. Place in a shallow bowl.

In a small bowl, mix together the vinegars and sugar, then pour over the cucumber. Add the salt and mix well.

Mound the cucumber on a small plate, sprinkle on the ginger, and serve as an appetizer or as a salad to accompany a rice meal.

SERVES *3 to 4 as an appetizer or part of a rice meal*

NOTE: *If you increase the amount of cucumber, you will need proportionately less dressing.*

POMELO SALAD

[*nyoom kroit t'long* — CAMBODIA]

Pomelos are big grapefruitlike fruits that are now becoming more available in North America. They are about twice the size of a grapefruit and have a very thick skin. The fruit ranges from quite sour to pleasantly sweet.

If you can't find a pomelo, use grapefruit. But grapefruits are far juicier than pomelos; pomelos are uniquely dry in texture. If using grapefruit, pour off excess juice; otherwise, it will be soggy. Be sure to adjust the seasonings to taste, as both pomelos and grapefruit have that wild range between sour and sweet.

3 tablespoons Thai fish sauce
3 tablespoons fresh lime juice
1 tablespoon palm sugar, or substitute brown sugar
1 pomelo or large grapefruit (approximately 1¼ pounds)
2 tablespoons Dry-Roasted Grated Coconut (page 308)
2 tablespoons Dry-Roasted Peanuts (page 308),
 coarsely chopped
1 tablespoon chopped shallots
1 cup mint leaves, chopped
2 to 3 bird chiles, finely chopped
Bibb lettuce leaves, washed and dried, for garnish

In a small bowl, mix together the fish sauce, lime juice, and sugar, stirring vigorously to dissolve the sugar completely. Set aside.

Peel the pomelo or grapefruit and separate into segments. Cut off the inside "seam" of each segment and then run your thumb between the membrane and the fruit to free it. Place the fruit in a bowl.

When ready to serve, pour off any juice that has accumulated at the bottom of the bowl; reserve for another purpose. Add the roasted coconut and peanuts, the shallots, mint, and chiles to the fruit and mix well. Pour the lime dressing over and mix well. Taste and adjust the balance of salt, sour, sweet (fish sauce, lime juice, and sugar) if you wish, then serve immediately on a bed of lettuce.

SERVES *4 as part of a rice meal*

Rice demands long days of labor, from plowing and smoothing the wet paddy before planting (LEFT), to planting and harvesting (RIGHT). Both photographs were taken near Taunggyi, Shan State, Burma.

VIETNAMESE GREEN PAPAYA SALAD
[*goi du du* — VIETNAM]

Papaya trees grow abundantly throughout Southeast Asia. They mature rapidly and produce large quantities of fruit, making papaya inexpensive and available year-round. As a consequence, there are a great many different versions of green papaya salad throughout the region, the most well known being *som tam,* from northeast Thailand and Laos (where it is called *tam som*). (See *Som Tam* with Yard-long Beans, page 76.)

This Vietnamese green papaya salad is quick to assemble and pleasingly tart and refreshing to eat. Serve it as a crisp contrast in texture and flavor to grilled or simmered meat dishes or hearty stews.

1 small green or half-ripe papaya

2 small star fruit, 1 cut into julienne strips and
   1 sliced crosswise

2 small tomatoes, 1 diced and 1 sliced

¼ cup fresh lime juice

1 tablespoon Vietnamese or Thai fish sauce

1 clove garlic, minced

1 bird or serrano chile, minced

1 shallot, minced

¼ cup Dry-Roasted Peanuts (page 308), finely chopped

1 tablespoon Roasted Rice Powder (page 308)

¼ cup coriander leaves

Peel the papaya, slice lengthwise in half, and remove the seeds. Using a coarse grater, grate into a large bowl. Add the julienned star fruit and diced tomato. In a small bowl, mix together the lime juice, fish sauce, garlic, chile, shallot, and peanuts. Pour over the salad and toss to blend.

Just before serving, sprinkle on the rice powder and top with the coriander leaves. Mound the salad on a plate and arrange the star fruit and tomato slices decoratively around it.

SERVES *4 as a side salad*

NOTE: *If green papayas are not available (they're nowadays a year-round staple at many Vietnamese and Thai groceries), substitute 3 or 4 Granny Smith apples, cut into small dice. Immediately after dicing the apples, toss with some of the lime juice to prevent the apples from discoloring.*

SOM TAM WITH YARD-LONG BEANS
[*som tam tua yai* — NORTHEAST THAILAND, LAOS]

We once ordered *som tam* from a restaurant menu in a tiny village in Thailand, and we were delighted when to the table came this beautiful version of the dish, made with yard-long beans instead of green papaya. The beans had been julienned, then pounded with chiles, dried shrimp, peanuts, garlic, lime juice, and fish sauce, just as shredded green papaya is in traditional *som tam*.

Som tam is traditionally pounded in a large Thai mortar with a pestle as it is blended. The "tam, tam" sound of the *som tam* maker is part of the sounds of morning markets in Laos and northeast Thailand. To make the salad, you need a large deep mortar or a bowl and a flat wooden spoon in which to soften and blend the beans with the flavorings. Use 1 chile for medium heat, 2 for traditional heat.

Serve a side platter of fresh greens and vegetables with *som tam* so guests can use the greens, and the cabbage, to scoop up the salad.

1 large clove garlic

¼ teaspoon salt

1 tablespoon Dry-Roasted Peanuts (page 308), coarsely chopped

1 tablespoon dried shrimp, minced

1 to 2 bird chiles, minced

Pinch of sugar, or more to taste

¼ cup fresh lime juice

2 tablespoons Thai fish sauce

2 plum tomatoes or 4 half-ripe cherry tomatoes, coarsely chopped

½ pound yard-long beans, or substitute green beans, trimmed, cut lengthwise in half, and then cut crosswise into 1½-inch lengths (see Note)

ACCOMPANIMENTS

Leaf or romaine lettuce, washed, dried, and torn into approximately 2-inch pieces

¼ head Savoy cabbage, cored and cut into small wedges

Place the garlic, salt, peanuts, dried shrimp, chiles, and sugar in a large mortar or in a food processor and pound or process to a paste. *If using a processor,* transfer the paste to a bowl. Stir in the lime juice and fish sauce, then add the chopped tomatoes and a generous handful of beans. *If using a mortar,* stir in the lime juice and fish sauce, the tomatoes and the handful of beans. Pound with the pestle or the back of the wooden spoon, being careful not to splash yourself, to mash the beans a little and combine them with the flavorings. Gradually add the remaining beans, mashing and blending as you do. (If your mortar is too small to handle the whole amount at once, prepare in two batches.) Taste for salty-hot-sweet balance and adjust the flavorings if you wish.

Mound onto a serving plate lined with lettuce leaves. Place the wedges of cabbage around the edge of the plate. Serve immediately.
SERVES *6*

NOTES: *If your beans are tough, first parboil them for several minutes in plenty of boiling water, then refresh them in cold water. Proceed to trim and chop them.*

The Shan have a version of som tam *called* mak sam paw saa *(mak sam paa being "papaya" in Shan). It's not a pounded salad, just a mixture of shredded green papaya, salt, dried red chile flakes,* tua nao *powder (see Shan Chile Paste, page 37), and tamarind water (made by dissolving tamarind pulp in water). It's tart and salty. If tamarind water is not available, they substitute minced pineapple to give a sour fruit note.*

*Sometimes hog plums (*makawk *in Thai and Lao) are mashed or squeezed into* som tam *to add another sour note. We've also eaten* som tam *made with pomelo (*som-u *in Thai) as the main ingredient— delicious.*

OPPOSITE: *Flower sellers by a busy highway in Sri Chiang Mai.* BELOW LEFT: *Pyrethrum flowers in full bloom. Pyrethrum is used in insecticides.* BELOW RIGHT: *Everyone dresses up at New Year's, although this Akha man was the first we'd seen wearing flowers.*

LUANG PRABANG FUSION SALAD

[*salat luang prabang* — LAOS]

This surprising salad is a brilliant fusion of French salad traditions and Lao flavorings. There are two dressings: First, a quickly cooked mixture of ground pork, garlic, and seasonings is poured, hot, over the lettuce and herbs. Then a lime juice and fish sauce dressing is added moments later, just before you toss and serve the salad. When you finish serving the salad, there will be a large, yummy puddle of dressing left on the platter; this is how it's done in Luang Prabang, and it's how it's meant to look, so don't worry.

You can serve Fusion Salad as a salad course, but we prefer it as a main dish, on its own or to accompany rice (the Lao way).

3 to 4 large or extra-large eggs, preferably free-range

2 medium heads leaf or Bibb lettuce, washed and dried

4 scallions, trimmed, smashed flat with the side of a cleaver,
   cut lengthwise in half or into quarters, and then cut
   crosswise into 2-inch lengths

1 cup coriander sprigs

1 cup loosely packed, coarsely chopped or torn Chinese celery
   leaves, or substitute flat-leaf parsley sprigs

LIME JUICE DRESSING

1 tablespoon minced ginger

2 bird or serrano chiles (optional)

1 to 2 cloves garlic, minced

3 tablespoons Thai fish sauce

2 tablespoons fresh lime juice

COOKED DRESSING

2 tablespoons peanut or vegetable oil or minced pork fat

8 cloves garlic, minced

½ pound ground pork

1 teaspoon salt

1 tablespoon sugar

¾ cup hot water

½ cup rice or cider vinegar

2 to 3 tablespoons Dry-Roasted Peanuts (page 308),
   coarsely chopped

Put the eggs in a saucepan with cold water to cover. Bring to a boil, then reduce the heat and cook at a gentle rolling boil for 10 minutes. Drain and set aside to cool.

Tear the salad greens into large coarse pieces. Place all the greens, including the scallions and herbs, in a large bowl and set aside.

Peel the hard-cooked eggs and cut crosswise in half. Transfer the yolks to a small bowl and mash; set aside. Slice the whites crosswise and set aside.

In a medium bowl, mix together all the lime juice dressing ingredients; set aside.

When you are ready to proceed, put the ingredients for the cooked dressing near your stovetop. Heat a wok or heavy skillet over high heat. Add the oil or fat and heat for 20 seconds, then add the minced garlic. Stir-fry briefly, until the garlic starts to change color, about 20 seconds, then toss in the pork. Use your spatula to break up the pork into small pieces as you stir-fry. Once all the pork has changed color completely, after 1 to 2 minutes, add the salt and sugar, then add the hot water and bring to a boil. Add the vinegar, add the reserved mashed egg yolks, and stir to blend.

Pour the hot liquid and pork over the prepared greens and toss gently. Pour the lime juice dressing and toss. Transfer the salad to a large flat platter (or to individual dinner plates) and mound it attractively. Sprinkle on the chopped roasted peanuts, arrange slices of egg white attractively on top, and serve immediately.

SERVES *6 to 8*

WHITE FUNGUS SALAD

[*yam het khao* — THAILAND]

Over the last few years, white fungus has become a dependable pantry item in our kitchen. It is tasty, cheap, easy to find, versatile, and fun. White fungus comes in a cellophane package, dry and lightweight, and keeps almost indefinitely (see page 319 for more details). Several times, when we have been waiting in line at a Chinese grocery with a package of white fungus, someone asked us how we were going to prepare it. When we would say we like to use it in salads, we got a rather weird look. The common use for white fungus in Chinese cooking is in a sugary light soup. We haven't yet tried the soup, but we sure do like the Thai salad version.

1 ounce dried white fungus, soaked in warm water
   for 10 minutes
1 tablespoon vegetable or peanut oil
2 tablespoons thinly sliced shallots
1 tablespoon minced garlic
4 to 5 ounces ground pork
2 to 3 Thai dried red chiles
2 tablespoons fresh lime juice
2 tablespoons Thai fish sauce
¼ cup coarsely torn coriander leaves

Drain the soaked fungus, rinse, and drain again thoroughly. Cut out and discard the hard core and any discolored patches. Cut the fungus into ¾-inch or teaspoon-sized pieces, and set aside in a bowl.

Place a wok or large heavy skillet over high heat. When it is hot, add the oil and swirl to coat the pan. Toss in the shallots and garlic, then, after 15 seconds, the pork and chiles. Stir-fry, breaking up any clumps of meat, until the pork is cooked through, about 1½ minutes. Add the lime juice and remove from the heat. Add the fish sauce, stir briefly, and add to the fungus.

Just before serving, add the coriander leaves and toss to mix. Turn out onto a plate and serve immediately.

SERVES *4 as part of a meal*

SPICY CUCUMBER SALAD

[*layou huanggua* — YUNNAN]

In this salad, the cucumbers are first dressed with a little vinegar, then dressed again with hot oil. The contrast of smooth chile-warm oil and crisp fresh cucumber is a knockout. The salad has a mild but not aggressive heat made with the 5 dried red chiles. Note that the cucumbers will soften if they're left standing, so don't pour the hot oil over them until just before you wish to serve the salad.

1 large or 2 medium European cucumbers (1 to 1¼ pounds)
2 tablespoons rice vinegar
1 tablespoon sugar
2 tablespoons peanut or vegetable oil
5 Thai dried red chiles, or 3 for milder heat
½ jalapeño, minced
7 Sichuan peppercorns
½ teaspoon salt
¼ cup packed torn coriander leaves

Peel the cucumber, leaving some thin strips of peel on if you wish, for a decorative effect. Cut lengthwise into quarters and scrape off and discard the seeds. Use the flat side of a cleaver or large knife to bash the cucumber pieces several times. Cut the pieces lengthwise into thinner strips, then cut crosswise into 2-inch lengths. Place in a medium bowl. In a small bowl, mix together the vinegar and sugar. Pour over the cucumber, mix well, and set aside.

Place a wok or skillet over high heat. When it is hot, add the oil and swirl to coat the pan. Toss in the dried chiles, jalapeño, and peppercorns and stir-fry for 20 to 30 seconds. Pour this over the cucumbers. Sprinkle on the salt and mix well.

Mound the salad in a shallow bowl. Sprinkle on the coriander leaves and serve immediately.

SERVES *4 as a salad or as one of many dishes in a rice meal*

NOTE: *The traditional way to make this uses 3 tablespoons of oil, giving a well-oiled texture that may be undesirable. If you wish, try both and see which you prefer.*

In present-day Burma, people can't talk openly about politics. They're afraid of informants and secret police, even while eating breakfast at the market.

OPPOSITE: SPICY CUCUMBER SALAD *(page 79).*

KAREN NEW YEAR: When our son Dominic was two, we lived in Chiang Mai for six months. We rented a little one-room house for seventy-five dollars a month, just off the river, and near the market. We asked around town about renting a secondhand vehicle, and before long we were driving an old blue pickup, which we came to love. Like many trucks in Thailand, it had a canopy over the back and two long benches, so it was easy to pick up anyone and everyone hitching a ride on the road.

The man we rented from turned out to be Karen, not Thai. The Karen live primarily in the Karen State, which Burma regards as Burma and the Karen regard as the Karen State. When the British left Burma in 1945, they recognized three different countries—Burma, the Karen State, and the Shan State. But the Burmese quickly moved on the others, and war broke out. And now, fifty years later, they are still at war. It is the world's oldest war, in fact. There are more than seven million Karen, not a small number: There are more Karen than there are Norwegians.

Anyway, not only was the man we rented from Karen, but he was also the political liaison officer for the Karen State in northern Thailand. One day, he asked us if we would like to go to Karen New Year, and we thought, sure. So off we went, he in his truck and we in ours. The first day, we got to the Salween River at a small town called Mae Sam Leap. The next day, we left our trucks and went on south by boat, down the Salween and then up the Moei River. We went through Karen immigration and continued up the river. Finally we arrived at a village in the jungle, and there we met the president of the Karen State, General Bomiya, and the prime minister. We slept in the house of a four-star general, next to the war hospital. The following day, before dawn, the general took us by boat even farther up the river, to the army headquarters at Manerplaw.

Dawn came just as we arrived, a heavy mist blanketing everything, fingering its way through the jungly terrain. At the military headquarters barefoot teenage soldiers with machine guns stared at us, stared at Dom, and we stared back. We made our way to a large field where the New Year ceremony was about to start. A little band with two electric guitars and a set of drums began to play. They played a slowed-down, a way sloweddown, blues-ish version of "Home on the Range." We took our seats and President Bomiya began to speak.

It was a beautiful rendition of "Home on the Range." It made us cry.

As we boarded the narrow boat that would take us back down the Moei River from Manerplaw, this man, a member of the Karen army, was waiting at the riverbank.

GRILLED EGGPLANT SALAD

[*yam makeua issaan* — NORTHEAST THAILAND, CENTRAL LAOS]

There are many versions of *yam makeua* in Thailand, and many related variations on the dressed grilled eggplant theme elsewhere in the region. No wonder, for eggplant, especially the long Asian eggplant, is so easy to work with, so full of flavor when grilled, and so spongelike when it comes to sopping up tasty dressings.

We learned this Lao-style version in northeast Thailand (Issaan): Eggplant is grilled whole alongside the familiar trio of shallots, garlic, and fresh chiles, then mashed with them in a mortar and seasoned. Unlike Bangkok-style grilled eggplant salad, there is no sugar in the flavorings, no dried shrimp. Though this salad traditionally has a fair amount of chile heat, we've made it only medium-hot. For less heat, use Hungarian wax chiles; for more, use Anaheims or the traditional, but sometimes hard to find, cayenne chiles.

Serve the salad as one of many dishes in a sticky rice or jasmine rice meal or as an appetizer to be scooped up with Thai-Lao Crispy Rice Crackers (page 106) or other crackers or sticky rice.

1 pound Asian eggplants (3 long or 5 short)

3 shallots, unpeeled

5 cloves garlic, unpeeled

1 to 2 cayenne chiles, or 2 Anaheim chiles, or 2 small banana
   or Hungarian wax chiles

2 small or 1 large scallion, trimmed and minced

½ cup coriander leaves, coarsely chopped, plus extra whole
   leaves for garnish

¼ cup mint leaves, finely chopped, plus extra for garnish

3 tablespoons fresh lime juice

3 tablespoons Thai fish sauce

2 tablespoons Dry-Roasted Sesame Seeds (page 308)

Salt to taste

1 medium European cucumber, sliced (optional)

Heat a grill or broiler. Prick the eggplants all over with a fork. Grill or broil about 5 inches from the heat, with the oven door closed, until well softened and browned, 10 to 15 minutes. If grilling, turn the eggplants to expose all sides to the heat. Remove from the heat and set aside to cool slightly.

Meanwhile, grill on a fine-mesh rack or broil the shallots, garlic, and chiles, turning often if grilling, until well softened; don't worry if there are some black spots. Remove from the heat and, when cool enough to handle, peel the garlic and shallots and coarsely chop together. Remove the chile stems and coarsely chop the chiles. Place the garlic, shallots, and chiles in a large mortar or in a blender or food processor and mash or process to a coarse paste.

Cut open the eggplants; scrape the flesh off the skin and discard the skin. Coarsely chop the flesh, then place it in a large bowl or in a mortar and mash with a spoon or pestle to a lumpy mass. Add the grilled flavorings and mash together. *Alternatively*, add the eggplant to the blender or processor and pulse briefly with the grilled flavorings; you don't want a completely smooth puree.

Turn the mixture out into a bowl (if necessary). Stir in the scallions and chopped coriander and mint, then stir in the lime juice and fish sauce. Add the sesame seeds, reserving a few for garnish if you wish. Taste and add a little salt if needed.

Serve the salad in a shallow bowl, garnished with a sprinkling of herbs and, if desired, sesame seeds. If you like, place slices of cucumber around the edge that guests can use to dip through the eggplant.

MAKES *about 2 cups; serves 4 to 6*

CARROT AND DAIKON PICKLED SALAD
[*dau chua* — VIETNAM]

This versatile and fresh-tasting salad-pickle-condiment combination will look familiar if you eat regularly in Vietnamese restaurants and/or sandwich shops. It's very easy to make at home. Instead of a blend of carrot and daikon, you can use a pound of just one of them. Serve as a side salad or as part of a Vietnamese salad plate. It also makes a great addition to rice paper roll-ups or Saigon Subs (page 287).

½ **pound carrots, peeled**
½ **pound daikon radish, peeled**
About ½ teaspoon kosher salt
1½ **cups water**
¼ **cup rice vinegar**
2 **tablespoons sugar**

Cut the tip off each carrot on a long diagonal. Use a Benriner or other vegetable slicer or a coarse grater to slice the carrots into strips, or use a knife to cut into matchsticks. You should have approximately 2 cups. Place the carrots in a large strainer and set aside.

Use the same method to make daikon strips. You should have approximately 2 cups. Add to the carrots in the strainer and mix well with your hands. Sprinkle on the salt and toss to mix. Place over a bowl or in the sink and let stand for 20 to 30 minutes.

Meanwhile, in a nonreactive saucepan, combine the water, vinegar, and sugar and bring to a boil. Remove from the heat; cool to room temperature. (Don't cook the vegetables, bathe them.)

Rinse the vegetables briefly with cold water, then squeeze dry and transfer to a medium bowl. Pour over the vinegar mixture and stir gently with a wooden spoon to ensure all the vegetables are well moistened. Let stand for 1 hour before serving.

To serve, lift the salad out of the vinegar bath (see Note) and mound attractively on a plate.
MAKES *about 2 to 3 cups; serves 6 as part of a meal*

NOTE: *If you have extra salad, leave it in the vinegar bath and store in a well-sealed container in the refrigerator. Leftovers keep for 2 to 3 days.*

PICKLED BEAN SPROUT SALAD
[*dua gia* — VIETNAM]

If you look into the kitchen of a Vietnamese restaurant, you will almost always see a very large bucket filled with fresh mung bean sprouts. Bean sprouts are served on the salad plate, served with noodles, served with wraps. They provide freshness as well as good crisp texture and taste.

This salad, like the Carrot and Daikon Pickled Salad, functions somewhere between a salad and a pickle. The bean sprouts are well flavored and more tender than raw sprouts, but they still have a refreshing crunch. Use this as a side salad or condiment, a topping in rice paper roll-ups, or a relish for grilled meat. The sprouts should be used the day they are prepared.

1 **pound mung bean sprouts (about 6 cups loosely packed)**
5 **large scallions or 8 smaller ones, trimmed, smashed flat with the side of a cleaver, sliced lengthwise into ribbons, and then cut crosswise into 2- to 3-inch lengths**
1 **tablespoon kosher salt**
½ **teaspoon sugar**
½ **cup rice vinegar**
4 **cups water**

Rinse the bean sprouts well in cold water, drain, and place in a large bowl. Add the scallions and set aside.

Place the remaining ingredients in a nonreactive saucepan and bring to a boil, stirring with a wooden spoon to dissolve the salt and sugar. Remove from the heat and let cool to room temperature.

Pour the vinegar mixture over the sprouts and scallions and stir gently to immerse all the vegetables. Let stand at room temperature for 1 to 2 hours.

Drain the bean sprouts and serve mounded on several plates.
SERVES *6 to 8 as an ingredient in rice paper roll-ups or as a salad dish in a larger meal*

RICE AND RICE DISHES

In the chill air of early-morning markets in the Mekong Delta and Cambodia, we're always seduced by the wonderful scent of jasmine rice. Most often it's simple plain rice, cooked in a steamer or rice cooker or a big heavy pot. But it may instead be rice bubbling gently in a rice soup, known in Cambodia as *babah* (see Rice Soup, Khmer Style, page 94) and in Vietnam as *chao* (see Shrimp and Rice Soup, page 95).

In Laos and northeast and northern Thailand, we're more likely to see or to sniff out sticky rice steaming over boiling water in a tall conical basket, shiny and aromatic long-grain sticky rice, the staple food in all three regions. Farther north again, in the Shan areas and beyond to southern Yunnan, rice most often means plain aromatic long-grain rice, eaten two or three times a day.

"Gin khao?" asks one Thai friend to another when they meet. "Have you eaten?" But the phrase literally means "Have you eaten rice?"

Rice is at the heart of most Southeast Asian meals, eaten plain, the essential food that anchors life. The rest of the meal may be made up of many dishes or may consist only of a dipping sauce or a salsa or a plate of vegetables to

The agricultural cycle in Southeast Asia alternates with the season. Rice harvest in northern Thailand is November to January, after the end of the rainy season. The rice is cut, leaving fields of golden stubble (OPPOSITE LEFT, near Chiang Mai). In winter, it's time to plant shallots (OPPOSITE RIGHT, near Hot in northern Thailand).

accompany the rice. Aromatic jasmine rice is quick to prepare, so if the pot runs low, more can be cooked up at any time; whatever else may be on the table, it's important never to run out of rice.

Rice cooked with other flavorings makes another whole category of food in the region, from Lao Yellow Rice and Duck (page 102) in Laos to the seductive Vietnamese Sticky Rice Breakfast (page 98) of southern Vietnam, sticky rice with herbs and coconut milk.

Dishes made with leftover rice are some of our favorite foods: Jasmine rice can be quickly stir-fried with garlic and a little meat, or in a flavor paste, then eaten with a sprinkling of coriander leaves and a squeeze of lime juice (see Thai Fried Rice, page 110, and Perfume River Rice, page 111). It can also be shaped into balls and deep-fried (see Deep-fried Jasmine Rice Balls, page 104) or dried and then deep-fried to make delicious crackers (see Thai-Lao Crispy Rice Crackers, page 106).

AROMATIC JASMINE RICE

[THAILAND, BURMA, CAMBODIA, VIETNAM, LAOS]

Jasmine rice is aromatic as it cooks, filling the house with its scent and a promise of good food to come. It is our favorite daily rice, soft and slightly clingy when cooked. We buy it in twenty-pound bags, usually labeled "Thai Jasmine" or "Thai Fragrant Rice" and also marked "superior quality" or "milagrosa." Perhaps sometime soon we'll also be seeing high-quality Cambodian and Vietnamese jasmine rice in the markets.

You can also substitute American-grown fragrant rice for Thai jasmine. The best-tasting jasmine rice from the United States we've found is produced by Lowell Farms in Texas. It's organically grown and carefully milled. It needs a little more cooking water than Thai jasmine and a few more minutes' cooking time (20 minutes at a simmer instead of 15).

Jasmine rice should be thoroughly washed in cold water, then cooked plain, with no salt and no oil. When cooked, it has an aromatic flavor and a good straightforward taste of grain. The dishes served with the rice supply all the seasoning needed.

3 cups long-grain Thai jasmine rice

Wash the rice thoroughly: Place it in a large wide heavy pot (3½-quart capacity or more) with a tight-fitting lid. Add cold water, swirl around several times with your hand, and drain; repeat twice more, or until the water runs clear. Add the cooking water: We add water measured the traditional way, that is, enough to cover the rice by about ½ inch, measured by placing the tip of the index finger on the surface of the rice and adding enough so that the water comes to the first joint. If you prefer to use more exact measured amounts, drain the washed rice well in a sieve, return to the pot, and add 3¾ cups cold water.

Bring the water to a full boil, uncovered, and let boil for about 15 seconds. Cover tightly, lower the heat to the lowest setting possible, and cook, *without lifting the lid,* for 15 minutes. Remove from the heat and let stand, covered, for 5 to 10 minutes. When you take off the lid, you will see the grains of rice standing up firmly on the top layer. Turn the rice gently with a rice paddle or wooden spoon, then place the lid back on to keep it warm. It's best served within 1 hour of cooking.

Store leftover rice in a sealed container in the refrigerator for up to three days. You can take it straight from there to make fried rice (see Index) or to add to hot broth.

MAKES *about 7 cups rice; serves 4 to 6*

NOTE: TO USE A RICE COOKER: *Rice cookers usually come with instructions listing the volume of water to use for a given amount of rice. The rice should be well washed as above, then cooked according to the rice cooker directions. If there are no water:rice proportions marked on your rice cooker, use just a touch less water than in the method above. If using a measured amount of water, drain the washed rice well in a colander before placing in the rice cooker and adding the water.*

AROMATIC JASMINE RICE *is pictured on page 240.*

BASIC STICKY RICE

[*khao neeo* — LAOS, NORTHERN AND NORTHEAST THAILAND, SOUTHERN YUNNAN]

If there is any one food that for us symbolizes the regional cuisines of Southeast Asia, it is sticky rice. It is the staple food, the staff of life, in Laos, northern Thailand, and northeast Thailand. It is also widely eaten in Cambodia, Vietnam, Yunnan, and other parts of Thailand, and it is often used for making sweets and ceremonial foods.

Sticky rice is medium to long grain and opaque white before cooking. It is a different variety of rice from jasmine, "sticky" when cooked because it contains a different form of starch (it is very low in amylose and is high in amylopectin). It is sometimes called sweet rice or glutinous rice. Sticky rice from Thailand is often sold marked *pin kao*, or with the Vietnamese term for sticky rice, *gao nep*.

Sticky rice is fun, liberating food. No utensils are needed. When it comes to eating sticky rice for the first time, children are usually better than adults; they have no problem eating with their fingers. For us, sticky rice is a way of eating, a way of organizing meals. To eat it, take a large ball of rice in one hand, then pull a smaller bite-sized piece off with your other hand and squeeze it gently into a firm clump. Then it's almost like a piece of bread: Use it to scoop up some salsa or a piece of grilled chicken.

To prepare sticky rice, you must first soak it overnight in cold water. It is then steam-cooked in a basket or steamer over a pot of boiling water. The long soaking gives the rice more flavor, but you can take a short-cut and soak it in warm water for just 2 hours.

People tend to eat a lot of sticky rice, or at least we do, and so do our friends, so we cook 3 cups for 4 to 6 hungry adults.

3 cups long-grain Thai sticky rice

EQUIPMENT NOTE: *You will need a large pot for soaking the rice and a rice-steaming arrangement; there are several different options for steaming sticky rice. By far the best is the traditional basket and pot. If you can shop in a Thai, Lao, or Vietnamese grocery, chances are you can buy the conical basket used for cooking sticky rice as well as the lightweight pot the basket rests in as it steams. You can also buy the basket and pot by mail-order (see Sources, page 325). This is the ideal equipment for cooking sticky rice—low-cost and made for the purpose. However, you can improvise by using a Chinese bamboo steamer or a steamer insert, or a large sieve. Line it with cheesecloth or muslin, place over a large pot of water, and cover tightly. The steamer must fit tightly so that no steam escapes around the edge and all the steam is forced up through the rice.*

Soak the rice in a container that holds at least twice the volume of the rice: Cover the rice with 2 to 3 inches of room-temperature water and soak for 6 to 24 hours. If you need to shorten the soaking time, soak the rice in warm (about 100°F) water for 2 hours. The longer soak gives more flavor and a more even, tender texture, but the rice is perfectly edible with the shorter soak in warm water.

Drain the rice and place in a conical steamer basket or alternative steaming arrangement (see Equipment Note). Set the steamer basket or steamer over several inches of boiling water in a large pot or a wok. *The rice must not be in or touching the boiling water.* Cover and steam for 25 minutes, or until the rice is shiny and tender. If using an alternative steaming arrangement, turn the rice over after about 20 minutes, so the top layer is on the bottom. Be careful that your pot doesn't run dry during steaming; add more water if necessary, making sure to keep it from touching the rice.

Turn the cooked rice out onto a clean work surface. Use a long-handled wooden spoon to flatten it out a little, then turn it over on itself, first from one side, then from the other, a little like folding over dough as you knead. This helps get rid of any clumps; after several foldings, the rice will be an even round lump. Place it in a covered basket or in a serving bowl covered by a damp cloth or a lid. Serve warm or at room temperature, directly from the basket or bowl. The rice will dry out if exposed to the air for long as it cools, so keep covered until serving. In Thailand and Laos, cooked sticky rice is kept warm and moist in covered baskets.

MAKES *about 6½ cups rice; serves 4 to 6*

BORDER TOWN: Border towns are always seedy—sometimes more, sometimes less, but always seedy.

Maybe it's because there are different rules (and different opportunities) on either side of the border, so inherently there is a bit of flimflam, zigzag, riffraff, whatever.

Mae Sai, a northern Thai town at the junction of Burma, Laos, and Thailand (the Golden Triangle), is no exception. Its one long commercial street, which leads directly to the bridge that crosses to Burma, looks like a frontier version of a strip mall that never ends. People come across from Burma every day, all day, shopping and selling up and down the long street, every once in a while stopping to eat. If you find a comfortable seat and watch long enough, you will see Shan, Akha, Burmese, Lahu, Kachin, and Kalaw, but you could watch a lifetime and not know exactly who everyone was and what they were up to, not really.

We didn't expect to spend much time in Mae Sai. We'd been there several times before and had never found it very appealing. Also, it's not a perfect family spot. We'd come only to see if it was possible to go by road to Kengtung, an important old town in the Shan hills in Burma. Someone had told us to go to Chad's Guest House, that Chad could help us (because it would have to be a less-than-official trip to Burma).

But Chad immediately said no. It had been possible for a time, but now, no. Maybe someone else could help us, but not him. So anyway, there we were, at Chad's, and so we stayed for the night. That night we got to talking with Chad's mother and sister, and with his niece Shieng, and

discovered that they were Tai Koen and Shan, and, sure, they would be happy to teach us about Tai Koen and Shan cooking (which was a big reason why we'd wanted to go to Kengtung). And meanwhile, Chad was working hard fixing up his vintage World War II jeeps, his true passion, and he didn't mind Dom and Tashi playing on the jeeps, or sitting on his antique motorbikes, so we decided we quite liked Mae Sai after all.

We stayed a while, hanging out in the kitchen and at the markets. We spent a lot of time at the markets, the morning market, the evening market, and the all-day cross-border everything-but-the-kitchen-sink market. The food markets in Mae Sai are incredible: There are Shan and Tai Koen specialties such as deep-fried donuts made of black sticky rice, flattened cakes of dried soybean used to flavor local dishes, tangled green piles of Mekong river weed (see River Weed, page 165), and *khao foon*, a dense yellowish jelly made of soured rice and eaten for breakfast with chiles, garlic, and black vinegar (see Khao Foon, page 108).

At night, after dinner, if we could get Chad talking, we'd hear wonderful tales of mystery and intrigue. Chad's parents once ran a small restaurant in town. For years Khun Sa, a famous drug warlord, would come once a week to play bridge with his mother, and Chad would watch and listen. But like all good storytellers, Chad would leave us hanging, leave us sitting on the edge of our chairs, when he decided it was time to start working again on his jeeps.

Tobacco is an important cash crop in northern Thailand along the Burmese border and is harvested and dried in the winter months.

RICE SOUP, KHMER STYLE

[*babah* — CAMBODIA]

All over Southeast Asia, there are versions of this one-dish meal, a thick soup of rice cooked in plenty of water or broth, then flavored with toppings and condiments. In Cantonese it's known as *juk*, in Thai as *khao tom*, in Vietnam it's *chao* (see page 95), and in Cambodia it's known as *babah*. I had my first bowl of *babah* as a snack on my way in from the airport and my last, in hurried regret, just before leaving Phnom Penh.

This is comfort food at any hour in any season, quickly prepared and very easy and satisfying. Make it on a chilly evening, or for lunch when you want your guests to feel taken care of. The whole dish can be made in just over half an hour, yet it tastes of slow simmering.

¼ pound ground pork

1 tablespoon Thai fish sauce

1 teaspoon sugar

6 cups water

2 stalks lemongrass, trimmed and smashed flat
   with the side of a cleaver

1 tablespoon dried shrimp

1-inch piece ginger, peeled and smashed flat

¾ cup Thai jasmine rice, rinsed well in cold water

2 tablespoons peanut or vegetable oil

5 cloves garlic

GARNISH AND ACCOMPANIMENTS

¼ cup Thai fish sauce

1 bird chile, chopped

2 tablespoons peanut or vegetable oil

2 shallots, chopped

4 leaves sawtooth herb, 6 sprigs rice paddy herb (*ngo om*),
   and/or about 12 leaves Asian basil, coarsely torn

2 cups bean sprouts, thoroughly rinsed in very hot water

2 scallions, trimmed and minced

Freshly ground black or white pepper

¼ cup Dry-Roasted Peanuts (page 308), coarsely chopped

1 lime, cut into wedges (optional)

In a small bowl, combine the pork with the fish sauce and sugar, mix well to blend, and set aside.

Place the water in a large heavy pot over high heat, add the lemongrass, dried shrimp, and ginger, and bring to a boil. Boil vigorously for 5 to 10 minutes, then sprinkle in the rice and stir gently with a wooden spoon until the water returns to a boil. Maintain a steady gentle boil until the rice is tender, 15 to 20 minutes, then turn off the heat. Remove and discard the lemongrass and ginger if you wish.

In the meantime, in a wok or heavy skillet, heat the oil. Add the garlic and stir-fry for 30 seconds, or until it is starting to turn golden. Toss in the pork and stir-fry, using your spatula to break up any lumps, until all the pork has changed color, about 2 minutes. Transfer the contents of the skillet to the soup and stir in.

Combine the fish sauce and chile in a condiment bowl; set aside.

Heat the oil in a small heavy skillet or in a wok over medium-high heat. Toss in the shallots and cook, stirring constantly, until golden, 2 to 3 minutes. Turn the shallots and oil out into a small bowl and set aside.

Just before serving, reheat the soup, stirring to prevent it from sticking. Divide the herbs you are using among four large soup bowls. Top the herbs in each bowl with ½ cup bean sprouts and a pinch of scallions. Pour the soup over top, then top each with another pinch of scallions, some shallots and oil, a very generous grinding of pepper, and a scattering of chopped peanuts. Serve with the fish sauce and chiles and lime wedges if you wish.

SERVES *4 as a one-dish meal*

SHRIMP AND RICE SOUP

[*chao tom* — SOUTHERN VIETNAM]

From China to Thailand, rice soup makes a great breakfast or between-meals snack or late-night supper. This quickly prepared Vietnamese rice soup has small pieces of shrimp cooked in a lightly flavored broth loaded with tender rice. A garnish of chopped roasted peanuts adds a pleasant change of texture and a nutty taste. The soup is traditionally served with a side dish of Vietnamese Must-Have Table Sauce so guests can add extra flavoring as they wish.

2 shallots, coarsely chopped

4 large cloves garlic, 2 minced and 2 peeled but left whole

½ teaspoon freshly ground black pepper or ¼ teaspoon
    freshly ground white pepper

2 tablespoons Vietnamese or Thai fish sauce

½ pound peeled and deveined shrimp (about ¾ pound
    in the shell), coarsely chopped

2 quarts water (or half pork or chicken broth, half water)

1 cup Thai jasmine rice, rinsed well in cold water

2 stalks lemongrass, trimmed and minced

2 tablespoons peanut or vegetable oil

2 medium tomatoes, coarsely chopped (optional)

GARNISH AND ACCOMPANIMENTS

2 to 3 tablespoons Dry-Roasted Peanuts (page 308),
    coarsely chopped

1 cup loosely packed coriander leaves

½ cup Vietnamese Must-Have Table Sauce (*nuoc cham*,
    page 28)

1 to 2 bird or serrano chiles, minced

Place the shallots, 1 whole garlic clove, and the pepper in a mortar and pound to a paste. Stir in 1 tablespoon of the fish sauce, then add the shrimp and pound together. *Alternatively*, mince the shallots and garlic clove, transfer to a bowl, and add the pepper and 1 tablespoon fish sauce. Finely chop the shrimp, add to the mixture, and turn to coat. Set aside.

Place the water (or stock and water) in a large pot. Add the rice and bring to a boil.

Meanwhile, pound the remaining whole garlic clove with the lemongrass in a mortar, or grind in a blender. Add to the rice water. Once the rice is boiling, lower the heat to medium and simmer, half covered, for about 15 minutes, or until the rice is very tender.

While the rice simmers, heat the oil in a skillet or wok over high heat. When it is hot, add the minced garlic and stir-fry for 30 seconds, or until golden, then add the shrimp with the marinade and stir-fry until the shrimp starts to change color, about 1 minute.

Add the fried shrimp mixture to the rice and toss in the tomatoes, if using. Scoop out about ½ cup of liquid from the soup to rinse out the skillet or wok and pour back into the soup. Continue simmering the soup for another 5 minutes, then serve. Or remove from the heat and let stand until just before you wish to serve (refrigerate if letting stand for more than 1 hour); reheat before serving.

Sprinkle a few roasted peanuts and some coriander leaves over each bowl of soup, then serve with side dishes of the remaining peanuts and coriander, the table sauce, and the minced chiles, so guests can adjust flavorings as they wish.

SERVES *6*

SHRIMP AND RICE SOUP *is pictured on page 96.*

LEFT: *There are many grades of rice to choose from in even the smallest market in the region; here, at the main market in Vientiane, the choice is particularly wide.*

RIGHT: *In northern Thailand, after the rice is harvested, the rice straw is often piled into stacks around a tidy conical pole.*

VIETNAMESE STICKY RICE BREAKFAST

[*xoi* — SOUTHERN VIETNAM]

Early-morning street vendors, steam rising from their pots of soup or their baskets of rice, are a welcome sight for the hungry early riser. Out taking photographs at dawn in Chau Doc, a Vietnamese town on the Mekong River right by the Cambodian border, I saw a small crowd of people hanging around an old woman vendor. She was selling *xoi*, sticky rice cooked with beans, in this case split mung beans. Unlike the northern Vietnamese version, in which the rice is cooked plain with some peanuts or whole beans, in the Delta version of *xoi*, I discovered a world of flavor choices that seemed both wild and wonderful.

The sticky rice steams with mung beans that have cooked in coconut milk. To eat it, you begin with a generous dollop of rice and beans in your bowl, then top them with some or all of the following: coconut cream, dry-roasted peanuts, dry-roasted sesame seeds, sugar, coriander leaves, and chopped scallions. That's the basic array (see Notes for options). Though these may not be the first toppings you'd think of for sticky rice, the flavorings come together beautifully to give richness, moisture, crunch, and, of course, lots of flavor, to this homey, simple, and nourishing breakfast-time street fare. Serve for breakfast or a snack, to be eaten with a spoon.

The total cooking time is less than 1 hour, and the beans can be cooked ahead, in which case the final cooking time is only the time it takes to steam the rice, about 25 minutes.

½ cup yellow split mung beans, soaked for 8 to 24 hours in cold water

About 1 cup canned or fresh medium to thin coconut milk (see page 315)

2 cups Thai or Vietnamese sticky rice, soaked for 8 to 24 hours in cold water (see Basic Sticky Rice, page 91)

TOPPINGS AND ACCOMPANIMENTS

About 2 tablespoons Dry-Roasted Sesame Seeds (page 308)

½ teaspoon salt

¼ to ¾ cup canned or fresh coconut cream or thick coconut milk

4 to 6 tablespoons Dry-Roasted Peanuts (page 308), coarsely chopped

2 to 3 tablespoons sugar (optional)

About ½ cup coarsely torn coriander leaves (optional)

Greens of 2 scallions, finely chopped (optional)

EQUIPMENT NOTE: *The soaked rice is steamed together with the cooked mung beans. You can use a Chinese bamboo steamer, lined with muslin or cheesecloth and placed over a wok or pot of boiling water, or a Lao-Thai sticky rice steaming basket (see Basic Sticky Rice, page 91, for details on steaming sticky rice). We've worked with both arrangements and find the rice steaming basket to be quicker and easier.*

Drain the mung beans and place in a pot with just enough coconut milk to cover. Bring to a rapid boil, stirring to prevent sticking, then lower the heat and cook at a simmer, half-covered, until the beans are very soft, about 20 minutes, stirring occasionally to prevent sticking or burning; if the beans do begin to stick, add a little more liquid. Remove from the heat and mash with a spoon or potato masher or in a food processor. Spoon the beans into a bowl and pat down firmly, pouring off any excess liquid. (*The beans can be made ahead and stored, covered, in the refrigerator, for up to 2 days.*)

If using a conical steamer basket, fill the pot with about 2 inches of water, place the basket in the pot, and put the rice in the basket. *If using a bamboo steamer,* line it with muslin, cheesecloth, or a cotton cloth and place it over a large pot or wok filled with 2 to 3 inches of water (the steamer should not be touching the water); spread the rice out in the cloth-lined steamer. Crumble the cooked mung beans over the rice. Mix the rice gently with your hands to distribute the beans through the top layer of the rice.

Place the pot over high heat and bring the water to a boil. *If using a basket,* cook for 25 minutes, or until tender, making sure the water doesn't run dry. *If using a bamboo steamer,* make sure that the steam is not escaping around the sides of the steamer; it must be forced through the rice. Once you see the steam coming up through the rice, cover the steamer tightly with a lid or aluminum foil and cook for 25 to 30 minutes, until tender. After about 12 minutes, lift the lid and turn the rice and bean mixture over. Using oven mitts to protect your hands from the steam, lift out the steamer and check the level of water in the pot. If it looks very low, add hot water, then place the steamer back over the water, cover, and continue to cook.

While the rice is cooking, briefly pound the roasted sesame seeds in a mortar or grind in a spice grinder and transfer to a small bowl. You can set the condiments out on separate small plates or bowls so guests can help themselves, or serve each guest an already garnished bowl of *xoi*.

Turn the cooked rice and bean mixture out into a bowl. Sprinkle on the salt and use a wooden spatula or spoon to turn the rice to blend. To assemble an individual serving, place about ¾ cup of the rice and bean mixture in a bowl, then top with 1 to 2 tablespoons thick coconut milk, about 1 teaspoon sesame seeds, 1 tablespoon chopped roasted peanuts, a generous sprinkling of sugar (begin with a heaping teaspoon), and a large pinch of coriander leaves and some minced scallions, if using.

SERVES *4 to 6*

NOTES: *You can also serve xoi as a flavored rice (without the sugar and coconut cream toppings) to accompany grilled meats or vegetables or roast pork or chicken in a Western-style meal. It makes a great contribution to a potluck supper.*

We like to make twice the amount of beans called for, then serve the extra beans as another optional topping for the rice.

In Ho Chi Minh City, we've eaten xoi with an even wider selection of toppings, including slices of Vietnamese Baked Cinnamon Pâté (page 259) or sliced cooked sausages. It then becomes a substantial meal, great for brunch or lunch, especially if you have a hungry crowd to feed.

ROADS TO EVERYWHERE: We're not particularly confident when it comes to handling motorcycles, especially larger ones, roadworthy ones, though we really wish we could be.

If we ever get to feeling comfortable with them, the first place we'll go is northern Thailand. Occasionally we meet people traveling there on motorbikes, and we're always jealous. The roads are so windy and deserted. The air is so fresh and clean. And the hills of northern Thailand always have that element of mystery. There are tribal people living in villages hidden in the hills; follow a dirt track, and sooner or later there will be a village. And then there is all the intrigue of the opium trade, though now everyone is growing strawberries instead of poppies. But there is still the intrigue.

We've often wondered about all the little roads in Thailand. Thailand has a lot of roads, and they are in pretty good condition. We used to think that the roads had all been built by U.S. drug enforcement money, to bring the poppy-growing tribals more into the fabric of Thai life, giving them access to schools and hospitals, and, in turn, giving the military and the police easier access in policing the poppy cultivation. But then we realized that it's not just the north, but other parts of the country as well.

"Why so many roads?" A Thai friend at last told us: "The reason we have so many roads is because so many of our politicians come from the construction industry. What is the English term? *Kickback?*"

Opium poppies bloom in the hills of Laos, Thailand, Vietnam, and Yunnan. During the colonial era, opium became an important cash crop.

LAO YELLOW RICE AND DUCK

[*khao cari ped* — CENTRAL LAOS]

This impressive dinner-party dish is easy to make and fun to serve. We learned it from Sivone Penasy, who lives with her husband, Sousath, and their two children, Melissa and Peter, in the "wild west" town of Phonsavan, near the Plain of Jars in eastern Laos (see The War, page 187).

4 cups jasmine rice

One 3½-pound duck

15 cloves garlic, peeled

1 tablespoon black peppercorns

2 teaspoons salt

1 tablespoon Madras curry powder

1 teaspoon ground turmeric (optional)

2 tablespoons Thai fish sauce

5 tablespoons vegetable oil or rendered duck fat

6½ cups water, or more if needed

6 small scallions, trimmed and cut lengthwise into fine ribbons

Place the rice in a bowl, add cold water to cover by 2 inches, and set aside to soak.

Use a cleaver to cut the duck into 12 to 15 pieces. Reserve the wing tips and neck for stock (see Notes). Trim off all the fat and thick skin and reserve for another purpose if desired.

Place the garlic cloves in a mortar with the peppercorns and the salt and pound to a paste. *Alternatively,* mince the garlic and place in a small bowl with the salt. Grind the peppercorns in a spice grinder and stir into the garlic, mashing with the back of the spoon. Add the curry powder and optional turmeric to the garlic paste and stir to blend, then stir in the fish sauce.

Place a large wide heavy pot over medium-high heat. When it is hot, add 2 tablespoons of the oil or fat and toss in the prepared paste. Cook for about 30 seconds, stirring to prevent sticking or burning, then add the duck pieces. Stir to coat all the duck with the flavored oil, then cook, stirring frequently, until all the pieces are lightly browned, about 10 minutes. (If your pot is narrow, you may have to cook the duck in two batches, using half the paste and oil for each, then return all the duck to the pot.) Add 2 cups of the water, bring to a boil, and simmer gently for 10 minutes.

Add the remaining 4½ cups water to the pot and bring to a boil. Drain the rice. Add the remaining 3 tablespoons vegetable oil or fat to the pot, then sprinkle in the rice; the liquid should cover the rice by a scant ½ inch. Add more water if necessary. Bring back to a boil, then cover tightly, lower the heat to medium-low, and cook until the rice is tender, 15 to 20 minutes. Remove from the heat and let stand 5 to 10 minutes.

Turn the rice and duck out onto a large platter and mound attractively. Garnish with the scallion ribbons and serve hot or at room temperature.

SERVES *8 as the centerpiece of a meal*

NOTES: *Sivone says she uses the same technique to cook beef or chicken. If using beef, use 2 to 2½ pounds boneless rump or shoulder, cut into rough 1-inch chunks. Add 2 tablespoons minced ginger to the paste, pounding it with the garlic and peppercorns.*

TO MAKE DUCK STOCK: *Place the duck neck, wing tips, and any other rejected bits in a large stockpot with 1 tablespoon black peppercorns, a 2-inch piece of ginger, 5 garlic cloves, peeled, and 5 shallots, peeled. Add water to cover. Bring to a boil, then reduce the heat and simmer for 2 hours. Remove from the heat and let stand until cool, then pour through a fine sieve, lined with cheesecloth if you wish. Discard the solids and transfer the broth to glass or plastic containers, cover tightly, and refrigerate. When chilled, the fat will congeal on the surface of the broth and can be scraped off and set aside for another purpose. Use refrigerated broth within 3 days, or freeze for up to 4 months.*

DEEP-FRIED JASMINE RICE BALLS
[LAOS]

The answer to "what to snack on?": rice balls at a street stall in Vientiane, Laos.

We think that these deep-fried rice balls may originally be Vietnamese, but we're not sure. We first had them while staying in Vientiane, in Laos. Whenever hunger struck, we'd walk down the street to a nearby market that specialized in prepared foods, and we'd pick up several rice balls. The rice ball vendor would break them open, then toss them with various fresh herbs and coarsely chopped pork skin. They were a great treat at any time of the day, a combination of savory rice, fresh tastes, and contrasting textures.

Once home, we worked on our own version of the recipe, as they seemed an ideal way to use leftover rice. In Vientiane, the balls were very large and deep-fried in oil. For our home-style version, we make them smaller and flatter. This way we can fry them in a shallow pan of hot oil and know that they'll cook right through. We also omit the pork skin, for the sake of convenience, and instead we serve them with a little chopped savory sausage or Vietnamese pâté.

The rice balls in Vientiane had a very golden glow, which we first assumed came from using a little tomato paste, but the women in the market assured us that they used only eggs and coconut to flavor the rice. Of course, the yolks of eggs from free-range hens are very richly colored. The coconut can be omitted, but it sure makes a great little extra taste. Serve these for lunch or breakfast.

1 large egg, preferably free-range

½ teaspoon salt

½ to 1 teaspoon sugar

4 cups freshly cooked or leftover jasmine rice

¼ cup finely chopped fresh or defrosted frozen, grated coconut
(optional)

Peanut or other oil for deep-frying

TOPPINGS AND CONDIMENTS

1 cup chopped cooked sausage, such as Spicy Northern
Sausage (page 256) or Issaan Very Garlicky Sausage
(page 258) or Vietnamese Baked Cinnamon Pâté (page 259)
(optional)

Sugar (optional)

¼ cup Thai fish sauce

2 to 3 limes, cut into wedges

½ cup minced scallions

½ cup chopped coriander

2 to 3 tablespoons dried red chile flakes (optional)

ACCOMPANIMENTS

Vietnamese Herb and Salad Plate (page 68)

½ cup Vietnamese Must-Have Table Sauce
(*nuoc cham*, page 28) (optional)

In a large bowl, whisk together the egg, salt, and sugar. Add the rice and the coconut, if using, and stir and turn to distribute the egg and coconut evenly through the rice.

Place a large heavy wok or large heavy pot on a burner and add oil to a depth of 1½ to 2 inches. Make sure the wok or pot is stable on the burner. Heat over high heat until the oil just begins to smoke, then lower the heat very slightly. A small clump of rice dropped into the oil should sink and then immediately rise back to the surface while browning but not turning black; adjust the heat as necessary.

Wet your hands, then scoop up a scant ½ cup of the rice mixture, place it in one palm, and use both hands to shape it into a flattened disk, like a hockey puck. Do not compress it; just handle it lightly, so that the grains of rice are not squashed and can still puff up in the hot oil. Using a slotted spoon, slide the patty into the hot oil. It will spatter and hiss mildly as it gives off moisture into the oil. Cook for 2 to 2½ minutes, turning it over after 45 seconds to 1 minute to ensure even browning and cooking. The rice on the outside of the ball will puff and turn golden as it cooks; you want it to be a medium brown, not just pale golden. When the patty is done, use the slotted spoon to lift it out of the oil, pausing to let excess oil drain off, and transfer it to a paper towel–lined plate or rack. Shape and cook the rest of the rice; you may have room to fry 2 patties at a time. You will have about 10 rice patties.

To serve, let the patties cool a little, so you can handle them. Put out a platter with piles of toppings on it, along with the salad plate, and, if you like, provide small individual condiment bowls of dipping sauce. Place 2 rice patties on each plate, or let guests serve themselves. Guests can dress their rice as they please. To prepare an individual serving, break open a patty into 3 or 4 pieces. Top with a generous sprinkling of chopped sausage or pâté, if using, then sprinkle on a little sugar if you wish, a dash of fish sauce, a generous squeeze of lime juice, and a dense sprinkling of scallions and coriander leaves. Top with sprinkled dried red chile flakes if you wish.

Use the lettuce and herb leaves to pick up pieces of the rice patties; drizzle on the table sauce if you wish. Eat the rice balls with your hands, the traditional way, or with a fork and spoon.

MAKES *10 rice balls; serves 5*

THAI-LAO CRISPY RICE CRACKERS

[*khao tang* — LAOS, THAILAND]

Leftover rice is the source of many wonderful rice dishes, from fried rice to these crisp savory rice crackers. Before the days of rice cookers, jasmine rice was often cooked in a heavy pot with a curving bottom that sat directly on the fire. The crust of toasty golden brown rice that stuck to the bottom of the pot became a treat in itself.

Drying sheets of cooked rice can yield a similar crispy toasted rice. The dried-out rice is broken into bite-sized pieces and then put away in well-sealed containers. Just before serving, the rice pieces are deep-fried until they puff, to make crispy crackers. It's a technique found in China and Thailand, as well as in many other parts of the rice-eating world. Where sticky rice is a staple, in Laos, and northern and northeast Thailand, it's shaped into flat disks that are dried, then deep-fried to make rice cakes known as *khao khop*.

Crispy rice crackers can be stored in a well-sealed container for several days. They make a handy pantry item: Drop them into hot soup as croutons, or serve them like chips, with salsa. In Laos, they are commonly eaten as an accompaniment to hot noodle soup.

2 cups or more just-cooked jasmine rice
Peanut or other oil for deep-frying

Use warm to hot rice. With a rice paddle or wooden spoon, spread the rice onto a lightly oiled baking sheet to make a layer about ½ inch thick. Press down with your paddle to compact the rice so that it sticks together. Don't worry about ragged edges, as you will be breaking up the rice into large crackers after it dries.

Place the baking sheet in a preheated 350°F oven and immediately lower the temperature to 250°F. Let dry for 3 to 4 hours. The bottom will be lightly browned.

When the rice is dry, lift it off the baking sheet in pieces. Break it into smaller pieces (about 2 inches across, or as you please), then store well sealed in a plastic bag until ready to use.

To fry the crackers, heat 2 to 3 inches of peanut oil in a large well-balanced wok, deep fryer, or large heavy pot to 325° to 350°F.

To test the temperature, drop a small piece of fried rice cake into the oil: It should sink to the bottom and immediately float back to the surface without burning or crisping . Adjust the heat as necessary.

Add several pieces of dried rice cracker to the hot oil and watch as the rice grains swell up. When the first sides stop swelling, turn them over and cook on the other side until well puffed and just starting to brown (about 30 seconds in all). Use a slotted spoon to remove them immediately to a paper towel–lined platter or rack to drain. Gather up any small broken pieces; these make delicious croutons. Fry the remaining pieces of rice cracker the same way, making sure that the oil is hot enough each time. Serve hot and fresh, to accompany soup or salsa. Store in a cool place for no more than a week.

N O T E :   *You can also use freshly cooked sticky rice to make these crackers.*

A new road links this Hmong village with the Thai towns lower down the river; before there were only footpaths between them.

LEFT: *Sticky rice being harvested in November around Chiang Mai.* RIGHT: *A Lisu child dressed in her New Year's finery. Grilled sticky rice cakes are eaten in quantity during the festivities.*

KHAO FOON: The Shan use rice or mung beans to make a wonderful snack, usually eaten in the morning, called *khao foon*. They snack in the market, or take a bag home.

Khao foon makers are specialists, like people who make tofu. The rice or beans are soaked in water, then ground to a smooth paste. The paste is cooked over low heat, stirred constantly. A coagulant is added (as it is in cheese or tofu making), and the paste thickens into a firm jellylike texture, with a neutral to slightly sour taste. If it's made from rice, *khao foon* is creamy white to pale yellow in color; if it's made from mung beans (as it is in the southern Shan State), it's a beautiful pale green. *Khao foon* is served in cubes, chunks, or slices, in a bowl. On top go all kinds of condiments and flavorings, from finely chopped scallions to chile paste, ginger paste, dark vinegar, chopped roasted peanuts, and more.

We ate the rice version of *khao foon* in Mae Sai and the mung bean version near Inle Lake, in the Shan State. The Phuan people, in the area around Phonsavan in eastern Laos, make a similar rice jelly that they call *khao poon*, as do the Bai near Dali, where it's called *mi lin fen*. It's sold in stalls in the market as a morning meal, topped in Dali with dark vinegar, and in Phonsavan with herbs, chopped scallions, and chile paste. The Phuan one we tried was very mild, with none of the fermented taste of the *khao foon* we'd eaten in Mae Sai.

In Mae Sai one late afternoon (see Border Town, page 92), Chad's niece Shieng took me off on her motorbike to a Tai Koen household that specialized in making *khao foon*. The family had moved to Thailand from the Shan State twenty years earlier. They were known, Shieng told me, as the finest *khao foon* makers in the area. By their beautiful traditional teak house, huge cauldrons of pale rice batter were slowly firming up into smooth jelly. In a few hours, the jelly would set completely; early next morning, well before dawn, it would be cut into chunks and carried off to the market to be sold.

In the southern part of Shan State, khao foon *is made with mung beans, so it's pale green in color. It's an appetizing sight in the morning market in Kalaw, Shan State, Burma.*

THAI FRIED RICE

[*khao pad* — THAILAND]

This is a simple, straightforward version of Thai fried rice, a dish we usually eat at least once a day in Thailand, and about half that frequently at home. While we like other versions of fried rice, for us it is the Thai version that is far and away the best. Maybe it is the combination of fish sauce, jasmine rice, and the taste of the wok. Maybe it is the squeeze of lime and fish sauce with chiles (*prik nam pla*) as condiments. Maybe it is the hundreds of different places where we've happily sat eating Thai fried rice, the totality of all those nice associations. Whatever it is, we love it. Thai fried rice is one of life's great simple dishes.

The following recipe is for one serving. If you have a large wok, the recipe is easily doubled to serve two; increase the cooking time by about 30 seconds. If you are serving more than two, prepare the additional servings separately. The cooking time is very short, so once all your ingredients are prepared, it is easy to go through the same cooking process—simply clean out the wok and wipe it dry each time. It is much easier to prepare *khao pad* when your wok isn't overly full. Total preparation time is about 8 minutes; cooking time is about 4 minutes.

2 tablespoons peanut oil

4 to 8 cloves garlic, minced (or even more if not using
   optional ingredients)

1 to 2 ounces thinly sliced boneless pork (optional)

2 cups cold cooked rice (preferably Thai jasmine)

2 scallions, trimmed, slivered lengthwise, and cut into
   1-inch lengths (optional)

2 teaspoons Thai fish sauce, or to taste

GARNISH AND ACCOMPANIMENTS

About ¼ cup coriander leaves

About 6 thin cucumber slices

1 small scallion, trimmed (optional)

2 lime wedges

¼ cup Thai Fish Sauce with Hot Chiles (page 33)

Heat a large heavy wok over high heat. When it is hot, add the oil and heat until very hot. Add the garlic and stir-fry until just golden, about 20 seconds. Add the pork, if using, and cook, stirring constantly, until all the pork has changed color completely, about 1 minute. Add the rice, breaking it up with wet fingers as you toss it into the wok. With your spatula, keep moving the rice around the wok. At first it may stick, but keep scooping and tossing it and soon it will be more manageable. Try to visualize frying each little bit of rice, sometimes pressing the rice against the wok with the back of your spatula. Good fried rice should have a faint seared-in-the-wok taste. Cook for approximately 1½ minutes. Add the optional scallions, then the fish sauce, and stir-fry for 30 seconds to 1 minute.

Turn out onto a dinner plate and garnish with the coriander. Lay a row of cucumber slices, the scallion, and the lime wedges around the rice. Squeeze the lime onto the rice as you eat it, along with the chile sauce—the salty, hot taste of the sauce brings out the full flavor of the rice.

SERVES 1

NOTES: *Once you've tossed the garlic into the hot oil, you can also add about ½ teaspoon Red Curry Paste (page 210 or store-bought) or Thai Roasted Chile Paste (nam prik pao, page 36 or store-bought). It adds another layer of flavor and a little heat too.*

Fried rice is very accommodating: If you have a little tomato or spinach or other greens, finely chop them and add after you've begun to stir-fry the rice.

Many people (we're among them) like to eat a fried egg on top of their fried rice. Wipe out your wok, heat about 2 teaspoons of oil, and quickly fry the egg, then turn it out onto the rice. It's delicious.

PERFUME RIVER RICE
[*com chien* — VIETNAM]

This Vietnamese version of fried rice is another great way to make a meal out of leftover rice. We first tasted it in Hue, on a rainy February day, at a street stall near the Perfume River. It was warming and sustaining, just what we were craving.

The rice is flavored with a paste of lemongrass, dried shrimp, and shallots. If you are not a dried shrimp lover, omit them and increase the fish sauce slightly.

4 cups cold cooked jasmine rice

1 tablespoon dried shrimp, soaked in a little hot water for 5 minutes

1 stalk lemongrass, trimmed and minced

1 small red onion, minced

3 shallots, minced

1 teaspoon sugar

Pinch of salt

2 tablespoons peanut or vegetable oil

2 tablespoons minced garlic

3 scallions, trimmed, smashed flat with the side of a cleaver, cut lengthwise into ribbons, and then cut crosswise into 2-inch lengths

2 tablespoons Dry-Roasted Sesame Seeds (page 308)

1 tablespoon Vietnamese or Thai fish sauce, or to taste

2 tomatoes, sliced, or 1 small European cucumber, thinly sliced

½ cup coarsely chopped coriander

Freshly ground black pepper

ACCOMPANIMENTS

Vietnamese Herb and Salad Plate (page 68) (optional)

Vietnamese Must-Have Table Sauce (*nuoc cham*, page 28)

Place the rice in a large bowl. Wet your hands with water, then break up any clumps of rice with your fingers. Set aside.

Place the shrimp and its soaking water, the lemongrass, onion, and shallots in a large mortar, add the sugar and salt, and pound to a paste. *Alternatively*, use a blender to grind the ingredients, adding just enough warm water to make a puree. Turn the paste out into a small bowl and set aside.

Heat a large heavy wok over high heat. Add the oil and heat until hot. Toss in the garlic and stir-fry for 10 seconds. Add the lemongrass paste and stir-fry for about 3 minutes, until it is golden. Add the scallions and stir-fry briefly. With wet hands, sprinkle the cold rice into the wok and stir-fry vigorously for 1 to 2 minutes, tossing and pressing the rice against the sides of the wok until all of it has been exposed to the hot pan. Add the sesame seeds and fish sauce and stir-fry for another 20 seconds or so. Taste and add a little more fish sauce if you wish, then turn out onto a plate. Arrange the tomato or cucumber slices around the rice and top with the coriander leaves and a generous grinding of pepper.

Serve with the salad and herb plate if you wish and with small condiment bowls of the table sauce, so guests can sprinkle it on as they eat.

SERVES *2 to 3 as a simple lunch*

NOODLES AND NOODLE DISHES

If rice is the bread of Southeast Asian food, then noodles are the potatoes. Noodles are extremely versatile; they can complement other foods or be eaten simply on their own. Fresh rice noodles, dried rice noodles, cellophane noodles, egg noodles, thin vermicelli noodles, and wide flat rice noodle sheets: At every hour of the day, they give comfort and sustenance. Noodles are stir-fried for lunch, heated in a steaming soup for breakfast, or eaten in a bowl with salad greens and herbs and an assortment of toppings for dinner.

Noodles come in many different shapes and sizes, made from rice, wheat, or mung beans. Most Southeast Asian noodles are now available in North America; when they aren't, there're good substitutes.

The classic Mekong noodle is fresh and round (like thin spaghetti) and made from rice. The other fresh noodles, used in stir-fries and occasionally in soups, are flat, like fettuccine, and also made of rice. In Asian

markets in larger North American cities, you'll find fresh noodles in the cooler near the tofu. You can also make your own (see Fresh Noodle Sheets, page 121) or substitute dried noodles.

Dried Asian noodles, like dried pasta, are widely available here, and are a wonderful pantry staple. They need only a short soaking or boiling in water, and then they can be stir-fried or served topped with sauces or flavorings.

We've pulled together in this chapter some of the many substantial noodle dishes from across the region, from noodle soups to stir-fries. Most are "meal-in-a-bowl"–style recipes that work as a main course or a simple meal. Ginger Chicken Noodle Soup (page 130), for example, is a hearty one-dish meal of rice noodles, broth, chicken, and herbs, easy to make ahead and then serve at a moment's notice. So too is rich and spicy Chiang Mai Curry Noodles (*khao soi,* page 134).

Noodle stir-fries, like the Chinese-influenced Thai classics Our Favorite Noodles with Greens and Gravy (page 116) and *pad thai* (page 124), make wonderful family suppers, winter or summer. You can also serve rice noodles plain with side dishes or toppings, in the same way rice would be, as a central anchor for a meal.

OPPOSITE: *Wheat flour noodles hanging over wooden poles to dry are a familiar sight in China, especially where there is a large Hui (Muslim Chinese) population.*
ABOVE: *The Kok River (Mae Kok in Thai) flows eastward from Burma into northern Thailand, heading past Chiang Rai and finally into the Mekong above Chiang Khong.*

OUR FAVORITE NOODLES WITH GREENS AND GRAVY

[*guaytio ladna* — THAILAND]

Guaytio ladna is one of those bottom-line great dishes we never get tired of eating, in the same category for us as Thai fried rice. In fact, in most neighborhood Thai restaurants, where you can order one, you can usually order the other, and we always have a hard time deciding between the two. When we're home in Toronto, this is an easy standby for a last-minute supper: tasty and satisfying and quick to make.

Ladna is a stir-fried noodle dish of fresh wide rice noodles (*guaytio*), dark green vegetables, and a little thinly sliced pork, all bathed in a flavorful "gravy." The gravy is salty with *dao jiao* (fermented soybean paste, known in Vietnamese as *tuong*) and slightly sour with vinegar. A simple mild chile-vinegar sauce, served on the side, brings out the flavors in the dish perfectly. All in all, *guaytio ladna* is a very good one-dish meal.

Although you can use dried rice noodles, the dish is at its very best when made with fresh rice noodles. If you have a Chinese or Southeast Asian community of any size in your region, almost certainly someone in the area is making fresh rice noodles or noodle sheets. Buy them fresh and store in the refrigerator (no more than two days) before using them. Otherwise, try making your own.

2 pounds fresh rice noodles or Fresh Noodle Sheets (page 121) (or substitute 1 pound wide dried rice noodles)

¼ cup peanut or vegetable oil

2 to 3 tablespoons minced garlic

Scant ½ pound boneless pork butt or shoulder, thinly sliced across the grain into 1- by ½-inch pieces (or substitute lean beef or boneless chicken, sliced similarly)

1 teaspoon sugar

1 pound bok choi, Shanghai bok choi, or other cabbage-family greens, cut lengthwise into ¼-inch-wide spears and well washed (3 to 4 cups loosely packed)

1 tablespoon fermented soybean paste (*dao jiao*), mashed until smooth

1 tablespoon soy sauce

1½ tablespoons Thai fish sauce

1½ tablespoons rice or cider vinegar

1¼ cups mild chicken, beef, or pork broth or water

1 tablespoon cornstarch, dissolved in 3 tablespoons water

Generous grinding of white or black pepper

ACCOMPANIMENT

½ cup Chile-Vinegar Sauce (recipe follows)

Our Favorite Noodles with Greens and Gravy *is pictured on page 118.*

If using fresh noodles or noodle sheets, rinse under warm running water. Stack the sheets, if using, slice into ¾-inch-wide noodles, and separate gently with your fingers; set aside. If using dried rice noodles, soak in warm water for 15 minutes to soften, then drain and set aside.

Place all the other ingredients by your stovetop. Have a platter and 3 or 4 dinner plates (one per guest) nearby.

Heat a large wok over high heat. Pour in 1½ tablespoons of the oil and swirl to coat the wok. When very hot, toss in approximately half the noodles and stir-fry gently for about 2 minutes, pressing them against the hot pan, then turn out onto the platter and repeat with the remaining noodles, using only 1 tablespoon oil. Divide the noodles among the four dinner plates.

Wipe out the wok, then place back over high heat. Add the remaining 1½ tablespoons oil and, when it is hot, toss in the garlic. Stir-fry briefly until starting to turn golden, about 20 seconds, then add the pork slices and a generous pinch of the sugar. Stir-fry for about 1 minute, or until all the meat has changed color. Toss in the sliced greens and stir-fry, pressing the vegetables against the hot sides of the wok, until they turn bright green, about 1½ minutes or more (depending on the size of your wok).

Add the soybean paste, soy sauce, fish sauce, vinegar, and the remaining scant teaspoon sugar and stir-fry to mix, then add the broth or water and the cornstarch mixture. Stir to mix, then cover for 30 seconds to a minute, until the liquid comes to a boil. Remove the cover and simmer, stirring carefully from time to time, for another 2 minutes, or until the liquid has thickened a little and the greens are tender.

Use your spatula or a ladle to distribute the meat, greens, and gravy over the noodles. Grind pepper over generously and serve hot, with a bowl or cruet of the chile-vinegar sauce.

SERVES *3 to 4*

NOTE: *For a vegetarian option, substitute ½ teaspoon salt (or more to taste) for the fish sauce and use about ½ pound pressed tofu (see Glossary) instead of pork. After frying the garlic, sear the tofu slices by pressing them against the hot sides of the wok for about 2 minutes, then proceed with the recipe as above.*

CHILE-VINEGAR SAUCE
[*nam som* — THAILAND]

Serve with stir-fried noodle dishes such as *pad thai* (page 124) or Our Favorite Noodles with Greens and Gravy: a little tart, a little sweet, and mildly hot.

½ cup rice vinegar

2 to 3 tablespoons sugar

½ mild chile (such as Cubanelle, Hungarian wax, or banana chile), sliced into rings

Put the vinegar in a small bowl and stir in the sugar until it is completely dissolved. Add the chile rings. Serve with a small spoon so guests can spoon a little onto their noodles.

Stored in a sealed container in the refrigerator, this will keep for 4 to 5 days.

MAKES *about ½ cup sauce*

LEFT: *In the cool of winter, early-morning mist shrouds the Mekong.* RIGHT: MORNING MARKET NOODLES *(page 138) are a welcome breakfast throughout the region.*
They're eaten with chopsticks, even by Thai, Lao, and Khmer people, and tribal people like this Akha woman, who do not normally use chopsticks for eating.

LEFT: *Monks in Phnom Penh make their morning alms rounds, collecting offerings of prepared food for their meals. Their vows prohibit them from eating between noon and the following morning.* RIGHT: *This Buddhist temple outside Muang Sing is airy and bright and open to the wind and the birds.*

FRESH NOODLE SHEETS

If you do not have a supply of fresh rice noodles or rice noodle sheets at your local Asian grocery store, you may want to make your own.

Homemade rice noodle sheets are surprisingly easy to make, once you get a little practice. They're white and supple, and irregularities don't matter because you'll use them sliced into noodles. If refrigerated, they will keep for up to forty-eight hours, but they really are at their best on the same day. Slice them into wide noodles and use them in soups or to make one of our household favorites, Our Favorite Noodles with Greens and Gravy (page 116).

1 cup rice flour
½ cup cornstarch
½ cup tapioca flour or potato starch
2¼ cups water
¼ to ½ cup vegetable oil (see Note)

In a large bowl, whisk together the flour, starches, and water. If necessary, strain through a sieve to get out any lumps. Let the batter stand for 30 minutes to 2 hours, covered. It will be very liquid, like a very thin crepe batter.

Place a heavy well-seasoned or nonstick 8-inch skillet with a tight-fitting lid over medium-low heat. Place a baking sheet beside the stove and spread about 2 tablespoons of oil on it, which you will use to coat the noodle sheets as they cool. Lightly oil a large plate and set it nearby.

After the skillet has heated for 5 minutes, drop a few drops of oil into it and rub the entire surface of the pan with a paper towel to distribute it evenly and remove any excess. Stir or whisk the batter well and, using a ladle or measuring cup, pour about ¼ cup of batter into the pan and swirl it around to coat the surface. Immediately cover with the lid and cook for 1 minute. (Steam will build up and cook the top surface while the bottom surface is cooked by the heat of the pan.) Lift the lid (do not let any water from the underside of the lid drip onto the rice sheet): The rice sheet should look shiny, with small bubbles; if it is still pasty and sticky, wipe the underside of the lid, replace it, cook for another 20 to 30 seconds, and then check again. When the rice sheet is no longer sticky on top, lift it out of the pan with a wooden spatula and place, top side down, on the oiled baking sheet.

Dry off the underside of the lid, whisk the batter well, and make the next sheet (you don't need to oil the pan each time, just for every second or third sheet—or not at all if your skillet is nonstick). When the cooked rice sheet has cooled slightly, flip it over to coat the other side well with oil, then transfer to the large plate; until the sheets are cool, they are sticky and may, even with the oil, stick together. Cook the remaining batter in the same way, remembering to stir or whisk the batter well before you lift out each ladleful. Once you get the temperature and procedure under control, you may want to speed up your production by using two pans in tandem. Make sure to keep the baking sheet well oiled; you will probably have to add more oil at the halfway mark.

MAKES *8 to 10 fresh rice noodle sheets, 7 to 8 inches across*

NOTE: *The oil you use to coat the noodles right after they're made is rinsed off before they are used in a dish, so don't be dismayed by the amount of oil called for.*

TROUBLESHOOTING: *Like crepes, Fresh Noodle Sheets take a while to master. Use the first one or two as test samples and adjust the pan temperature and batter thickness and quantity as necessary.*

If the batter is immediately sticking to the pan rather than swirling around when you pour it in, lower the temperature slightly. If there is still a problem, add a little more water to make the batter more liquid.

Once the sheets have cooled, store on the plate wrapped in plastic wrap in the refrigerator. They will harden a little, but will soften again when sliced and stir-fried or heated in broth.

CHIANG MAI: We don't know why, but people visiting Thailand for the first time often go up north to Chiang Mai expecting a quaint, arty, traditional sort of place. Chiang Mai is Thailand's second city. It's noisy, crowded, polluted, and frustrating, full of high-rises, department stores, and ugly buildings.

We love Chiang Mai. If we had to choose to live any one place in Thailand, it would probably be here. We don't know why exactly, but it must be something about its people. People here are quirky, almost cosmopolitan, deliberate. They open little specialized shops and assume that other people will be interested (and sure enough, they are right). Vegetarian Thai cooking, which is a stretch in Thailand considering the prevalence of fish sauce and the use of meat as a flavoring, abounds in Chiang Mai. A modest little place across from the railway station serves incredible, inventive vegetarian fare, and it even has a good selection of wines to drink with dinner. We recently met a man from England, retired, who had come to Chiang Mai as a visitor and he had never gone home. He had started an English "chip" stall on the street near the night market and happily made a go of it; in Chiang Mai, he fit right in.

Chiang Mai is also, in essence, deceptive. While Bangkok is a mere two hundred years old, Chiang Mai has been a center of power in northern Thailand for almost seven centuries. There are old temples here, traces of Burmese architecture, and traditional Lanna-style buildings. Chiang Mai people are proud of their northern heritage, their distinctive language and culture.

Outside the city is a fertile rice-growing plain that stretches in all directions until it bumps up against the steep mountains that rim the valley. To the west, the high dome-shaped Doi Sutep, a mountain topped by a monastery, and the location of the Thai Royal Family's northern palace, seems to be looking down on the city. It can be seen from almost everywhere in Chiang Mai but, like most people, we're usually too busy enjoying the life on the streets and in the markets to spare a thought for the countryside round about.

It's rare these days to come upon a cycle rickshaw in Chiang Mai. As the region prospers, there's a shift toward motorized rickshaws.

PAD THAI CLASSIC STIR-FRIED NOODLES
[*pad thai* — THAILAND]

Pad thai literally means "Thai fry," and it is the dish many foreigners think of first when they think about Thai food. It's a satisfying one-dish noodle stir-fry, dry rather than sauced, and full of different isolated flavors that come together in a balance of salty, sour, and sweet. There are salty dried shrimp, soft pieces of cooked egg with a little succulent pork, and seared pressed tofu, all scattered throughout pan-seared thin rice noodles.

Once you have your ingredients prepared, cooking time is less than 6 minutes. You need a large wok to prepare this amount (the noodles take up a lot of room and you need to be able to push ingredients up the sides of the wok while you cook others). If your wok is small, make the recipe in two batches.

CONDIMENTS AND ACCOMPANIMENTS

1 cup **Chile-Vinegar Sauce (page 117)**

Cayenne pepper

Sugar (optional)

½ to 1 **European cucumber, thinly sliced**

1 small head **leaf lettuce, washed, dried, and separated into leaves (optional)**

1 **lime, cut into small wedges**

NOODLES

2 ounces **boneless pork thinly sliced, and cut into narrow strips about 1½ inches long**

1 teaspoon **sugar**

1 heaping tablespoon **tamarind pulp, dissolved in 2 to 3 tablespoons warm water, and pressed through a sieve, or substitute 1 tablespoon rice vinegar plus 1 tablespoon water**

1 tablespoon **soy sauce**

1 tablespoon **Thai fish sauce**

3 large **eggs**

Pinch of **salt**

3 tablespoons **peanut or vegetable oil**

2 to 3 cloves **garlic, minced**

1 cube (2 to 3 ounces) **pressed tofu, cut into narrow 1½-inch-long strips**

½ pound **narrow dried rice noodles, soaked in warm water for 20 minutes and drained**

½ pound (scant 4 cups) **bean sprouts, rinsed and drained**

3 **scallions, trimmed, smashed flat with the side of a cleaver, and cut into 1½-inch lengths**

1 tablespoon **dried shrimp**

1 tablespoon **salted radish (optional)**

1 cup **Dry-Roasted Peanuts (page 308), coarsely chopped**

2 to 4 tablespoons **coriander leaves (optional)**

Before you begin cooking, place the chile-vinegar sauce in a bowl on the table as a condiment, along with a small condiment plate of cayenne and another small bowl of sugar if you wish. Arrange the cucumber slices around the edge of your serving platter or individual plates, together with the lettuce leaves, if using, and lime wedges. (If you wish, arrange extras of all three on a serving plate.)

Place the pork in a small bowl, add the sugar, and toss to mix. In a medium bowl, mix together the tamarind water (or rice vinegar and water), soy sauce, and fish sauce. In a small bowl, lightly beat the eggs with the salt. Place all the ingredients by your stovetop.

Place a large wok over high heat. Add about 1½ tablespoons of the oil and, when it is hot, add the garlic and stir-fry briefly until it begins to change color, about 15 seconds. Toss in the pork and stir-fry until it has all changed color, 1 minute or less. Add the tofu and press it against the hot sides of the wok to scorch it a little, 10 to 20 seconds. Pour in the egg mixture and let cook until it starts to set around the pork and tofu slices, less than a minute. Use your spatula to cut it into large pieces, then transfer all onto a plate and set aside.

Place the wok back over high heat, add remaining 1½ tablespoons or so oil, and swirl to coat. Toss in the drained noodles and stir-fry vigorously, pressing them against the hot wok to sear and heat them, then turn and press them again. They will seem dry and unwieldy, but don't worry, just keep folding them over and pressing them onto the wok—after about 1 minute, they will all have softened more and be warm.

Move the noodles up the sides of the wok and toss in 2 to 2½ cups of the bean sprouts and the scallions. Stir-fry vigorously for about 20 seconds, pressing and turning to wilt them against the hot wok. Add the dried shrimp and salted radish and toss briefly with your spatula, then add the soy sauce mixture. Stir-fry for about another 30 seconds, gradually incorporating noodles into the bean sprout mixture. Add the reserved egg-meat mixture and toss gently to mix everything together.

Turn out onto the platter or onto individual plates. Place the remaining bean sprouts on a plate on the table. Sprinkle some of the chopped peanuts onto the noodles, and place the rest in a bowl as a condiment so guests can add extra as they wish. Sprinkle on the coriander leaves, if using, and serve. If serving from a central platter, serve guests (chopsticks or tongs are easiest for the job) or invite everyone to use their chopsticks to serve themselves. As they eat, guests can flavor their portions as they wish, with a sprinkling of cayenne, a squeeze of lime juice, a sprinkling of sugar (traditional in Thailand, but usually not loved by foreigners), a little more chopped peanuts, some bean sprouts, and a drizzle of chile-vinegar sauce.

SERVES *3 to 4 as a one-dish meal*

NOTES: *If not using salted radish, add a pinch of salt to the soy sauce mixture. You can omit the pork, or use chicken or beef, cut into slices instead. If not using pork, add the sugar to the soy sauce mixture.*

If you have a very large wok, you can, instead of removing the egg and meat mixture, use the traditional method and just push it up the sides of the wok while you stir-fry the noodles and bean sprouts. Then just push everything back down when you wish to incorporate it with the noodles.

PAD *THAI* CLASSIC STIR-FRIED NOODLES *is pictured on page 126.*

Tribal people, such as this Akha woman in northern Laos, may walk three or four hours to get to the market, their strong woven baskets on their backs.

HEARTY VIETNAMESE BEEF NOODLE SOUP
[*pho bo* — VIETNAM]

Pho (pronounced like the French word for fire, *feu*) means "noodle," as well as "noodle soup," and *bo* means "beef." In this classic *pho*, a slowly simmered beef broth, aromatic with star anise, cinnamon, and ginger, is poured over rice noodles, thinly sliced beef, and fresh basil leaves. The hot broth cooks the beef almost instantly.

The soup is originally from the north, but it is now a classic throughout Vietnam. We first tasted it at a restaurant outside Saigon as we were setting off on a long trip by car to northern Vietnam; the seductive flavors of the soup, and the combination of salt, pepper, and lime juice into which we dipped tender pieces of beef, made us happy to be on the road.

In Vietnam, beef noodle soup is traditionally eaten as we ate it that first time, for breakfast; people sit at little food stalls, chopsticks in one hand and spoon in the other, eating large bowls of the fragrant noodle soup.

NOTE: *In Vietnam, beef bones, unlike pork bones, are washed before using; the recipe starts the traditional way, with instructions for boiling the oxtails or ribs, then discarding the water and starting to make the stock.*

SOUP

5 pounds oxtails or beef short ribs

6 quarts water

5 star anise

One 2-inch cinnamon stick

5 cloves

1 teaspoon black peppercorns

2- to 3-inch piece (about 2 ounces) ginger

2 medium onions, cut in half

1 pound stewing beef, trimmed of excess fat

5 tablespoons Vietnamese or Thai fish sauce, or to taste

Salt to taste

1 pound thin or medium dried rice noodles, soaked in warm water for 15 minutes and drained

GARNISH AND ACCOMPANIMENTS

2 cups bean sprouts, rinsed

Lime Juice Yin-Yang (recipe follows)

1 pound eye of round or other boneless lean beef, very thinly sliced across the grain into 1- to 2-inch-long slices

½ cup Asian basil or sweet basil leaves

½ cup coriander leaves

3 shallots, thinly sliced

1 or 2 bird or serrano chiles, minced

Place the oxtails or ribs in a large pot, cover with cold water, and bring to a boil. Boil vigorously for 5 minutes, then drain. Rinse out the pot well, rinse off the oxtails or ribs and place back in the pot.

Add 4 quarts of the water and bring to a boil. Add the star anise, cinnamon stick, cloves, and peppercorns. Using tongs, char the ginger over a gas flame, then add to the pot; use the same method to char the onion pieces, then add to the pot. *Alternatively*, heat a heavy skillet over high heat, add the ginger and onion pieces, and scorch well on all sides before adding to the pot.

Let the broth boil gently, uncovered, skimming off foam and scum, for about 30 minutes. Add the remaining 2 quarts water, bring back to the boil, and continue to boil gently, skimming off foam. When foam has stopped rising to the surface, lower the heat to medium-low and simmer for another hour.

Add the stewing beef and fish sauce, bring back to a boil, and simmer, uncovered, until the meat is very tender, about 2 hours. Leaving the soup at a simmer, remove the stewing beef and cool slightly. Slice as thin as possible and set aside.

Remove the soup from the heat and remove and discard the bones and solids. For a traditionally clear broth, line a colander with a double layer of cheesecloth and strain the soup into a clean bowl. Let the stock cool, then refrigerate, covered, for at least 2 hours.

Skim off the layer of fat from the top of the stock and discard. (*The soup can be made ahead to this point and stored in the refrigerator, beef and stock in separate well-sealed containers, for up to 2 days, or frozen for up to 1 month.*)

About 20 minutes before you wish to serve the soup, remove the meat and stock from the refrigerator and set the meat aside. Transfer the stock to a pot and heat until warm. Strain through cheesecloth as described above, return to the pot, and bring to a boil. Taste for seasonings and add fish sauce or salt as desired, then simmer gently, half covered, while you prepare the accompaniments.

Bring a large pot of water to a boil. Drop in the rice noodles and cook until just tender but not mushy, 30 seconds to 1 minute. Transfer to a colander, rinse with cold water, and set aside. Blanch the bean sprouts briefly in the same boiling water, then set aside.

Provide each guest with a spoon and a pair of chopsticks, as well as a small side plate with the Lime Juice Yin-Yang—a generous pile of salt, another of black pepper beside it, and a lime wedge or two—to be used as a condiment for the beef slices (see below). Set out the raw beef, along with small dishes of the herbs, shallots, bean sprouts, and sliced chile.

To serve, divide the noodles among 6 to 8 large bowls. Top each serving with a generous pinch of bean sprouts, a few shallot slices, several basil leaves, slices of cooked beef, and slices of raw beef. Ladle the hot broth over and sprinkle with the coriander.

MAKES *about 3 quarts broth; serves 6 to 8*

NOTE: *If you freeze the beef stock, you may wish to serve it as a clear broth on its own or simply poured over thin slices of lean beef, shallot slices, and perhaps several sprigs of basil. Sprinkle with coriander leaves and, if including beef slices, serve with Lime Juice Yin-Yang.*

LIME JUICE YIN-YANG

Simple but elegant, this little condiment is still our favorite combo with beef of every kind, as well as a brilliant way of serving salt and pepper any time. We learned it from a man named Lam, long ago on our first trip to Vietnam.

Coarse sea salt or kosher salt
Very coarsely ground black pepper
Small wedges of lime

Place the salt and pepper in separate shallow bowls, with a spoon for each. Place the lime wedges on a small plate. Give each guest a very small condiment dish. Demonstrate how to combine flavors by first placing a generous pile of salt on one side of your condiment dish, then a heap of pepper separately on the other side. Squeeze a little lime juice over the space in between. Use a chopstick to gently mix the proportion of salt and pepper that you wish into the lime juice, making a black-and-white paste.

GINGER CHICKEN NOODLE SOUP

[*pho ga* — VIETNAM]

This warming noodle soup is a good introduction to the pleasures of making your own Southeast Asian noodle soup, as it is easy to prepare and always a big hit. The broth is poured over rice noodles, bean sprouts, and fresh herbs, then served topped with a little ginger paste.

SOUP

One 3½-pound chicken, excess fat removed

3 quarts cold water

1 teaspoon black peppercorns

2- to 3-inch piece (2 to 3 ounces) ginger

1 large or 2 medium onions, cut into quarters

2 tablespoons Vietnamese or Thai fish sauce, or to taste

Salt to taste

GARNISH AND ACCOMPANIMENTS

1½ cups loosely packed bean sprouts, rinsed

1 pound thin or medium dried rice noodles, soaked in warm water for 15 minutes and drained

2- to 3-inch piece (2 to 3 ounces) ginger

Pinch of salt

2 to 3 shallots, thinly sliced

1 cup loosely packed coarsely chopped coriander

½ cup loosely packed Vietnamese coriander leaves (*rau ram*), or substitute chopped mint

1 to 2 limes, cut into wedges

Rinse the chicken, including the heart, neck, and giblets, thoroughly with cold water (reserve the liver for another use). Place in a large pot and add the water and peppercorns. (If the chicken is not covered with water, you will have to turn it once or twice during cooking.) Bring to a boil over high heat.

As the water is heating, scorch the ginger and the onion pieces, either over a gas flame, using tongs to hold the pieces in the flame until they scorch, or together in a dry heavy skillet over high heat. Turn the pieces until they are blackened on all sides, then add to the soup.

Once the water comes to a boil, skim off the foam, lower the heat, and let simmer, partially covered, until the chicken is cooked, about 45 minutes, skimming off the foam occasionally. If the chicken is not completely covered with water, turn it several times during cooking. Remove the chicken from the broth and set aside to cool slightly. Remove the meat from the bones, coarsely shred, and set aside; discard the bones, giblets, and skin.

Line a colander with a double layer of cheesecloth and strain the broth into a bowl. Let cool, then transfer to several containers and refrigerate, covered, for at least 3 hours. When the broth has chilled completely, skim off the layer of fat on the surface with a large spoon and reserve it for use in the soup (traditionally a little of this fat is dolloped onto the soup when it is served) or for another purpose. (*The soup can be made ahead to this point and the broth and chicken stored separately in the refrigerator, in well-covered containers, for up to 2 days. The broth can also be frozen for up to 3 months.*)

About 30 minutes before you wish to serve the soup, remove the broth and shredded chicken from the refrigerator. Place the soup in a pot, add the fish sauce, and bring to a boil, then lower the heat and let simmer until ready to serve. Taste for seasoning and add fish sauce or salt to taste.

Meanwhile, bring a large pot of water to a vigorous boil. Place the bean sprouts in a sieve or a colander and blanch them in the boiling water for 20 to 30 seconds. Remove and set aside to drain. Bring the water back to a boil, drop in the rice noodles, and cook just until softened but not mushy, 30 seconds to 1 minute. Drain, rinse with cold water, and set aside.

Using the technique described above, scorch the piece of ginger. Coarsely chop it, then place in a large mortar, add the salt, and pound to a paste. *Alternatively*, mince the ginger, place it in a bowl, add the salt, and use the back of a spoon to mash the ginger; add a little water, if necessary, to make a paste.

To serve, divide the noodles among six large soup bowls. Place about ¼ cup bean sprouts in each, then top with the chicken. Add several shallot slices, separated into rings, ladle the hot broth over, and add a dollop of the ginger paste and a dollop of the reserved chicken fat, if you wish. Sprinkle on some coriander and Vietnamese coriander or mint. Serve at once, with small plates of the remaining shallot slices and herbs, a small bowl of the remaining ginger paste, and the lime wedges, so guests can adjust flavorings to taste.

MAKES *about 11 cups broth (and 18 to 20 ounces cooked chicken); serves 6 as a one-dish meal*

VIETNAMESE NOODLE COMBOS
[VIETNAM]

Starting with a coil of soaked and cooked noodles, Vietnamese cooks and market stall vendors construct wonderful meal-in-a-bowl combos. Here are some suggestions for embarking on this flexible approach to noodles.

1 pound rice vermicelli or dried rice noodles, soaked in warm water for 15 minutes and drained, then briefly boiled and drained

About 2 cups chopped salad greens

1 cup Carrot and Daikon Pickled Salad (page 85) (optional)

1 cup bean sprouts, rinsed and drained, or pickled (see page 85) (optional)

TOPPINGS: CHOOSE TWO OR THREE

Classic Vietnamese Spring Rolls (page 274), cut into 1-inch lengths

Vietnamese Grilled Pork Balls (page 252)

Aromatic Lemongrass Patties (page 251)

Grilled Lemongrass Beef (page 225)

Other sliced grilled meats or vegetables

GARNISH

Coriander leaves or mint leaves

ACCOMPANIMENT

Vietnamese Must-Have Table Sauce (*nuoc cham*, page 28)

The noodles can be cooked up to 2 hours ahead and set aside.

To serve, distribute the salad greens and vegetables, if using, among four large bowls. Distribute the noodles among the bowls. Place the toppings over and sprinkle on the herbs. Serve with the dipping sauce in a small bowl with a small spoon so guests can drizzle on sauce as they wish.

SERVES *4*

MUANG SING: We know we are in a good place when our children are awakened early one morning by the sound of their hotel room door slowly squeaking open, and in through the doorway come the horns and the curious head of an enormous water buffalo. "Come quickly," they call to us. Water buffalo may look mighty big when they are munching on rice straw in a field, but when you see one standing in the doorway of your children's small room, their size takes on a whole new dimension.

We will never forget our time in Muang Sing, a tiny town way up in the northwestern corner of Laos, just a few miles south of the Chinese border. Our hotel was a simple one-story structure by a rice field. For a few hours each evening, we had electricity powered by a generator; the rest of the time we had just sunshine in the day and candles at night. For entertainment, we'd walk up and down the town's two dusty main roads, or we'd hike or bicycle out into the hills, or we'd simply hang around. We'd go for dinner to a local restaurant, and while we ate, we'd watch the villagers as they watched television, Chinese operas and Thai fight-it-out dramas. By nine o'clock, the generator would turn off, and along with everyone else, we'd walk home in the dark, voices in the dark.

The big event of the day, the local market, got started every morning hours before dawn. Muang Sing's streets would begin to fill with tribal people walking in from the hills: Akha, Mien, Tai Dam, Hmong. They'd be laughing and carrying on, coming to the market to buy, to sell, to have a good time. Many came from villages far away, having walked in darkness for hours carrying big baskets of jungle-gathered specialties: bamboo shoots, medicinal plants, small wild game. For a few hours each morning, Muang Sing became the bustling center of its world, the Chicago of northwestern Laos, and for us it was absolutely thrilling.

One morning I sat down for a bowl of noodles next to an Akha man who was also having a bowl of noodles. We checked each other out, the way you do in the market. "Nice trousers," I said, motioning to his hand-spun, handwoven cotton pants, which were a little dusty and worn but still incredible. He couldn't understand what I had said, and I couldn't understand what he then said (maybe something about my trousers), but we acknowledged each other and continued to check each other out. And then we ate our bowls of noodles, and moved on.

Well, later we ran into each other again, and again we admired each other's trousers, only this time somehow more intently. A friend of his came by, and then another, and soon we had a little crowd. Before I knew it, I was bargaining for his trousers. It was a wild session: yes, no, maybe, too dirty, too much, too little, made by hand, much better than mine, yes. He walked away, I walked away, then we returned and it went on. At last we settled on a deal, a fair price, or so I thought. And then he solemnly turned around and walked home, back into the hills.

Next morning, right at dawn, there he was at our small hotel. He was wearing the same trousers, dusty and worn, and he stood there with the same serious expression that never changed. When he saw me he held out a pair of trousers, new trousers. They were hand-spun, handwoven, ready to wear.

I hope they will last a lifetime.

When we bicycled out of Muang Sing one hot sunny day, heading toward the Chinese border, we came upon these water buffalo, looking rested and oh-so-cool.

CHIANG MAI CURRY NOODLES

[*khao soi* — NORTHERN THAILAND]

We're told by friends in Chiang Mai, Thailand's northern capital (see Chiang Mai, page 122), that this noodle dish is originally from the Shan State of Burma; others say it came with Muslim traders from Yunnan. Whatever the story, *khao soi* is now known as a Chiang Mai specialty. It's an easy-to-make, very rich and delicious one-dish meal.

The broth that bathes the noodles is flavored with a little curry paste, turmeric, and garlic and is smooth and thick with coconut milk. Traditionally *khao soi* is made, as it is here, with beef; you can also make it with chicken.

The recipe calls for Chinese egg noodles, available from most Chinese groceries. They come in one-pound packages and are about linguine width and pale yellow. The cooked noodles are placed in large individual bowls and the curry sauce is poured over them when the dish is served. *Khao soi* is usually topped with a small nest of crispy noodles, egg noodles that have been briefly deep-fried; they add a delightful contrasting texture. There is a small array of condiments traditionally served with *khao soi*; don't worry if you don't have pickled cabbage.

2 to 3 cloves garlic, peeled

1-inch piece fresh turmeric, minced, or 1 teaspoon ground turmeric

1 teaspoon salt, plus a pinch

1 tablespoon Red Curry Paste (page 210 or store-bought)

1 tablespoon peanut or vegetable oil

3 cups canned or fresh coconut milk (see page 315), with ½ cup of the thickest milk set aside

½ pound boneless flavorful beef (sirloin tip or trimmed stewing beef), cut into ½-inch chunks

1 tablespoon sugar

1 cup water

3 tablespoons Thai fish sauce

1 tablespoon fresh lime juice

Peanut oil for deep-frying noodles (optional)

1 pound Chinese egg noodles (*bamee*)

TOPPINGS AND CONDIMENTS

Fried noodle nests (optional; see below)

½ cup coarsely chopped shallots

½ cup minced scallions

½ cup Pickled Cabbage, Thai Style (page 311 or store-bought)

1 lime, cut into wedges

Place the garlic in a mortar with the turmeric and the pinch of salt and pound to a paste. *Alternatively,* finely mince the garlic and whole turmeric, if using, and place the garlic and turmeric in a small bowl with the pinch of salt. Stir in the red curry paste and set aside.

Place a large heavy pot or wok over high heat. Add the 1 tablespoon oil and, when it is hot, toss in the curry paste mixture. Stir-fry for 30 seconds, then add the reserved ½ cup thick coconut milk and lower the heat to medium-high. Add the meat and sugar and cook, stirring frequently, for 4 to 5 minutes, until the meat has changed color all over. Add the remaining 2½ cups coconut milk, the water, fish sauce, and the remaining 1 teaspoon salt and bring to a boil, then reduce the heat to medium and cook at a strong simmer for about 10 minutes. Remove from the heat and stir in the lime juice. *(The soup can be prepared up to an hour ahead, then reheated just before serving.)*

Meanwhile, make the optional crispy noodles: Place a plate lined with several layers of paper towels by your stove. Place a large wok or heavy pot over high heat and add about 1 cup peanut oil, or ½ inch oil. When the oil is hot, drop in a strand of uncooked noodle to test the temperature. It should sizzle slightly as it falls to the bottom, then immediately puff and rise to the surface; adjust the heat slightly, if necessary. Toss a handful (about 1 cup) of noodles into the oil and watch as they puff up. Use a spatula or long tongs to turn them over and expose all of them to the hot oil. They will crisp up very quickly, in less than 1 minute. Lift the crisped noodles out of the oil and place on the paper towel–lined plate. Give the oil a moment to come back to temperature, and then repeat with a second handful of noodles. *(The noodles can be fried ahead and left standing for several hours.)*

To serve, bring a large pot of water to a vigorous boil over high heat. Drop in the remaining noodles (or all noodles, if you didn't make crispy noodles), bring back to a boil, and cook until tender but not mushy, about 6 minutes. Drain well.

Divide the drained noodles among four large bowls. Ladle over the broth and meat. Top with crispy noodles, if you have them, and a pinch each of shallots and scallions. Serve with the remaining condiments set out in small bowls so guests can garnish their soup as they wish. Provide each guest with chopsticks and a large spoon.

SERVES *4*

CHIANG MAI CURRY NOODLES *is pictured on page 137.*

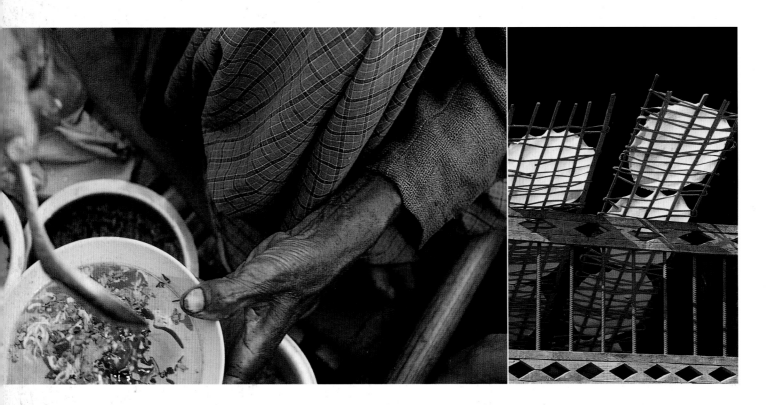

LEFT: *A soup vendor serves up fresh noodles bathed in broth. Even when the noodle stall is on a boat, as here on Inle Lake in Burma's Shan State, the broth is always hot and the choice of toppings generous.* RIGHT: *The rice batter that makes noodles can also be used to make rice wrappers, although making them thin and fine is an art.*

MORNING MARKET NOODLES
[MEKONG REGION]

Early morning in the village markets in Southeast Asia, there's a chill in the air and the smell of wood smoke from cooking fires. Women cook at open-air stalls, each with a table and a few stools, some bowls and jars of condiments, and a platter of fresh ingredients. (In the floating markets of the Mekong Delta, the stalls are small boats, rocking gently.) Clouds of steam rise from simmering pots of soup. Shoppers, whether tribal people in from the hills in Muang Sing, or Dai women slender in sarongs and cotton blouses in Menghan, or foreign travelers out for an early stroll in Vientiane, find themselves perched on stools, side by side with strangers, eating Morning Market Noodles, usually in a hot soup.

The details vary, but in all places the soup bowl is large, the broth is hot and aromatic, and there are a few pieces of meat and the occasional fragment of vegetable, lost in a tangle of noodles.

Morning Market Noodles are wonderful to serve for breakfast, lunch, or supper, anytime. Make the broth ahead, then prepare the condiments and toppings and let everyone assemble his or her own soup noodles. Serving this way accommodates a wide variety of eaters, from those who like only mild tastes to those who adore chiles.

We've listed an array of optional accompaniments; you can keep things very simple or provide a wider choice of flavorings (see Notes for suggestions). However you proceed, your guests will feel welcomed, cared for, satisfied.

10 to 12 cups Basic Southeast Asian Broth (page 50) or
    other mild chicken or pork broth
1 pound chicken thighs, coarsely chopped, or ½ to 1 pound
    fresh ham or lean pork roast, cut into 2-inch chunks
Salt and/or Vietnamese or Thai fish sauce to taste
1½ pounds thin dried rice noodles or rice vermicelli, soaked
    in warm water for 15 minutes and drained, or 2 pounds
    fresh rice noodles

OPTIONAL INGREDIENTS

Bean sprouts

Chopped napa cabbage

Pea tendrils

OPTIONAL TOPPINGS

Minced scallions

Coriander leaves

Dry-Roasted Peanuts (page 308), coarsely chopped

**Spicy pork filling from Green-Wrapped Flavor Bundles
    (page 269)**

Fried Shallots (page 310)

OPTIONAL CONDIMENTS

Black rice vinegar

Rice vinegar mixed with soy sauce

Garlic Oil (page 310)

Roasted sesame oil

**Yunnanese Chile Pepper Paste (page 27) or store-bought
    chile paste**

Chile-Vinegar Sauce (page 117)

Sugar

Fish sauce

Lime wedges for squeezing

Salt and freshly ground black or white pepper

Place the stock in a large pot, add the meat, and bring to a boil. Lower the heat and simmer until the meat is tender, about 30 minutes. Taste and add salt or fish sauce, or a combination, as you wish. Lift out the pieces of meat, discard any bones, and cut the meat into bite-sized pieces. Keep the broth warm over low heat until you wish to serve. (*You can make the soup ahead and let the broth and meat cool to room temperature, then store them in separate sealed containers in the refrigerator for 2 days or in the freezer for up to 1 month. Bring the meat to room temperature before proceeding.*)

About 20 minutes before you wish to serve the soup, put a large pot of water on to boil. Put the optional ingredients you have chosen near your stovetop and set out the toppings and condiments on the table. Bring the broth to a steady simmer. Add the reserved meat to the soup, or, place it on a plate so you can offer it to your guests separately. Set out a sieve or colander to use for dipping the noodles and vegetables into the boiling water and a pair of tongs or long chopsticks for fishing the meat out of the broth. Put out a large soup bowl, a spoon, and chopsticks for each person.

Serve each person individually: Ask each guest which of the ingredients he or she would like in the soup. Place a coil of noodles in the sieve and dip into the boiling water for 30 seconds. Lift them out, pausing to let them drain, then place them in the guest's bowl. Ladle over a generous quantity of hot broth and some chopped meat, if using. If you want to parboil the raw ingredients (bean sprouts, napa cabbage, or pea tendrils) your guest has chosen, dip them briefly into the boiling water before placing them in the soup bowl.

Invite your guests to add flavorings as they wish. You may find that when they return for seconds, they want their noodles "dry," with little or no broth; another option in this very flexible way of eating.

SERVES *8*

NOTES ON REGIONAL DIFFERENCES: *In Yunnan, at markets in the Dali region, flavorings on vendors' tables generally consist of hot chile paste, black rice vinegar mixed with soy sauce (a blend known as* suan su*), garlic oil, roasted sesame oil, ground roasted peanuts minced and mixed with sugar, minced scallions, and chopped coriander.*

In southern Yunnan, in the Dai area near the Lao border, condiments are similar, though instead of vinegar with soy sauce, there are fried shallots and a paste made of ginger mashed with a pinch of salt and moistened with water.

In Muang Sing, in northern Laos, pea tendrils are usually on offer and so is a spicy pork paste (the filling for Green-Wrapped Flavor Bundles, page 269) that is dolloped on top of the soup, then stirred in. There is also chile oil or chile paste, along with chopped scallions and coriander, but there is no sesame oil or peanuts. Similarly, in Luang Prabang and Vientiane, there is no soy or vinegar, no sesame oil or peanuts. There is often, however, chopped celery leaf, a dish of fish sauce, extra pieces of boiled meat, and padek *(fermented fish paste).*

In northeast Thailand and southern Laos, there is fish sauce, sometimes shrimp paste or padek*, sugar, a mild chile-vinegar sauce, chile oil, and sometimes scallion oil or fried shallots or fried garlic.*

In Cambodia, with a bowl of k'tieu *you might have optional toppings of dried shrimp, bean sprouts, soy sauce, chopped bird chiles, coriander leaves, pickled cabbage, fried garlic, and, often, sugar.*

In southern Vietnam, hu tieu is a close cousin of the Cambodian soup k'tieu. *It comes as two dishes: thin rice vermicelli in one bowl and the broth served on the side. Other noodle soups in Vietnam are usually called* pho, *after the flat rice noodles they contain. Hu tieu usually comes with the flavorings similar to those with* k'tieu: *coriander leaves, sometimes roasted sesame oil or scallion oil, always bean sprouts but not pea tendrils, soy sauce, lime wedges, bird chiles, and pepper. For other noodle soups in southern Vietnam, there might also be ground peanuts, assorted fresh herbs, including mint and Asian basil and sometimes sawtooth herb but less commonly coriander leaves, and fish sauce.*

NORTHERN RICE NOODLE STEW

[*kanom jiin nam ngio* — NORTHERN THAILAND]

This is a dish of simmered meat with lots of thin gravy that is served over fresh round white rice noodles known as *kanom jiin*. Since fresh rice noodles can be hard to find outside Southeast Asia, we use dried rice vermicelli or the narrowest dried flat rice noodle available.

We first tasted this dish at a restaurant in Chiang Mai, where our friend Guk Gai had taken us for traditional northern food. The place was jammed. When the dish came, it was delicious, though a little hard to figure out. There was a lot of broth, chile-hot and a little lime-sour, very unlike the sweet coconut milk curries of central Thailand, with pieces of well-cooked pork scattered through it.

This is the closest we can come to reproducing that dish. It comes originally from the Shan, hence the flavoring with Shan Chile Paste. You'll notice there's no fish sauce, just salt, in the Shan tradition. When you taste for salt, remember that the sauce is going over noodles, so it needs to be a little saltier than if you were eating it on its own.

Tai Lu villagers in northern Laos live in graceful wooden houses built on stilts and placed close together along narrow tree-lined lanes.

NOODLE STEW

1½ pounds pork spareribs, chopped into 3 or 4 pieces

5 cups water or light chicken or pork broth

2 to 3 tablespoons peanut or vegetable oil

3 tablespoons Shan Chile Paste (page 37), or substitute
   1 tablespoon Red Curry Paste (page 210 or store-bought)
   mixed with 1 tablespoon fermented soybean paste (*dao jiao*)

½ teaspoon ground turmeric

½ cup chopped shallots or mild onions

½ pound ground pork

1 medium to large (about ½ pound) tomato, coarsely chopped,
   or 2 to 3 canned tomatoes, drained and coarsely chopped

½ teaspoon salt (2 teaspoons if using red curry paste),
   or to taste

2 tablespoons fresh lime juice

1 pound dried rice vermicelli or narrow dried rice noodles,
   soaked in warm water for 15 minutes and drained

TOPPINGS AND ACCOMPANIMENTS

½ cup Fried Garlic (page 310)

½ cup loosely packed torn coriander leaves

¼ cup minced scallions

2 cups bean sprouts, rinsed and drained

1 cup Pickled Cabbage, Thai Style (page 311 or store-bought),
   coarsely chopped (optional)

5 to 6 Thai dried red chiles, quickly fried in oil until softened
   (see Note) (optional)

1 lime, cut into wedges

Rinse the ribs in cold water, then place in a pot with the water or broth and bring to a boil. Simmer for 20 minutes, or until the ribs are cooked, skimming off any foam on the surface. Remove from the heat, lift the ribs out of the broth, and cool a moment. Cut the meat from the bones, coarsely chop, and return to the pot. Set aside.

Heat a wok over high heat. Add the oil and swirl to coat the wok. Toss in the chile paste, or the curry paste and soybean paste, and stir-fry for 15 seconds, using your spatula to break up the paste. Toss in the turmeric and shallots or onions and stir-fry vigorously for about 15 seconds. Toss in the pork and stir-fry, using your spatula to break up any lumps, until the pork is cooked through, about 5 minutes. Add the chopped tomato and simmer 5 minutes more.

Add the stir-fried mixture to the reserved broth and bring to a simmer. Add the salt and lime juice and stir until well blended. Taste for salt and add a little more if you wish. The sauce should be thin, with a hot, slightly sour tang. (*The dish can be prepared ahead to this point, then cooled to room temperature, transferred to a well-sealed nonreactive container, and stored in the refrigerator for up to 3 days or in the freezer for a month. When ready to proceed, place the meat and broth back in a pot and bring to a simmer.*)

Bring a large pot of water to a boil. Add the noodles and cook until tender, 1 to 2 minutes; drain.

To serve, place a coiled heap of noodles in each bowl and ladle over a generous amount of broth and some meat. Sprinkle fried garlic, coriander leaves, and minced scallions over each serving; put the remaining broth and meat in a bowl with a serving spoon so guests can add more to their bowls as they wish. Place the accompaniments in piles on a platter or make up small individual plates for each guest, as you wish. The bean sprouts, pickled cabbage, and fried chiles can be stirred into the broth and noodles or eaten separately as accompaniments, and the lime wedges can be squeezed over to give an extra sour note.

SERVES *6*

NOTE: *To fry dried chiles, place about ¼ cup peanut or vegetable oil in a wok or heavy skillet and heat over medium-high heat. When they are hot, toss in whole chiles and fry for about 1 minute, or until soft. Remove from the pan and drain in paper towels.*

THE NOODLE MAKER: I don't know her name, but I always think of her as the noodle maker. She lives in a small village in northern Laos near the Chinese border. She's a slender, hardworking mother of a large family, Tai Lu in her ethnicity. Her house is made of wood, built high up on stilts. There is a narrow wooden staircase running up to the veranda, where most of the household chores take place, and a doorway through to the inside, where there are several rooms for sleeping. Down below, under the house, she stores her loom, millstones for grinding rice, two large cauldrons, and other miscellaneous tools and utensils. Every day, underneath the house, she makes fresh rice noodles (known as *khao soi* in northern Laos) for sale at the nearby morning market in Muang Sing.

I came by one day, camera in hand, and saw her working under the house, though at what I couldn't see. She motioned, so I came in to get a closer look. She was grinding soaked rice between two millstones, transforming it into a wet dough. It was hard work, grinding by hand, going round and round, and continuously feeding rice and water into the top hole of the millstones. A pasty dough came oozing whitely out the sides, then gathered in a trough below the bottom stone.

Once she'd finished grinding, she kneaded the dough, over and over, for what felt like forever and was probably close to twenty minutes, until it was perfectly smooth. She already had a large pot of water heating over a fire (haul the wood, light the fire, haul the water, place the pot on the fire and fill it, tend the fire . . .). We moved over near the pot. She took out a cloth bag, like a pastry bag, with a small wooden disk at one end pierced with small holes, and she put some of the dough in the bag. Then, leaning over the boiling water in the cauldron, squeezing the bag hard until the sinews corded in her strong, slender arms, she squeezed long fine lengths of the white dough into the pot in continuously swirling spirals. They sank, then rose in the bubbling water. She used a mesh strainer to lift them out and laid them on a banana leaf, then she filled the bag again with dough and began squeezing out the next batch.

The next day, there she was in the market, way before dawn. Her beautiful white coils of noodles were nearly all gone, sold for pennies a kilo. It was almost time for her to head back to the village, time to start grinding more rice.

Fresh round rice noodles are known as kanom jiin *in Thai,* khao poon *in central Laos, and* khao soi *in the north. In more remote areas, they are still laboriously handmade; elsewhere the process is a little more mechanized.*

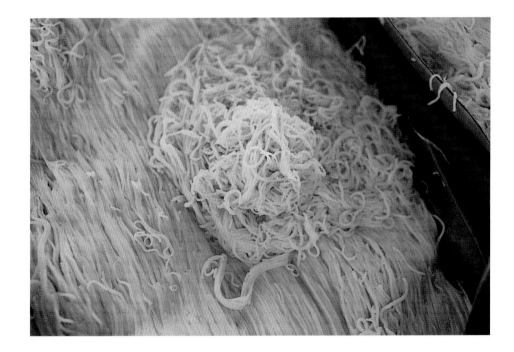

CELLOPHANE NOODLE SALAD
WITH OYSTER MUSHROOMS

[*yam wun sen* — THAILAND]

If you order *yam wun sen* from a Thai menu, the only thing you know for sure is that the salad will include cellophane noodles. Apart from that, few *yam wun sen* are ever much alike. The noodles provide a base for the salad, as in a pasta salad, and the other ingredients bring flavor and contrasting color and texture. In this recipe, oyster mushrooms and a small amount of pork add flavor, while coriander leaves and scallions bring added color. Be sure to serve with plenty of tender leaf lettuce and/or cucumber slices to use for scooping up the noodles.

SALAD

1 pound oyster mushrooms, cleaned

About 3 tablespoons peanut or vegetable oil

3 to 4 cloves garlic, minced

¼ pound (about ½ cup) ground pork

½ teaspoon salt

Pinch of sugar

3 bundles (about 3 ounces) cellophane noodles, soaked in warm water for 20 minutes and drained

1 medium scallion, trimmed, cut lengthwise into thin slices, and then cut crosswise into 2-inch lengths

1 cup loosely packed coriander leaves

Several whole tender leaf lettuce leaves for lining the plates and/or about 6 inches European cucumber, finely sliced

1 lime, cut into small wedges

Freshly ground black or white pepper

DRESSING

4 to 5 tablespoons fresh lime juice

4 to 5 tablespoons Thai fish sauce

½ to 1 teaspoon dried red chile flakes or 1 Thai dried red chile, crumbled

1½ teaspoons sugar

Prepare a grill fire or preheat the boiler. Separate the clumps of oyster mushrooms into individual mushrooms. Brush lightly with oil, then grill or broil until moist and tender right through, turning them partway through cooking. Let cool slightly, then cut into bite-sized pieces, discarding any tough stems, and set aside.

Heat 2 tablespoons oil in a wok or heavy skillet over high heat. When it is hot, toss in the garlic and stir-fry until golden, about 30 seconds, then add the pork and stir-fry briefly, using your spatula to break up any lumps. Stir in the salt and sugar and stir-fry until all the meat has changed color, then remove from the heat and set aside in a bowl.

Bring a medium pot of water to a boil. Cut the soaked cellophane noodles into 2- to 3-inch lengths (we use scissors and snip through clumps). Dump the noodles into the boiling water for 1 minute, then drain into a sieve or colander and refresh with cold water.

Place the noodles in a large bowl. Add the pork mixture and the mushrooms, toss, and set aside.

In a cup or small bowl, mix together all the dressing ingredients, starting with the lesser amount of each, then taste and adjust the balance of hot, sour, salty, and sweet if you wish. Pour about 6 tablespoons of dressing over the salad and toss gently; reserve the remaining dressing. (*The salad can be made ahead to this point and set aside, covered—and refrigerated if the wait will be longer than 30 minutes—for up to 2 hours. Bring back to room temperature before proceeding.*)

Add the scallion and most of the coriander leaves to the salad, reserving a few for garnish. Toss gently. Just before serving, pour over the remaining dressing. Line individual plates with lettuce leaves, if you wish, then mound the salad on top and sprinkle on the reserved coriander leaves. Or mound the salad, then arrange 5 or 6 overlapping cucumber slices around the edge of each salad. Place a lime wedge or two on each plate, and serve. Set out a pepper grinder so guests can grind pepper over if they wish.

SERVES *4*

SHAN SALAD WITH CELLOPHANE NOODLES AND GINGER

[*neen* — SHAN STATE]

We were taught how to make this salad by Shieng in Mai Sai, on the Thai border with the Shan State (see Border Town, page 92). She made it with celtuce, a celery-lettuce hybrid, but told us that any firm lettuce or cabbage green would be appropriate. After some experimenting, we now use the bottom half of a head of napa cabbage. It has good taste and a pleasing crunch, even after standing in the salad dressing for a while.

The dressing is tart with rice vinegar, and has some warmth from both minced ginger and dried chile, a wonderful complement to the cool crispness of the cabbage and the silkiness of the cellophane noodles.

SALAD

2 cups julienned napa cabbage (see Note)

3 bundles (about 3 ounces) dried cellophane noodles, soaked in warm water for 20 minutes and drained

1 cup coarsely chopped coriander

DRESSING AND FLAVOR PASTE

3 tablespoons vegetable or peanut oil

¼ cup chopped garlic

2 to 3 Thai dried red chiles, or 1 teaspoon dried red chile flakes, or less for less heat

2 tablespoons minced ginger (about 2 inches)

2 teaspoons dried shrimp

1 teaspoon salt

2 tablespoons water

2 tablespoons rice vinegar

1 tablespoon white wine vinegar or fresh lime juice

Place the cabbage in a large bowl of cold water and set aside.

Bring a large pot of water to a boil. Add the cellophane noodles and cook until softened, about 1½ minutes. Drain thoroughly in a sieve or colander. Coarsely chop.

Drain the cabbage and place in a bowl, add the noodles, and toss with your hands to mix well.

In a small heavy skillet, heat the oil over medium-high heat. Add the garlic and cook over medium heat until lightly browned, about 4 minutes. If using whole dried chiles, break into small pieces and stir into the oil. Or, stir in the chile flakes. Continue cooking and stirring for 1 minute, then transfer the garlic, chiles, and oil to a medium bowl.

Place the ginger in a mortar and pound to a paste, then add the shrimp and salt and pound to a paste. *Alternatively,* mince the ginger and shrimp very fine, place in a bowl with the salt, and use the back of a large spoon to mash and blend together. Stir the water into ginger-shrimp mixture, then add to the reserved garlic and chile oil. Stir in the vinegars. Pour the dressing over the salad and toss well. Add the coriander and toss well. Let stand for 15 minutes before serving to allow the flavors to blend.

SERVES *4 to 6 as part of a meal*

NOTE: *To prepare the cabbage, cut a napa cabbage crosswise in half. You will be using the bottom half. Reserve the remaining cabbage for another purpose. Cut out and discard the very tough core, then cut the cabbage into julienne strips about 2 inches long.*

VARIATION: *If you'd like to serve this as a more substantial dish, you can include oyster mushrooms: Grill or parboil about 4 oyster mushrooms, then coarsely chop. Add after mixing together the cabbage and noodles. You may want to increase the salt, chiles, and vinegar slightly and the oil to ¼ cup.*

MOSTLY VEGETABLES

Once the rainy season ends in early October, the waters of the Mekong and its tributaries begin to fall. From swiftly flowing muddy torrents, they gradually shrink through the dry months, only to start to swell again with the early rains in May. As the rivers fall, huge sloping riverbanks emerge on either shore, and wherever there's a village nearby, people begin to cultivate the riverbanks.

Gardens are planted, vegetable gardens. Sometimes little terraces are constructed, sometimes plots are divided with bamboo poles and bits of string. Over time, the riverbanks become an intricate maze of garden plots, one with corn, one of peas, one with scallions or coriander. At dawn and dusk each day, people carry buckets of water up the bank from the river, then carefully water the growing green plants. There's sometimes a song or a passing comment as they walk to and fro, or crouch by their plots looking for weeds to pluck.

We've come to think of these intensive vegetable gardens as a symbol of the Mekong region, given life by the rivers, and also by all the attentive work of people who live here.

Vegetables are everywhere on the Southeast Asian table, in practically every dish. They're sliced as a raw accompaniment or parboiled or stir-fried. In jungle areas and in the countryside, people use wild leafy greens and herbs that they gather in addition to the harvest of their gardens.

Many of the best vegetable dishes are the simplest, such as Chinese Greens, Thai Style (page 156) and Quick and Tasty Yunnanese Potatoes (page 162). But in Southeast Asia, vegetables are rarely just vegetables. Often there's a little meat to give some depth of flavor to a stir-fry, or to a simmered dish like The Best Eggplant Dish Ever (page 159).

In this chapter, we've also included dishes that feature tofu or eggs. One of our favorites on a cool evening is Luscious Chile-Oil Tofu (page 168), with its fabulous contrast of cool silky tofu and hot chile oil. Eggs seem made for stir-frying: As they blend with vegetables or cellophane noodles, they transform textures and are wonderfully transformed in the process (see Stir-fried Eggs with Cellophane Noodles, page 169).

TOP: *As the water level of the Mekong drops in the dry season, terraces of green vegetables take shape on the newly exposed riverbanks. There is a constant coming and going as people carry water up from the river to their gardens.* BOTTOM: *Greens drying on baskets near Xieng Khuang in Laos before being pickled.*

SEARED PEPPER-SALT TOFU

[jiaoyan dougan — YUNNAN]

Pressed tofu, also known as firm tofu or *doufu gan* (in Mandarin), looks a little like cheese. It comes in small firm blocks that may be white, pale tan, or darker brown on the outside (see Glossary for more details). Firm tofu is always smooth and easy to slice. For our children, we often serve it simply sliced and dressed with a little thick soy sauce and a sprinkling of minced scallion or coriander leaves, a dish we first tasted in noodle shops in Taiwan.

Look for pressed tofu in Chinese grocery stores, in the cooler. If you do find a good reliable source, you'll discover what a versatile, nutritious, tasty food it is.

When quickly stir-fried in a very lightly oiled wok, as here, pressed tofu puffs a little and takes on a good seared texture from the hot pan, yet it remains smooth on the tongue. There's a little warmth here from the Sichuan pepper, but the dish is not highly spiced. Pair it with a soup and a stir-fried green vegetable such as Yunnan Greens (page 151).

½ **pound pressed tofu (2 to 3 blocks)**
Peanut or vegetable oil
¼ **teaspoon salt, or to taste**
⅛ **teaspoon Chinese Pepper-Salt (page 309) or
   Two Pepper–Salt Spice Dip (page 309)**
1 **to 2 tablespoons chopped chives or scallion greens**
¼ **cup coriander leaves (optional)**

Thinly slice the tofu into 2- by ½-inch slices. Set aside. Rub an oiled paper towel over the inside of your wok. Place the wok over high heat and, when it is hot, toss in the tofu slices. Lower the heat to medium-high and stir-fry, pressing the slices against the hot sides of the wok to sear and brown them but trying not to break them up, until browning well. Add the salt, the spice blend, and the greens and stir-fry for another 30 seconds. Turn out onto a plate, taste for salt, and add a little more if you wish.

Serve topped with the coriander leaves.

SERVES *2 to 4 as part of a rice meal*

NOTE: *When purchasing pressed tofu, pay close attention to the expiration date, as it isn't a very long keeper.*

CLASSIC MIXED VEGETABLE STIR-FRY
[*pad pak* — THAILAND, LAOS]

A perfect marriage of wok and ingredients, *pad pak* is a welcome addition to any meal (or a good meal on its own, served simply with jasmine rice). As always with stir-frying, make sure your wok is very hot before you start cooking. The essential ingredient here is *dao jiao*, fermented soybean paste (see Glossary), which creates a tasty light sauce for the vegetables.

You can make this dish with just one vegetable, napa cabbage, for example, but a combination of vegetables, as in the recipe below, is more interesting. To make the dish vegetarian, substitute ¾ teaspoon salt for the fish sauce. Also, if you are like us, you might look at the 2 tablespoons of oil and think, oh, I can do it with only 1 tablespoon, but in this case it really needs the 2 tablespoons.

2 tablespoons peanut or vegetable oil
2 cloves garlic, smashed
½ pound napa cabbage, cut crosswise into ½-inch strips
¼ pound snow peas (about 1½ cups)
¼ pound mushrooms, cleaned and sliced (about 1½ cups)
1 tablespoon Thai fish sauce
1 tablespoon fermented soybean paste (*dao jiao*)
¼ teaspoon freshly ground black pepper, or to taste

Heat a large wok over high heat. Add the oil and swirl gently to coat. When the oil is hot, toss in the garlic and stir-fry until starting to turn golden. Add all the vegetables and stir-fry until starting to soften, 1½ to 2 minutes. Add the fish sauce, cover, and cook for 2 minutes. Add the soybean paste and stir-fry briefly to mix well, then turn out onto a plate. Season with the black pepper and serve.
SERVES *4 with rice*

YUNNAN GREENS *is pictured on page 153.*

YUNNAN GREENS
[*sunni cai* — YUNNAN]

If you're a vegetarian and planning a trip to China, don't let anyone convince you that you'll have a hard time finding good food to eat. With rice, excellent tofu dishes, and fresh stir-fried green vegetables, eating as a vegetarian in China can be pure pleasure, especially so in someplace relatively warm and fertile like Yunnan.

In this simple stir-fry, the bok choi is first parboiled, then stir-fried. Dried chiles and ginger are added to give warmth and a little bite to the beautiful dark green vegetables. The same method can be used with green beans or cabbage, and the result is equally tasty.

1 pound bok choi or Shanghai bok choi (5 to 8 heads)
Salt
2 tablespoons peanut or vegetable oil
2 Thai dried red chiles
½ teaspoon minced ginger
½ cup mild vegetable broth or water
1 teaspoon cornstarch, dissolved in 2 tablespoons water

Place a large pot of water on to boil. Meanwhile, cut the bok choi lengthwise into thirds or quarters and place in a sink full of cold water to soak for several minutes. Wash thoroughly to get any dirt out of the base of the stalks.

When the water is boiling, add about 1 tablespoon salt, bring back to the boil, and add the bok choi. Stir with a long-handled wooden spoon to make sure all the greens are immersed. Bring back to a boil, boil for under a minute, drain, and set aside.

Heat a large wok over high heat. Add the oil and swirl to coat the wok. Toss in the chiles and ginger. Stir briefly, then add the greens and stir-fry for 30 seconds, pressing them against the sides of the wok to sear them a little. Add the broth and let it boil for about 30 seconds. Stir the cornstarch paste well, then add it together with ½ teaspoon salt. Stir-fry for another 15 to 30 seconds, turn out onto a small platter, and serve. (Warn your guests that the chiles are not for eating, just for flavor.)
SERVES *4 as one of several dishes in a meal*

LEFT: *Here in Sangkhom, Thailand, the cultivation along the riverbanks is so intensive, with many tiny plots and the narrowest of paths between them, that each small piece of the patchwork is "fenced off" with small sticks or twigs to mark the line between cultivated garden and pathway.* RIGHT: *In Menghan, a Dai woman walks back and forth across the wide sandy riverbank, carrying water from the river to her vegetable garden.*

LUANG PRABANG: It's strange now to remember first planning to go into Luang Prabang, the old capital of Laos. In 1989, we had tried to get from Vientiane to Luang Prabang, but the police had threateningly told us that we couldn't go. It had all been a bit creepy.

Now we were planning to go in by boat, a two-day trip down the Mekong. We knew that things had changed for the better in Laos from the tourism point of view, but still we were feeling cautious. We'd play it really safe, we thought, and not stay long.

Very early in the morning, we took a small boat from Chiang Khong, Thailand, across the river to the Lao town of Huay Xai, crossing through Lao customs. Then we ran down the road to another dock and jumped onto a cargo boat just about to head down the river. Like everyone else, we climbed up onto the flat roof of the boat, found a place to call our own, and then sat back. Pretty pleasant.

All day we traveled down the river. Dom and Tashi were thrilled, sitting cross-legged at the very front of the boat, playing cards with other passengers and occasionally looking up at the mountains and forests all around. Along the river there were beautiful long, inviting sandbars, the river being very low in the dry season, and every once in a while the driver would deftly maneuver around a sand spit in our course.

By the end of the day, we had arrived at the village of Pak Beng, where the boat docked, and we went looking for a place to spend the night. Pak Beng had no electricity, no amenities, but a smiling woman fed us dinner at a table set up outside and then we slept in a tiny little cement room with four cots and no windows, the local hotel and restaurant.

Next day, we were back on a boat, though not the same boat, and not as big a boat, and we were told we had to sit inside because the rapids made the roof too dangerous a perch. The inside was cramped with hens and bags and cargo, and it wasn't as easy to see the river, but we all had a good day nonetheless. As on the day before, the river was absolutely beautiful, but with virtually no sign of people. Vietnam has nearly eighty million people; Thailand nearly sixty million. Laos has only four and a half million people; now this scarcity of population all began to make more sense.

By late afternoon, we came around one last bend in the river and there before us was Luang Prabang. Up high on the banks we could see golden shrines and temples, and suddenly all around us there were boats, people, noise, and action. In an instant, we were stretching our cramped limbs and making sure we had all children, bags, and wits collected. We scrambled like everyone else, hustling up the embankment, waving for a rickshaw.

An hour later, we were in a guest house, unpacked, arrived. At dusk we strolled along the river, stopped in at an evening market lit with candles, snacked on grilled chicken and sticky rice. The kids found an ice cream place, and we found some Lao beer. Luang Prabang seemed pretty nice, wonderful, in fact. We settled in and past worries became a distant memory.

Every evening, it seems, there is a light show on the Mekong in Luang Prabang, as the glow of the sunset lights up the river.

In Cambodia, shoppers can buy finely sliced ginger and lemongrass ready to be ground into flavorful pastes of all kinds.

CHINESE GREENS, THAI STYLE
[THAILAND]

Our preferred vegetable for this Chinese-Thai dish is the Chinese leafy green known in Cantonese as *gai laan* and in Mandarin as *jie lan*, sometimes called Chinese broccoli in English. It has thick round stalks topped with leaves and small white flowers. Because the stalks are tough, it needs a brief parboiling in plenty of water before being stir-fried with flavorings. You can use this parboil-then-stir-fry-and-simmer method for any green from bok choi to broccoli rabe. If you're using a more tender-stalked vegetable, reduce the final cooking time to 30 seconds or less to avoid overcooking.

1 pound Chinese leafy greens (see Headnote)
1 tablespoon salt
1 tablespoon vegetable or peanut oil
1 tablespoon minced garlic
1 tablespoon fermented soybean paste (*dao jiao*)
1 tablespoon Thai fish sauce
½ cup water

Wash the greens thoroughly in cold water. Cut off and discard any discolored leaves. Slice any thick stems lengthwise in half.

Bring a large pot of water to a rolling boil and add the salt. Toss in the greens, bring back to a boil, and boil for 1 minute, then drain and set aside.

Heat a large wok over high heat. Add the oil and swirl to coat the wok. Toss in the garlic and stir-fry for 30 seconds, then toss in the greens. Stir-fry vigorously for about 1½ minutes, then add the soybean paste and fish sauce. Stir-fry for another 30 seconds, then add the water, bring to a boil, and cover. Cook for about 2 minutes, then remove the lid. The greens should be tender and still bright green. Turn out onto a plate and serve hot or at room temperature.

SERVES *4 to 6 as part of a rice meal*

STIR-FRIED CABBAGE WITH DRIED CHILES AND GINGER

[*lajiao baicai* — YUNNAN]

Cabbage is the great winter staple wherever there's a long cold season to endure, from Scotland and rural Minnesota or Saskatchewan to northern India and Korea. In China, in late fall, especially in northern rural areas, you'll see stacks of cabbages in fields and markets. They're stored in a number of ways: dried and then salted, just dried, stored as is in a cool place, or pickled (see Pickled Cabbage, Thai Style, page 311).

When we drove south from Dali through Yunnan on a cold day in February, we stopped the first day for lunch at a small family-run restaurant in the country. Among the home-style dishes we were served was this one, the cabbage wilted but still a little crunchy, and well flavored by its searing in ginger-chile-and-anise-flavored oil.

1 small Savoy or green cabbage (about 1 pound)

2 tablespoons peanut or vegetable oil

1 ounce pork butt, with its fat, sliced, or 2 slices bacon,
   cut into 1-inch lengths

4 cloves garlic, minced

3 Thai dried red chiles

Three ¼-inch slices ginger

1 star anise, broken in two

1 teaspoon salt, or to taste

2 teaspoons soy sauce

Thinly slice the cabbage, then coarsely chop. Or grate it on a coarse grater. Discard any tough stems. You should have about 4 cups cabbage. Set aside.

Heat a large wok over medium-high heat. Add the oil and swirl it around to coat the wok. Toss in the pork slices (or bacon) and garlic, lower heat to medium, and stir-fry for about 2 minutes, until the garlic begins to change color and the pork fat begins to melt. (It is important that the wok not be over the highest heat, so that the pork fat can melt gradually without the meat scorching.) Add the dried chiles, ginger, and star anise and continue to stir-fry for 2 minutes longer. Raise the heat to high, toss in the cabbage, and stir-fry for about 1 minute, pressing the cabbage against the sides of the wok. Add the salt and continue to stir-fry until the cabbage wilts and softens, about 5 minutes. Add the soy sauce and then stir-fry for another minute or so, again pressing the cabbage firmly against the hot sides of the wok, until the cabbage is quite soft and wilted, with the occasional very slight bit of crunch. Taste for seasoning and adjust if you wish.

Turn out onto a plate and mound attractively. Serve hot.

SERVES *4 as part of a rice meal*

NOTE: *The ginger, chiles, and anise are there to flavor the oil, not to be eaten.*

SIMPLE DALI CAULIFLOWER

[*dali huacai* — YUNNAN]

Travel, it sometimes seems, is all about luck. And were we lucky to meet a young Englishman named Oran Feild. Oran had been living in China for several years, initially as a language student from his university in England, but later as a "dropout" seriously intent on pursuing his passion for traditional Chinese food and martial arts. He'd found himself a place to live in Kunming, a well-respected martial arts teacher, and a master cook who'd taken him on as an apprentice.

We first met him in Dali, where he was staying for the lunar new year. We started talking, and discovered that he was a serious student of Yunnanese culinary traditions. One day, he ran into us in the market and invited us to a meal he was making for a number of friends, casually met travelers like us as well as longtime China residents of one kind or another.

In the feast he prepared, this ordinary dish stood out because of its intentional simplicity. As Oran explained, every Yunannese meal must have one plain simple dish, without heat or dramatic color or complication. Cauliflower took to the role perfectly.

1 medium head cauliflower
Salt
2 tablespoons peanut or vegetable oil
2 teaspoons minced garlic or 3 to 4 whole cloves garlic,
  smashed (see Note)

Put a large pot of water on to boil. Meanwhile, cut off and discard the cauliflower leaves and cut out the core. Cut the cauliflower into florets.

Once the water is boiling, add about 1 tablespoon salt, bring back to a boil, and toss in the cauliflower florets. Use a long-handled spoon to stir gently as water comes back to a boil. Boil for about 1 minute, or until the cauliflower is tender but still firm. Drain and set aside.

Heat a large wok over high heat. Add the oil and swirl to coat the wok. Toss in the garlic and stir-fry until it starts to turn golden, 15 to 20 seconds. Toss in the cauliflower and stir-fry for 30 seconds to 1 minute, pressing it against the side of the wok to sear it, being careful not to mash it. Add ½ teaspoon salt, stir-fry briefly, turn out onto a colorful plate, and serve.

SERVES *4 as part of a rice meal*

NOTE: *We like the look and taste of fried minced garlic scattered over the cauliflower. However, if we're making this for children, who usually don't like eating garlic, we leave the cloves whole and just smash them before adding them to the hot oil. The oil takes on the garlic flavor, but the cauliflower remains pristine-looking, perfect for the children (and we end up with lovely large pieces of golden garlic).*

THE BEST EGGPLANT DISH EVER

[*makeua oop* — SHAN STATE, NORTHERN THAILAND]

The Tai Koen and Shan people who live in Burma's northern Shan State have a category of dishes called *oop*. *Oop* refers to the cooking method: steaming without water in a tightly sealed pot. To make this *oop*, once you've placed all the ingredients in a heavy pot with a tight-fitting lid, you need only check it every 5 or 10 minutes and give it a quick stir, until the flavors have blended and the eggplant has cooked to a softened tender mass. Though the pork and turmeric can be omitted, we highly recommend that you include both. "The best eggplant dish ever!" was our friend Cassandra's reaction when she tested the recipe.

Eggplant *oop* is traditionally served as part of a rice meal, but it can also be used, very nontraditionally, as a spread on bread.

**3 Thai dried red chiles, soaked in warm water
for 15 minutes to soften**

¼ cup finely chopped shallots

5 cloves garlic, minced

1 heaping tablespoon dried shrimp

1 teaspoon salt

1 medium tomato, coarsely chopped

2 tablespoons vegetable oil

¼ cup (about 2 ounces) ground pork (optional)

½ teaspoon ground turmeric (optional)

**1½ pounds Asian eggplants (4 to 5 medium),
cut into ¼-inch slices**

5 to 8 leaves mint or coriander, coarsely torn

Drain the chiles, reserving the water. Coarsely chop them, discarding the tough stems, and place in a mortar or blender together with the shallots, garlic, shrimp, and salt. Pound or process to a paste (if using the blender, you will probably need to add some of the chile soaking water). Add the tomato and pound or blend briefly, then transfer the spice paste to a bowl and set aside.

Place a 3½- to 4½-quart heavy pot with a tight-fitting lid over high heat. Add the oil and swirl to coat the bottom of the pot with oil. Add the pork, if using, and brown briefly, then add the spice paste and optional turmeric. Lower the heat to medium and cook, stirring, until aromatic, about 2 minutes. Add the eggplant slices and stir briefly, cover tightly, and reduce the heat to low (do not add water). Cook, checking every 5 minutes or so to ensure that nothing is sticking and to give the ingredients a brief stir, for 45 minutes to 1 hour, or until the eggplant is very tender and shapeless. (*The dish can be prepared ahead to this point and then reheated; refrigerate if making more than an hour in advance.*)

Turn out into a shallow bowl and top with the mint or coriander. Serve warm or at room temperature.

SERVES *4 as part of a rice meal*

NOTE: *The Shan also use this technique to cook* pak gooed, *a fiddleheadlike vegetable. To cook ⅔ to ¾ pound of fiddleheads, double the quantity of pork and tomatoes given here and cut back on the dried chiles, then follow the recipe. The fiddleheads should be bright green and tender when done.*

THE FABRIC OF IT ALL: At home, we have an old cherry wood dresser where we keep treasures

from the Mekong. In it there are Hmong baby carriers painstakingly embroidered in reverse appliqué. There are Mien cross-stitch women's pants, and Akha bodices, shoulder bags, and leg wraps, all in the rich earthy colors so distinctive to the Akha. There are indigo children's shirts and vests made by the Tai Dam, hand spun, handwoven, and bleached by wear and many a river washing. There are elegant silk sarongs, Lao *phaa nung*, as fine in our fingers as a string of seed pearls. Every once in a while we open a drawer of the dresser and simply browse, transported by a wonderful faraway smell of wood fires and kerosene lanterns, of clothing made by hand, of memories of a way of life very different from our own.

Food and textiles are for us equally full of meaning. Both are art disguised as domesticity, personal expression woven into necessity, care and nurturing transformed into color, taste, and feel. We get the same tingly goose bumps watching an Akha family arrive in the Muang Sing market (see page 133), dressed for the occasion, as we do being taught a new recipe by Mae in Menghan (see page 60). There is a sense of a tradition kept alive, and there is also incredible beauty.

When we are out on the road traveling in Laos, or in Yunnan, or in northern Thailand, often at night we'll sit in our hotel room, or out on a porch somewhere, and simply marvel at a piece of embroidery we were able to purchase in a local market. Or we'll work at repairing an old handwoven bag, or a pair of falling-apart indigo pants made from hemp.

It's so satisfying to feel the fabric, to decipher how the embroidery is stitched, to study the coarse weave of the cloth.

On several trips, we have taken with us a patchwork quilt in a state of semicompleteness, a quilt we can work on in the evening or when waiting for a bus to come. It covers our bed at night, it gives a simple two-dollar-a-day hotel room a sense of home, and it is fun to have something to share with women who are always curious and appreciative (even though our skills are so crude by comparison).

When we walk into a Mien or Hmong village, someone is always embroidering: a young woman, an old woman, a group of women. A mother will be standing in a doorway, keeping an eye on toddlers playing outside, and in her hands will be a needle and thread, working away at a piece of embroidery. When we look closely at the fineness of the work, a minuscule Mien cross-stitch or Hmong reverse appliqué that demands the tiniest piece of cloth being turned over and stitched down, it is unimaginable to us how someone simply stands there casually and sews so meticulously.

And if we walk into an Akha village, or a Tai Dam village, or into practically any village in the region and look around, sooner or later we will find someone weaving or spinning. And when we watch Dominic and Tashi watch a woman as she spins or weaves, studying her feet and hands as she manipulates the wonderfully mysterious and complicated process, and out comes cloth, we realize we are just like them. We're in awe.

In a small Akha village perched on a hill, we came upon a woman at her loom, weaving cloth from cotton she and her husband had grown and then spun into strong thread. Every once in a while she'd stop to mend a broken strand or adjust the loom or speak to a nearby child. Gradually, the fabric took shape beneath her fingers.

QUICK AND TASTY YUNNANESE POTATOES
[*jiaxiang tudou — YUNNAN*]

This is slightly chile-hot and very, very good, either hot from the wok or at room temperature. Serve as part of a rice meal with grilled or stir-fried meat, some lightly flavored Chinese greens, and a soup. It also makes great leftovers, cold or reheated. We like the leftovers topped by lightly stir-fried greens and a fried egg. No extra seasoning needed.

2 pounds potatoes (see Note)
3 tablespoons peanut or vegetable oil
5 Thai dried red chiles
**1 cup finely chopped scallions or a mixture
    of scallions and chives or garlic shoots**
1 teaspoon salt

Wash the potatoes well but do not peel unless the skins are very old and tough. Boil the potatoes in a large pot of salted water until just cooked. Drain and put back in the hot pot to dry. When cool enough to handle, slide off the skins if you wish. Coarsely chop the potatoes or break them into large bite-sized pieces.

Heat a wok over high heat. Add the oil and swirl to coat the pan, then toss in the chiles. Stir-fry briefly until they puff, about 30 seconds, then add the potatoes and stir-fry for about 3 minutes, pressing the potatoes against the hot sides of the wok to sear them. Add the chopped scallions or greens and salt and stir-fry for another 2 minutes. Turn out onto a plate and serve hot or at room temperature.

SERVES *4 to 6 as part of a rice meal*

NOTE: *You can use leftover boiled potatoes for this dish. The proportions above are for about 6 cups cut-up potatoes. If you begin with less, reduce the amount of greens and chiles proportionately. And your potatoes may already be salted, so be cautious as you add salt to taste.*

OPPOSITE: *Scallions displayed at the market in Laos.* ABOVE LEFT: *These round eggplants, sometimes called Thai eggplants, are often used in curries in Laos and Thailand.* ABOVE RIGHT: *The best time to visit Wat Xieng Thong, which sits high above the Mekong in the old section of Luang Prabang, is when the warm light of the late-afternoon sun lights up the glittering mosaics on the buildings in the temple complex.*

RIVER WEED: River weed, or *khai*, as it's known in Laos and northern Thailand, grows in the Mekong and also in all the smaller rivers that flow into the Mekong. When it is first pulled out of the water, it looks like a mass of fine seaweed, very green in color. It's harvested in the winter, from November to January.

We first saw river weed in the market in Chiang Khong, a small town on the Mekong in northern Thailand. We had no idea what it was. Then, as seasonal things tend to go, we began to see it everywhere, great huge bright green bundles drying on railings and bamboo screens in the sunshine. In Luang Prabang, sitting down by the Khan river one afternoon, we watched a father and his two sons as they went out into the river, then emerged a few minutes later looking like three large bushy Boston ferns walking down the beach.

Having finally clued in to *khai*, we started to notice strange blackish sheets that looked a little bit like thick *nori* seaweed in the market in Luang Prabang. When we looked closely, we could see that there were dried tomatoes pressed into the sheets, like pressed flowers, and the sheets were often dotted with sesame seeds. We learned it was *khai pen*, dried river weed. People cut it into strips and use it as a flavoring in vegetable dishes or fried rice, or fry it as a topping or condiment. *Khai pen* is relatively expensive in Laos, about a dollar for four sheets, astronomical in a country where a laborer might get paid only twenty-five cents an hour. But it's dense and flavorful; a little goes a long way.

Like many foods we encounter in Southeast Asia, we put both *khai* and *khai pen* down as foods we'd be able perhaps to describe but never to cook with at home, but we were wrong. A few months later, when we arrived home, there was a package from Lotus Foods in California, deep in the stack of mail that had accumulated while we were away. When we finally got around to opening it, there was a little package of *khai pen*, beautiful dark dried sheets, flavored with sesame seeds. "Thought you might be interested," said a nice little note. "Just received this river algae from Laos."

If you ever come across these sheets of dried river weed, now being imported from Laos, buy a package or two. Use it sliced into ribbons and quickly fried, as a flavoring for rice.

On the other hand, if you ever have fresh sun-dried river weed to work with, here's how to prepare it: It should be a bright green cloud of soft strands. For 4 to 5 cups loose river weed, the Shan way is to pound together about ½ cup garlic cloves, 3 tablespoons chopped galangal, several dried red chiles, and salt. Heat a wok over high heat and add about ¼ cup of oil. When it's hot, add the flavor paste, lower the heat to medium and stir-fry gently for 3 to 4 minutes, then turn off the heat and toss in the river weed. Turn and toss to moisten thoroughly with flavored oil. You might want to stir-fry a little chopped tomato or some sesame seeds, before you add the river weed. Turn out onto a plate and serve hot. It will melt in your mouth.

And while you eat, please picture those three big Boston ferns walking down the beach!

Once the huge piles of freshly gathered river weed have spent several days drying in the sun, they are divided into small bundles, then again put back in the sun to dry.

ABOVE: *Monks busily preparing for a temple festival, cleaning statues and climbing up bamboo scaffolding to erect a banner.* OPPOSITE: LUSCIOUS CHILE-OIL TOFU *(page 168)*.

LUSCIOUS CHILE-OIL TOFU
[*layou doufu* — YUNNAN]

A kind of Yunnanese *mapo doufu*, this dish of fresh tofu flavored with a little pork, Sichuan pepper, and a generous dollop of chile oil is a great midwinter standby. Not only is its hot and spicy warmth welcome on a cold winter day, but we think of tofu as an ideal food at a time when our selection of fresh seasonal vegetables is limited.

Sichuan pepper, common in Yunnan, gives a pleasant numbing heat, while the chile oil is hot in a different way. You can increase the pepper to ¼ teaspoon, or more if you wish. Serve with rice and a vegetable dish such as Chinese Greens, Thai Style (page 156).

1 tablespoon peanut or vegetable oil

3 scallions, trimmed, smashed flat with the side of a cleaver, cut lengthwise into strips, and then cut crosswise into 1-inch lengths

¼ cup (about 2 ounces) ground pork

4 blocks fresh tofu (about 1½ pounds), cut into ¾-inch cubes

2 to 3 tablespoons Hot Chile Oil (page 310 or store-bought)

1 teaspoon salt, plus a pinch

⅛ teaspoon freshly ground Sichuan pepper, or more to taste

1 teaspoon cornstarch, dissolved in 1 tablespoon water

Place all the ingredients near your stovetop . Heat a wok over high heat. Add the oil and swirl to coat, then toss in the scallions, reduce the heat to medium-high, and stir-fry briefly. Add the pork and stir-fry, breaking up any clumps with your spatula, until it has all changed color, about 1 minute. Pour off any water that has drained out of the tofu cubes and add the tofu, chile oil, salt, and pepper to the wok. Raise the heat, turn the ingredients gently to mix well, and cook for 30 seconds to 1 minute. Stir the cornstarch paste, add to the wok, stir to blend, and cook for another 20 to 30 seconds until the sauce thickens.

Turn out onto a plate or into a shallow bowl. Serve hot or at room temperature, to accompany rice or noodles.

SERVES *3 to 4 with rice and one or more other dishes*

EGGS SCRAMBLED WITH TOMATO
[*fanqie jidan* — YUNNAN]

The first time we visited the town of Dali, in Yunnan, was in the spring of 1984 (see Fish Heads and Fat, page 40). Dali had been "open" to outsiders for only a short time, so there were just two small restaurants, and one hotel. The restaurants were basic, but as they were the main meeting places for travelers in town, they were fun.

This simple egg and tomato stir-fry was a frequently ordered dish in both restaurants. The eggs were good, the tomatoes were good, and, served with a hearty bowl of rice and a little Yunnanese chile pepper paste, it made for a very welcome meal.

Serve with Yunnanese Chile Pepper Paste (page 27), a plate of simply dressed cooked vegetables, such as Simple Dali Cauliflower (page 158) or Yunnan Greens (page 151), and perhaps a soup.

3 large or extra-large eggs

¾ teaspoon salt

½ teaspoon freshly ground black pepper

1 tablespoon peanut or vegetable oil

1 tablespoon minced garlic

3 scallions, trimmed and cut into 1-inch lengths

2 large half-green to semiripe tomatoes (just under 1 pound total), coarsely chopped

Coriander leaves for garnish

Break the eggs into a medium bowl and whisk well. Whisk in the salt and pepper and stir to mix, then set aside.

Heat a large wok or heavy skillet over high heat. Add the oil and swirl to coat the pan, then toss in the garlic. Stir-fry for 15 seconds, then add the scallions and stir-fry for another 15 seconds. Add the tomato chunks and stir-fry for 2 minutes, or until softened and heated through. Add the eggs and stir-fry vigorously for 2 minutes, then turn out onto a plate and top with the coriander leaves. Serve hot.

SERVES *3 to 4 as part of a rice meal*

STIR-FRIED EGGS WITH CELLOPHANE NOODLES

[*yam kai* — LAOS, THAILAND]

This is a fresh-tasting cross between a stir-fry and a warm salad; the lime juice dressing on the noodles meets the pepper and the softness of the egg. After taking us shopping in the market in Phonsavan, Sivone (see The War, page 186) made it as part of a late lunch, with a plate of *pad pak* (Classic Mixed Vegetable Stir-fry, page 151) alongside. Try to find free-range eggs; their flavor and color make the dish very special.

Serve as part of a rice-based meal, or serve as a main dish for lunch, accompanied by a salad or greens of some kind and rice.

3 large or extra-large eggs

¼ teaspoon salt

Generous grinding of white or black pepper

1 bundle (about 1 ounce) dried cellophane noodles, soaked in warm water for 20 minutes, drained, and cut into approximately 2-inch lengths (see Note)

1 tablespoon Thai fish sauce

1 tablespoon fresh lime juice

¼ teaspoon dried red chile flakes, or more to taste

2 tablespoons peanut or vegetable oil

¼ cup chopped shallots

3 small scallions, trimmed, smashed flat with the side of a cleaver, and cut into 1-inch lengths

Coriander leaves for garnish

Whisk the eggs in a medium bowl with the salt and pepper; set aside. Bring a medium pot of water to a boil. Drop in the cellophane noodles and simmer for 30 seconds, or until soft; drain, refresh with cold water, and drain again. Place the noodles in a bowl.

In a small bowl, mix together the fish sauce, lime juice, and chile flakes, then pour over the noodles, toss, and set aside.

Place all the ingredients near your stovetop. Heat a wok over high heat. Add the oil and swirl to coat the bottom of the wok. Toss in the shallots and stir-fry until softened and starting to change color, about 45 seconds. Add the scallions and stir-fry for about 15 seconds, then pour in the eggs and tilt the wok to spread them. As the eggs set against the hot wok, use your spatula to lift up one section and turn it toward the center, then tilt the wok to make more liquid egg flow onto the hot pan. Repeat the folding and tilting until all the eggs are starting to set, about 1 minute. Add the noodles and continue to toss and cook for 30 seconds to 1 minute. The eggs will be broken into pieces and distributed through the noodles. Try not to shred them too much; they should still be in bite-sized or larger chunks.

Turn out onto a platter or onto individual plates, garnish with the coriander leaves, and serve.

SERVES *3 to 4 as part of a rice meal or 2 as a main dish for lunch*

NOTE: *We find it easiest to cut soaked cellophane noodles with a large pair of scissors, picking up a clump from the bowl of drained noodles and snipping off lengths into another bowl.*

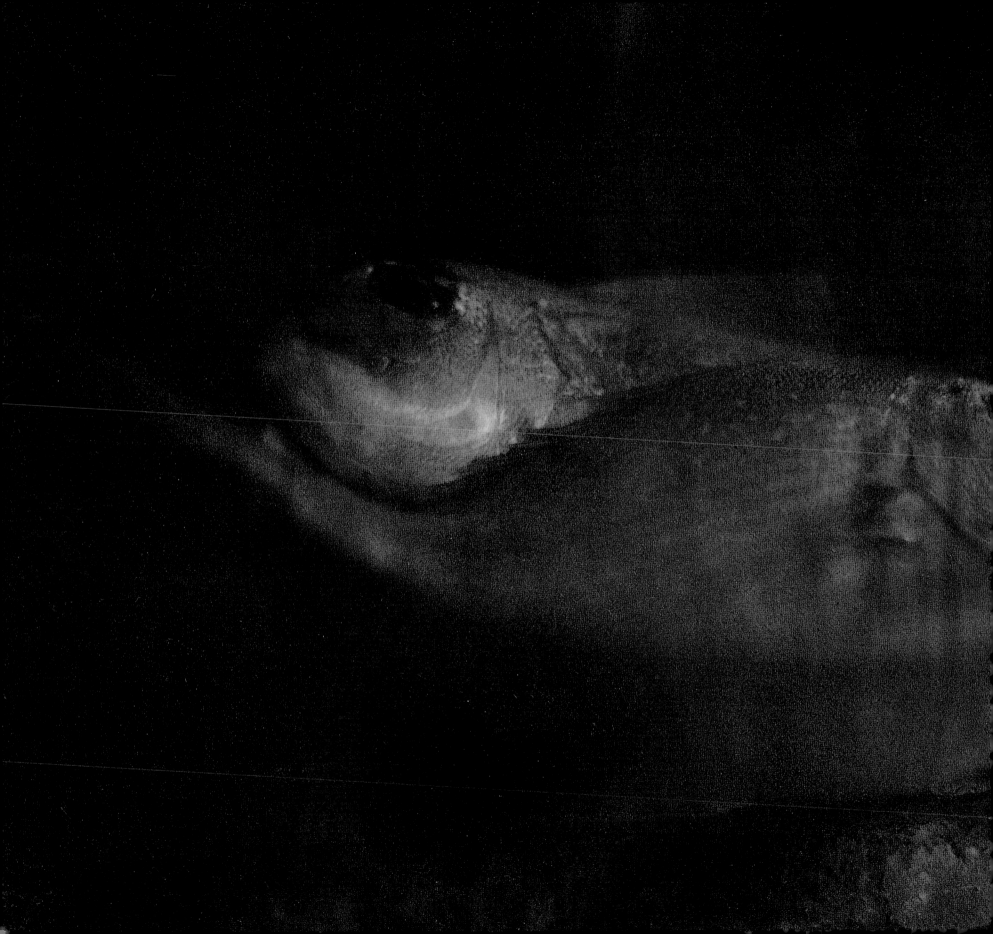

FISH AND SEAFOOD

There is a large and varied repertoire of fish dishes in Southeast Asia, and no wonder, for historically, fish and seafood from the rivers and lakes and from the ocean have been an easily available source of food. Village people, especially the Tai Lu in northern Laos and in Yunnan, often have fish ponds outside their homes. In the late afternoon, men and children wade into the ponds to catch fish for supper, sometimes with a net, but often using only their hands and quick reflexes. The fish are fairly small, like lake perch. The ponds are a good source of snails too, and a place for ducks to feed on pond weed.

Fresh fish and seafood are sold in morning and evening markets throughout Southeast Asia. Shrimp and squid are easy to find here, but much of the fish eaten in the region is freshwater. Far from Southeast Asian rivers and lakes, we suggest substitutions, using fish available here in North America. Dishes include salads, as well as grilled, stewed, simmered, and stir-fried fish, cooked alone or combined with vegetables.

Shrimp and smoked fish, with their distinctive tastes, are often combined very simply with fresh ingredients (see for example, Smoked Fish and Green Mango, page 174, and Rice Paper Roll-ups with Shrimp and Herbs, page 177).

In markets in the region, you can buy salt-grilled fish to take home and serve with rice and other dishes. The technique is easy for the home cook, using a grill or a broiler (see Salt-Grilled Catfish, page 190). Another simple technique uses whole fresh fish that are rubbed or stuffed with a flavor paste, then wrapped and grilled or baked (see Baked Bass with Spicy Rub, page 184, and Dai Grilled Stuffed Fish, page 189). Fish steaks or fillets may be grilled or stir-fried or simmered with flavorings (see, for example, Khmer Fish Stew with Lemongrass, page 181, and Slow-Cooked Sweet and Spicy Fish, page 191).

LEFT: *We had visited several small villages on the Thai side and then, on our way back downriver to Chiang Khong, we stopped in at a sandbar. It was technically Lao territory, at the time off-limits to foreigners without a visa, but these fishermen didn't seem at all troubled by our being there.* RIGHT: *In Vientiane, you can buy delicious salt-grilled fish at the market and take it home to serve with rice and vegetables and soup for lunch or dinner. It's also easy to make at home.*

SMOKED FISH AND GREEN MANGO
[CAMBODIA]

Around the Tonle Sap, Cambodia's great inland lake, Khmer and Vietnamese fishermen live in "floating villages." During rainy season, the lake rises as the Mekong's waters flow up to the lake, flooding the rice fields and making the land fertile. As the level of the Mekong falls in October/November at the start of the dry season, water flows back down toward the Mekong. This is the good fishing season. Though some of the catch is eaten fresh, most of it must be preserved. Some is salted and sun-dried, some is smoked, and some is made into *prahok* and *tuk traey*, fermented fish paste and fish sauce.

We love this dish, with its unique combination of smoky fish and tart green mango. Serve it as an appetizer or as a salad.

2 green mangoes

1 small smoked trout

½ cup packed chopped coriander leaves, or substitute chopped celery leaves or finely chopped mint

DRESSING

2 tablespoons rice, brown rice, or coconut vinegar

1 tablespoon Thai or Cambodian fish sauce

1 tablespoon sugar

1 teaspoon minced garlic

1 tablespoon minced shallots

1 tablespoon minced galangal, or substitute 1 teaspoon minced ginger plus a pinch of grated lemon zest

Peel the mangoes, then coarsely grate, discarding the pits. Or cut the peeled mangoes into fine julienne. Place in a medium bowl.

Remove and discard all the skin and bones from the fish. Chop into small pieces (you should have about 1 cup) and add to mangoes. Stir in the coriander, then set aside.

In a bowl or cup, combine all the dressing ingredients. Just before you wish to serve, spoon 5 tablespoons of the dressing onto the salad, then toss gently to blend well. Taste and add a little more dressing if you wish.

Serve mounded on a serving plate or on individual plates.

SERVES *3 to 4 as part of a rice meal or 6 as an appetizer*

NOTE: *For a different (nontraditional) crisp texture, try quickly frying the fish in a little oil, in a hot wok or skillet, then chop and proceed with the recipe.*

There's always a crowd at the morning market, wherever you are in the Mekong region. But at floating markets, such as this near Cantho in the Mekong Delta, people arrive in boats of all sizes and "morning rush hour" takes on a whole different look.

SQUID WITH GINGER-GARLIC SAUCE

[*muoc tuoi* — VIETNAM]

All along the coast of southern Vietnam, squid boats, small round coracles, sit out on the beach in the sun. Come evening, they're loaded into larger boats and carried offshore. There they're put into the water, each one manned by a fisherman with a bright light. The squid swim up, attracted by the light, and the fishermen use a net to haul them in.

These days cleaned flash-frozen squid is widely available; there's no more cleaning and peeling to be done (though instructions for cleaning squid are given below, just in case). We like this simple dish. It takes us back to a beach outside Da Nang, where we sat one afternoon long ago, on our first trip to Vietnam, eating freshly caught, freshly cooked squid at a small beachside stand. We dipped it, mouthful by mouthful, into a garlicky ginger sauce and washed it down with local beer.

SQUID

2 pounds cleaned squid or 3 pounds small or medium whole squid

2 to 3 tablespoons fresh lime juice

½ cup coriander leaves (optional)

GARNISH AND ACCOMPANIMENTS

Leaf lettuce or Vietnamese Herb and Salad Plate (page 68)

Ginger-Garlic Sauce (recipe follows)

1 lime, cut into wedges

Salt and freshly ground black pepper

Wash the squid thoroughly. If using whole squid: To clean, hold the body of the squid in one hand and gently pull the head and tentacles off (taking care not to break the ink sac). The intestines will automatically come away with the head. Separate the tentacles from the rest, wash thoroughly, and set aside. Peel off the outer red-brown skin from the body. Turn the squid body inside out; remove the cartilage and wash again thoroughly until no longer gritty. Turn right side out.

Slice the squid bodies into ¼-inch-wide rings or into 1½- to 2-inch slices. Leave the tentacles whole or cut in half, as you like.

Fill a large pot with water and bring to a boil. Toss in the squid and cook until tender, 4 to 6 minutes. Drain well, place in a bowl, and pour over the lime juice. Toss to coat. Add the coriander leaves if you wish, and toss.

Transfer the squid to a shallow serving bowl or place on a bed of lettuce on a small platter. Serve with the salad and herb plate if you wish, and with condiment dishes of the ginger-garlic sauce, wedges of lime, and salt and pepper. Use the lettuce or salad greens and herbs to pick up the squid, then drizzle on a little sauce or squeeze on lime juice and season to taste, mouthful by mouthful.

SERVES *4 to 6 as an appetizer or as part of a rice meal*

GINGER-GARLIC SAUCE

2 tablespoons minced ginger

2 cloves garlic, minced

1 bird or serrano chile, finely chopped

1 teaspoon sugar

3 tablespoons Vietnamese or Thai fish sauce

3 tablespoons fresh lime juice

1 to 2 tablespoons water

If you have a mortar and pestle, crush and blend together the ginger, garlic, chile, and sugar. If you don't, simply combine the ingredients in a small bowl. Add the fish sauce, lime juice, and water to taste and blend well.

Leftovers will keep in a well-sealed glass container in the refrigerator for 3 days.

MAKES *about ⅓ cup sauce*

RICE PAPER ROLL-UPS WITH SHRIMP AND HERBS
[*goi cuon* — VIETNAM, CAMBODIA]

Long ago in Paris, I learned to make these roll-ups from Salme, the aunt of a friend. Salme had fled Estonia during the Second World War and taken refuge in France. When I met her, she had been married to a Vietnamese doctor for almost thirty years. They'd spent several years in Vietnam in the late forties, then had returned to France.

Salme made wonderful Vietnamese food. She was quick in all her movements and alert, the last person you'd expect to have the patience to hand-roll rice paper roll-ups. In fact, she'd figured out, like many gifted cooks before her, that the work goes quickly if you have many hands doing it, someone to talk with as you work, and an efficient system for getting the work done. So the basic recipe for rice paper roll-ups should begin: "Gather one or two friends round your work area to help." The work goes quickly, and it is fun when done in good company. You can make these up to two hours ahead, then cover them with a damp towel until ready to serve.

Serve whole or cut in half, as appetizers or as part of a meal.

12 medium shrimp, fresh or frozen

3 to 4 ounces dried rice vermicelli, soaked in warm water
    for 20 minutes and drained

15 rice papers (about 8 inches in diameter)

1½ cups bean sprouts, blanched in boiling water
    for 30 seconds and drained

¾ cup Carrot and Daikon Pickled Salad (page 85), or
    substitute ¾ cup grated carrot tossed with 1 teaspoon
    sugar and 1 tablespoon rice vinegar

½ cup packed mint leaves

30 chives or Chinese chives, or substitute greens from
    6 to 8 scallions, cut lengthwise into slivers

½ cup packed coriander leaves

ACCOMPANIMENTS

Vietnamese Herb and Salad Plate (page 68)

Vietnamese Must-Have Table Sauce (*nuoc cham*, page 28)
    or Vietnamese Peanut Sauce (*nuoc leo*, page 28)

Bring a large pot of salted water to a boil. Drop in the shrimp, bring back to a boil, and cook just until pink and firm to the touch, 1 to 3 minutes. Lift out immediately with tongs or chopsticks and transfer to a plate to cool.

Bring the water back to a boil. Drop in the soaked vermicelli, cook for 2 minutes, or until soft, and drain. Refresh with cold water, drain, and set aside.

Remove the shrimp shells, devein, and cut the shrimp lengthwise in half down the back. Set aside.

Place a large bowl of warm water by your work area. Moisten a tea towel or cotton cloth thoroughly with water and lay it flat on the work surface. Working with 1 rice paper at a time, immerse the rice paper in the water. It will soften in less than 30 seconds. Lift it out and place it flat on the wet cloth. Place about 1 tablespoon of noodles on it, spreading them in a line across the wrapper about one third of the way from the bottom edge. Lay about 1 tablespoon bean sprouts and a heaping teaspoon carrot salad along the line of noodles and then sprinkle several mint leaves along it. Start to roll up the fillings in the wrapper, then place 2 shrimp halves along the length of the roll. Fold over the ends to seal in the filling, then roll up another half-turn. Place 2 chives or a sliver or two of scallion along the crease, letting one end stick out past the end of the roll. Place several coriander leaves along the crease, then finish rolling up. Moisten the edge with water and set on a plate, seam side down. Cover with a damp cloth and with plastic wrap, then repeat with the remaining rolls.

Serve immediately, or set aside for up to 2 hours, covered with the damp cloth and plastic wrap to prevent the rice paper wrappers from drying out. Serve on a platter or on individual plates, whole or cut crosswise in half.

To eat, place a leaf of lettuce in your palm and lay a roll-up on it. Wrap the lettuce leaf round one end of the roll-up (as if you were wrapping a cone in a napkin). Use a small spoon to drizzle on the sauce as you eat, mouthful by mouthful.

MAKES *15 roll-ups; serves 10 as part of a rice meal*

VIENTIANE: Vientiane (pronounced "Venjiang" in Lao), the modern-day capital of the Lao People's Democratic Republic, is not what we would call a cosmopolitan city. There is a large UN and NGO presence here, and there are many embassies and consulates, but basically Vientiane is more of a town than a city. There is life at night on its four or five main roads, with fancy UN four-wheel-drive vehicles and secondhand Japanese imports sharing space with scooter rickshaws, bicycles, and pedestrians. The foreign community goes out to dinner: a Swedish bakery-café, a nice Italian restaurant with pizza, a fancy hotel. And there are wine shops, good wine shops, an oddity in Southeast Asia, but still. . . .

The first time we were in Vientiane, in 1989, there was almost no traffic in the capital, and for dining there were only two streets downtown where we could find small restaurants open at night. They were serving primarily Vietnamese food, good food. Walking at night, we'd see foreigners, but they'd never look our way. They were mostly Russians, stationed in Laos (as many were at that time also in Vietnam). They never seemed to smile.

We like Vientiane a lot. We wish someone would offer us a job there, or at least give us a very long visa. We'd hang out at the Raintree Book Store and chat with the proprietor, Mr. Hodgson, who has run his bookstore through thick and thin for a long time. And we'd stop and chat with Carol Cassidy at Lao Textiles, maybe sit in the back and watch the weavers.

For lunch, probably most days we'd end up at the river, eating sticky rice and grilled chicken bought from a street vendor with a table and stools set up under a big tree, or we'd order a spicy grilled sausage salad, or *laab* (spicy chopped pork or chicken salad with herbs—see page 196), or *som tam* (see page 76).

For dinner, well, dinner would be no problem in our family, living in Vientiane. Apart from all the places with good Lao food, there is an Indian restaurant, also down by the river, called Nazim. It serves both North and South Indian food and prepares both remarkably well. There are *masala dosas, chapatis, pakoras* and *samosas, dal, baingen bharta, naan,* and *uppuma,* the whole works! Dominic and Tashi love it all. They like sticky rice a lot, but not more than *masala dosas.*

And Nazim also serves french fries with ketchup.

Vientiane has many reminders of the French colonial era, including old-style two-story shop-houses with gracefully fading painted plaster walls.

AROMATIC STEAMED FISH CURRY

[*mawk pa* — LAOS, THAILAND]

Steaming fish or chicken with aromatics in banana leaf packets is a technique found from Yunnan to Cambodia. The technique is *mawk* in modern Thai, Lao, and Khmer, and the word and technique may originally be Khmer. Making the packets is difficult here, so we steam the mixture in bowls placed in a steamer. (We use several small bowls, to ensure quicker and more even cooking.) The bowls of curry get turned out onto a platter afterwards, smelling wonderful and tasting even better. Serve with rice and a clear soup.

Use catfish or red snapper or whatever firm-fleshed fish you prefer. Buy a whole fish, so you can see that it's very fresh, and then ask that it be cleaned and filleted.

1½ pounds fish fillets (see Headnote)

1 Thai dried red chile, soaked in ½ cup warm water
    until softened

2 stalks lemongrass, trimmed and minced very fine

½ cup chopped shallots

2 tablespoons chopped coriander roots

1 tablespoon fresh lime juice

2 tablespoons Thai fish sauce

½ teaspoon salt, or more to taste

1 cup chopped scallion greens

¼ cup packed Asian basil or sweet basil leaves, coarsely torn

Cut the fish into bite-sized pieces, about 1½ inches across, discarding any bones or other tough bits, and set aside in a bowl.

Reserve the chile soaking water and mince the soaked chile, discarding the tough stem. Place in a large mortar or in a blender, add the lemongrass, shallots, and coriander roots, and pound or blend to as smooth a paste as possible. Add the chile soaking liquid and lime juice and stir or blend together.

Pour the flavor paste over the fish and stir. Add the fish sauce and salt and stir, then taste and add a little more salt if you wish. Stir in most of the scallion greens, reserving about 2 tablespoons for garnish. Stir in the basil leaves.

Divide the mixture between two or three wide shallow heatproof bowls (most large cereal bowls will do just fine). Make sure there's a good ½ inch left at the top of each bowl so the contents have room to expand during cooking. Place the bowls in a steamer (you may need to stack two steamers) set over water in a large pot.

Bring the water to a boil, cover, and steam until the fish is tender and opaque, about 40 minutes. Turn out into a shallow bowl or deep platter, garnish with the reserved scallion greens, and serve.

SERVES *4 to 6 as part of a rice meal*

NOTE: *The Khmer version of this dish is known as* ah mawk. *It includes coconut milk and is often topped with a dollop of coconut cream and some finely shredded lime leaves rather than with scallion leaves.*

KHMER FISH STEW WITH LEMONGRASS

[*samla' metchou peng pa* — C A M B O D I A]

Samla' are "wet dishes," somewhere between a stew and a hearty soup. They are the standard accompaniment for rice in Cambodia, hot and tasty, often sour, and usually loaded with lemongrass and other aromatics. The most common *samla'* is made with fish, fish from the river or from the Great Lake, the Tonle Sap.

This fish *samla'* is easy, needing no special broth and no long cooking. It's a close cousin of *canh chua*, the Vietnamese sour soup so common in the Delta, but heartier. Perhaps *canh chua* is originally Khmer, or maybe it's an inevitable combination, because a lightly sour and lemony broth goes so beautifully with fish.

Serve this from a large bowl at the table, ladling it into individual small bowls, accompanied by rice, and perhaps a simple vegetable stir-fry, to make an easy meal.

4 cups water

4 stalks lemongrass, trimmed and smashed flat
   with the side of a cleaver

3 tablespoons tamarind pulp

¾ pound fish steaks (catfish, tilapia, or other freshwater fish
   of your choice)

1 tablespoon minced garlic

1 tablespoon Cambodian or Thai fish sauce

½ teaspoon salt

½ pound green or half-ripe tomatoes, seeded and cut
   into scant ½-inch pieces

2 small scallions, trimmed and cut into ½-inch lengths

4 sawtooth herb leaves, coarsely chopped

12 Asian basil or sweet basil leaves, coarsely chopped

4 to 6 sprigs rice paddy herb (*ngo om*), coarsely chopped

1 teaspoon sugar, or to taste

Put the water in a large pot, add the lemongrass, and bring to a vigorous boil. Boil for 5 minutes, half-covered, then lower the heat and simmer over medium heat for a few minutes.

Once the broth is simmering, scoop out about 1 cup of the liquid into a small bowl. Add the tamarind pulp to the bowl, stir well to dissolve it thoroughly, and set aside.

Rinse off the fish. If using large steaks, cut into roughly 1½- to 2-inch pieces. If using small steaks, cut in half. Add to the broth, together with the garlic, bring to a boil, and simmer until the fish is opaque. Add the fish sauce and salt. Place a sieve or fine strainer over the soup and pour the tamarind liquid through it. Use the back of a wooden spoon to press the tamarind pulp against the strainer, then discard the remaining seeds and pith. Stir the stew well and let it simmer for several minutes.

Add the tomatoes, scallions, herbs, and sugar to the stew and simmer for 5 minutes. Serve hot.

S E R V E S *4 as part of a rice meal*

SPICY FISH CURRY WITH COCONUT MILK

[*pa sousi haeng* — LAOS, NORTHEAST THAILAND]

This Lao freshwater fish dish is a kind of curry, moist and savory, but with relatively little sauce (*haeng* means dry). A simple medium-hot spice paste is cooked in a little coconut milk and then used to flavor sliced fish fillets as they cook over low heat. We've adapted this recipe from Phia Sing's cookbook, a remarkable collection of recipes by the chef to the Lao royal family, who died in 1967. His notebooks were given to Alan Davidson in the early seventies and then edited by Alan and Jennifer Davidson into a wonderful cookbook and reference (see Bibliography). Phia Sing calls for a kind of catfish known in Lao as *pa ling*. Use whatever freshwater fish you prefer.

This is a good dish to make whenever you come across fresh wild lime leaves at the store, or when you've got a stash of frozen leaves in your freezer that you want to share with friends. Serve with a fresh salad or another dish with crisp, contrasting textures.

1 pound fish fillets (catfish, tilapia, or other freshwater fish
   of your choice)
½ teaspoon salt, plus a pinch
½ teaspoon freshly ground black pepper
2 Thai dried red chiles, soaked in a little warm water
   until softened
5 scallions
2 small shallots, chopped
2 tablespoons rendered pork fat or peanut or vegetable oil
1 cup canned or fresh coconut milk (see page 315),
   divided into ½ cup thicker milk and ½ cup thinner milk
1 to 2 tablespoons Thai fish sauce
3 to 5 fresh or frozen wild lime leaves
Freshly ground black pepper
¼ to ½ cup coarsely chopped coriander

Slice the fish into pieces less than ½ inch thick. Place in a medium bowl, add the ½ teaspoon salt and the pepper, and toss to coat: set aside, covered.

To prepare the spice paste, reserve the chile soaking water and coarsely chop the chiles, discarding any tough stems. Place the chiles and a pinch of salt in a mortar or in a blender. Cut the greens off the scallions, leaving the bulbs and green stems, and set aside. Trim off the roots, then finely chop the bulbs and stems. Place in the mortar or blender, add the shallots, and pound or blend to a paste, adding a little of the reserved chile soaking water to the blender as necessary. Set the paste aside in a bowl.

Finely chop enough of the reserved scallion greens to make ½ cup and set aside.

Heat a wok or heavy skillet over medium-high heat. Add the pork fat or oil and when it is hot, add the fish pieces. Stir-fry until browned on both sides, then transfer to a plate and set aside.

Place the pan back over high heat, add the ½ cup thick coconut milk, and lower the temperature to medium-high. Cook until the oil begins to separate, about 5 minutes, then stir in the spice paste. Cook, stirring, for another 5 minutes, or until the mixture begins to smell fragrant. Add the remaining ½ cup coconut milk and the fish sauce and bring to a simmer. Add the fried fish pieces and the lime leaves, move the fish around gently to coat it well with sauce, and add most of the chopped scallion greens. Taste for seasoning and adjust if you wish. Let cook for 30 seconds, then transfer to a shallow bowl and serve, topped with a grinding of black pepper, the remaining scallion leaves, and the coriander. Serve with plain jasmine rice.

SERVES *4 as part of a rice meal*

STIR-FRIED FISH WITH GINGER

[*traey cha k'nye* — CAMBODIA]

In this simple Khmer stir-fry, a close cousin of Khmer Stir-fried Ginger and Beef (page 219), ginger is the vegetable as well as the flavoring. Use catfish or snapper or any other firm-fleshed fish.

Serve with rice, a clear soup, and a fresh-tasting salad, such as Pomelo Salad (page 72), Vietnamese Green Papaya Salad (page 75), or a Western-style tossed salad.

1 pound fish fillets (see Headnote)

½ pound ginger, preferably young ginger

3 tablespoons vegetable or peanut oil

¼ cup minced shallots

4 scallions, trimmed, smashed flat with the side of a cleaver, sliced lengthwise in half, and then cut into 2-inch lengths

2 tablespoons Thai fish sauce

2 teaspoons sugar

1 teaspoon salt, or to taste

1 tablespoon fresh lime juice

Slice the fish fillets into strips about 2 inches long and less than ½ inch thick. Peel the ginger, then cut into fine matchstick-length julienne (this is most easily done by cutting thin slices, then stacking these to cut them into matchsticks). You should have about 2 cups, loosely packed.

Heat a wok over medium-high heat. Add the oil and, when it is hot, add the ginger. When the ginger is starting to turn golden, after about 3 minutes, toss in the shallots. Stir-fry until the ginger is golden brown, 2 to 4 minutes. Toss in the scallions, reserving a few shreds for garnish, and stir-fry briefly, pressing the scallions against the hot wok to sear them. Add the sliced fish and stir-fry gently for 1 minute, using your spatula to separate the slices and to expose them all to the hot wok. Add the fish sauce, sugar, and salt, stir gently, and cook for 3 minutes, or until the fish is just cooked through. Add the lime juice, taste and adjust the seasonings if you wish, and turn out onto a platter. Garnish with the reserved scallion shreds and serve hot.

SERVES *4 as part of a rice meal*

NOTE: *A similar dish, very common in the rainy season and in places near streams, is frogs' legs, coarsely chopped and stir-fried with plenty of ginger.*

Salted fish arranged in threesomes in Luang Prabang's central market.

BAKED BASS WITH SPICY RUB

[*pa pao* — LAOS, NORTHEAST THAILAND]

In Laos and northeast Thailand, fish and curries are often cooked in banana leaf wrappers over a small fire. Wrapping keeps in moisture and flavor, so it lends itself perfectly to fish prepared with a marinade or with aromatics.

You don't have to have banana leaves for this dish, just aluminum foil, but if you do come across banana leaves fresh or in the freezer section at a Southeast Asian grocery store, buy a package and keep it in your freezer. Banana leaves give a pleasant scent to the food as it cooks and they're easy and fun to work with.

Two 1- to 1½-pound gutted and scaled whole firm-fleshed fish (striped bass or lake trout, for example, or a saltwater fish such as snapper)
2 tablespoons Peppercorn–Coriander Root Flavor Paste (recipe follows)
2 stalks lemongrass, trimmed, smashed flat with the side of a cleaver, and cut into 1-inch lengths
2 limes, cut into wedges
Salt and freshly ground black pepper (optional)

Preheat the oven to 400°F, or light a grill to produce a medium heat.

Wash the fish inside and out and wipe dry. Make three shallow diagonal slashes on each side of each fish. Put some flavor paste in each slit and then smear the rest over the outside and a little on the inside of the fish. Put the chopped lemongrass inside the fish.

Place two 18-inch square pieces of heavy-duty aluminum foil side by side on your work surface. If you have fresh or frozen banana leaves, use them: Lay one or more overlapping pieces of banana leaf (strip out the central rib of the leaf first) on top of each. Lay one fish on each set of wrappings, diagonally or whichever way allows a complete wrap. Wrap each fish firmly in the banana leaf, if using, and then in foil, tucking in the ends as you roll it up to seal it well.

Bake on a baking sheet in the center of the oven for 30 to 40 minutes, or grill on a grill rack 5 to 6 inches from the flame for 15 to 20 minutes a side. The fish should be moist and tender. Remove from the heat and place on one or two platters. Serve in the banana

leaf wrapping or turned out onto the platter(s), as you please. Accompany with lime wedges and, if you wish, salt and pepper.

SERVES *4 as part of a rice meal*

PEPPERCORN–CORIANDER ROOT FLAVOR PASTE

Here the essential flavors of the Thai repertoire all come together: black pepper (*prik thai*), coriander roots, and garlic, salted with a little Thai fish sauce. Use this paste as a marinade for fish, grilled chicken (see Grilled Chicken with Hot and Sweet Dipping Sauce, page 199), or pork.

Because the paste is so versatile, it's handy to have a stash of coriander roots in the freezer. Whenever you have a bunch of coriander, after you have used the leaves, chop off the roots, wash, and store them in a plastic bag in the freezer. You don't need to defrost them before using, as they can be chopped and pounded still frozen.

This recipe makes a small quantity of flavor paste, just over 2 tablespoons; double the quantities if you'd like to make more.

2 teaspoons black peppercorns
5 to 6 large cloves garlic, coarsely chopped (about 2 tablespoons)
3 tablespoons coarsely chopped coriander roots
Pinch of salt
1 teaspoon Thai fish sauce

Place the peppercorns in a mortar with the garlic and pound to a paste. Add the coriander roots and salt and pound to a paste. This will take 5 to 10 minutes; if you have a small blender or other food grinder that can produce a smooth paste, use it instead. Stir in the fish sauce.

Store in a well-sealed glass jar; this keeps for 4 days.

MAKES *2 to 3 tablespoons paste*

THE WAR: In Laos, we flew in a fourteen-seater up to Phonsavan, a new town in the northeastern part of the country. The old town, Xieng Khuang, about twenty-five miles away, was totally destroyed in the war, and Phonsavan grew up in its place. As we approached Phonsavan, the jungly mountain landscape, littered with thousands of small and not so small bomb craters, looked as if it had a terrible case of the chicken pox; later we discovered that the town of Phonsavan has no big trees left whatsoever. The area is still denuded as a result of Agent Orange.

When we got out of the plane onto the small airstrip, the sun was just setting and the sky was ablaze. There was a crowd of tribal Hmong waiting to greet family members arriving on the plane, family members who had long ago escaped and ended up in the United States as refugees, in San Diego, Missoula, Minneapolis. When we got to the terminal, a tiny little building, the sun had set, and it was pitch black. The town's electricity hadn't yet come on; it would be another twenty minutes.

That night we found a nice place to stay run by a Lao family. There were two kids in the family, just the ages of our kids, and all of them immediately hit it off and started to play. We ate dinner with the family, then we drank a local brew with the parents, Sivone and Sousath, and settled in for some late-night conversation. The mother, Sivone, from Sainyabuli, in western Laos, is tall and calm. The father, born into an upper-class family in Vientiane, had been shipped off to school and safety in China in the late sixties at the age of ten. At thirteen, homesick, he had run away from the school, heading back to Laos, but he encountered the Pathet Lao and enlisted with them as a soldier. He lived in the caves of northeast Laos with them and fought for the rest of the war.

Sousath is my age, maybe a year or two younger. I didn't fight in the war; my friends and brothers didn't fight. I had a high lottery number in the draft, so I didn't have to go. In 1977, I went to Bangkok for the first time, and I lived in a house just on the edge of what had been the main U.S. airbase. The war was still there: the fatherless children left behind, the bars, and the edginess. Thousands of Thais died in the war, fighting for terrible low wages.

In Phonsavan, we learned immediately not to walk off the trail, not to wander around carelessly for fear of unexploded ordnance. We all took a certain keen interest in studying the enormous bomb casings that littered the road as we walked to and from the market. One day we took a jeep to the old town of Xieng Khuang. An ancient town, capital of the old Tai Phuan kingdom of Xieng Khuang, it is a town we'd read about in books, a town entirely tribal in composition and forever isolated in the far northern mountains of Laos. People have trickled back into Xieng Khuang, inhabiting the ruins and building new shops. We went to the market and had lunch. An old monk came by wanting to speak English with Dom and Tashi.

It's twenty-five years since the fall of Saigon.

The big skies, dirt roads, and traces of war we saw around Phonsavan gave it a Wild West feel, far from the apparent sedateness of Vientiane.

VIETNAMESE SHRIMP AND PORK STIR-FRY

[*tom thit heo* — SOUTHERN VIETNAM]

Walk through any small market in the Mekong Delta and you'll see small food stands with a counter or some small tables and a scattering of stools. Some serve bowls of noodles over salad greens, topped with an assortment of offerings from spring rolls to roast pork; others specialize in rice combos. The food is usually very tasty and very fresh. The only problem, as always with street food, is deciding what to have each time.

Some toppings for rice and noodles, like this one, are so simple and straightforward that they can easily become part of your standard repertoire here in North America. When you want to get good flavor on the table quickly, try this stir-fry. It is eaten in homes, street stands, and restaurants all around the Delta. Serve as part of a rice meal or as a topping for noodles (see Notes), with Vietnamese Must-Have Table Sauce (*nuoc cham*, page 28) and fresh salad greens.

½ **pound medium to small peeled and deveined shrimp (about ¾ pound shrimp in the shell, peeled and deveined)**

¼ **pound boneless pork butt or shoulder, thinly sliced (about ½ cup)**

2 tablespoons Vietnamese or Thai fish sauce

1 teaspoon sugar

2 tablespoons peanut or vegetable oil

1 tablespoon minced garlic

2 tablespoons minced lemongrass

Freshly ground black pepper to taste

2 tablespoons chopped mint or coriander, for garnish (optional)

Place the shrimp and pork slices in a bowl. In a small bowl, mix together the fish sauce and sugar, then pour over the shrimp and pork and turn to make sure all the pieces are coated. Set aside, covered, to marinate for 30 minutes.

Heat a wok over high heat. Add the oil and swirl to coat the pan. When the oil is hot, add the garlic and stir-fry for 10 seconds, then add the lemongrass and stir-fry until the garlic starts to change color. Toss in the shrimp and pork and any remaining marinade and stir-fry vigorously until the pork is cooked through. Transfer to a plate, grind black pepper over, and garnish with the fresh herb if you wish.

SERVES *4*

NOTES: *If serving over rice noodles and you are starting with dried rice noodles, soak them in warm water for 15 minutes, then drain. Just before serving, bring a large pot of water to a boil and cook the noodles for about 30 seconds, then drain well and serve topped by the stir-fried shrimp and pork. Or, instead of heating the noodles in boiling water, add them to your wok once the pork is cooked through and toss them with the sauce. Add a little water if the mixture seems too dry. Stir-fry for several minutes, long enough to fully soften the noodles and coat them with sauce, then turn out onto a platter or onto individual plates and garnish with the fresh herb if desired.*

Use a little Stir-fried Shrimp and Pork as a filling for Vietnamese Savory Crepes (banh xeo, *page 280*) *if you wish.*

DAI GRILLED STUFFED FISH

[SOUTHERN YUNNAN]

In Menghan, we'd watch Mae (see Menghan, page 60) as she prepared home-style dishes in her outdoor kitchen, then we'd move over to our table in the large main room to eat, meal after meal. Grilled stuffed fish, fresh from the pond down the road, was one of our favorites. First she filled them with a simple flavor paste, then she placed them in a simple grilling holder made of split bamboo and grilled them over a small fire. They were crisp on the outside and tender inside.

We've tried to reproduce Mae's method many times, but have not yet found a fish that lends itself perfectly to her technique. Admitting defeat, we've adapted the recipe we were shown. We grill or bake small striped bass wrapped in banana leaf (if available) and in foil. If you can't get banana leaves, use lettuce leaves instead; heat them briefly in a microwave or dip them into boiling water to soften them. The fish lacks the crispness of the original, but it has all its succulence and flavor.

Two 1-pound striped bass, cleaned and scaled

1 teaspoon salt

1½ teaspoons Two Pepper–Salt Spice Dip (page 309)

FILLING

2 cups chopped scallions (white and tender green parts)

¼ cup minced pork fat (see Note)

2 serrano or cayenne chiles

4 cloves garlic

Light a grill or preheat the oven to 350°F.

Rub the fish all over with the salt. Slash both sides of each fish two or three times. Rub the pepper-salt all over the fish, inside and out, including into the slashes.

In a large mortar or in the food processor, combine all the filling ingredients and pound or process to make a pale green paste. Stuff the slashes of the fish with some of the filling and place the rest inside the cavities of the fish. Wrap each fish well in a banana leaf if available (or a lettuce leaf) and then in aluminum foil (see page 184 for detailed instructions).

Grill over medium heat about 5 inches from the flame, or place on a baking sheet and bake in the center of the preheated oven, allowing about 10 minutes per inch of thickness, measured at the thickest part of the fish. If grilling, turn the fish over partway through cooking. Turn out onto a serving platter.

SERVES *4 as part of a rice meal*

NOTE: *We've learned what good flavor a little pork fat can give. We trim the fat off pork roasts or other cuts when we bring them home, then freeze the fat in small quantities in plastic bags, so it's there when we need it. You can also buy pork trimmings from your butcher.*

SALT-GRILLED CATFISH

[*pa yang* — LAOS, NORTHEAST THAILAND]

In the Lao and northeast Thai village markets along the Mekong, vendors set up small grills on which they cook slender freshwater fish coated in coarse salt. There's usually a chopstick-sized stake, like a wooden skewer, running the length of each fish to hold it straight over the fire. When done, the fish are a little blackened, with traces of salt crystals in the slits cut in their sides.

Like many simple foods, salt-grilled fish is delicious, especially if the grilling is done over a wood or charcoal fire. Serve whole, either hot off the grill or at room temperature, and let guests lift the chunks of tender meat off the bone. If you think your guests may hesitate to take on whole fish, though, you can instead lift the flesh off the bones after grilling and serve it in pieces on a platter, with some tender lettuce or a salad plate on the side, and wedges of lime.

Serve with sticky rice or jasmine rice, a spicy salad such as *Som Tam* with Yard-long Beans (page 76), and a salsa such as Grilled Tomato Salsa (page 44). Guests can eat with their fingers, wrapping pieces of fish in a lettuce leaf, or with chopsticks or a fork and knife.

Four ½-pound catfish or other firm-fleshed fish, cleaned and scaled

About ½ cup kosher salt

OPTIONAL ACCOMPANIMENTS

Lime wedges

Salad greens or Vietnamese Herb and Salad Plate (page 68)

Hot and Sweet Dipping Sauce (page 199) or Vietnamese Must-Have Table Sauce (*nuoc cham*, page 28)

Heat a grill or preheat a broiler.

Once the grill or broiler is hot, rinse the fish thoroughly; do not rub dry. Make three shallow diagonal slashes on each side of each fish. Place the salt on a large platter. Working with one fish at a time, place the fish on the salt and press down so the salt adheres; rub some salt into each slash, then turn the fish over and repeat on other side.

If using a grill, place each salted fish directly on the grill as you prepare it. Cook for about 4 minutes, then turn over and cook for about 4 minutes longer. *If using a broiler*, place the salted fish on a rack in a broiling pan as you prepare them. When all the fish have been salted, place about 5 inches from the heating element and broil for 8 to 10 minutes, turning the fish over after about 4 minutes. When done, the fish will be tender and flake when tested with a fork.

Place the fish on individual plates or on a platter with the lime wedges, and serve the salad greens separately. Give guests individual small bowls of whichever table sauce you choose to serve.

SERVES *4 as part of a rice meal*

NOTE: *You can use salt-grilled fish in many ways: as an extra topping for noodles, for example, or dressed in a simple Thai or Vietnamese salad with a lime juice and fish sauce dressing like that for Vietnamese Chicken Salad with* Rau Ram *(page 197).*

SLOW-COOKED SWEET AND SPICY FISH

[*ca kho tieu* — SOUTHERN VIETNAM]

To make this dish, you need a heavy cast-iron skillet. Thin small fish steaks, preferably with the backbone in, are briefly seared, then simmered in a hot-sweet-salty sauce that cooks down in about fifteen minutes. The fish often used in the Delta for *ca kho tieu* is called *ca bac*, firm-fleshed and sweet-tasting. You can use any small freshwater fish, the freshest possible. Serve with plenty of rice and with a sour or tart vegetable or meat dish, such as Stir-fried Pork and Tomato (page 244) or Buddhist Sour Soup (page 58), to balance the sweet saltiness of the sauce.

½ **pound firm fish steaks**

½ **teaspoon freshly ground black or white pepper,**
   plus extra for serving if desired

2 **tablespoons palm sugar, or substitute brown sugar**

¼ **cup warm water**

2 **tablespoons Vietnamese or Thai fish sauce**

1 **to 2 tablespoons peanut or vegetable oil**

1 **tablespoon finely minced lemongrass**

2 **scallions, trimmed, smashed flat with the side of a cleaver,**
   sliced lengthwise into 2 or 3 pieces, and then cut crosswise
   into 2- to 3-inch lengths

1 **tablespoon Fried Garlic (page 310) or Fried Shallots**
   (page 310), optional

Place the fish on a plate, sprinkle both sides with the pepper, and set aside. In a medium bowl, dissolve the sugar in the warm water, then stir in the fish sauce. Set aside.

Place a heavy medium (no larger than 8 inches in diameter) skillet over high heat. When it is hot, add the oil and swirl around to coat the pan. Toss in the lemongrass, then immediately place the fillets in the hot oil and sear for 10 to 15 seconds, then turn over and repeat. Add the liquid ingredients. Bring to a fierce boil, then lower the heat to medium and toss in the scallions. Cook for 10 minutes, uncovered, turning the fish over after about 5 minutes. As the liquid cooks down, lower the heat little by little, just enough to prevent the sauce from burning. It will reduce gradually to a texture somewhere between a heavy syrup and a paste.

Serve hot, in the skillet or in a shallow serving dish, topped with a generous grinding of pepper if you wish, and the fried garlic or fried shallots. Put out a serving spoon so guests can spoon a little sauce over their fish.

SERVES *4 as part of a rice meal*

POULTRY

Chickens and ducks, like pigs, are part of daily life in villages and small towns all through Southeast Asia. They wander at will, foraging across clean-swept courtyards and along well-worn paths. In rural areas, they are especially valued as egg layers, and, consequently, dishes featuring chicken or duck (such as Duck in Green Curry Paste, page 211) are something of a luxury outside cities and towns. And because most of the birds are truly free-range, they have wonderful flavor (so too, of course, do their eggs).

Here in North America, we suggest that you seek out organic or free-range birds; they're worth the extra trouble and expense. As people do in Laos, you can make the most of a good-tasting chicken by combining it with potatoes and coconut milk to make a simmered dish of mild Chicken and Potato Curry (page 203). Or, in the summer, boil

OPPOSITE LEFT: *A small boy holds a chicken in Luang Prabang.* OPPOSITE RIGHT: *On our first trip to northeast Thailand, long ago, we'd sit on a wooden balcony overlooking the Mekong in Chiang Khan and watch the sun set over the river.*

a whole chicken, use the broth for soup, and shred the meat to make Vietnamese Chicken Salad with *Rau Ram* (page 197), bright with lime juice and aromatic with fresh herbs, ideal for a warm summer evening.

Lao and Thai people have a brilliant way with grilled chicken. All along the Mekong valley, vendors sell it in markets and at roadside stands, with a hot-sweet dipping sauce and plenty of sticky rice. This is one of our favorite treats, and one that's very easy to make at home, on the grill or under the broiler (see Grilled Chicken with Hot and Sweet Dipping Sauce, page 199). Prepare it for guests, whatever the time of year.

MINCED CHICKEN WITH FRESH HERBS

[*laab gai* — NORTHERN AND NORTHEAST THAILAND, LAOS]

Laab is a category of dishes made from minced pork, beef, chicken, or fish. What makes *laab* distinctive is the way the meat is prepared: It is hand chopped, using one or two cleavers and chopping continuously, to a coarse minced texture. We helped make a *laab* from water buffalo meat (*sin khouai*) when we were staying in Luang Prabang, but there the texture we needed was a smooth paste, so it took a lot of chopping and then pounding in a mortar. Here it's all done in about five minutes. The effect of using the cleaver in this way is that the meat resembles ground meat, but it is much more irregular in texture, and a lot more interesting in the dish.

The minced chicken is quickly poached in a little boiling water before being dressed with fresh herbs, dried chiles, and a lime juice and fish sauce dressing. Vietnamese coriander is wonderful with chicken, but if you don't have any available, substitute regular coriander or mint leaves, or a mixture.

1 pound boneless skinless chicken breasts and/or thighs, rinsed, or substitute lean ground chicken

¼ cup thinly sliced shallots, slices separated into rings

1 or 2 Thai dried red chiles, stemmed and chopped

¼ cup fresh lime juice

3 tablespoons Thai fish sauce

½ teaspoon sugar

¼ teaspoon freshly ground black pepper

¼ cup packed Vietnamese coriander (*rau ram*) leaves, or substitute mint leaves or regular coriander leaves, coarsely torn, plus small sprigs for garnish

3 tablespoons Aromatic Roasted Rice Powder (page 309) or Roasted Rice Powder (page 308)

ACCOMPANIMENTS

Steamed Vegetable Plate (page 69) or wedges of raw Savoy cabbage

A handful of tender young green beans or yard-long beans

3 or 4 scallions, trimmed

If using chicken parts, with a cleaver, slice the chicken, then mince it until it resembles the consistency of ground beef.

In a small saucepan, bring 2½ cups water to a boil. Toss in the chicken and cook until all the meat has changed color, about 2 minutes. Drain the chicken, and save the stock for another purpose if desired.

In a medium bowl, mix the chicken with the shallots, chiles, lime juice, fish sauce, sugar, black pepper, herbs, and roasted rice powder. Mound on a plate and garnish with fresh herb sprigs. Put out a platter of the accompaniments and serve with plenty of sticky rice.

SERVES *4 as part of a rice meal*

VIETNAMESE CHICKEN SALAD WITH *RAU RAM*
[*ga xe phai* — VIETNAM]

This fresh-tasting chicken salad is a favorite of ours, both at home and in Vietnamese restaurants. We first ate it in Hue, at a small family-run restaurant many years ago. It was our first taste of Vietnamese coriander, known in Vietnamese as *rau ram* and in Thai as *pakchi wietnam*. It doesn't resemble regular coriander at all except that it is a strong distinctive-tasting herb, but "Vietnamese coriander" is what it translates into in Thai. It's a member of the *Polygonum* family.

We grow Vietnamese coriander year-round; as long as it's well watered, it thrives in our garden in the summer and then comes inside for the winter. We love it. It has soft, smooth narrow pointed leaves and a strong distinctive taste. Luckily, in the last few years it has become widely available in Vietnamese groceries. If you can't find Vietnamese coriander, substitute Asian basil or fresh mint.

The salad is dressed with a tangy, mildly hot, mildly sweet lime juice and fish sauce dressing.

2 pounds chicken legs and/or breasts, rinsed (see Note)
3 tablespoons fresh lime juice
3 tablespoons Thai or Vietnamese fish sauce
2 tablespoons rice or cider vinegar
1 teaspoon sugar, or to taste
2 to 3 bird or serrano chiles, minced
2 cloves garlic, or more to taste, minced
3 shallots, thinly sliced
1 cup bean sprouts, rinsed
2 cups shredded napa cabbage, or substitute finely shredded
  Savoy cabbage
2/3 cup Vietnamese coriander leaves (*rau ram,* see Headnote),
  coarsely torn, or substitute Asian basil or sweet basil leaves,
  torn, or 1/2 cup finely chopped mint leaves plus extra
  whole leaves for garnish
Freshly ground black or white pepper

Place a heavy pot with about 4 cups water in it on the stove to boil. When simmering, add the chicken and poach until the juices run clear when the flesh is pierced with a skewer, 25 to 30 minutes. Remove the chicken from the cooking liquid and let cool; reserve the broth for another purpose. (*The chicken can be cooked ahead, and stored, once cooled to room temperature, in a well-sealed container in the refrigerator, for up to 48 hours. Before proceeding, bring back to room temperature.*)

Remove and discard the chicken skin, lift the meat off the bones, and pull into shreds. There should be about 2 cups of meat.

In a small bowl, stir together the lime juice, fish sauce, vinegar, sugar, chiles, and garlic. Separate the shallot slices into rings, then add to the dressing. Let stand for 30 minutes, if you have time.

Blanch the bean sprouts in boiling water (or the reserved chicken broth) for about 30 seconds, then refresh with cold water and drain thoroughly. In a large bowl, combine the chicken, bean sprouts, cabbage, and herbs. Pour the dressing over and toss gently to blend well.

Mound the salad decoratively on a plate. Grind pepper over if you wish, and garnish with herb leaves.

SERVES *4 with rice or noodles*

NOTE: *If you already have 2 cups or more of cooked chicken, you can use it. Just shred it into bite-size pieces, then mix up the dressing and assemble the salad as directed. This salad is traditionally served with deep-fried shrimp chips. We like it simply with rice or noodles.*

GRILLED CHICKEN WITH HOT AND SWEET DIPPING SAUCE

[*gai yang, ping gai* — NORTHEAST THAILAND, LAOS]

In markets all over northeast Thailand, each day vendors set up small charcoal grills for cooking *gai yang*, the region's most famous dish. The pieces of chicken are large, butterflied whole breasts and legs, that are held flat over the grill pinched in holders of split bamboo. As the chicken goes on the grill, there's a sizzle and puffs of smoke. Soon the smell of grilling chicken, with the traditional Thai-Lao marinade of coriander root, black pepper, and garlic, becomes mouthwateringly irresistible. We find ourselves heading for the grill, ordering a piece or two of chicken and of course a bag of sticky rice to go with it. The dipping sauce comes in a little plastic bag, bright orange with chile and sticky with cooked sugar. Heaven.

Back at home, we cut our chicken into smaller pieces. It makes grilling easier and gives more surface for the marinade to cling to.

MARINADE

2 tablespoons Pepper–Coriander Root Flavor Paste (page 184)

2 to 3 tablespoons Thai fish sauce

3 pounds chicken breasts or breasts and legs, chopped into 10 to 12 pieces (see Note)

ACCOMPANIMENT

Hot and Sweet Dipping Sauce (recipe follows)

Place the coriander root paste in a large bowl and stir in the fish sauce. Place the chicken pieces in the marinade and turn to coat well. Let stand, covered, at room temperature for about 1 hour or in the refrigerator for as long as 3 hours.

Heat a grill or preheat the broiler. *If using a grill,* place the chicken pieces 4 to 5 inches from the flame, bone side down, and grill until the bottom side is starting to brown, about 6 to 8 minutes. Then, turn over and cook until golden brown on the other side and the juices run clear when the meat is pierced.

If using a broiler, put the chicken pieces in a lightly oiled broiling pan, bone side up, place 4 to 6 inches from the broiler element, and cook for 8 to 10 minutes, or until the chicken is starting to brown. Turn the pieces over and broil for another 8 minutes, or until the juices run clear.

Transfer the chicken pieces to a platter and serve with the dipping sauce and plenty of sticky rice.

SERVES *6 as part of a rice meal*

NOTE: *You will need a cleaver to chop the chicken into smaller pieces: A whole 2-pound chicken breast should be chopped in half, then each half chopped into 4 pieces; legs are chopped into drumstick and thigh.*

HOT AND SWEET DIPPING SAUCE

[*nam jeem*]

The classic dipping sauce for grilled chicken, this also makes a simple condiment for sticky rice or grilled pork, lamb, or fish. Serve it in individual condiment bowls so guests can dip their chicken and their sticky rice into it as they eat.

½ cup rice or cider vinegar

½ cup sugar

1 to 2 cloves garlic, finely minced

¼ teaspoon salt

1½ teaspoons dried red pepper flakes

Place the vinegar in a small nonreactive saucepan and heat to a boil. Add the sugar, stirring until it has completely dissolved, then lower the heat to medium-low and let simmer for 5 minutes.

Meanwhile, using a mortar and pestle or a bowl and the back of a spoon, pound or mash the garlic and salt to a smooth paste. Stir in the pepper flakes and blend well. Remove the vinegar mixture from the heat and stir in the garlic paste. Let cool to room temperature. Store sealed in a glass jar in the refrigerator for up to 2 days.

MAKES *about ½ cup sauce*

SANGKHOM: Recently we went back to Sangkhom, a small northeastern Thai village on the Mekong where we had spent several pleasurable weeks ten years earlier. When we first arrived, we were quite disoriented. The bungalows we had stayed in before were no longer there, having been washed away by a flooding Mekong. But after a little searching, we found a group of new bungalows not far away, built in the same simple style, each with a porch looking out over the river.

The new bungalows are owned by Yigal and Nupiit. "Food is available in the village," Yigal explained as we checked in, "or, if you tell us ahead of time, you can eat with us. Nupiit is a great cook; she has even cooked for the Rolling Stones."

As it happened, we never learned more about the Rolling Stones, but Yigal was right: Nupiit is a great cook. Born in Sangkhom and raised there and in southern Laos, where her father worked, she cooks in a northeastern Thai-Lao way, and is particularly knowledgeable about wild edible plants. Yigal, born in Israel and raised in New York City, met Nupiit on a trip to Thailand many years ago, and they have been together ever since. Half the year they live on the big island in Hawaii, and half the year in Sangkhom. They live well but modestly, charging only two to three dollars a night for a bungalow, and about the same for a meal. Yigal has a satellite dish, and at night he loves to point it around at different places in the sky and watch Russian television, Polish, Burmese. It's fun, watching Polish television sitting in a little village in Thailand, listening to the Mekong and feeling its breeze.

But it's not nearly as much fun as eating Nupiit's cooking and learning kitchen ways from her. "This is the way we eat sticky rice," she said to Dom and Tashi the very first lunch we ate together. "You take a good amount of rice in your hand, and then with your other hand, tear off a much smaller piece from the big piece, like this." With her little bite-sized piece of rice she then reached for a bit of fried beef jerky. On the table there were at least ten different dishes, far more food than six of us would finish. As in Laos, there was a plate of steamed vegetables: chunks of pumpkin, wedges of cabbage, long beans. There was an herb plate with fresh coriander, green onion, Chinese celery. And then there was all the hot stuff: a *tom yum* hot enough to singe our lips; a salsa (*jaew*), rich-tasting with grilled chiles and shallots; a *laab*, chile-hot and fragrant with roasted rice powder; a plain-looking salt-grilled fish from which we'd pick small chunks of tender meat. . . . Some of the tastes were bitter and wild, others easy and wonderfully familiar. It was a beautiful table of food, green, earthy, and abundant.

We'd planned to spend a few nights in Sangkhom, but it was a good two and a half weeks later when we finally rolled out of town, very sad to be leaving, thanks to Nupiit and Yigal.

Up a small stream valley near the Mekong in Sangkhom, a small bungalow and footbridge emerge from the morning mist.

STIR-FRIED CHICKEN WITH HOLY BASIL
[*gai pad bai gaprow* — THAILAND]

Holy basil and hot chiles combine to make a class of quickly stir-fried spicy Thai dishes, using chicken, beef, or seafood. If you want a milder dish, reduce the quantity of chiles. Holy basil has little flavor until it is cooked, when it becomes intense and wonderful. If using Asian or sweet basil leaves, add them at the last minute.

5 cloves garlic

2 to 3 serrano or bird chiles, stemmed

3 tablespoons peanut or vegetable oil

1 pound boneless, skinless chicken breasts and/or thighs, rinsed, thoroughly dried, and minced or chopped into bite-sized pieces

2 red cayenne chiles, cut lengthwise into strips (optional)

1 tablespoon Thai fish sauce

1 teaspoon soy sauce

1 teaspoon sugar

¼ teaspoon freshly ground black pepper

1 cup holy basil leaves, or substitute Asian basil or sweet basil leaves (see Headnote)

Place the garlic and whole chiles in a mortar and pound to a paste. Or finely mince them.

Place a large wok over high heat. When it is hot, add the oil and swirl gently to coat the pan. Toss in the garlic and chiles and stir-fry for 30 seconds, or until the garlic is just golden. Add the chicken and stir-fry for 3 to 4 minutes, or until the chicken has turned white throughout, using your spatula to separate any clumps and to press the meat against the hot wok. Add the chiles, if using, the fish sauce, soy sauce, sugar, and pepper and stir-fry briefly. Add the holy basil, if using, and stir-fry until wilted, about 1½ minutes, then turn out onto a large plate or shallow serving dish. If using Asian or sweet basil, after adding the herbs, just give the dish one good stir, then turn it out onto the platter. Serve immediately.

SERVES *4 with rice and one or more other dishes*

TURKEY WITH MINT AND HOT CHILES
[LAOS]

It's a strange sight the first time you see it: a turkey strolling unconcernedly along a path near a small Lao village. "What's a turkey doing here, in this tropical place?" was our first reaction. But then we realized that turkeys are raised in many households in Laos. We don't know who introduced them, or when. But now they're a standard domestic fowl, used to make curries and soups, just like chickens.

Leftover turkey from a North American–style roasted Thanksgiving bird lends itself beautifully to this good-tasting Lao salad, fresh with mint and lime juice, a little chile-hot with bird chile—far from the usual turkey leftovers!

8 to 10 ounces cooked light and dark turkey meat, roughly cut into ½-inch chunks (about 2 cups packed) (see Note)

2 tablespoons thinly sliced shallots, separated into rings

½ cup loosely packed coarsely torn coriander leaves

½ cup loosely packed coarsely chopped mint leaves

1 teaspoon minced bird chile, or more to taste

Freshly ground black pepper to taste

2 tablespoons Thai fish sauce, or to taste

3 tablespoons fresh lime juice

1 tablespoon Roasted Rice Powder (page 308) or Aromatic Roasted Rice Powder (page 309), or more to taste (optional)

Combine the meat and shallots in a shallow bowl. Add the coriander and mint leaves and mix well.

In a small bowl, combine all the remaining ingredients except the rice powder and stir to mix well. Pour over the salad and toss to distribute the dressing thoroughly. Just before serving, sprinkle on the rice powder, if using.

SERVES *4 as part of a rice meal, with a soup or curry*

NOTE: *You could, of course, substitute leftover chicken for the turkey.*

CHICKEN AND POTATO CURRY

[*khoua kai* — LAOS]

This dish from Laos is a kind of mild curry, with plenty of fragrant broth. The potatoes are an unexpected pleasure in the midst of the tender chicken and the coconut milk–based sauce. Use a good firm boiling potato such as Yukon Gold that will hold its shape during long simmering.

The recipe needs a little attention for 15 to 20 minutes, then the chicken can be left to simmer until done. You can also make the whole dish ahead and then reheat it just before serving, giving the flavors even more time to blend. If you prepare the dish more than 2 hours ahead, let cool, then refrigerate covered until ready to reheat and serve. Like many simmered dishes, this curry makes great leftovers.

**2½ pounds chicken legs and breasts or 1½ pounds boneless
    breasts and legs, rinsed**
Salt and freshly ground black pepper
**8 medium Yukon Gold or other boiling potatoes (about
    2 pounds), peeled**
2 cups water
3 Thai dried red chiles, soaked in warm water until softened
2 tablespoons minced garlic
5 small shallots, coarsely chopped
2 tablespoons vegetable oil
2 tablespoons Thai fish sauce
**2 cups canned or fresh coconut milk (see page 315),
    ½ cup of the thickest milk set aside**
6 fresh or frozen wild lime leaves
½ cup packed chopped scallion greens (optional)
1 cup loosely packed coriander leaves

If using chicken on the bone, use a cleaver to cut each leg into 2 pieces and whole breasts into 6 to 8 pieces (discard any bone splinters). If using boneless chicken, cut into large pieces about 1 by 2 inches.

Place the chicken in a medium bowl, sprinkle on 1 teaspoon each salt and pepper, and toss to coat. Set aside, covered, while you prepare the potatoes and the spice paste.

Chop the potatoes into approximately 1- to 1½-inch cubes. Place in a pot with 2 cups water, bring to a boil, and cook for 10 minutes. Drain, reserving 1½ cups of the water. Set the potatoes aside.

To prepare the spice paste, reserve the chile soaking water and coarsely chop the chiles, discarding the tough stem ends. Place in a mortar with a pinch of salt and pound briefly, then add the chopped garlic and shallots and pound all to a coarse paste. *Alternatively,* combine the chiles, salt, garlic, and shallots in a blender or food processor and process to a paste; you may need to add a little of the chile soaking water. Set aside the chile paste in a small bowl.

Heat a wide heavy pot or a large wok over high heat. Add the oil and swirl to coat the pan. Add the spice paste and stir-fry briefly, until starting to brown. Add the chicken and cook, turning frequently to prevent sticking, for several minutes. Add the fish sauce and continue to cook until the chicken is browned on all sides, about 10 minutes in all, or slightly less for boneless chicken.

In a medium bowl, stir together the 1½ cups thinner coconut milk and the reserved potato water. Add to the chicken, together with the potatoes, and bring to a vigorous boil, then lower the heat, cover, and simmer until the chicken is very tender, about 30 minutes.

Add the lime leaves and the ½ remaining cup thicker coconut milk, bring to a boil, and simmer until the cream starts to separate, about 8 minutes. Taste for salt and adjust if necessary. Stir in the scallion greens if you wish.

Transfer to a large shallow bowl. Garnish with the chopped coriander and a generous grinding of black pepper. Serve with plenty of plain jasmine rice.

SERVES *6 generously, with rice*

NOTE: *To reheat leftovers, place the curry in a heavy pot, stir in a little warm water to help thin and melt the coconut milk, and reheat gently.*

An older woman gardening in northeast Thailand pauses from her labors.

KHMER CHICKEN *SAMLA'* WITH COCONUT MILK

[*samla' daung* — CAMBODIA]

Lemongrass features so prominently in Khmer cooking that in local produce markets it is impossible to miss the lemongrass vendors. They sit there with huge piles of finely slivered lemongrass in front of them, always slivering more while at the same time measuring out lemongrass by the bag to shoppers. They're a beautiful sight, the piles of freshly slivered lemongrass, and fragrant as well.

Khmer *samla*'s are somewhere between soup and stew, ideal for eating with rice (see Khmer Fish Stew with Lemongrass, page 181). The curry paste used (with lots of lemongrass) is traditionally made by pounding all the ingredients in a stone mortar long and hard until they make a paste; using a food processor or blender, you can reduce them quickly and easily to a fine chopped texture that, while not as smooth as a pounded paste, is very acceptable.

CURRY PASTE

6 to 10 stalks lemongrass

2 small wedges wild lime, mostly peel, or substitute chunks
of regular lime, minced (about 1 teaspoon)

½ teaspoon minced fresh turmeric or ground turmeric

Several pinches of salt

3 tablespoons minced galangal

10 to 12 tiny mauve Asian shallots, coarsely chopped, or
substitute 4 to 5 regular shallots, coarsely chopped
(about 1 cup)

10 medium to large cloves garlic, coarsely chopped

4 Thai dried red chiles, soaked in warm water until softened

2 tablespoons shrimp paste

2 whole chicken legs (1½ to 2 pounds), rinsed

3 tablespoons vegetable oil

3 cups coconut milk, canned or fresh (see page 315), divided
into 1½ cups thinner milk and 1½ cups thicker milk

2 teaspoons salt

1 teaspoon sugar

Cut the tough root ends and dry upper stalks off the lemongrass; peel off the tough outer layers and discard. Very thinly slice the remaining 2 to 3 inches of each stalk. You should have 1¼ cups (the number of stalks you need will vary greatly depending on their size and freshness).

If using a large mortar with a pestle, place the lime and turmeric in the mortar with a pinch of salt and pound to a paste. Add the galangal and pound well. Add about one third of the lemongrass and pulverize to a smooth texture. Gradually add more lemongrass, continuing to pound; empty out some or all of the mixture if your mortar is getting full. Once the lemongrass is broken down, add the shallots and then the garlic, along with another pinch of salt, as you continue pounding. Once you have a smooth, even paste, transfer to a medium bowl and set aside.

If using a food processor or blender, place the lemongrass in the processor or blender and process until very finely chopped. Add the lime, turmeric, a pinch of salt, and the galangal and process until finely chopped. Add the shallots and garlic and another pinch of salt and process to a fine paste. Transfer to a bowl and set aside.

Reserve the chile-soaking water and chop any tough stem ends off the soaked chiles and discard. Cut the chiles open and remove and discard the seeds (or set aside for another purpose). Mince the chiles, then place in a mortar or a blender or processor, with a pinch of salt, and pound or process to a coarse paste. If using a blender or processor, add a little chile-soaking water if necessary to help create a paste, and use a spatula to push the mixture back down the sides to the blade. Add to lemongrass paste, stir to mix well, and set aside.

Spread the shrimp paste on a piece of aluminum foil, fold the foil over to seal, and flatten into a thin package. Place in a hot skillet over medium-high heat for 3 to 4 minutes. Turn over and cook for another 3 to 4 minutes, pressing the package flat against the skillet occasionally with a spatula. Remove from the skillet, unfold the foil, and crumble the toasted shrimp paste into the curry paste, stirring thoroughly to blend it in. Set the curry paste aside.

If you wish, remove the skin and any excess fat from the chicken and discard. Use a heavy cleaver to cut the drumsticks and thighs apart, then halve each drumstick and cut each thigh into 3 pieces.

Heat a large heavy pot over medium-high heat. Add the oil and when it is hot, stir in the curry paste. Cook, stirring, until smooth and aromatic. Add the chicken pieces and stir to turn and coat. Cook, stirring occasionally, for 7 to 10 minutes, until starting to change color. Add the 1½ cups thinner coconut milk, the salt, and the sugar and bring to a boil. Boil gently for 10 minutes. Add about half the thicker coconut milk, bring back to a boil, and simmer, half-covered, for 20 minutes. Skim off any scum, then add the remaining coconut milk and simmer for another 10 to 15 minutes, until the chicken is very tender. Serve hot, giving each person 2 pieces of chicken and lots of sauce.

SERVES *5 as part of a rice meal*

NOTE: *If you wish, you can include eggplant in this curry. Use round green or white Thai eggplants, halved or quartered, or Asian eggplants (see Glossary), unpeeled, cut into rough 1-inch chunks. Add the eggplant about 10 minutes after you add the first coconut milk.*

KHMER CHICKEN *SAMLA* WITH COCONUT MILK *is pictured on page 208.*

SRI CHIANG MAI: At first glance, the town of Sri Chiang Mai looks a lot like any other small Thai highway town. Cars, big trucks, and big buses zoom through town in a blink of the eye, pausing only if by chance someone needs a bite to eat, or if it's time to refill the gas tank. The highway cuts a wide swath through the town, and on either side there are shops and shop houses, along with several gas stations, a police hut, and a bus stop.

But if you stop in town, and turn down a side street, Sri Chiang Mai (like most small highway towns) has grace and personality, small lanes covered in bougainvillea, fruit trees in people's front yards. There is a schoolyard of ample proportions, a quiet local hospital, a beautiful outdoor produce market. Sri Chiang Mai is situated on the Mekong, and all along the river there is a wide walkway (newly built) where people stroll and food vendors gather in the late afternoon and evening. Across the river is Laos, Vientiane, in fact, and it's fun to watch the action on the river as you eat a piece of grilled chicken and a little bag of sticky rice.

But while Sri Chiang Mai looks and feels much like any other pleasant northeast Thai town, it is in another way a unique place. In the 1950s, when the Vietnamese were fighting for independence against the French, a group of Vietnamese came as refugees to Thailand and ended up in Sri Chiang Mai. They were allowed to stay, though they were not allowed to go anywhere outside a thirty-five-kilometer radius of the town. Now, almost fifty years later, the Vietnamese community still exists, though we're told the thirty-five-kilometer restriction has ended.

So if you're wandering through the market and the food seems a little bit different, it is. It's Vietnamese. And it has fused with Thai. It's great.

In Thai villages, monks leave their monastery to make their regular morning alms round at dawn. Some monks, rather than staying in a monastery, travel on foot from place to place, carrying all their possessions in a single shoulder bag; at dawn they, too, make their alms round in whatever village they find themselves in.

OPPOSITE: *In warm climates, there's a premium on freshness: Both chickens and fish are often sold live.* ABOVE: *The work of watering and weeding the riverbank vegetable gardens in Sangkhom, as elsewhere in northeast Thailand and in Laos, seems mostly to fall to the women in the family.*

QUICK RED CHICKEN CURRY

[*gaeng ped gai* — THAILAND]

We confess to sometimes taking shortcuts with culinary traditions, and this curry is a good example of a modern "under thirty minutes" version of a traditional dish. The dilemma of an unexpected guest or a last-minute panic about what to make for supper is easily and gracefully resolved if you have canned coconut milk, a supply of homemade or store-bought curry paste, and some chicken in the refrigerator or freezer. If you have a supply of frozen lime leaves and some Asian or sweet basil around, so much the better.

Serve with jasmine rice, a simple stir-fried or parboiled vegetable dish such as Yunnan Greens (page 151) or Simple Dali Cauliflower (page 158), and a small plate of sliced cucumbers or Pickled Cabbage, Thai Style (page 311 or store-bought).

5 cups canned or fresh coconut milk (see page 315), divided
    into 1 cup thicker milk and 4 cups thinner milk

3 tablespoons Red Curry Paste (recipe follows, or store-bought)

1 pound boneless skinless chicken breasts or thighs (or a
    mixture), rinsed and cut into ¼-inch slices

2 tablespoons Thai fish sauce

4 fresh or frozen wild lime leaves, torn into pieces

2 red chiles (cayenne or serrano, or substitute ½ red bell
    pepper), cut into long thin strips (optional)

½ cup Asian basil or sweet basil leaves

Heat a wok or heavy-bottomed large saucepan over medium-high heat. Add ½ cup of the thicker coconut milk. When it is bubbling, add the curry paste and cook, stirring, for 2 minutes, then add remaining ½ cup thicker milk and cook for 5 to 8 minutes, until the oil begins to separate.

Add the chicken pieces, stir well to coat with the flavored oil, and cook over high heat for about 4 minutes, until the chicken has changed color and become somewhat firmer. Add the remaining 4 cups coconut milk and bring to a boil. Lower the heat and simmer for 5 to 10 minutes.

Stir in the fish sauce and lime leaves. Reduce the heat and simmer for 5 minutes. Just before serving, stir in the chile or bell pepper strips, if using, and the basil.

SERVES *4 to 6 as part of a rice meal*

NOTE: *If you wish to include a vegetable in the curry, the classic is eggplant. Cut round Thai eggplant in half or into quarters, or Asian eggplant into rough ¾-inch chunks, and add once all the coconut milk has come to a boil. Cook for another 5 to 10 minutes.*

RED CURRY PASTE

[*krung gaeng deng* — THAILAND]

You can buy good red curry paste at the market or by mail-order, but, as with most things, homemade has an especially good flavor and aroma. We like to use a little of it as a flavoring in soup or to flavor the oil when we fry rice or stir-fry vegetables.

Red curry paste gets its heat from dried Thai red chiles; it has an aromatic citrusy flavor from galangal, lemongrass, and lime zest. The paste keeps well in the refrigerator.

1½ cups (about 1½ ounces) Thai dried red chiles

1½ tablespoons coriander seeds

1 teaspoon cumin seeds

⅛ teaspoon black peppercorns

2 stalks lemongrass, trimmed and minced

1 tablespoon coarsely chopped coriander roots

¼ cup coarsely chopped galangal

1 teaspoon minced wild lime zest, or substitute regular lime zest

¼ cup coarsely chopped garlic

¼ cup coarsely chopped shallots

1 teaspoon salt

1½ teaspoons shrimp paste

Break the stems off the chiles and discard, together with seeds. Break the chiles into pieces, place in a bowl, and cover with hot water. Place a small lid on to keep them submerged. Let soak for 20 to 30 minutes, or longer if more convenient.

Meanwhile, heat a small heavy skillet over medium-high heat. Add the coriander seeds and dry-roast, occasionally shaking the pan or stirring, until aromatic and beginning to change color, about 3 minutes. Transfer to mortar or a bowl and repeat with the cumin seeds, for about 1 minute. Repeat with peppercorns, roasting just long enough to heat them well, about 1 minute. Use a pestle or spice grinder to pound or grind the spices together to a powder; set aside.

If using a large mortar with a pestle, place the ground spices in the mortar, add the lemongrass, coriander roots, and galangal and pound thoroughly until reduced to a paste. Add the lime zest and pound to blend. Add the garlic, shallots, and salt and pound and mash to a smooth paste. Transfer to a bowl and set aside.

Drain the chiles, place in the mortar, and pound to a paste. (This will take a few minutes.) When the chiles are fairly smooth, add the shrimp paste and pound together. Add the reserved spice paste and pound together.

If using a blender, chop the coriander roots, galangal, garlic, and shallots fairly fine and, with the blades whirling, add to the blender. Add the reserved ground spices, the lemongrass, lime zest, salt, and shrimp paste and continue to blend until you have a paste. You may need to stop and scrape down the sides of the blender with a spatula; add a little water if the mixture seems very dry, then blend until fairly smooth. Drain the chiles, reserving the soaking water. Add the chiles to the blender with a little of the soaking water and blend to a paste, adding a little extra soaking water if necessary.

Store in a well-sealed glass container in the refrigerator. The paste keeps for 2 to 3 months (with a slight loss of intensity over time).

MAKES *about 1¼ cups thick paste*

DUCK IN GREEN CURRY PASTE

[*gaeng kiao wan ped* — THAILAND]

Duck is a treat, and so is green curry; they make a great combination in this Thai classic. The green curry paste can be freshly made for the occasion, retrieved from the stash in your refrigerator, or store-bought.

Once the curry paste is made and the duck cut up, the dish takes about 45 minutes of cooking, most of that easy simmering. You can also begin the dish a day ahead, as described below, then finish cooking and flavoring it just before serving.

If you don't have wild lime leaves, you can do without, but you should have the basil leaves. Both stay a beautiful bright green atop the curry. The dish is quite chile-hot. Serve with plenty of rice, or fresh rice noodles, and some fresh crisp vegetables for contrasting cool texture.

One 3- to 3½-pound duck

3 to 3½ cups canned or fresh coconut milk (see page 315), ¼ cup of the thickest milk set aside

1 teaspoon freshly grated nutmeg (optional)

4 to 5 tablespoons Green Curry Paste (recipe follows, or store-bought; see Notes)

2 tablespoons Thai fish sauce

8 to 10 round Thai eggplants, stems removed and halved lengthwise, or substitute 1½ cups coarsely chopped (1-inch chunks) Asian eggplant

8 to 10 fresh or frozen wild lime leaves (optional)

½ teaspoon salt, or to taste

½ to 1 cup sliced (½-inch-wide slices) mild to medium-hot green and red chiles (optional; see Notes)

About 25 Asian or sweet basil leaves

continued

Use a cleaver to cut the duck into pieces, leaving the meat on the bone. Cut the legs crosswise in two; otherwise, generally try to end up with pieces not more than 2 inches long. Trim off all the fat and fatty skin (and reserve for another purpose).

Place a heavy 6-quart or larger pot over medium heat. Add the ¼ cup thick coconut milk and stir as it heats and melts, then cook for 5 minutes over medium-high heat, or until the oil starts to separate. If using nutmeg, stir it into the curry paste. Add the paste to the cooking coconut cream, together with 1 tablespoon of the fish sauce. Stir to blend well and continue to cook for about 5 minutes, stirring frequently. The paste will become very aromatic.

Add the duck pieces and turn to coat with the paste. Raise the heat to high and cook, turning occasionally, for about 5 minutes. Add the remaining coconut milk and bring to a boil. Reduce the heat and cook at a strong simmer for 15 to 20 minutes. (*The curry can be prepared ahead to this point and set aside for up to 24 hours, once cooled, in a well-sealed container in the refrigerator. Return to the heavy pot and bring to a simmer over medium heat when ready to proceed.*)

Add the eggplant, 5 to 6 of the lime leaves, the salt, and the remaining 1 tablespoon fish sauce and bring back to a boil. Simmer for another 15 minutes. Taste and adjust the seasonings if you wish.

Just before you wish to serve the dish, add the chile slices, if using, the remaining lime leaves, and the basil leaves. Cook 1 more minute, then turn into a bowl and serve.

SERVES *4 to 6 as part of a rice meal*

NOTES: *Several older Thai cookbooks we've used for guidance suggest adding nutmeg to green curry paste when making duck curry. We like it, so it's included as an option.*

Since green curry pastes, like all others, vary in chile heat, if you're using a ready-made paste, you may find that it's hotter than our Green Curry Paste recipe and that you need use less of it. If you find that your sauce tastes hotter than you want, dilute it by adding more coconut milk or water. (You may then have to add a little salt.)

Traditionally, whole red and green chiles of medium heat are added to the curry near the end of cooking, as beautiful contrast. We've had trouble finding those chiles here, so instead we suggest slicing long slender green chiles (the ones we've found are medium-hot), and red ones if available, into fat rings. If you wish to substitute half a sweet red bell pepper cut into strips, do so, for the purpose of the chiles is as much decorative as it is flavoring.

Another green curry tradition is the use of the tiny berry-sized green Thai eggplants called makeua puong *as garnish. They have a much-prized bitter taste. They're still hard to find in North America, but if you find them, add them about 5 minutes before you add the chiles and basil leaves.*

GREEN CURRY PASTE

[*krung gaeng kiao wan* — THAILAND]

Green curry paste is special because, unlike most curry pastes, it's made with fresh green chiles rather than dried red chiles. It's often used for flavoring duck or chicken and served with plenty of basil and lime leaves, green on green.

All curry pastes vary widely according to the tastes and habits of the maker. We like this version of green curry paste, chile-hot but still not as intensely hot as some, and very citrusy with lemongrass, galangal, and wild lime zest. You can, of course, substitute a store-bought paste (they're now widely available), as many people in Thailand do.

We make this paste in our large Thai mortar, not so much because we love the long job of pounding it, but because we find that our food processor does not get it chopped finely enough. You could use the processor or a blender and then finish the paste off smoothly in a large mortar. Some small blenders do a good job of grinding finely; if you have one, do use it. We find the whole pounding process takes us about 20 minutes using our large ceramic mortar and wooden pestle. A stone mortar and pestle works faster. The paste needs to be smooth and free of coarse bits that would make a cooked curry sauce grainy.

We like to make this quantity, enough for four curries, since the paste keeps for about a month in the refrigerator.

1 tablespoon coriander seeds

2 teaspoons cumin seeds

1 teaspoon black peppercorns

¼ cup minced coriander roots

1½ teaspoons salt

½ cup minced lemongrass (4 to 8 stalks)

¼ cup coarsely chopped garlic

¼ cup coarsely chopped shallots

2 tablespoons chopped galangal, or substitute 1 tablespoon
  minced ginger plus 1 tablespoon fresh lime juice

1 tablespoon minced wild lime zest, or substitute
  regular lime zest

½ cup bird chiles (preferably green ones),
  stemmed and coarsely chopped

1 tablespoon shrimp paste

Place a heavy skillet over medium-high heat. Add the coriander seeds and dry-roast, stirring frequently with a wooden spoon, until aromatic and beginning to change color, about 3 minutes. Transfer to a mortar or spice grinder and grind to a powder, then set aside. Use the same method to dry-roast the cumin seeds, about 1 minute, then grind to a powder and add to the ground coriander. Grind the peppercorns and add to the spice mixture.

Use a large mortar (or food processor or blender; see Headnote), to reduce the ingredients to a paste: Place the coriander roots in the mortar with a pinch of the salt and pound until well softened and breaking down. Add the lemongrass and pound until it is well mashed. Add the garlic and another pinch of salt and continue pounding. Once the garlic is shapeless and breaking down, add the shallots and continue until broken down. Add the galangal and lime zest and pound and mash with another pinch of salt to a coarse paste. Add the spice blend and mash and pound until well combined. Add the chopped chiles and the remaining salt and pound until broken down and smooth. Set aside.

Place the shrimp paste on a piece of aluminum foil about 8 by 4 inches. Spread it out in a thin layer, then fold the foil over it to seal and make a flat package. Place a heavy skillet over high heat, put the foil package in the skillet, and cook for about 3 minutes on the first side, pressing it down onto the hot surface. Turn over and repeat on the other side. You should start to smell the hot shrimp paste. Remove from the heat, unwrap it, and add to the curry paste blend. Pound or stir thoroughly to blend. You'll smell all the aromas in the curry paste as it mixes with the hot shrimp paste.

Store the curry paste in a clean, dry, well-sealed glass jar in the refrigerator. It should keep for about a month.

MAKES *1 cup paste*

BEEF

You don't see herds of Herefords grazing their way along the banks of the Mekong, nor

Aberdeen Angus, for that matter. But you do see some fine-boned Asian cattle grazing, and

lots of water buffalo, lazing in mud wallows, calmly lifting their big heads with black swept-

back horns to watch you as you walk by. Water buffalo are the region's beast of burden, used for plowing and

milking, and, eventually, for meat. The buffs are docile and amiable, a good thing, given

their size. They graze in the rice stubble and along the edges of the road, often tended or

watched by village children.

The recipes we've grouped together here all call for beef, though some of them have

their origins in recipes using the meat of the water buffalo. Along the Mekong, beef is

The Khmer empire once stretched from western Thailand to the Mekong Delta. Many Khmer people who still live in the Mekong Delta region are descendants of the Khmer who controlled the area until two centuries ago. In the countryside near Tra Vinh lies Ba Om, an important Khmer temple lively with monks of all ages.

grilled, stir-fried, or sun-dried and then deep-fried (see Fried Beef Jerky, page 218), but rarely stewed. One exception is a delicious slow-simmered dish from Yunnan, Hui Beef Stew with Chick-peas and Anise (page 231), very warming on a cold winter's evening.

Beef and water buffalo meat are sometimes eaten spiced and uncooked in northern Thailand, the Shan State, Laos, and parts of Yunnan. The meat is first minced or sliced, then dressed with chiles and salt (see Dai Beef Tartare with Pepper-Salt, page 230) or with lime juice (see Chiang Mai Carpaccio, page 230).

LEFT: *Water buffalo are used for plowing and, when the day's work is done, for a slow ride home.* CENTER: *One of the huge carved faces at the Bayon, in Angkor Thom, dwarfs Khmer visitors.* RIGHT: *With its beautiful carvings and lovely proportions, the temple of Banteay Srei is perhaps the most aesthetically pleasing of the ancient Khmer temples.*

FRIED BEEF JERKY

[*neua kaem* — NORTHEAST THAILAND, SOUTHERN LAOS]

In northeast Thailand, sun-drying marinated beef produces *neua kaem*, salty strips of flavorful dried beef. These days it's not dried out completely, unlike jerky, though in earlier times perhaps it was, a way of keeping meat indefinitely without spoilage. The drying helps it keep for a few days without refrigeration, changes the texture, and intensifies the taste of the meat and the flavorings it's marinated in. Though it's often eaten dry, like jerky, *neua kaem* is even more delicious if briefly fried; you can also grill it, brushed with a little oil.

This aromatic marinade is a pounded combination of coriander seeds, coriander roots, lemongrass, and seasonings that we also use as a rub for beef before grilling.

Traditionally, the beef strips are coated in the marinade, then sun-dried. But sun-drying needs hot sun and a way of protecting the meat from contamination, so we suggest that you simply slow-dry the beef strips in a warm oven. It takes about 6 hours in the oven to get semidry, the texture we prefer. If you want a completely dried-out jerky (for taking on a camping trip, say), leave the strips in the oven for 10 to 15 hours (see Notes).

You can make the dried beef, then store it in the freezer until you want to serve it. It makes a great last-minute dish.

1 pound boneless lean beef (such as tenderloin, flank steak, or center round)

MARINADE

½ teaspoon coriander seeds

1 tablespoon minced lemongrass (about 1 stalk)

½ teaspoon salt

3 tablespoons chopped coriander roots

2 medium cloves garlic, chopped

½ teaspoon black peppercorns

1 teaspoon sugar

2 tablespoons Thai fish sauce, or more as needed

Peanut oil or other oil for deep-frying

Slice the beef into very thin strips and set aside in a shallow bowl.

Using a large mortar and a pestle, pound the coriander seeds to a coarse powder, then add the lemongrass and pound until well broken down. Add the salt and coriander roots and pound to a coarse paste, then add the garlic, peppercorns, and sugar and pound to a paste. Stir in the fish sauce, then pound a little to make a smooth paste. If it seems very dry, add a little more fish sauce, or a little water. You want the paste to be moist and smooth enough to coat the meat. You'll have about 3 tablespoons marinade.

Alternatively, you can use a blender to make the paste. (With a processor, it's difficult to get a fine-enough texture.) You may need to use a spice grinder or coffee grinder to grind the coriander seeds and pepper first, then add the ground spices to the other marinade ingredients in the blender and reduce to a paste. Use a spatula to scrape the sides down as necessary.

Add the marinade to the meat and toss and turn to coat the meat thoroughly. If you have time, cover the meat and refrigerate for at least 2 hours, or as long as overnight.

Preheat the oven to 150°F. Drain off any liquid that has been drawn out of the meat. Place a rack over a baking sheet (to catch any drips), arrange the pieces on the rack, laying them as flat as possible, and place in the upper third of the oven. Let dry for 6 hours, leaving the oven door propped open several inches to let moisture escape.

After 6 hours, the meat will have changed color right through and it will be drier, but not completely dried out. This is the ideal texture, we think, for making fried jerky. You can fry it immediately, or cool it and store it in the freezer in a well-sealed bag or container until ready to use. Bring the jerky back to room temperature before frying.

Place several plates lined with paper towels near your stovetop and have tongs or long chopsticks handy. Place the oil in a well-balanced (not tippy) wok or a large heavy skillet: You want the oil to be about ½ inch deep in a skillet, or slightly more at the deepest point of the wok. Heat the oil until it's just starting to smoke. Gently slide about one quarter of the meat into the wok or skillet and fry for about 30 seconds, turning and moving it constantly with your tongs or chopsticks. Lift the meat out onto a paper towel–lined plate.

Bring the oil back to almost-smoking hot and cook the remaining meat in batches. Serve hot or at room temperature as a snack or as part of a rice meal.

SERVES *6*

NOTES: *Once you have finished frying, place the wok or skillet at the back of the stove until the oil has cooled to room temperature, then pour the oil through a piece of cheesecloth into a glass jar and store, covered, in the refrigerator.*

If you want very dry jerky, traveling food, leave the strips in the oven for 10 to 12 hours, or until they are very lightweight and dry. (One pound of meat will give you about ¼ pound dry jerky.) This makes good food for camping or hiking. (It's salty, so you'll want to know you have plenty of drinking water.)

To use this marinade for grilled beef, rub over a piece of beef tenderloin, then place the beef under a preheated broiler or on a hot grill. Broil or grill, turning halfway through the cooking, to the desired doneness. Remove from the heat and let stand for 10 minutes. Serve thinly sliced, with Lime Juice Yin-Yang (page 129), or as a grilled beef salad, tossed with thinly sliced shallots and a lime juice and fish sauce dressing.

You can use the same recipe to make fried pork jerky; increase the sugar to 2 teaspoons and, if you wish, omit the lemongrass and coriander seeds. This is a very delicious plain country version.

KHMER STIR-FRIED GINGER AND BEEF

[*saiko cha k'nye* — CAMBODIA]

Sao Pheha (see Phnom Penh Nights, page 242) introduced me to several easy dishes from the Khmer home-cooking repertoire. This was perhaps the simplest, and also the most surprising. It's a stir-fry in which ginger has the role of featured vegetable, warming and full of flavor. The ginger is cut into julienne twigs and then fried with a little beef. The result is a mound of beef slices and tender ginger, all bathed in plenty of gravy, a great companion for rice.

Be sure to buy firm ginger for this dish (ginger with wrinkled skin will be tough and stringy), and, if there's a choice, young ginger rather than the tan mature ginger. Serve with a sour stew or soup, such as Khmer Fish Stew with Lemongrass (page 181) or Buddhist Sour Soup (page 58), and some simple greens, such as Classic Mixed Vegetable Stir-fry (page 151).

**Generous ½ pound boneless sirloin, eye of round, or
    other lean beef**
½ pound ginger, preferably young ginger
3 tablespoons vegetable or peanut oil
3 to 4 cloves garlic, smashed and minced
2 tablespoons Thai fish sauce
2 teaspoons sugar

Thinly slice the beef across the grain and set aside. Peel the ginger, then cut it into fine matchstick-length julienne (this is most easily done by cutting thin slices, then stacking these to cut into matchsticks). You'll have about 2 cups.

Heat a wok over medium-high heat. Add the oil and, when it is hot, add the garlic. Cook until golden, 20 to 30 seconds. Add the meat and stir-fry, using your spatula to separate the slices and to expose them all to the heat, until most of the meat has changed color. Add the fish sauce and sugar, toss in the ginger twigs, and stir-fry until just tender, 4 to 5 minutes. Serve hot with rice.

SERVES *4 with rice and another dish*

FERMENTED FISH: New foods can be intimidating, scary even, especially if they're soured or fermented, or transformed in a way that's unfamiliar. Those of us who were raised in some blend of European–North American culinary tradition tend to love cheese. The fact that it's a fermented product doesn't bother us—in fact, for many of us, the smellier, the better. But for many Southeast Asians, the first reaction to cheese, or yogurt, is an appalled aversion: "Yuck!" sums it up.

Similarly, when we venture into traditional fermented foods from other cultures, we often have a hard time learning to like them. The Japanese fermented soybeans, *natto*, sour, slimy, and, yes, delicious, come to mind. So does stinky bean curd, *zhou doufu*, in China.

In Laos, Thailand, Cambodia, and Vietnam, the precursor to fish sauce is a very strong tasting fermented fish paste, with bits of fish floating in a briny liquid. In Cambodia it's known as *prahok*, in Thailand as *pla raa*, in Laos and Issaan as *padek*, in Vietnam as *mam*. Fish sauce was originally the liquid poured or pressed from fish paste (*nuoc mam*, for example, means "liquid from *mam*"). Though salty fish sauce–like flavorings can in fact also be made with fruits or vegetables, salted and fermented, *prahok*, *pla raa*, *padek*, and *mam* need fish. The fish are packed with salt, and often rice bran or rice powder, in a ceramic barrel and left to ferment. It's a way of preserving the catch and supplying amino acids in a diet high in rice and vegetables and low in animal products.

Padek and *prahok* are still made in the countryside, and people raised with them can't live without their punchy, salty kick (the closest taste analogy is preserved anchovies). Many of the Lao and Khmer dishes in this book were originally made with *padek* or *prahok* instead of fish sauce (though, we're always told, you must never use *padek* to make *laab*). With more people living in cities, fewer people in Thailand seem to be eating *pla raa* or *padek*. For one thing, you need to be in the countryside to make it. Also, it's now become much easier to buy a bottle of fish sauce than to make your own, though they don't have the same taste, not at all.

As for foreigners, the assertive salty fermented fish taste of *padek* or *prahok* or *pla raa* or *mam* is more than many are prepared to take on. All of which is to say that we've left out the *padek* or *prahok* or *pla raa* or *mam*. For a dish with a strong *padek*-type flavor, try Issaan Salsa with Anchovies (page 38). It's salty and delicious when eaten with rice, very intense, almost overpowering, on its own.

Beside many Khmer temples lies a calm pond sheltered by tall trees. Here at Ba Om temple (see photograph on page 221), a Khmer man fishes in the temple pond.

CAMBODIAN HOT POT

[CAMBODIA]

One dish that lends itself to a convivial evening with friends is hot pot. It's like fondue, but with the ingredients cooked in a hot broth. It's a fun way to eat, and once the ingredients and the broth are on the table, the host is free to join the party.

Although I first ate Cambodian Hot Pot on a warm tropical night at a small streetside restaurant in Phnom Penh, it is a great any-time-of-year meal. We sat, four of us, on stools around a low table set out on the sidewalk. Out came the hot pot, full of broth. The flame was lit under it and soon the broth was bubbling. We had ordered a simple array of ingredients, and they came on two platters: some thinly sliced beef, chopped greens, fresh herbs, mushrooms, a coil of soft noodles, some dipping sauces. Using chopsticks, we dropped a little meat and a few mushrooms into the broth, then began fishing treasures out and eating them. The pace was leisurely. Gradually, in a rhythm of fishing out cooked morsels and adding more, we worked our way through the platters. Finally the noodles went in. They simmered briefly, then we each ended with a bowl of richly flavored noodle soup, carefully ladled out from the hot pot, a wonderful way of finishing the feast.

Use the recipe below to get you started; feel free to add ingredients to the platter or to improvise other sauces, as you wish.

Serve wine or, more traditionally, very weak whiskey-and-sodas with this meal. Put out a platter of raw vegetables—cucumber slices, leaf lettuce, and carrot sticks—so guests can chew on something crisp as they wait for their next mouthful from the hot pot.

BROTH

2 pounds oxtails or ¾ pound stewing beef, coarsely chopped into 8 pieces

8 cups water

3 shallots, coarsely chopped

4 cloves garlic, coarsely chopped

10 black peppercorns

1 teaspoon salt

1 tablespoon Thai fish sauce

3 scallions, trimmed and cut into 2-inch lengths

PLATTER

¾ pound to 1 pound boneless beef, thinly sliced

2 cups assorted mushrooms (such as button, oyster, and portobello), cleaned and cut into large bite-sized pieces

4 sawtooth herb leaves

1 cup Asian or sweet basil leaves

3 sprigs rice paddy herb (*rau om*)

2 cups loosely packed coarsely chopped romaine lettuce or napa cabbage

2 large eggs (optional)

1 pound fresh egg noodles or ½ pound dried rice noodles

CONDIMENTS AND SAUCES

Thai fish sauce

2 tablespoons minced bird chiles

Yunnanese Chile Pepper Paste (page 27), Fresh Chile-Garlic Paste (page 26), or store-bought Sriracha sauce (see page 26)

Lime wedges

Salt and freshly ground black pepper

To prepare the broth, place the meat in a large pot with cold water to cover. Bring to a boil and boil for 2 or 3 minutes, then drain. Rinse both the pot and meat, then place the meat back in the pot. Add the 8 cups water, shallots, garlic, and peppercorns and bring to a boil. Skim off and discard any foam, then lower the heat and simmer, halfcovered, for 1 hour.

Add the salt and fish sauce and simmer for another few minutes, then taste for salt and adjust if necessary. Remove from the heat.

Remove the meat from the broth. Pull the meatiest bits off the oxtail bones and set aside; discard the bones. Or, if using stewing beef, set aside. Strain the broth through a fine strainer or a colander lined with cheesecloth and discard the solids. You should have about 6 cups broth; if necessary, add water to make a total of 6 cups liquid. If you have time, set the broth aside to cool, refrigerate for 2 hours, and then skim off the surface fat. (*The broth can be made ahead and stored in a well-sealed nonreactive container for 3 days in the refrigerator or up to 2 months in the freezer. The meat can be stored in a well-sealed container for up to 3 days in the refrigerator.*)

About 30 minutes before serving, prepare the platter ingredients and set out on one large or several smaller platters. Place the eggs, if using, uncracked, in a bowl. If using fresh noodles, rinse them off and arrange in several coils on a plate. If using dried rice noodles, soak in warm water for 20 minutes, then drain and coil on a plate. Set out a condiment bowl, a soup bowl, a plate, a pair of chopsticks, and a soupspoon for each guest.

Just before serving, reheat the broth. If you used stewing beef, slice the meat. Add some or all of the reserved oxtail or stew meat and the scallions to the broth. Lower the heat to a simmer while you set up a hot pot or other pot heated over a low flame (see Note). Pour the hot broth, with the meat and the scallions, into the hot pot. The heat should be enough to keep the broth at a slightly bubbling simmer. Invite your guests to the table.

Begin by tossing some of the sawtooth herb and rice paddy herb into the broth. Invite your guests to add a few items from the platter to the soup; then, a few minutes later, invite them to "go fishing" with their chopsticks for the cooked morsels, which they can lift out onto their plates and eat, perhaps after dabbing on one or more condiments. As the meal goes on, gradually add more herbs and greens to the soup.

When the platter is just about empty, break the eggs, if using, into the bowl, beat them briefly with chopsticks, and add them to the soup. Stir to spread the skeins of egg. Toss in the noodles, and stir gently. When the fresh noodles are tender or the dried ones are hot, use a ladle and chopsticks to serve the soup and noodles to each guest. Invite them to sprinkle any remaining fresh basil leaves onto their soup as they eat.

SERVES *4 to 6*

NOTE: *The traditional serving implement used for hot pot is available from Chinese and Vietnamese cookware shops. These days, the most commonly available are lightweight aluminum pots. A hot pot has a cylindrical "chimney" in the center that is placed over a can of Sterno or other small flame. Around the chimney is the doughnut-shaped "pot" in which the broth and other ingredients simmer, heated by the chimney. You can also use a large heatproof pot set over a Sterno flame, fondue style.*

SPICY GRILLED BEEF SALAD

[*neua nam toke* — LAOS, NORTHEAST THAILAND]

The name of this substantial dish means "beef with dripping liquid." The beef is lightly grilled or broiled, then thinly sliced. The slices are cooked a little more in a hot broth-based dressing before being tossed with sliced shallots and fresh mint leaves. The meat emerges tender, moist, and lightly spiced with chiles. It makes a great main-course dish accompanied by sticky rice or aromatic jasmine rice.

SALAD

One 1-pound boneless beef sirloin steak, approximately ¾ inch thick

1 teaspoon freshly ground black pepper

½ cup beef or chicken broth

3 tablespoons fresh lime juice

2 tablespoons Thai fish sauce

1 teaspoon sugar

1 teaspoon Roasted Rice Powder (page 308) (optional)

⅓ cup thinly sliced shallots, separated into rings

4 scallions, trimmed, sliced lengthwise in half, and cut into ½-inch lengths

2 bird or serrano chiles, minced

½ cup mint leaves

ACCOMPANIMENTS: CHOOSE TWO OR THREE

1 small cabbage, cored, cut into wedges, and separated into leaves

8 to 10 leaves tender leaf or Bibb lettuce

4 to 6 leaves napa cabbage, cut crosswise into 1- to 2-inch slices

5 or 6 yard-long beans, trimmed, cut into 2-inch lengths, and (optional) blanched in boiling water for 1 minute

1 European cucumber, cut into ¼-inch slices

2 or 3 scallions, trimmed and sliced lengthwise in half

Prepare a grill or preheat the broiler. Rub the meat with the black pepper. If grilling, place the meat 3 to 4 inches above the coals or flame; if broiling, place in the broiler pan about 3 inches below the element. Grill or broil until rare, 2 to 3 minutes per side. Very thinly slice the meat across the grain.

In a medium saucepan, mix the broth, lime juice, fish sauce, and sugar together and bring to a boil over high heat. Toss in the rice powder and meat and quickly stir to coat the meat. Immediately remove from the heat and transfer the meat and dressing to a large bowl (you must be quick so as not to overcook the beef). Add the shallots, scallions, chiles, and mint and toss gently. Let stand while you arrange your choice of accompaniments on a platter.

Mound the salad on a plate and pour the extra dressing over. Serve with the platter of accompaniments and plenty of jasmine or sticky rice.

SERVES *4 to 6 with rice*

SPICY GRILLED BEEF SALAD *is pictured on page 227.*

GRILLED LEMONGRASS BEEF
[*thit bo nuong* — VIETNAM]

Bo Bay Mon means "Beef in Seven Ways" and is the name given to a style of restaurant found in Ho Chi Minh City and now, lucky for us, in some North American cities. It's a place to go for a special occasion, especially in a culture that doesn't eat lots of meat, for each of the dishes on the menu is made with beef. Sometimes the restaurant adds several more dishes to the classic lucky seven.

We love the taste of grilled lemongrass, so we generally choose this grilled beef whenever we're dining at a Vietnamese restaurant, *Bo Bay Mon* style or otherwise. Tender slices of beef are marinated in a lemongrass-based marinade and then grilled or broiled. Serve as one of several dishes with rice, as a topping for noodles, or as an ingredient in rice paper roll-ups (see Note).

MARINADE

2 stalks lemongrass, trimmed and minced

2 to 3 cloves garlic, finely chopped

2 shallots, finely chopped

1 bird or serrano chile, finely chopped

2 tablespoons Vietnamese or Thai fish sauce

1 tablespoon fresh lime juice

1 tablespoon water

1 tablespoon roasted sesame oil

1 pound beef rump roast or eye of round, trimmed of all fat

2 tablespoons Dry-Roasted Sesame Seeds (page 308)

ACCOMPANIMENTS

Vietnamese Herb and Salad Plate (page 68)

1 cup Vietnamese Peanut Sauce (*nuoc leo*, page 28) or
  Vietnamese Must-Have Table Sauce (*nuoc cham*, page 28)

To prepare the marinade, combine the lemongrass, garlic, shallots, and chile in a mortar and pound to a paste. Or, combine in a blender and blend, adding a little water if necessary to make a paste. Transfer the paste to a bowl, add the fish sauce, lime juice, and water and blend well. Add the sesame oil and stir well. Set aside.

Cut the meat into very thin slices (less than ⅛ inch) against the grain (this is easier if the meat is cold). Then cut the slices into 1½-inch lengths. Place the meat in a shallow bowl, add the marinade, and mix well, making sure that the meat is well coated. Cover and marinate for 1 hour at room temperature or up to 8 hours in the refrigerator.

If using wooden skewers, soak them in water for 30 minutes before using. Prepare a grill or preheat the broiler.

Thread the pieces of meat onto wooden or fine metal skewers and sprinkle with the sesame seeds. Lightly oil the grill rack or broiler pan. Grill or broil the meat for 1 minute per side for medium-rare.

Arrange on a platter and serve with the salad plate and peanut sauce or table sauce.

SERVES *4 to 6 as part of a rice or noodle meal*

NOTE: *To serve the beef in rice paper roll-ups, set out, in addition to the salad plate and dipping sauce, about 25 dried rice papers, preferably small rounds; 1 pound rice vermicelli, soaked in warm water for 15 minutes, drained, cooked in boiling water, and drained; ¼ cup Dry-Roasted Peanuts (page 308), finely chopped (optional); and 2 bird or serrano chiles, minced (optional). Make sure there is plenty of soft leaf lettuce on the salad plate, and set out a bowl of warm water for wetting the rice papers. Show your guests how to roll up the beef: Moisten a rice paper in warm water until soft. Place a lettuce leaf on your plate and lay the rice paper on it. Place a small bunch of noodles, perhaps some minced chiles or chopped peanuts, or whatever else you please, on it, then add some herb sprigs and pieces of grilled beef. Roll up, tucking in the sides. Use the lettuce leaf to hold the roll. Dip it in the sauce, or drizzle on a little sauce with a spoon, and eat.*

GRILLED LEMONGRASS BEEF *is pictured on page 226.*

SIAM RIEP: It's terrible to admit in an opener to Angkor Wat, but I'm not a big temple person. I'm terrible with iconography, and with old temples and ruins my imagination is slow to get into gear. I want kitchens, food, clothing, agriculture, daily life.

But don't get me wrong, I loved Angkor Wat; I mean, I loved being there. The temples are human in scale, not overpowering, while the surrounding countryside is jungly, vast, and mysterious. These days the whole Angkor region is treated as a national park. Each day I entered, I was required to pay a twenty-dollar entrance fee, plus six dollars for a guide. The system was fine by me: Dawn to dusk I had a guide who drove me around on the back of his motorbike.

The first few days, we visited temple after temple on Heang Ly's motorbike. He got me to Bayon at sunrise, Angkor at sunset; we did the "small circuit," and then started on the "long circuit." Our days were long, varooming around on the motorbike, climbing up and down temple stairs. But as we went along, we talked, and we got to be friends.

Heang was born near Angkor in a village a day's walk from Siem Riep. His father had been an odd-job man in the village, fixing things, sometimes working as a doctor ministering to patients with medicinal roots and herbs, especially people suffering from allergies. Heang's grandfather had come to Cambodia from China, so when the Khmer Rouge came through the village looking for anyone with Chinese ancestry, his father's life was in danger. But the village people hid him; he was their friend, after all, and he helped them. His father then sent Heang and his older brother to the city, to Siam Riep, thinking they would be safer there, and they were. Heang was twelve.

Like every family in Cambodia, Heang's family suffered much tragedy. "Salt had greater value than gold," Heang told me one morning as we were driving along. "Gold meant nothing. There was no food to buy." Before going to the city, Heang, like many Cambodian children, had the daily job of shepherding cows from grassy field to grassy field. Then, as now, the job was horribly dangerous because the fields were strewn with land mines. "The only thing is," Heang explained as we were watching children one morning with a herd of cows on the road, "sometimes the cows save the children: They hit the mines before the children do."

But Heang does more than look back. At twenty-six years old, he is an incredibly good guide. He is multilingual, intelligent, nice, funny. When I at last admitted to him that I was more interested in food than in temples, he took me to markets, to a fish-fermenting factory, and to a Vietnamese village entirely afloat on the Tonle Sap. At dawn, we no longer drove to ruins, but instead met for *babah* (see page 94) and talked food. Every meal had a purpose, and an explanation.

On my last day, my last morning, a different guide showed up. He had a note from Heang, explaining that he'd gotten a better offer that day, a German tour group in a minivan. I was disappointed, but pleased for him. What Heang deserves, what everyone in Cambodia deserves, is for each day to be better than the last.

One's first sight of Angkor Wat: calm, mysterious, beautiful. In the fifteenth century, the Khmer court moved from Angkor to establish a new capital at Phnom Penh.

CHIANG MAI CARPACCIO

[*saa jin* — NORTHERN THAILAND]

We learned this simple traditional dish from a friend in Chiang Mai. It's ideal as an appetizer, or as one of several dishes in a rice meal. The transparently thin slices of beef are "cooked" by the lime juice they're bathed in, then flavored with a scattering of distinctive tastes: minced lemongrass, shallots, and fresh ginger and herbs.

¼ pound beef tenderloin or other boneless tender lean cut

3 tablespoons fresh lime juice

¼ teaspoon salt, or more to taste

1 tablespoon minced shallots, or substitute mild onion

½ teaspoon minced lemongrass

¼ teaspoon minced ginger

¼ cup torn coriander leaves or minced mint leaves

Very thinly slice the beef across the grain (this is easier if the meat is frozen or at least well chilled), then cut the slices crosswise into bite-sized pieces, about ¾ inch long. Place in a shallow bowl with the lime juice, turn to mix well, and let stand for 5 minutes.

Lay the beef slices on a flat plate in a single layer, slightly overlapping if you wish. Pour any remaining lime juice over. Sprinkle on the salt, then sprinkle on the remaining ingredients in order, ending with the fresh herbs. Serve immediately.

SERVES *4 as an appetizer or as part of a rice meal*

DAI BEEF TARTARE WITH PEPPER-SALT

[*saa dai* — SOUTHERN YUNNAN]

We've come across this delicious spiced minced beef several times in southern Yunnan. Each time, we used pieces of cabbage to scoop up small mouthfuls, hot and salty and good; you could also use cucumber slices. It is a great pairing with beer. Serve winter or summer, as an appetizer. If you prefer your beef cooked, then shape the seasoned meat into patties and grill or broil them (see Note).

¼ pound boneless lean beef (such as tenderloin)

½ teaspoon Chinese Pepper-Salt (page 309)

¼ cup coriander leaves, coarsely torn

ACCOMPANIMENTS

Small wedges of Savoy cabbage, parboiled, or cucumber slices or fresh leaf lettuce

Two Pepper-Salt Spice Dip (page 309)

Use a cleaver to slice the meat very thin and then to chop it until finely minced: Chop it fine in one direction, then fold it over on itself and chop fine in the other direction. Transfer to a large mortar or a food processor, add the pepper-salt, and pound or process until very smooth. Stir in the coriander leaves, or pulse briefly. Mound on a small plate, and serve with your chosen accompaniments and sticky rice or Thai-Lao Crispy Rice Crackers (page 106).

MAKES *over ½ cup tartare; serves 4 as an appetizer*

NOTE: *If you hesitate to serve raw beef, you can shape the beef paste into small patties (this recipe makes 12 patties about ½ inch across), slide them onto small skewers if you wish, brush them with a little sesame oil, and grill or broil them. Serve as an appetizer, as one dish of many in a rice meal, or as an ingredient for wrapping in rice paper roll-ups (see Note, page 177).*

HUI BEEF STEW WITH CHICK-PEAS AND ANISE

[*niu rou fang zang* — CENTRAL YUNNAN]

Hui is the name given in China to people of Han Chinese ethnicity who are Muslim. There are large communities of Hui in western Yunnan, perhaps descendants of the soldiers of Kublai Khan's army who swept through conquering the region in 1237. Hui cuisine has a strongly Central Asian flavor: flatbreads, simmered meats without many vegetables, and, of course, no pork, just lamb or beef. This hearty stew is great for cold winter evenings. Make plenty, because it makes wonderful leftovers. (You can also make it with lamb.)

Serve with rice or flatbreads and a plate of Yunnan Greens (page 151) or Simple Dali Cauliflower (page 158). To spice things up, put out a dish of Yunnanese Chile Pepper Paste (page 27).

2 cups dried chick-peas, 4 cups cooked chick-peas,
    with their cooking liquid, or 4½ cups canned chick-peas,
    rinsed and drained
Water
3 tablespoons peanut or vegetable oil or beef drippings
2 pounds stewing beef, cut into approximately 2-inch chunks,
    or substitute stewing lamb
2 cups coarsely chopped onions
2 star anise (3 if using lamb)
1 tablespoon salt, or to taste
¼ teaspoon Sichuan peppercorns, ground to a powder
2 Thai dried red chiles
4 scallions, trimmed, cut lengthwise in half, and then cut into
    2-inch lengths (optional)
3 tablespoons Dry-Roasted Sesame Seeds (page 308) (optional)

If using uncooked chick-peas, place in a large pot with water to cover by 3 inches. Bring to a vigorous boil, then boil for 15 minutes. Drain, then return to the pot and add 8 cups water. Bring to a vigorous boil and skim off any foam, then reduce the heat to maintain a strong simmer and cook half-covered until the chick-peas are just tender, 2 to 3 hours. Remove from the heat and set the pot aside.

While the chick-peas are cooking, prepare the beef: In a large wok or a large heavy skillet, heat the oil or drippings over high heat. Add the meat (in two batches if your wok or skillet seems small) and sear, turning and stirring to expose all surfaces to the hot pan, until all the surfaces have changed color. Add the onions and star anise, lower the heat to medium, and cook until the onions are very soft, about 10 minutes. Add 1 teaspoon salt and the Sichuan pepper and cook for another 5 minutes. Remove the pan from the heat and set aside.

When ready to proceed, place the pot of cooked chick-peas back on the stove, or, if using previously cooked or canned chick-peas, place them in a large heavy pot. Add the meat mixture to the chick-peas, then add water, enough to just cover the meat. Add the dried chiles and the remaining 2 teaspoons salt, raise the heat, and bring the stew almost to a boil. Lower the heat and cook at a simmer, uncovered, for about 3 hours, until the meat is very tender and the chick-peas almost melting. Stir occasionally, and add extra water if the stew seems to be getting dry. (*Once cooked, the stew can be set aside until 10 minutes before serving; if the wait will be longer than 2 hours, cool to room temperature, then refrigerate in a covered container, for up to 3 days. The stew can also be frozen for up to 2 months. Place it in a large pot over medium heat and bring almost to a boil before proceeding.*)

About 5 minutes before serving, if you wish, stir the scallions and sesame seeds into the stew. Taste for seasonings and adjust if necessary.

SERVES *8*

SALT AND SALTY: A few years ago, we discovered a book entirely on the subject of salt and brining in Southeast Asia, called *Le Sel de la vie en Asie du Sud-est* ("The Salt of Life in Southeast Asia"; see Bibliography). It discusses salt extraction in Cambodia and Thailand. It describes in detail *prahok*, *padek*, and *mam*, the Khmer, Lao-Thai, and Vietnamese fermented fish pastes. It discusses the modern-day fish sauces, liquid and milder than the pastes: *tuk traey* in Cambodia, *nam pla* in Thailand, *nam pa* in Lao, and *nuoc mam* in Vietnam (see Fermented Fish, page 220).

The book is a treasure, but, unfortunately, nowhere does it address one of our basic questions: What is it about fish sauce that makes it mildly addictive? We know it's not just us. Whole nations feel the same way. And, as with olive oil, people always prefer the fish sauce they've grown up with, the fish sauce from their region.

In the spring of 1975, I was in Paris, staying with the uncle of a friend. He was a retired doctor of Vietnamese origin named Tanh, a longtime resident of France. His older brothers' families were still in Vietnam. Over the years, he'd bought several apartments in Paris, just in case they ever needed to leave.

We sat in the living room watching the fall of Saigon on television. As events moved swiftly on the other side of the world, Tanh predicted that Vietnam would be cut off from trade and contact with the West for some time. "We won't be able to get *nuoc mam*," he said, "only that mild Thai fish sauce." So he sent me off to buy what bottles of Vietnamese fish sauce I could find. Others had had the same idea; in each shop, there were only a few bottles left on the shelves. Tanh stored his carefully in the cellar.

Ten months later, on a cold gray February day, nineteen members of his family, aged six to seventy-four, arrived in Paris, on twenty-four hours' notice, with only the clothes on their backs.

We love the array of bottled fish sauces sold at markets, but how to choose one? The best fish sauce, we think, is light colored and fairly clear (rather than dark and cloudy), contains no sugar, and has only three ingredients: anchovies, salt, water. We prefer fish sauces made in Thailand; they're a little milder than the Vietnamese.

PORK

We once spent the lunar new year in a large Lisu village not far from Pai, in northern Thailand. For three days and nights, people in their New Year's finery danced, ate, and played music, but what we most remember, more than all the color and sound, is the abundance of pigs: piglets roaming in packs, bigger pigs nosing in the red dirt for scraps, and pigs in the evening coming at a run when whistled home like children, eager for their supper of more scraps. When we'd go for a walk on a trail out of the village, we'd be followed by pigs. Pigs, pigs, pigs.

It's impossible to overestimate the value of pigs in Southeast Asia. Pork is a main ingredient in everything from stir-fries to simmered dishes to grilled sausages. Even in a vegetable dish, or a green salad, there will often be a

RIGHT: *You don't need to go to the market in Phonsavan, Laos, for good-tasting pork sausages; making your own is remarkably easy (see* SPICY NORTHERN SAUSAGE, *page 256, and* VERY GARLICKY SAUSAGE, *page 258).* OPPOSITE: *At ease in boats from childhood, like most people in the Mekong Delta, this man stands in his boat at a floating market near Cantho, Vietnam.*

small amount of pork to give an extra depth of flavor. The words for meat and pork are often the same.

In this chapter, we've grouped all the dishes that use pork as an important ingredient (except pork soup, which is in the Soup chapter), from easy stir-fries like Quick Khmer Pork with Green Beans (page 238) to simmered dishes such as Luang Prabang Pork Stew with Bitter Greens (page 245). Many of the dishes in the Mekong pork repertoire start by mincing fresh ham or other pork roast meat. It's so versatile. We've discovered that with a food processor, finely chopping pork and then combining it with other flavorings to make, for example, Spicy Northern Sausage (page 256), Aromatic Lemongrass Patties (page 251), or Vietnamese Grilled Pork Balls (page 252), is very, very easy. Then onto the grill they go.

For scooping up Mekong salsas at home, we can buy fried pork skin in packages labeled "chicharrones," but in northern Thailand and Laos, fried pork skin is made fresh at the morning market.

QUICK KHMER PORK WITH GREEN BEANS

[*cha sangdek khoua* — CAMBODIA]

This mild-tasting meat and vegetable dish from Phnom Penh makes an ideal complement and balance for hot-and-sour soup or dishes with strong chile heat. It is traditionally made with yard-long beans (*sangdek khoua* in Khmer), but you can substitute green beans (called *sangdek barang*, or "foreign beans," in Khmer).

Serve with rice and a soup or stew. Put out a condiment dish of *tuk traey* ("fish sauce") with a bird chile, whole or minced, floating in it.

2 tablespoons vegetable or peanut oil or lard

4 to 6 cloves garlic, smashed and minced
  (about 1½ tablespoons)

½ pound boneless lean pork (such as fresh ham or trimmed
  pork shoulder), thinly sliced across the grain

1 teaspoon sugar

½ teaspoon salt, or to taste

1 tablespoon Thai fish sauce, or to taste

2 cups green beans or yard-long beans cut into 1½-inch lengths

¼ cup water

2 tablespoons coriander leaves (optional)

In a large wok or wide heavy pan, heat the oil or lard over medium-high heat. When it is hot, add the garlic and cook until golden, about 20 seconds. Add the pork, sugar, and salt, and stir-fry, using your spatula to separate the slices of pork, and expose all the surfaces to the hot wok, until all the meat has changed color. Splash in the fish sauce, add the beans, and cook for 2 minutes, then add the water. Bring to a boil and cook for about 3 more minutes (time will vary depending on the tenderness of the beans); the beans should be cooked but still have some crunch and life and be very green. Taste for seasonings and adjust if necessary. Sprinkle on the coriander leaves, if you wish, and serve on a flat plate or in a shallow bowl.

SERVES *2 to 4 as part of a rice meal*

QUICK KHMER PORK WITH GREEN BEANS *is pictured on page 240, with* AROMATIC JASMINE RICE *(page 90).*

STIR-FRIED YUNNAN HAM
[YUNNAN]

In the course of our long bumpy journey through southern Yunnan, we stopped for lunch one day at a small family-run restaurant/truck stop. We sat in the sunny courtyard behind the restaurant, sheltered from the wind. There were cabbages hanging on a line to sun-dry, and in the kitchen, there were hams hanging alongside strings of garlic and dried chiles. The owner's children came out to eye us, then shyly invited us over to watch their small television, turning it up louder. There was a procession, and solemn martial music, for this was the day of Deng Xiao Ping's state funeral. Beijing felt very far away.

One of the dishes we were served at the restaurant was a version of this simple Yunnanese classic: pork slices fried in flavored oil. It can be made with Yunnan ham or the famous (but hard to find here) three-layered pork of Yunnan. Far from Yunnan, we substitute prosciutto, salted air-dried pork from Italy. Buy it in slices, or more economically, see if you can find an "end," the tip of the joint that is too difficult for the butcher to turn into beautiful slices and thus costs much less. If you are using prosciutto or ham, follow the recipe; if you have access to three-layered pork, deep-fry it in 2 inches of hot oil with the flavorings.

Be sure to accompany the ham with a moist dish such as Yunnan Greens (page 151) and a soup, as well as rice.

2 tablespoons peanut or vegetable oil or lard

½ teaspoon five-spice powder, or substitute ⅛ teaspoon ground cinnamon, 2 whole cloves, and 1 star anise (or ¼ teaspoon anise seeds)

1 teaspoon sugar

¼ pound thinly sliced Yunnan or other cured ham or prosciutto, *not* trimmed of fat, cut into pieces about 1 by ½ inch

¼ cup coriander leaves or flat-leaf parsley sprigs (optional)

Heat the oil or lard in a large wok or a heavy skillet over medium-high heat. Toss in the spice powder or spices and stir-fry briefly. Add the sugar and stir to mix well. Toss in the ham and stir-fry for about 1½ minutes, pressing the meat against the hot wok, until it is changing color and the fat on the meat is crisping and browning. Transfer to a plate lined with a paper towel. (Once the oil has cooled, pour it through a cheesecloth-lined sieve into a clean dry container and discard the debris. Store the flavored oil in the refrigerator to use for stir-frying.)

Serve the meat on a small plate, hot or at room temperature, plain or garnished with fresh coriander or parsley sprigs.

SERVES *4 as part of a rice meal*

NOTE: *Leftovers are very good in sandwiches (Saigon Subs, page 287, or others) or, finely chopped, as a topping for congee or noodles or an ingredient in fried rice.*

Evening light on the Mekong in Luang Prabang.

PHNOM PENH NIGHTS: My seatmate on the Bangkok–Phnom Penh flight was a Belgian engineer-entrepreneur named Sandy who'd been living in Phnom Penh for about three years. The coup (Hun Sen pushing Ranariddh out) had taken place a month earlier, and many in the foreign community had left town, so Sandy was taking care of a friend's house for a while.

He offered me his apartment, a beautiful loft space overlooking the river, and I happily settled into a routine. Every morning I'd go out early to take photographs, then come back in time to go to the market with Sao Phenha, Sandy's maid. She was in her twenties, shy, but also confident. She'd grown up in the countryside and was now working in Phnom Penh to avoid her unhappy marriage. We had the language of gesture, but not spoken language, in common. We'd snack on noodles in the market and taste samples as we shopped. She taught me so much, both there and in the kitchen. Sometimes her girlfriends would come by and giggle at the sight of me. One spoke French; I was dismayed when she explained that they thought it strange that a foreign woman wanted to learn about Khmer food, rather than preferring French or Thai or Vietnamese.

In the evening, Sandy would turn up with his Vietnamese girlfriend and we'd all go out together. One night we ate out on the street, delicious Cambodian hot pot. Another night, we dined at a large fancy restaurant that catered to expats and to businessmen with money. On the menu were Thai and Vietnamese dishes as well as a few Cambodian specialties, and onstage a singer-dancer from the Philippines.

After eating, we'd go barhopping. This was Sandy's world, and everybody knew him. He had sold his very successful bar just before the coup, lucky for him. One night we stopped in there and found the place nearly empty. There were mirrors on two walls and a sparkling ball to make glittery reflections round the room. Several women in sleek long satin dresses were hanging around, chatting or moving to the music, waiting for action that wasn't happening. We went on to another bar, which was more of the same.

Then a group of men arrived. They were mostly French diplomats, partying in honor of one man who was leaving the next day for a post in Africa. There was a little dancing, the women undulating with each other, the men drinking and occasionally fondling the women. The women were Vietnamese who'd come to Phnom Penh looking for work, mostly of the long-term-mistress variety. One, beautiful in a bare-backed green silk sheath, told me she'd left her child in Vietnam five years ago, with her parents. She sent money back to them each month. She'd had a two-year relationship in Phnom Penh with a man from France, and had borne his child. Now the lover had gone back home, taking the baby. She had pictures. "My baby will have a better life there," she said, "and maybe someday I'll have the money to visit them."

Next day, on my plane out, there was the French diplomat, looking a little the worse for wear, off to new fields, new bars, new women.

Near the Mekong in the center of Phnom Penh, not far from the royal palace, is a shrine where people come to pray at all hours.

STIR-FRIED PORK AND TOMATO

[*hong san du* — YUNNAN]

Chunks of tart green tomato, softened in the hot wok, give this Yunnanese stir-fry a fresh distinctive taste, though it also works well with ripe red tomatoes. There is some heat from the chiles (this will vary with the chiles you have available) and a smooth succulence from the chopped pork and the dash of sesame oil that rounds out the dish. Make this just before you wish to serve it; it will take you less than ten minutes. Leftovers (if you're lucky) are delicious the next day.

⅓ pound pork (such as trimmed shoulder or butt)
2 to 3 long medium-hot green chiles (such as Cubanelles,
    Anaheim, or Hungarian wax)
2 tablespoons peanut or vegetable oil
½ pound tomatoes, preferably mixed red and green,
    cut into ¾-inch dice (about 2 cups)
¾ teaspoon salt, or to taste
1 teaspoon roasted sesame oil
1 teaspoon cornstarch, dissolved in 2 tablespoons water

Use a cleaver to thinly slice the pork, then cut crosswise to coarsely mince. Set aside.

Trim the stems from the chiles, then make one cut lengthwise in each to expose the seeds; strip them out and discard. Roll-cut the chiles crosswise on the diagonal into approximately ¾-inch chunks: Lay each one on the cutting board and slice, rotating the chile a quarter turn between slices. You should have about 1 cup.

Place all the ingredients near your stovetop. Have a serving plate ready.

Heat a wok or large heavy skillet over high heat until hot, then add the oil. When the oil is hot, add the pork and stir-fry, separating the meat to expose all surfaces to the heat, until it has all changed color, about 2 minutes. Add the chiles and tomatoes and stir-fry for about 3 minutes, until the chiles are beginning to soften and the tomatoes are getting tender. Add the salt and stir-fry for another minute or so, until the chiles are softened and the tomatoes are soft but still have some shape, then add the sesame oil. Stir briefly, then stir the cornstarch mixture well and add it to the wok. Stir-fry for about 30 seconds, until the sauce thickens, then turn out onto the serving plate and serve hot.

SERVES *2 to 4 as part of a rice meal*

LUANG PRABANG PORK STEW
WITH BITTER GREENS

[*oaw' moo sai pakkat* — LAOS]

Home from our first time in northern Laos, we tried to describe to friends the distinctive taste of Luang Prabang food. There's a certain acid-bitter aroma and taste that appears in at least one dish per meal and is strangely appetizing. But all the words we used didn't convey how special and delicious that taste was. It wasn't until we figured out how to make this stew, and then fed it to friends, that we felt we had communicated the pleasures of Luang Prabang food. It made our guests reach for more: seconds, and then third helpings. . . .

The secret to this flavor balance is the long, slow cooking of the dill, greens, and wild lime leaves. This dish is another incentive for buying lots of wild lime leaves whenever you find them, then sealing them in plastic and storing them in the freezer.

You might accompany this stew with Simple Dali Cauliflower (page 158) or Classic Mixed Vegetable Stir-fry (page 151), as well as a salsa, such as Rich Lao Salsa (page 39) or Grilled Tomato Salsa (page 44).

About ½ pound fairly lean pork (shoulder or trimmed butt)

2 tablespoons minced pork fat or vegetable oil

¼ cup coarsely chopped shallots

2 tablespoons minced garlic

4 cups water

¾ pound Chinese mustard greens, Chinese broccoli, or
    broccoli rabe, cut into 2-inch lengths

3 to 4 stalks dill (about 1 ounce)

About 5 Chinese chives, cut into 1-inch lengths (approximately
    ¼ cup), or substitute ¼ cup sliced regular chives

5 fresh or frozen wild lime leaves

2 tablespoons Thai fish sauce

Greens from 3 scallions, finely chopped

Freshly ground black pepper

Thinly slice the pork into strips about 1½ inches long and ½ inch wide and set aside.

If using pork fat, place a large heavy pot over medium heat and toss in the fat; when it has melted, raise the heat to high. Or, if using vegetable oil, place the pot over high heat, add the oil, and heat until very hot. Toss the shallots and garlic into the pot and stir as they start to soften and change color. Add the sliced pork and stir-fry, using your spatula to separate the pieces and expose all surfaces to the heat, until the pork has changed color. Add the water and then toss in the greens, dill, and chives. Stir to immerse the greens in the water and bring to a boil.

Tear 3 of the lime leaves into coarse pieces and add to the pot. Stir to make sure all the ingredients are immersed, then lower the heat and simmer gently, half covered, for 1 hour. Stir occasionally to make sure nothing is sticking. The dish will cook down, leaving 2½ to 3 cups liquid and very melting greens. Add the fish sauce, stir, and taste for seasonings. (*The stew can be made ahead to this point and set aside until just before you wish to serve it. If leaving for longer than 2 hours, let cool completely, place in a well-sealed nonreactive container, and refrigerate. About 5 minutes before you wish to serve the stew, bring back to a gentle simmer.*)

Add the chopped scallion greens to the stew, stir, and add the remaining lime leaves. Transfer to a serving bowl and generously grind black pepper over. Put the stew on the table with a serving spoon so guests can help themselves. Serve as one of several dishes in a rice meal. Invite your guests to begin with a mound of rice on their plates and then top with some stew, or provide small individual bowls for the stew, so guests can eat it on its own or with their rice.

SERVES *4*

NOTE: *In Luang Prabang, the stew would also be flavored with pieces of a woody stem called* sakhan. *It has dark brown bark that is peeled off before using and a very white interior; it gives an aromatic taste and a slight bitterness, too.*

JUNGLE CURRY

[*gaeng paa moo* — NORTHERN THAILAND]

One of the best jungle curries we ever ate was sniffed out by our friend Oie in a small town in western Thailand near the Burmese border. We'd been to visit Three Pagodas Pass and on our way back stopped in Sangkhlaburi to eat. Oie, being from the north, loves jungle curry and makes disparaging remarks about Bangkok food, with its coconut milk and sweetened flavors; Supote, her husband, is from Bangkok, and he just smiles tolerantly. This is our closest approximation of that long-ago jungle curry, a pleasure, especially when eaten with dear friends.

Coconuts don't grow in the jungle and are not a mainstay in northern Thai cooking. The name "jungle curry" is a way of saying "no coconut milk." We're told it was traditionally made with wild boar, for which pork is the usual substitute. For people who like Thai curries but are watching their consumption of coconut milk, this curry is a great discovery. It's also a good introduction to a Southeast Asian rhizome, a relative of ginger known in Thai as *krachai*, that goes into both the curry paste and the curry (see Glossary for more information). The curry is chile-hot, best eaten with lots of sticky rice as well as plain vegetables, raw or steamed, to balance out the heat.

1 pound boneless pork (shoulder or butt)
2 tablespoons vegetable oil or lard
2 tablespoons minced garlic
¼ cup Jungle Curry Paste (recipe follows), or less for less heat
2 cups mild chicken or pork broth or water
¾ pound Asian eggplants (about 3 medium), coarsely chopped
3 round Thai eggplants (see Glossary), quartered (or increase the Asian eggplant to 1 pound)
½ pound yard-long beans or green beans, trimmed and cut into 1-inch lengths
3 tablespoons Thai fish sauce
¼ cup thinly sliced *krachai* (optional)
4 fresh or frozen wild lime leaves, coarsely torn
1 cup Asian basil leaves, or substitute sweet basil leaves
1 teaspoon salt, or to taste

Cut the pork into ¼-inch thick 1- by 2-inch slices and set aside.

Heat a large wok or heavy skillet over high heat. When it is hot, add the oil or lard and swirl to coat the cooking surface, then toss in the garlic. Stir-fry until the garlic begins to turn golden, then add the curry paste and stir-fry for 30 seconds, pressing it against the hot wok. Add the pork slices and stir-fry for 2 to 3 minutes, separating the slices with your spatula. When the slices are lightly browned all over, add the broth or water and bring to a boil. Add the eggplants, beans, fish sauce, the *krachai*, if using, and half the lime leaves and cook for about 8 minutes, or until the vegetables are tender. Add the remaining lime leaves and simmer for another 15 seconds.

Remove from the heat and stir in the basil leaves. Taste for salt and adjust as you wish, stir well, then transfer to a serving bowl and serve with sticky rice.

SERVES *6 with sticky rice*

JUNGLE CURRY PASTE

[*krung gaeng paa* — NORTHERN THAILAND]

This paste is hot, aromatic, and wild-tasting. It's quick to make up, even in a large mortar, and even quicker if you use a blender. Make it whenever you come across fresh *krachai*, and then use it to make Jungle Curry.

¼ cup chopped shallots

1 tablespoon chopped garlic

½ teaspoon salt

1 tablespoon minced galangal

1 heaping tablespoon minced lemongrass (about 1 stalk)

8 Thai dried red chiles, stemmed and minced (with seeds)

1 tablespoon minced coriander roots

1 tablespoon minced *krachai* (optional)

2 fresh or frozen wild lime leaves, deveined and minced

1 tablespoon shrimp paste

Place the shallots and garlic in a large mortar with a pinch of the salt and pound and grind to a paste. Add the remaining ingredients one by one, pounding and grinding them together to make a coarse paste and adding the remaining salt little by little to help with the grinding. *Alternatively*, use a blender to reduce all the ingredients to a paste. If the paste seems very dry, stir in a little water to moisten. Use immediately, or store in a well-sealed glass jar in the refrigerator for up to 5 days or in the freezer for several months.

MAKES *about ⅓ cup paste*

In the villages and towns along the Mekong, even in Phnom Penh, the measured daily rhythms of farming and fishing are never far away.

THE RAW AND THE COOKED: In 1978, I worked in Bangkok with two fellows from northeast Thailand. On Saturday nights, together with several of their friends, we often went out to disco-bar-restaurant sorts of places, enormous places where people would dance and eat, dance and eat. On these occasions, they often gave me a hard time because I wouldn't eat any dish containing raw pork, dishes like *laab dip*, which is made with uncooked meat. I'd tell them they were crazy, that they were going to get trichinosis, but they would laugh and continue to give me a hard time. I sometimes wondered whether or not Thai people are immune to trichinosis, because so many people seemed to eat the raw pork dishes.

One night, in an especially low-lit disco place, I was eating away at the spicy hot dishes on the table and suddenly I realized everyone around me was staring or laughing. "Do you like that one?" they asked, pointing to one particular dish. "Yes, a lot," I replied, and just as I said it I realized . . . raw pork.

Some versions of *laab* are cooked: The Shan cook their pork *laab*, (see Aromatic Minced Pork, Shan Style, page 250) and chicken *laab* is always made with minced chicken that is poached, then dressed with flavorings (see Minced Chicken with Fresh Herbs, page 196). In northern Laos, we learned how to make *laab* from water buffalo meat; some of the meat was poached in boiling water, then added, with the broth and the seasonings, to the finely pounded uncooked meat.

In northern Thailand and among the Bai people in Yunnan, *laab* is most often eaten as *laab dip*, or uncooked *laab*. This horrifies not only many foreigners, but also many people from other parts of the region. In Bai villages, raw pork *laab* is a market food eaten with pleasure by tired and busy buyers and sellers at the weekly markets. The pork is minced with a cleaver, then mixed with salt and chopped hot red chiles. Perhaps the chiles and salt have an antibacterial role. We certainly didn't see any obvious ill effects. . . .

A young pig being carried home from the Shiapin market, near Dali in Yunnan, for fattening up.

AROMATIC MINCED PORK, SHAN STYLE

[*laab moo tai yai* — SHAN STATE]

This pork *laab* is chile-hot, brightened with fresh herbs, and cooked. Unlike the *laab* dishes we've eaten in Thai or Lao households (see Minced Chicken with Fresh Herbs, page 196, for example), here the finely minced meat is fried, not poached. It's flavored as it cooks with a wonderful blend of lemongrass, galangal, chile, and toasted sesame seeds. Don't be surprised at the amount of shallots and garlic in the dish. By the time everything has briefly cooked together, they've blended into the other flavors. For less intense heat, reduce the dried chiles to 4.

Serve this mounded on a plate to accompany sticky or jasmine rice, a simple vegetable dish such as Simple Dali Cauliflower (page 158) or Classic Mixed Vegetable Stir-fry (page 151), and a soup such as Silky Coconut-Pumpkin Soup (page 51). Serve the steamed or fresh vegetables on the side.

6 to 8 cloves garlic, unpeeled

3 tablespoons minced lemongrass (2 to 3 stalks)

2 tablespoons chopped galangal

6 Thai dried red chiles

1 teaspoon salt

1 tablespoon Dry-Roasted Sesame Seeds (page 308)

2 tablespoons peanut or vegetable oil

½ cup chopped shallots

¾ pound ground pork

⅓ to ½ cup chopped scallion greens

½ cup coarsely chopped coriander

¼ cup minced fresh mint

ACCOMPANIMENTS

Steamed Vegetable Plate (page 69) or sliced cucumber and
   leaf lettuce or small wedges of Savoy cabbage

Heat a heavy skillet over medium-high heat, add the garlic cloves, and dry-roast until the skins are well browned or blackened. (Or place the garlic cloves on a fine-mesh rack on a gas or charcoal grill and cook until well blackened.) When the cloves are cool enough to handle, peel off and discard the skins and place the garlic in a large mortar or in a blender or food processor. Add the lemongrass, galangal, chiles, and salt and pound or process to a paste. Add the sesame seeds and pound or process briefly, then set aside.

Heat a heavy skillet or a wok over high heat. When it is hot, add the oil and swirl to coat the pan, then toss in the shallots and reduce the heat to medium. Cook, stirring frequently, until the shallots are tender and golden brown, about 4 minutes. Add the chile paste and stir to break it up and expose it to the heat. Add the pork and cook, stirring to break up any larger clumps and expose all the meat to the heat, until all the meat has changed color, then let simmer for another 2 minutes. Stir in the scallion greens, coriander, and half the chopped mint.

Remove from the heat and mound on a plate. Sprinkle over the remaining mint. Serve with rice and with the vegetable plate or sliced cucumber and lettuce or cabbage. Use the fresh ingredients to scoop up mouthfuls of meat, or spoon it over the rice.

SERVES *4 as part of a rice meal*

NOTE: *There's a similar version of this dish made by the Tai Lu people in and around Muang Sing, in northern Laos, where they call it* saa. *They cook the coarsely minced pork with lemongrass, scallions, garlic, and salt.*

AROMATIC LEMONGRASS PATTIES
[*mak paen* — LAOS]

There's a small evening market in Luang Prabang, just between the post office and the river. Tiny candles light the tables where vendors sit selling grilled fish, dark red salsas, sticky rice, grilled chicken, spicy curries, and piles of fresh and plain-cooked vegetables to eat with whatever foods you buy.

One of our favorite local specialties in the market is *mak paen*, small aromatic grilled meat patties. Luckily, we've discovered that they are almost as easy to make at home as they were to pick up at the evening market (though minus a considerable element of atmosphere . . .).

Serve these hot, or set aside on a plate to cool, then wrap well and store in the refrigerator for up to 3 days. Use, thinly sliced, as a topping for Vietnamese Savory Crepes (page 280), or for noodles, or as an ingredient in Saigon Subs (page 287).

½ **pound boneless reasonably lean pork (shoulder or butt, trimmed of most fat)**
¼ **cup sliced shallots**
1 **stalk lemongrass, trimmed and minced**
¼ **teaspoon salt**
¼ **teaspoon freshly ground black pepper**

Thinly slice the pork. Transfer to a food processor, add the shallots lemongrass, salt, and pepper and process for about 30 seconds or until the mixture forms an even-textured ball. Turn out into a bowl. *Alternatively*, use a cleaver to finely chop the pork, first in one direction and then in the other, then fold the meat over on itself and chop again until smooth, discarding any fat or connective tissue. Add the shallots and lemongrass and continue mincing until the mixture is smooth, then transfer to a bowl.

Set out several plates. Working with wet hands, pick up a scant 2 tablespoons of the pork mixture and shape it into a flat patty 2 to

3 inches in diameter. Place on a plate and repeat with the remaining mixture; do not stack the patties. You'll have 7 or 8 patties.

Heat a large heavy skillet (or two smaller heavy skillets) over medium-high heat. Rub lightly with an oiled paper towel and add the patties. Lower the heat to medium and cook until golden on the first side, then turn over and cook for another 3 to 4 minutes, until golden and cooked through. As the patties cook, use a spatula to flatten them against the hot surface. (You can also grill or broil the patties until golden and cooked through, turning them over partway through cooking.)

Serve hot, with rice, a vegetable dish, and a salsa.

MAKES *7 or 8 patties; serves 4 as part of a rice meal*

NOTES: *A close relative of these patties, called* cha heo, *is made in markets in the Mekong Delta. The minced flavored meat is shaped into fairly thin strips about 2 inches long and ¾ inch wide, then threaded onto skewers and cooked over a grill. As the meat cooks, it's brushed with a little sweetened coconut milk, making it very succulent. To try it, before you begin grilling, warm some coconut milk and dissolve some palm sugar and a little fish sauce in it.*

TO MAKE A THAI-LAO SALAD *(a yam) with this aromatic flavored pork, slice the cooked patties into thin strips and place in a bowl with an equal volume of thinly sliced shallots, along with some finely chopped fresh mint and/or coarsely torn coriander leaves. If you have some leftover cooked sausages (see Index) or Vietnamese Baked Cinnamon Pâté (page 259), or Vietnamese Grilled Pork Balls (page 252), cut them into bite-sized pieces and add to the salad. Dress with a lime juice and fish sauce dressing such as the one used for Turkey with Mint and Hot Chiles (page 202). Don't be shy about using hot chiles in the dressing, and use plenty of Aromatic Roasted Rice Powder (page 309) if you have any handy. Serve with sticky rice or jasmine rice.*

VIETNAMESE GRILLED PORK BALLS
[*nem nuong* — VIETNAM]

If you want to please children or guests who are cautious about "foreign food," make up a batch of these easy-to-eat treats. They're prepared all over Vietnam, in restaurants, street stalls, and home kitchens. They're also sold at Vietnamese-run restaurants and street stands in northeast Thailand, Laos, and Cambodia.

With a food processor, reducing the pork to a smooth paste is very easy. Shaping the balls is surprisingly quick, and it can be done several hours ahead of cooking if it's more convenient. Leftovers freeze well, wrapped in foil.

1 pound lean pork (such as fresh ham or trimmed shoulder), thinly sliced

¼ cup minced shallots

¼ cup minced garlic

2 tablespoons Vietnamese or Thai fish sauce

1 teaspoon sugar

Generous grinding of black pepper

2 ounces minced pork fat (about ¼ cup)

2 tablespoons Aromatic Roasted Rice Powder (page 309) or Roasted Rice Powder (page 308)

Peanut or vegetable oil

ACCOMPANIMENTS

Vietnamese Herb and Salad Plate (page 68), including plenty of leaf lettuce, herb sprigs, and cucumber slices

Vietnamese Must-Have Table Sauce (*nuoc cham*, page 28) or Vietnamese Peanut Sauce (*nuoc leo*, page 28)

Place the pork slices in a bowl with the shallots, garlic, fish sauce, sugar, and black pepper. Turn to mix well, then cover and refrigerate for at least 1 hour and as long as 24 hours. Before proceeding, transfer to the freezer for 30 minutes.

Place the fat in the processor and process to a paste. Add the chilled pork slices with the marinade and process briefly, in pulses, until a ball of rubbery paste forms; you may need to use a rubber spatula to scrape down the sides of the processor bowl. Add the rice powder and process very briefly to blend, then turn out into a bowl. You will have about 2 cups dense-flavored paste. (*The paste can be refrigerated, covered, for up to 24 hours before proceeding.*)

Prepare a grill or preheat the broiler. If using bamboo skewers, soak in water for at least 30 minutes.

Place a little oil in a shallow bowl and use it to oil your hands and two large plates. Scoop up a scant tablespoon of the pork paste and squeeze in the palm of one hand to make a tight round ball. Set on one of the oiled plates, then repeat with the remaining paste. You will have about 35 balls. Slide the balls onto the presoaked bamboo skewers or onto metal skewers, placing 3 or 4 on each skewer. (If the grill is not ready, cover the meatballs with plastic wrap and refrigerate until ready to grill.)

Place skewers on the grill or 5 inches from the broiler heating element and grill or broil for 10 minutes. Turn and continue cooking, then turn again to ensure that all sides get exposed to the heat. The meatballs will be cooked through but still succulent after about 20 minutes. (To check for doneness, cut a meatball in half; the meat should be firm and should have changed color.) Remove to a platter and serve on the skewers, or slide off the skewers and serve on individual plates, 5 or 6 balls per guest.

Serve hot or at room temperature, with the salad plate and small bowls of the dipping sauce.

SERVES *6 as an appetizer or as part of a rice meal*

NOTE: *To serve the pork balls in rice paper roll-ups, follow the instructions on page 177.*

You can also serve the pork balls as a topping for a bowl of noodles (see Morning Market Noodles, page 138, for example) or as an ingredient in a spicy Thai-Lao–style salad (see Notes, page 251).

THE MARKET: To describe a Southeast Asian open-air market, what comes first to mind is the normal, the everyday. There is a meat section, a fish section, colorful fruits and vegetables, people with their bicycles and scooters and their woven baskets held in at the elbow. There is the rich warm light at dawn and then again at dusk, when the market gets crowded and shoppers nudge and twist their way between the stalls. There are the florists, rice merchants, knife sharpeners, coconut graters, ice cutters, eel peelers. There are the pyramids of Day-Glo red and green curry pastes, the mounds of pink shrimp paste, the jars of multicolored pickles, the rows of sausages arranged in wonderful symmetry. At night there is the light of candles and the tired voices of the market people who have been working since dawn, and there is all the roughage, slippery roughage underfoot, from trimming vegetables and peeling fruit.

Markets breathe, they rest, they laugh, they yell. They absorb all the life around them and multiply it. A basket of garlic and shallots is laid out in a Mandalay market garnished with strands of fragrant jasmine and a single red rose. In Phonsavan, in northern Laos, violence erupts at the end of a long day and sixteen people are killed in gunfire.

Early one morning in Phnom Penh, my first morning in Cambodia, I walk, somewhat reluctantly, with my cameras into the busy morning market on 154th Street. I squeeze my way in between rickshaws piled high with passengers and produce. I'm thinking about Cambodia, about all the terrible things that have happened here. I'm a little afraid, afraid to be with my cameras the way I usually am, a little pushy, silly, engaged.

But I make my way into the crowd. I arrange my camera bag, take hold of my two cameras. People are wearing a lot of stripes, clean cotton striped shirts. Must be a fashion; it's a nice fashion. The market has rich blues and greens, overcast tones. There are piles of slivered lemongrass, huge piles. Everything is moist and fresh. There is jicama, good-quality jicama. Good-quality everything, I think. There are tiny take-home packets of sawtooth herb, bird chiles, lemongrass. Beautiful.

I stop for a bowl of hot noodle soup. The morning is still cold; the sun hasn't yet arrived. People are laughing, shopping. I squat against a wall with my bowl and a pair of chopsticks, my cameras awkwardly hanging from around my neck. I'm visible in the market but it's okay.

Back on my feet, working my way through the market, it's slow going. So much to see. On a side street, there is a busy wholesale section, shop houses and trucks with coconuts, papayas, and bananas. I photograph without hesitation; there's more space to move, and it's easier to frame. There're monks passing by with pale pastel umbrellas. There's a family noodle stand, three generations of women working. Maybe four? There's . . .

Suddenly there is noise, commotion, lots of noise. I look away from my cameras and, yikes, an elephant, *an elephant*, coming toward me. People are laughing. There is an elephant coming toward me, and people are laughing. I leap to one side, a leap-to-avoid-an-elephant leap. I'm okay, red in the face, but okay. The elephant is after someone else, having fun. It steals a dozen bananas, scarfs them down.

No one argues with an elephant.

SPICY NORTHERN SAUSAGE

[*sai ouah* — NORTHERN THAILAND, LAOS]

This delicious succulent sausage from northern Thailand has some chile heat and complex aromatic flavors. If you don't want to make link sausages, use the recipe to make patties, for grilling or frying.

Sausage making is easy, we've found, and requires no special equipment, apart from an easily contrived homemade tool for stuffing (see method). It's easier and more fun to work with a friend, especially the first time you do it, so there's an extra set of hands to help as you get familiar with the gestures you need to make to get the filling into the sausage casing. The work is not finicky and the results are truly dazzling.

The sausages should cure for 24 to 48 hours in a cool place. If you wish, after 24 hours, you can wrap them in a plastic bag and freeze them until you're ready to grill, fry, or broil them.

The cooked sausages or patties make a delicious snack or appetizer. They can be eaten with tasty accompaniments, as described below, or used as an ingredient in a Thai-Lao-style salad (see Notes, page 251, for instructions).

¼ pound pork fat, coarsely chopped

1 pound boneless lean pork, cut into approximately ½-inch cubes

½ cup chopped shallots

4 medium to large cloves garlic

5 fresh or frozen wild lime leaves, sliced into ribbons (about 2 tablespoons packed)

¼ cup chopped coriander roots and stems

2 tablespoons minced lemongrass (1 large stalk)

1 tablespoon minced galangal, or substitute 1 teaspoon minced ginger

5 bird chiles, preferably red, stemmed and minced

¾ teaspoon salt

Approximately 45 inches pork sausage casings

ACCOMPANIMENTS

3 tablespoons ginger cut into matchsticks

1 cup coriander leaves

3 scallions, trimmed, sliced lengthwise, and then cut into 1-inch lengths

2 to 3 bird chiles, minced

1 European cucumber, sliced

Generous heap of lettuce leaves

Place the fat in a food processor and process to a paste. Add the meat and process just until a springy pink ball forms. Turn out into a bowl.

Place the shallots and garlic in the food processor and mince. Add the lime leaves, coriander roots, lemongrass, galangal or ginger, and chiles and mince, using a spatula to wipe down the sides as necessary. Add the meat mixture together with the salt, and pulse several times to blend all the ingredients well. Transfer back to the bowl, cover, and place in the refrigerator.

To make the sausages, untangle the sausage casing and rinse under cold water. Then open one end with your fingers and place under a gently running tap so that the water flows through the casing and rinses it. Squeeze the water out of the casing, then tie a simple knot at one end.

Unless you have a mechanical sausage maker, the easiest way to stuff the sausages is to use a large clean clear plastic 2-liter soda bottle: Cut it in half, about 6 inches from the bottom. The top half is your new sausage-making tool.

Fit the open end of the sausage casing over the top of the soda bottle, then slide it up along the neck of the bottle as far as it will go (about 1 inch). With the cut edge braced against your torso, use both hands to slide the rest of the sausage casing up onto the neck of the bottle. It may seem as if it won't fit, but it will; once it's all on except the knotted end, hold it firmly on the neck with the fingers of one hand.

Take the sausage mixture out of the refrigerator. With your free hand, scoop up a small handful of the sausage filling mixture, place it inside the bottle, and use your index finger to push it through the neck of the bottle and into the casing. It's easiest to fill the casing if you're working very close to the bottle, so hold tightly to the casing and bottle top with the fingers of one hand to maintain tension as you stuff the casing, gradually releasing a little more until you have 4 inches of tightly stuffed casing. Try to keep air out of the casing. Twist the casing to seal off the first sausage, twisting it four or five times to make a space before the next one. Let it hang down as you make the next sausage. Repeat to make the remaining sausages, maintaining tension and trying to fill each full without any air pockets. Your hands will soon get comfortable and you'll be surprised how quickly you reach the end of your length of casing. *Note:* As you twist the later sausages, make sure the earlier ones don't come untwisted. If they do, twirl them again. The stuffing is soft, so twist to force it tightly into the casing.

Tie a knot to seal off the last sausage (like tying off a balloon) and lay sausages on a plate in a loose coil. You'll have about 8 sausages. (If you have any filling left over, you can use it for patties to fry or grill like Aromatic Lemongrass Patties, page 251.) Cover loosely and leave in the refrigerator to stand for at least 24 hours. They'll give off a little liquid, which you should pour off, and they'll firm up. Cook within 72 hours.

You can fry these in a little oil in a heavy frying pan over medium heat or grill them over a medium fire for about 10 minutes, turning them to expose all surfaces to the heat until nicely browned on all sides. Prick them all over with a fork, toothpick, or fine skewer before cooking.

To serve, cut into long diagonal slices and present on a plate with a platter of the accompaniments. Place a piece of sausage in a lettuce leaf, top with any or all of the other accompaniments, then wrap up and eat.

MAKES *about 8 sausages; serves 4 to 6 as an appetizer*

ISSAAN VERY GARLICKY SAUSAGE

[*sai krok issaan* — NORTHEAST THAILAND, LAOS]

These pork and sticky rice sausages are flavored with the traditional Thai-Lao flavors: coriander roots, black pepper, and garlic, lots of garlic. They're firm and a little chewy, and delicious. The sticky rice seems to soften and blend all the flavors beautifully. They make a wonderful appetizer.

The sausages are traditionally shaped into round 1-inch balls. We make longer (3-inch) sausages, then slice them after cooking. Make whatever version you please.

2 ounces pork fat, coarsely chopped

½ pound boneless lean pork roast or fresh ham, chopped into roughly ½-inch pieces

1 tablespoon minced coriander roots

½ cup chopped garlic

½ teaspoon salt

1 teaspoon freshly ground black pepper

2 cups cooked sticky rice

Approximately 45 inches pork sausage casings

ACCOMPANIMENTS

3 tablespoons ginger cut into matchsticks or small cubes

1 cup coriander leaves

¼ cup Dry-Roasted Peanuts (page 308), coarsely chopped

2 to 3 bird chiles, minced

1 European cucumber, sliced

Generous heap of lettuce leaves

Place the fat in a food processor and process to a paste. Add the meat and process briefly, until a coarse, springy mass forms. Transfer to a bowl.

Place the coriander roots, garlic, salt, and pepper in a mortar or in the processor and finely mince. If using a mortar, transfer to the processor. Add the fat and meat mixture and the cooked rice, breaking it into small chunks as you add it. Pulse several times to mix well. Transfer to a bowl, cover, and refrigerate.

To make the sausages, follow the instructions for Spicy Northern Sausage on page 257, but make the sausages shorter, either the traditional 1-inch round ones or, our preference, about 3 inches long. You'll have about 12 sausages if you make them each about 3 inches long. (If you have any filling left over, you can use it for patties to fry or grill like Aromatic Lemongrass Patties, page 251.)

Refrigerate for at least 24 hours, loosely covered. The sausages will dry out slightly and firm up. Pour off any water they release. Cook within 72 hours.

You can fry these in a little oil in a heavy frying pan over medium heat or grill them over a medium fire for about 10 minutes, turning them to expose all sides to the heat until they are browned all over. Prick them all over with a fork, toothpick, or fine skewer before cooking.

To serve, cut into diagonal slices and present on a plate with a platter of accompaniments. Eat the sausages wrapped in lettuce leaves, topped as you please.

MAKES *about twelve 3-inch sausages; serves 4 to 6 as an appetizer or as part of a rice meal*

VIETNAMESE BAKED CINNAMON PÂTÉ

[*cha que* — VIETNAM]

Food processors have made making sausages and pâtés so easy. Here, lean fresh ham (leg of pork) is flavored and chilled before being processed to a paste with a little fat. The mixture bakes in a medium oven, then is usually served at room temperature.

This smooth-textured pâté has a subtle flavor and is a handy standby to have in your refrigerator or freezer. Serve as a snack, a topping for rice or noodles or noodle soup, or a filling for Saigon Subs (page 287). You can also use the pâté, sliced or cubed, in a Thai- or Vietnamese-style salad, combined with shallots and herbs and dressed in a fish sauce–lime juice dressing (see Notes, page 251, for details).

MARINADE

1 tablespoon potato starch
2 tablespoons Vietnamese fish sauce
1½ teaspoons sugar
¼ teaspoon freshly ground black pepper
2 teaspoons ground cinnamon

1 pound boneless lean fresh ham or trimmed shoulder
   or other roast
1 ounce pork fat

In a medium bowl, stir together the potato starch and fish sauce, then stir in the remaining marinade ingredients. Add enough water to make a fairly liquid paste.

Trim the pork of fat, cut into ¼-inch slices, and put into the marinade. Turn to coat with the marinade, then cover and refrigerate for at least 4 hours, or as long as 24 hours. Before proceeding, place the meat and fat in the freezer for 30 minutes.

Preheat the oven to 350°F. Grease an 8-inch square baking pan.

Place the fat in a food processor and process to a paste. Remove and set aside. Place the chilled meat mixture in the processor and process to a fine paste. Add the fat and pulse briefly to blend the two. Transfer the mixture to the baking pan and press it evenly into the pan with wet hands. Smooth the top and place in the center of the oven.

Bake until browned on top, about 40 minutes. Cool in the pan. Slice into long narrow slices or cut into cubes. Store, well wrapped, in the refrigerator for up to 3 days or in the freezer for up to a month.

MAKES *about 1 pound firm pâté*

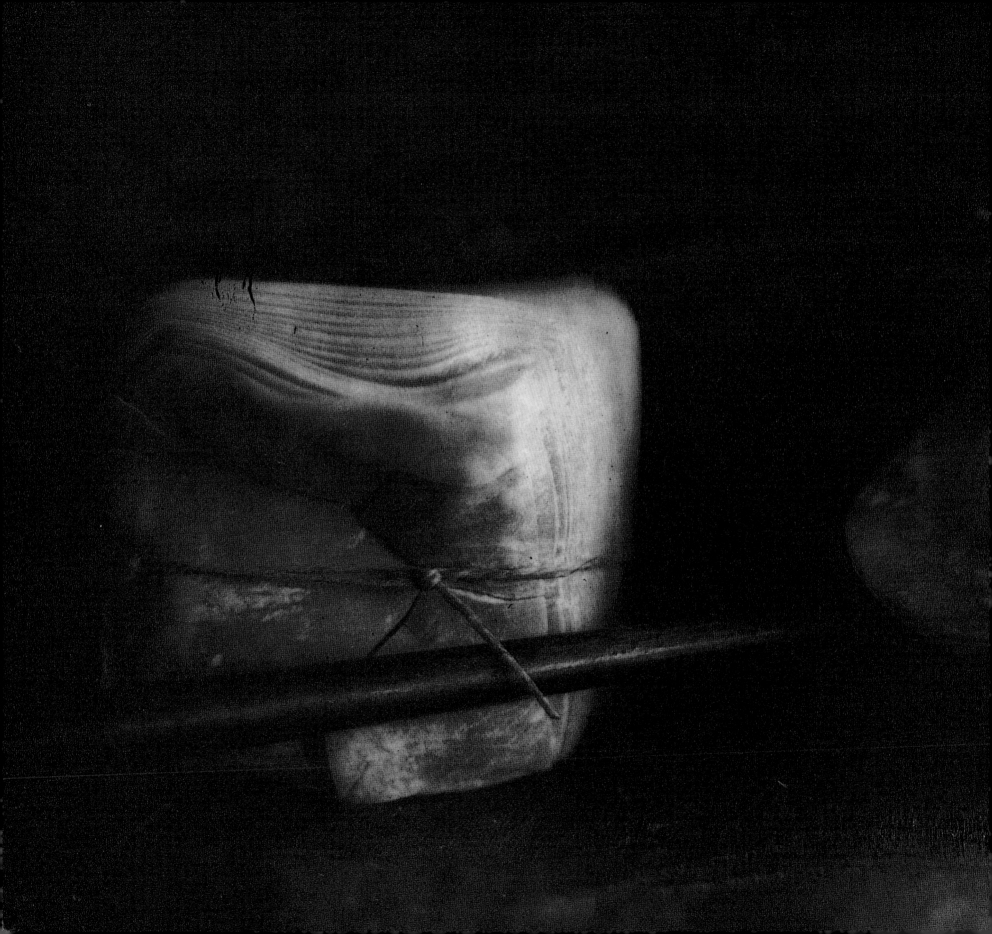

SNACKS AND STREET FOOD

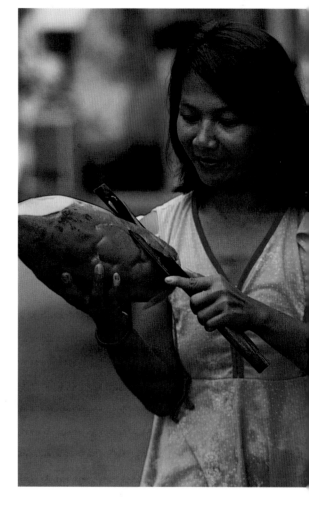

Snacking is a much-loved pastime in Southeast Asia and the preparation of street foods is high art. In larger towns and cities, street foods are available at almost any hour of the day or night, and even in rural areas, even in the smallest village, there is seldom a time when there isn't a snack to be had. Southeast Asia is a snacker's paradise and we love it all, the savory and the sweet, the ingenious combinations of both.

Here we've included recipes for some of our favorite savory snacks and street foods that we think also translate easily into the North American kitchen (sweet snacks are in the next chapter). Some are flavor bundles that guests can nibble (or devour) as they sip drinks and wait to sit down for a meal. These wrapped treats are part of a Lao tradition of *miang,* or small wrapped foods: A highly flavored filling,

often with meat and distinctive spicing, is wrapped in a leaf of lettuce or other green, topped with fresh herbs, drizzled with a little sauce, and then rolled up and eaten in one or two quick mouthfuls. Hot and Spicy Leaf Wraps (page 264) and Beef and Lettuce Roll-ups (page 268) are best served on a platter as roll-your-own treats, because that way they're flexible, allowing each guest to flavor mouthfuls to taste.

Other street foods, like Vietnamese Savory Crepes (page 280) or the familiar and delicious Classic Vietnamese Spring Rolls (page 274), can be served as an appetizer course or as part of a meal, with salad greens, herbs, and rice or noodles. Here too we've included sandwiches—we call them Mekong subs—made with the French-style bread that is a legacy of the French colonial years in Indochina. Like any good snack, they're flexible, flavorful, and easy to eat at any hour.

OPPOSITE RIGHT: *Like mangoes, papayas are eaten both as a vegetable (when green) spiked with salt and chiles, and as a fruit (when ripe).* ABOVE: *A young Akha woman snacks at the morning market in northern Laos.*

A street vendor sits for most of the day assembling Green-Wrapped Flavor Bundles *(page 269) and selling them to passersby.*

HOT AND SPICY LEAF WRAPS

[*miang kham* — CENTRAL LAOS, NORTHEAST THAILAND]

We once helped a young Thai woman and her mother learn how to make bread. They were running a little restaurant in Nathon, on the island of Koh Samui, and wanted to serve sandwiches. They also wanted to learn how to make peanut butter, for many of the young foreign tourists coming to the island were asking for bread and peanut butter.

We spent a great afternoon with them making bread, grinding fresh peanut butter, and chatting. Then we all sat down and snacked on *miang kham,* a delicious little snack from northeast Thailand that we'd never eaten before. They showed us how to put a little roasted coconut on a leaf and top it with a pinch each of ginger, lime, chile, dried shrimp, roasted peanuts, and coriander leaves, then drizzle on the thick salty-sweet sauce, roll up the bundle, and pop it into our mouths. Mouthful after mouthful, we experimented with different proportions of hot and sweet, salty and sour, each time loving the array of bursting flavors as we bit into a bundle.

Since then we've run across *miang kham* in Bangkok as well as in homes in rural Issaan (northeastern Thailand). The sauce ingredients differ from place to place, but the sauce is always salty and sweet; the piles of filling ingredients seldom vary.

This makes a great appetizer for a party or a group of friends.

1 tablespoon shrimp paste

1 tablespoon dried shrimp, minced

2 tablespoons minced shallots

1 tablespoon chopped galangal, or substitute 1 teaspoon
   minced ginger

Pinch of salt

½ cup Dry-Roasted Grated Coconut (page 308)

1 cup water

½ cup palm sugar, or substitute brown sugar

Thai fish sauce or salt to taste

FILLING INGREDIENTS

2 tablespoons fresh lime juice, mixed with 2 tablespoons
   water (optional)

3 tablespoons peeled and cubed ginger, preferably young
   ginger

¼ cup chopped shallots

1½ cups Dry-Roasted Grated Coconut (page 308)

½ cup Dry-Roasted Peanuts (page 308), coarsely chopped

½ cup dried shrimp

1 lime, cut into tiny wedges or cubes (including peel)

1 cup coriander leaves

3 tablespoons minced bird or serrano chiles

2 heads Bibb lettuce, well washed, dried, and separated into
   leaves (or 25 to 30 pepper leaves, if available)

Spread the shrimp paste on a piece of foil wrap about 8 inches by 4 inches, fold it over and seal, then flatten. Place in a hot skillet and dry roast, pressing the package against the hot pan, for about 2 minutes. Turn over and repeat on the other side, then remove from the heat and set aside.

Place the dried shrimp, shallots, galangal or ginger, and salt in a mortar or blender and pound or grind to a paste. Add the shrimp paste and coconut and blend well.

Heat the water in a small nonreactive saucepan and stir in the flavor paste. Add the sugar and stir to dissolve. Bring to a boil, then reduce the heat and simmer until the mixture thickens, about 10 minutes. Remove from the heat. Taste and add fish sauce or salt if you wish; the sauce should be sweet and salty. (*The sauce can be made ahead and then stored, once cooled, in the refrigerator. Before serving, warm it slightly to loosen it.*)

If you have time, place the lime juice and water mixture in a small bowl, add the chopped ginger, and let stand for 5 to 10 minutes. Remove the ginger and place the chopped shallots in the lime juice mixture for 5 to 10 minutes, then drain. This will help prevent the ginger and shallots from discoloring as they sit out on the platter.

Arrange the filling ingredients in attractive piles on a large platter: Put the grated coconut (since it's a larger pile than the others) in the center, either directly on the platter or in a bowl. Place a platter or large bowl of the leaf lettuce nearby. Put out several bowls of the sauce, each with a small spoon to use for drizzling the sauce on the bundles.

Show your guests how to assemble a flavor package (see Headnote), then leave them to it.

SERVES *6 to 8 as an appetizer*

HOT AND SPICY LEAF WRAPS *is pictured on page 266.*

LEFT: *Salad greens displayed in a village market in Laos.* RIGHT: *At the market in Sri Chiang Mai (see page 206), Vietnamese specialties are sold alongside Thai and Lao street foods.*

BEEF AND LETTUCE ROLL-UPS

[*miang neua* — NORTHEAST THAILAND, LAOS]

Like *miang kham* (page 264), this savory snack makes a great appetizer. All the ingredients are set out on a platter, ready to be rolled up into lettuce leaf packets. Guests take a leaf of lettuce, spoon a little beef onto it, and add a pinch or so of each of the other fillings, to taste. Then they spoon on a drizzle of the hot-sour-sweet sauce, roll up the leaf to make a packet, and eat with pleasure.

FILLING INGREDIENTS

½ pound boneless lean beef (such as tenderloin or sirloin),
    cut into ½-inch cubes

½ cup canned or fresh coconut milk (see page 315)

½ teaspoon salt

½ cup Dry-Roasted Peanuts (page 308), coarsely chopped

3 tablespoons peeled and cubed ginger, preferably young
    ginger

½ cup chopped shallots

1 lime, cut into tiny wedges or cubes (including peel)

1 cup chopped mint or celery leaves

2 tablespoons minced bird or serrano chiles

2 medium heads tender leaf lettuce or Bibb lettuce, washed,
    dried, and separated into leaves

SAUCE (SEE NOTE)

1 bird or serrano chile, minced (or use 2 for more heat)

¼ teaspoon salt

1 tablespoon sugar

½ cup sour orange juice, or substitute ¼ cup regular orange
    juice mixed with ¼ cup lime juice

2 tablespoons Dry-Roasted Peanuts (page 308),
    very finely chopped

Place the beef in a heavy pot with the coconut milk and salt. Bring to a gentle boil, reduce the heat and then simmer, stirring occasionally, for 10 minutes. Transfer to a shallow bowl and set out on the table with a small serving spoon. Arrange the remaining filling ingredients in piles on a platter. Put the lettuce leaves on the platter or in a shallow bowl to one side.

To prepare the sauce, place the chile in a mortar with the salt and pound to a paste, then transfer to a bowl and stir in the sugar and juice. Or finely mince the chile, place in a bowl, and stir in the salt, sugar, and juice. Just before serving, stir the peanuts into the sauce. Taste and adjust the seasonings if you wish. Transfer to one or more condiment bowls and set out on the table with several small spoons so guests can drizzle sauce onto their roll-ups.

Show your guests how to assemble a roll-up, then invite them to try.

SERVES *6 as an appetizer*

NOTE: *You can instead use ½ cup Hot and Sweet Dipping Sauce (page 199), with the addition of 2 tablespoons finely chopped Dry-Roasted Peanuts.*

GREEN-WRAPPED FLAVOR BUNDLES
[*miang lao* — L A O S]

Each day we'd pass a smiling woman street vendor who sat deftly rolling up these flavor bundles by the Mekong in Luang Prabang. It was always a pleasure to stop briefly for several good mouthfuls before continuing on our way. Serve these as an appetizer or as part of a meal.

FILLING

½ **pound boneless lean pork (such as fresh ham or loin) or lean ground pork**

1 **tablespoon tamarind pulp, dissolved in ¼ cup warm water**

3 **tablespoons peanut or vegetable oil or pork lard**

½ **cup chopped shallots**

3 **tablespoons minced garlic**

2 **tablespoons palm sugar, or substitute brown sugar**

1 **or 2 tablespoons Thai fish sauce, or to taste**

½ **to 1 teaspoon salt, or to taste**

1 **tablespoon minced ginger**

2 **tablespoons Dry-Roasted Peanuts (page 308), finely chopped**

WRAPPING AND TOPPING

About 30 pieces Pickled Cabbage, Thai Style (page 311 or store-bought) or Bibb lettuce or tender leaf lettuce leaves (or pepper leaves, if available)

1 **stalk lemongrass, trimmed and minced**

2 **tablespoons minced ginger**

2 **to 3 scallions, trimmed and minced**

½ **cup chopped coriander leaves and stems**

If not using ground pork, cut the pork into thin slices, then stack the slices, cut into strips, and then cut crosswise into cubes. Use a cleaver to mince the pork to a reasonably even consistency. Set aside.

Place a sieve over a bowl and press the dissolved tamarind through the sieve; discard the pulp. Set the tamarind juice aside.

Heat a wok over high heat. Add the oil or lard, and, when it is hot, add the shallots and garlic. Stir-fry until golden, then add the pork and stir-fry until it has all changed color, about 4 minutes. Add the sugar, the reserved tamarind juice, the fish sauce, and salt and cook until the liquids have almost evaporated, about 5 minutes. Add the ginger and peanuts and stir-fry for another minute. The mixture should be the consistency of paste and somewhat salty tasting. Adjust seasonings if you wish. Remove from the wok and let cool. You will have about 1½ cups filling. (*The filling can be made ahead and stored in a sealed container in the refrigerator for up to 3 days.*)

To make a flavor package, put a leaf of pickled cabbage or lettuce on the palm of one hand, then scoop up a scant tablespoon of the filling and place it on the leaf. Sprinkle on a pinch of minced lemongrass, a little ginger, a pinch of scallions, and another of coriander. Fold the leaf over to make a bundle, or leave it open, like a filled cup, and place on a platter. Repeat with the remaining ingredients and greens. Or instead, serve these roll-your-own style: Show your guests how to assemble a bundle, then invite them to serve themselves.

MAKES *about 2 dozen flavor bundles*

NOTE: *The flavored filling also makes a great topping for noodles, with or without broth (see Morning Market Noodles, page 138). You could also use it as a filling for Saigon Subs (page 287).*

STEAMED PORK DUMPLINGS

[*sakhoo sai moo* — NORTHEAST THAILAND]

These yummy treats are sold in village markets in Issaan (northeastern Thailand), early in the morning, before sunrise, as mist comes off the river in the pink dawn. People buy them in batches of ten, with a separate bag of condiments, toppings, and leafy greens, and take them home for eating later.

Sakhoo sai moo are small round steamed dumplings made with a simple tapioca dough and filled with a savory pork mixture. They're a beautiful translucent white when cooked, and they can be made several hours ahead, for they're best served not hot, but at room temperature. (They also freeze well, so you can make them days in advance, then resteam them to defrost them before serving.)

Serve them as a snack or an appetizer. Steamed pork dumplings are always served with hot chiles, fried garlic, and fresh herbs, so you can wrap each one, with the extra flavorings, in a small leaf of lettuce and make a delicious couple of mouthfuls. The tapioca dough is a little chewy, yet soft; the filling has crunch and a seductive sweet-salt taste.

14 ounces small Asian-style tapioca pearls
2 cups boiling water
½ pound boneless lean pork (such as fresh ham or trimmed shoulder)
3 tablespoons vegetable or peanut oil
2 tablespoons minced garlic
1 tablespoon minced coriander roots
¼ cup finely chopped salted radish, rinsed and drained
¾ cup finely chopped Dry-Roasted Peanuts (page 308)
2 tablespoons Thai fish sauce
3 tablespoons palm sugar, or substitute brown sugar
½ tablespoon coarsely ground black pepper
Banana or cabbage leaves to line the steamers

GARNISH

1 medium head leaf or Bibb lettuce, washed, dried, and separated into leaves, large leaves torn in half
About 1 tablespoon Garlic Oil (page 310)
2 to 3 tablespoons Fried Garlic (page 310) or Fried Shallots (page 310)
¼ cup coriander or mint leaves
2 tablespoons chopped bird or serrano chiles

Place the tapioca in a medium bowl and gradually add the water, stirring. Knead to a smooth paste, then cover with plastic wrap and set aside for 1 to 1½ hours.

Meanwhile, very thinly slice the pork into strips (this is easier if the meat is cold) and then cut crosswise into very small cubes; set aside.

Heat the oil in a wok or large heavy skillet and, when it is hot, toss in the garlic and coriander roots. Stir-fry until the garlic starts to turn golden, about 15 seconds, then toss in the pork. Stir-fry until all the pork has changed color, about 3 minutes. Add the radish, peanuts, fish sauce, sugar, and pepper and stir-fry briefly until the sugar has melted and the ingredients are blended. Set aside to cool.

When ready to proceed, line two steamer racks with banana or cabbage leaves and oil the leaves lightly. Cut the tapioca dough in half. Work with one half at a time, leaving the remaining dough covered with plastic wrap.

On a lightly oiled work surface, roll the dough back and forth under your palms into a smooth cylinder about 12 inches long and 1½ inches in diameter. Slice crosswise in half, then cut each half into 8 slices.

With lightly oiled hands, on the lightly oiled surface, flatten a slice of dough to a disk about 1½ inches in diameter. Lay it on the palm of one hand and place a slightly heaping teaspoon of the filling in the center. Wrap the dough over the filling, then pinch the ends and roll in your palm to shape a ball. If the dough cracks, don't worry, it's easy to patch and will be fine. The first few shaping attempts may feel awkward because the dough is not very pliable, but the work goes quickly, and as the dough cooks, it will seal any holes.

Place the ball on a steamer rack. Repeat with the remaining dough and filling, making sure the balls are not touching each other on the rack.

Once one steamer rack is full, place it over water in a pot or wok and bring to a boil. Cover and steam for 10 to 15 minutes, until the dough is translucent and tender. Remove from the steamer and set aside while you assemble and cook the remaining dumplings. *(The dumplings can be made ahead and left at room temperature for up to 2 hours.)*

To serve, arrange the balls on a serving plate lined with lettuce leaves and sprinkle on a little garlic oil, then top with the fried garlic or fried shallots. On another plate, arrange a pile of the remaining leaf lettuce, the coriander or mint leaves, and the chopped bird chiles.

To eat, wrap a dumpling, some coriander or mint, and a little chile in a lettuce leaf. Each dumpling makes two or three very flavorful mouthfuls.

MAKES *32 dumplings; serves 6 to 8*

NOTE: *To freeze leftover dumplings, place in a plastic container (we use large yogurt containers), cover, and freeze. Don't pack the balls in too tightly, and be sure to discard any lettuce or other greens. You can take them out of the freezer several hours ahead or at the last minute; either way, you'll want to resteam the dumplings. Place them in a steamer rack above boiling water and steam until tender, about 10 minutes (take one from the steamer and cut it open to check that the center has reached room temperature). Serve as described above, at room temperature, with the accompaniments for wrapping and flavoring.*

BICH: An alert little face, a gravelly voice, clean clothes on an undernourished half-grown frame, dirty bare legs and feet, this was Bich. She traveled with a sidekick, an even smaller girl. Bich was ten years old. She picked me up one day in Chau Doc, tried to sell me lottery tickets, and then just hung around. Some of the people in the market would give her food; others chased her harshly, aiming the odd blow. She had a mother and no father. She wasn't in school, because it costs a little. Anyway, she needed to be earning money and scrounging food to feed herself during the day.

She could count, and knew what value each *dong* note had, but at some point I realized that she couldn't read numbers. Over several glasses of soda and several days, using whatever fragments of Vietnamese I could scratch up, I tried to teach her to match the shapes of the numbers from 1 to 10 to meaning. Every once in a while I bought some lottery tickets from her.

My last morning in Chau Doc, I ran into Bich at the market. I told her I was leaving and asked her to join me for a drink. We sat down and ordered, then I gave her some money and a pen and a small pad of paper so she could practice her numbers. She sat tall in her chair, looking pleased, rattling the ice in her glass as she stirred her soda with a straw between sips. Soon it was time to go. I caught the proprietor's eye. Bich waved her hand imperiously, stopping me. She pulled out the money I'd given her and handed some over to pay for the drinks. She was firm, unpersuadable, awe-inspiring.

A small Khmer boy stands holding a string of heavily aromatic frangipani flowers in a fishing village on the Tonle Sap, near Siam Reap.

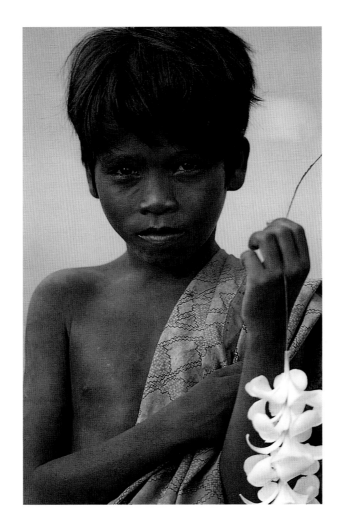

CLASSIC VIETNAMESE SPRING ROLLS

[*cha gio* — VIETNAM]

In Vietnam, deep-fried spring rolls are mostly market and restaurant food. They can be made small or long, but either way, they're eaten in the hand, wrapped in a lettuce leaf with some fresh herbs, served occasionally with vinegared carrots and cold cooked rice noodles.

You can assemble the rolls several hours ahead and refrigerate until you are ready to deep-fry. Once fried and drained on paper towels, they can be reheated in the oven or in hot oil.

Use either small round rice paper wrappers or wedge-shaped wrappers if you can. We like Red Rose brand best. If you can only find large wrappers, you will be making longer rolls, and fewer of them.

FILLING

½ **pound ground pork**

2 **ounces peeled and deveined medium shrimp, briefly rinsed**
   and finely chopped (about ½ cup)

½ **medium onion (or large shallot), finely chopped**

2 **cloves garlic, minced**

2 **to 3 shallots, minced**

½ **cup finely chopped jicama or carrot (optional)**

1 **ounce cellophane noodles, soaked in warm water for**
   20 minutes, drained, and cut into 1-inch lengths with scissors
   (just over ½ cup)

¼ **teaspoon freshly ground black pepper**

2 **tablespoons Vietnamese fish sauce**

40 **small round rice papers (about 5 inches across) or wedge-**
   shaped papers, or substitute ten 8-inch round rice papers

Peanut oil for deep-frying

ACCOMPANIMENTS

½ **pound thin dried rice noodles, soaked in warm water for**
   20 minutes, drained, cooked in boiling water for about
   2 minutes, and then drained, rinsed with cold water,
   and drained again (optional)

Vietnamese Herb and Salad Plate (page 68), with plenty of
   lettuce leaves

1½ **cups Vietnamese Must-Have Table Sauce (*nuoc cham*,**
   page 28)

Place the pork in a medium bowl, add all the other filling ingredients, and mix very well. You will have about 2 cups of filling. Set aside. (*You can prepare the filling ahead and store in a well-sealed container in the refrigerator for up to 12 hours.*)

Set out two large plates or a flat tray. Wet a tea towel well, then wring out and place on your work surface. Fill a wide bowl or basin with 2 inches of warm water. (Or, fill with 1 inch beer and add 1 inch hot water, to make a warm mixture; see Notes.)

If using small round papers or wedges, immerse a paper in the warm soaking liquid until well softened, then lay on the damp tea towel (place the wedge with the point facing away from you). Place a generous teaspoon of the filling onto the paper in a 2-inch-long line near and parallel to the round edge nearest you. Roll that edge over the filling, then fold over the sides of the rice paper and roll up tightly. Place the finished roll on the plate or tray, seam side down, and cover with a damp cloth. Repeat for the remaining rolls.

If using large papers, wet 1 paper thoroughly until softened, then place on the damp tea towel. Place a scant 2 tablespoons filling in a line about 5 inches long across the wrapper, well below the midline, leaving a ¾-inch border at either end of the line. Fold the edge nearest you over the filling, fold over the sides of the rice paper, and roll up tightly. Place on the plate or tray, cover with a damp cloth, and repeat with the remaining papers and filling.

(The rolls can be assembled up to 3 hours ahead and stored, well-sealed, in the refrigerator.)

When ready to fry, set out several racks or large plates lined with paper towels, and have extra paper towels ready. Also set out a slotted spoon. Place two stable woks or large heavy skillets over medium-high heat. (You can use only one, of course; it will just take longer.) Add peanut oil to a depth of about 1 inch in each wok at its deepest point or ¾ inch in the skillets, and heat until hot. (Use slightly more oil if frying longer or larger rolls.) Test the temperature by dropping a piece of moistened rice paper into the oil. It should sink and then immediately rise back up slowly, without darkening. If it darkens and rises up quickly, the oil is too hot; lower the temperature slightly if necessary. We find a setting somewhere between medium and medium-high to be ideal.

Add the rolls one at a time to the pans, being careful not to splash yourself with hot oil, without crowding; make sure the rolls aren't touching. (You will probably have to make two batches at least, even if using two large skillets or woks.) After you add the rolls to the oil, they will hiss vigorously as they release moisture into the hot oil, then they'll bubble and the rice paper will change texture. Use a spatula to turn the rolls so they cook evenly, but be gentle with them so you don't tear the skins. Cook for 7 to 10 minutes, until golden all over, then use the slotted spoon to transfer to a paper towel–lined rack or plate. Repeat with the remaining rolls.

Arrange the cooked noodles, if using, and the salad plate on one or more platters, so guests can serve themselves as they wish. Or, arrange an individual plate of noodles and salad ingredients for each guest. Put the table sauce in individual condiment bowls so each person has a personal dipping sauce. Serve the rolls on one or more plates; if serving long rolls, cut in half or into thirds.

MAKES *about 40 small rolls or 10 long rolls; serves 6 to 8*

NOTES: *Everyone has his or her tricks and theories about how to make a perfect Vietnamese spring roll. When we asked the chef-owners at our favorite local restaurant Pho Hung, in Toronto, for their advice, they told us that they use beer to moisten the rice papers. It helps make the paper crisp when it fries, they said. But, as they pointed out, in Vietnam beer is too expensive, so people just use water. We've tried soaking in plain water and in beer, and both work well; over time, we've come to think the beer might give a slightly crisper and more golden result, but it's a close call.*

We've also read recipes that advise putting sugar in the soaking water. We've tried it and didn't like it; it made the rolls too dark. (When asked about sugar water, the people at the Pho Hung shook their heads: "Bad idea," they said firmly.)

Sometimes the paper bubbles and boils in the oil as it fries, making blisters; this is not a problem. And even if you overcook the rolls a bit, they're still very good.

You can also use the restaurant approach to deep-frying spring rolls: Fry the rolls lightly until an almost-done pale golden color, then take them out and drain well on a paper towel–covered rack. Just before serving, reheat your oil, then quickly fry them for a minute or two more so you can serve them hot and crisp.

CLASSIC VIETNAMESE SPRING ROLLS *is pictured on page 277, with* VIETNAMESE MUST-HAVE TABLE SAUCE *(nuoc cham, page 28).*

LEFT: *That Panom, a small town on the Mekong in northeast Thailand, is famous throughout the country for its temple.* RIGHT: *When we photographed this older woman harvesting rice in southern Vietnam, she had already lived through many changes and hardships: She was born under French colonial rule, then came the Japanese war followed by a period of peace, and then more years of war and loss and uncertainty, and finally, in 1975, the unification of Vietnam under the Hanoi government.*

VILLAGE LUNCH: Anh is a cyclo driver, skinny and sinewy, like most of the breed. He has a little

English and a lot of heart. He spends his days pedaling around Chau Doc (in southern Vietnam, just by the Cambodian border; see map, page 6) looking for fares and doing short hauls, especially to and from the market. He found me at the bus station, in the rain. I'd just arrived after a five-hour trip from Ho Chi Minh City, a little disoriented from all the slow, bumpy miles on the road, and without a clue about where to stay or what I'd find in town.

In the end, I spent a lot of my week in Chau Doc exploring outside town with Anh. We went on the river to visit floating fish farms, we traveled on a borrowed motorbike to the Cham villages across the river (see The People, page 9), where we saw large cool mosques and people weaving lengths of striped and checked cotton cloth in their houses.

Some miles beyond the Cham villages, we came to a silk-weaving factory, with women and children working hard amid the clatter of old machinery. We also traveled out of town to visit the temples at Sam Mountain; from the top, we could see green rice fields stretching off westward into Cambodia, and the river, brown and swollen in the rainy season, cutting a wide path through the green.

One day, Anh took me home to meet his Cambodian-born Vietnamese wife. Over a small wood fire, they made a wonderful lunch: rice, sour soup, and slow-cooked sweet and salty fish. We ate with two of their children, all sitting on a bamboo mat in the main room of their small wood house. Then we sat quietly chatting in the drowsy warm afternoon, as the sun slanted in through the open doorway.

In many parts of the region, rivers are the main roads and boats the main mode of transportation. Here in central Vietnam, what looks like the population of an entire village travels home from a weekly market, loaded with shopping.

VIETNAMESE SAVORY CREPES

[*banh xeo* — VIETNAM]

Banh xeo are often called Vietnamese crepes, but at first glance they look more like crispy filled omelets. The surprise is that although they are fine, pale yellow filled crepes, there is no egg in them whatsoever, and no wheat flour. Instead, the batter is made from soaked and ground mung beans (they're golden yellow, hence the color), combined with coconut milk and some rice flour, like a cousin of a South Indian *dosa*. The batter is traditionally cooked on a hot well-oiled wok; the crepe is not turned over but instead steams under a lid, while the bottom gets crispy.

Though *banh xeo* are sometimes made in restaurants, usually with complicated fillings, some of the best we've tasted have been the simplest, made as street food at roadside stands. One of our favorites was the *banh xeo* we ate in Cantho in the Mekong Delta. The filling was mostly greens and herbs, with bean sprouts and a small dollop of chopped cooked shrimp. Another, even simpler, made by a street vendor in the old section of Luang Prabang, in Laos, was entirely vegetarian.

This recipe is for a basic *banh xeo*, crispy and delicious, a wonderful snack or a fun dish at a multidish meal.

Make the batter as long as a day ahead and then prepare the crepes short-order style, so they come to the table hot and crisp. Put the crepes out one at a time, as they come off the hot wok: Guests can help themselves from a serving plate, using chopsticks or serving spoons to lift pieces of crepe onto their plates.

Serve with plenty of tender lettuce leaves and fresh mint and basil, as directed below. To eat, use chopsticks (or a spoon and fork). Place a piece of *banh xeo* and an herb sprig, together with some shredded carrot and radish, on a lettuce leaf, then drizzle on a little sauce, roll up loosely, and enjoy.

CREPES

¼ cup yellow split mung beans, soaked in water
   for 30 minutes and drained

1½ cups canned or fresh coconut milk (see page 315)

½ cup water

1 cup rice flour

½ teaspoon sugar

½ teaspoon salt

¼ teaspoon ground turmeric (optional)

Vegetable oil for cooking

FILLINGS

3 cups bean sprouts, rinsed and drained

1 cup coarsely chopped coriander

1 cup minced scallions (4 to 5)

OPTIONAL FILLING

1½ cups Vietnamese Shrimp and Pork Stir-fry (page 188)

ACCOMPANIMENTS

2 large heads leaf lettuce or Bibb lettuce, washed, dried,
   and separated into leaves

2 cups Carrot and Daikon Pickled Salad (page 85) (optional)

Mint leaves and/or Asian basil leaves

2 cups Vietnamese Must-Have Table Sauce (*nuoc cham*,
   page 28) or Vegetarian *Nuoc Cham* (page 29)

Place the mung beans and coconut milk in a blender and process to a puree. Add the water and rice flour and process until smooth, then add the sugar, salt, and turmeric, if using, and process briefly. Place a fine sieve over a bowl and pour the batter through to strain out any lumps. Cover the bowl with plastic wrap and set aside in the refrigerator for at least 30 minutes, or up to 24 hours.

Before starting to cook, set out the fillings you will be using near your stovetop, as well as the plates on which you plan to serve the crepes and a lid for covering the wok during cooking. Arrange the fresh accompaniments on one or more platters, and set out the dipping sauce in individual condiment dishes.

Stir the batter for several minutes. It will have thickened in the refrigerator, but after stirring, it should be quite liquid, not thick and heavy. If necessary, add a little water to thin it. Place a large wok over high heat. When it is hot, add about 2 tablespoons oil, swirl to coat the wok well, and then pour off the oil (make sure no oil runs down the outside of the wok; wipe it off if it does). Place the wok back over high heat. (If using an electric stovetop, turn on another burner to medium heat.) Scoop up ⅓ cup of the batter and pour it into the wok. Lift the wok and tip it to swirl the batter around thinly into a circle about 8 inches in diameter. Place the wok back on the heat. There will be small bubbles and holes in your crepe; don't worry—in fact, these give delicious crispy edges. Sprinkle some bean sprouts, coriander, and scallions onto one side of the crepe. If you wish, add a heaping tablespoon of the shrimp-pork mixture. Lower the heat to medium (or move the wok onto the burner set at medium), cover the wok, and let the crepe cook for about 3 minutes, until the edges are brown and the underside is crispy; the top, having steam-cooked, will be soft and pale yellow. Use your spatula to ease the edges of the crepe off the wok, then fold the crepe in half and slide it onto a waiting plate. Serve immediately, or wait until you've cooked two and serve them together.

Show your guests how to serve themselves, using chopsticks (or a spoon and fork) to help themselves to pieces of crepe (see Headnote for eating instructions).

Wipe the wok thoroughly with a well-oiled cloth or paper towel, then cook the remaining crepes. Once you are comfortable with the cooking technique, you may want to work with two woks at once, thus speeding up your production.

MAKES *about 12* banh xeo, *about 8 inches in diameter; serves 6 to 8*

NOTES: *Whoever is doing the cooking will be busy turning out crepes until the last of the batter has been cooked. The crepes are so much better, crispy and fresh-tasting, when hot from the wok, that your guests will love you, even as they miss your company while you're cooking.*

It's important that your wok be lightly oiled, but that there not be too much oil. Excess oil will make the batter slip and slide when you pour it in, rather than spreading and cooking on the hot metal. If you're having this problem, use a paper towel or cloth to wipe off excess oil. On the other hand, if the batter is too thick, it won't spread as you tip and tilt the pan: Add a little water to thin it.

HUI HONEY-FILLED FLATBREADS

[*huizhou mien bao* — YUNNAN]

We were delighted to find flatbreads in Dali (in China's Yunnan province; see map, page 6), breads baked in a small tandoor oven out in the street. Some were meat-filled, some plain, and some a little sweet. They came hot from the oven, made to order as we stood watching. They're made by members of the large Hui (Chinese Muslim) community in Dali, a reminder of the cultural links between the Hui and Muslim cultures in Central Asia.

Oran, a student of Yunnanese culinary traditions (see Headnote, page 158), told us about a delicious variant on Hui flatbread. The bread is made in the same way as regular Hui tandoor bread, but it is filled with a little honeycomb and nutmeg before baking. We've worked with the idea, using liquid honey rather than comb honey, and freshly grated nutmeg. It's delicious and surprising too. Oran had told us that these honey breads are particularly good with chile-hot dishes, or just dipped in a little chile paste. The sweetness of the honey balances the chile heat. He was right. Try them. Serve as a snack on their own or with a salsa, or serve to accompany Hui Beef Stew with Chick-peas and Anise (page 231) or other savory dishes.

2½ cups lukewarm water
1 teaspoon instant dry yeast
6 to 7 cups unbleached all-purpose flour
1 tablespoon salt
About 5 tablespoons honey
½ teaspoon freshly grated nutmeg (optional)

Place the water in a large bowl and sprinkle on the yeast. Add 2 cups of the flour and stir, always in the same direction, until well mixed. Add another cup of flour and stir it in. Stir the batter 100 times in the same direction (to help develop the gluten strands), then, if it's convenient, cover the bowl with plastic wrap and set aside for 30 minutes to 3 hours in a cool place. (You can also just continue making the dough, if it suits your schedule better.)

Sprinkle the salt onto the dough and stir in. Add more flour, ½ cup at a time, always stirring in the same direction. As the dough gets heavier, you may have to turn and fold it rather than stirring to incorporate the flour. When the dough is too stiff to work with

a spoon, flour a work surface generously and turn the dough out of the bowl. Let stand while you clean out the bowl and wipe it dry.

Knead the dough for 10 minutes, folding the dough over on itself, then turning it a quarter turn and repeating. Add flour to your work surface and hands as necessary to keep dough from sticking; use a dough scraper or knife to clean the surface of sticky bits of dough. Properly kneaded, the dough will be smooth and elastic.

Lightly oil the bread bowl, place the dough in the bowl, cover with plastic wrap, and put in a cool place to rise until doubled in volume, 2 to 3 hours, or overnight if you wish. (If the temperature in the house is warm [over 75°F], if rising overnight, refrigerate the dough, then bring back to room temperature at least 1 hour before proceeding.)

Preheat the oven to 500°F and place a baking stone or unglazed quarry tiles on a rack in the center to upper third of the oven. Make sure there is enough space (at least ½ inch) between the stone or tiles and the oven walls so that air can circulate freely.

Flour a work surface. Pull the dough away from the sides of the bowl, turn it out, and knead briefly. Using a sharp knife, divide the dough into 16 equal pieces. Shape each into a ball, cover with plastic wrap; and set aside for 20 minutes.

Place the honey in a medium bowl and stir in enough warm water to make it easily spreadable. Then stir in the optional nutmeg.

To shape the breads, work with two breads at a time, rolling out one and letting it rest for a moment while you roll out the other. Roll out the first ball of dough to a flattened round about 6 inches in diameter. Spread a teaspoon of honey on the round, leaving a clear narrow border all around. Fold the sides up over the honey, pleating the dough as necessary to cover it completely, like a filled pouch, then flatten the dough with a lightly floured palm; repair any gaps by pinching them together. Repeat with a second ball of dough. Then, using a rolling pin or your hands, roll or stretch each bread out to a flat round 6 to 7 inches in diameter. If the breads spring back, set aside to let the dough relax while you begin shaping the next two breads, then return to them in 2 or 3 minutes.

Prick each bread lightly 4 or 5 times with a fork and place on the hot tiles or baking stone. Begin shaping two more breads as they cook. Cook for about 4 minutes, or until the bottom is golden and the top begins to have golden spots. Use a long-handled spatula to lift the breads out of the oven; set aside on a rack to cool slightly, then wrap in a towel to keep warm. Repeat with remaining breads.

MAKES *16 breads*

LEFT: *Cyclo drivers are tough, resourceful people, working hard to earn a living. With growing prosperity, cyclos are being forced out of central Ho Chi Minh City.*
RIGHT: *But in Phnom Penh, cyclos are still the most useful form of taxi. Outside each market a row of cyclo drivers waits for customers to emerge.*

MEKONG SUBS: These sandwich combos, made with long rolls like mini French baguettes, are standard street fare from Ho Chi Minh City (Saigon) to Phnom Penh to Vientiane. The French introduced bakery-produced baguettes to their Southeast Asian colonies (Vietnam, Cambodia, and Laos) and they became an entrenched part of the food traditions in towns and cities. Mekong subs are a brilliant example of a colonized cuisine co-opting a good idea (the baguette sandwich) and going it one better.

Since wheat doesn't thrive in the tropics, wheat flour for all this bread has to be imported. It came first from France, then from the United States; after 1975, it was shipped in from the USSR, and now it comes mostly, we're told, from Australia. Bakeries in the region turn out a modified baguette-style roll, light, white, with a crisp crust.

Butter and mayonnaise, two other French introductions, have a big role in Mekong subs, though you can ask for a sandwich without. Fillings range from Vietnamese pâté to cooked sausage to ham, combined with any one or more of a range of choices, including pickled carrot shreds, hot chiles, and fresh herbs.

These days, the flow of ideas is going the other way, and Mekong subs are conquering North America. It's no wonder: They're unbeatable.

Ferry crossings are odd places: Everyone wants to move on across the river, yet they may get hungry or have the urge to shop, hence vendors of all kinds. Often the food is very good, freshly prepared. At this Mekong Delta crossing, a sandwich vendor sells Mekong subs filled with small grilled birds, a local delicacy.

Market people, like this jackfruit vendor in Hue, often have a real sense of theater and are prepared to engage in banter of all kinds.

SAIGON SUBS
[*banh mi* — VIETNAM]

This is the model of the Mekong sub that has traveled to North America. It's spicier than the Phnom Penh version (see Note). Most ingredients are optional; what makes the sandwich distinctively Southeast Asian is the combination of fresh coriander, strong-tasting meats, and pickled carrot shreds. (Some would say that mayonnaise is another must-include ingredient.)

FOR EACH SANDWICH

One 6- to 8-inch length French bread/baguette, split, or substitute a kaiser roll, sliced open

Butter (optional)

Mayonnaise (optional)

ONE OR MORE OF

Vietnamese Baked Cinnamon Pâté (page 259 or store-bought) or other pork pâté, Vietnamese or French—pâté de campagne is a good option (homemade or store-bought)

Filling from Green-Wrapped Flavor Bundles (page 269)

Thinly sliced cured ham, such as Black Forest ham

Thinly sliced headcheese

Aromatic Lemongrass Patties (page 251), sliced into strips

Chopped cooked sausage, such as Spicy Northern Sausage (page 256)

PLUS

Carrot and Daikon Pickled Salad (page 85) (optional)

Minced bird chiles (optional)

Coriander sprigs

To make each sandwich, spread both cut sides of the bread lightly with butter and one side with mayonnaise, if using. If using pâté, spread or smear it on the other cut side. Lay pieces or slices of any meats you are using on it. Top with carrot and daikon shreds and a few pieces of minced chiles, if using, and coriander, spreading them along the length of the sandwich. Close and press firmly but gently to make the sandwich hold together. Serve whole or cut crosswise in half.

To serve assemble-your-own subs, set out all the ingredients on plates or platters, with plenty of knives for spreading and chopsticks for lifting the meat slices.

NOTE: *In Phnom Penh, the sandwich tradition is a little different from that of the Vietnamese. The bread is split and both sides are lightly grilled or toasted, then served alongside meats and other fillings. A small knife and a fork come with each sandwich plate. The choice of fillings is similar to Saigon Subs, with the addition of options like green tomato cut into wedges, sliced scallions, and slices of cucumber. The other distinctive part of Phnom Penh Subs is that they are served with bowls of condiments alongside: fish sauce, soy sauce, chile paste, and Maggi sauce, this yet another European idea adapted to a new purpose.*

SWEETS AND DRINKS

Dessert is not usually part of a meal in Southeast Asia; instead, sweets are eaten as a snack at almost any hour of the day. Fried Bananas (page 299), for example, one of our all-time favorite street foods, makes a wonderful mid-morning snack.

We're not going to give a recipe for another one of our favorite Thai sweets. Not a formal recipe, that is: It doesn't need a formal recipe. And it's not that we eat this particular sweet treat very often, we don't. But we love it, well, we love the fact of it. So here it is: Take a hot dog bun, fill it with several scoops of coconut ice cream, and pour sweetened condensed milk over the ice cream, gooping it on. An ice cream sandwich, Thai style.

Better yet, try some of the easy sweets that follow, from Tashi's Favorite Black Rice Pudding (page 292) to Sweet Corn Fritters (page 296) and Classic Banana Shake (page 303). Another surprising and simple dessert is Tapioca and Corn Pudding

with Coconut Cream (page 294); it may transform your idea of tapioca, as it has ours.

We confess that, when traveling, we often arrange our days around a good source of Thai or Lao or Vietnamese Iced Coffee with Sweetened Condensed Milk (page 304); luckily, it's easy to make at home, so once back from travels, we need not go without.

OPPOSITE: *Deep-frying is a quick way of cooking sweet treats, from* FRIED BANANAS *(page 299) to* SWEET CORN FRITTERS *(page 296).* ABOVE LEFT: *At a morning market, a woman carries freshly made rice doughnuts and fritters.* ABOVE RIGHT: *In Mae Sai, on the Thai-Burmese border, vendors fry up rice doughnuts for hungry shoppers.*

TASHI'S FAVORITE BLACK RICE PUDDING

[*khao neeo see dam* — THAILAND]

Since black rice is a big favorite of Tashi's, over time we've developed a quick version of black rice pudding, aromatic, sweet, and satisfying. You can prepare it and have it in bowls for impatient rice pudding fans in under an hour, with no presoaking of the rice. Serve it for dessert or as a snack, or even for breakfast. The rice is moist, almost soupy, when first made, but if it's left to stand in a cool place, it firms up into a pudding-cake texture and can be eaten in slices (see Note below). Eat it on its own or topped with sesame seeds, coriander leaves, or fried shallots, or a combination.

2 cups black sticky rice

3 cups water

2 cups canned or fresh coconut milk (see page 315)

¾ cup palm sugar, or substitute brown sugar

½ teaspoon salt

OPTIONAL TOPPINGS

2 tablespoons Dry-Roasted Sesame Seeds (page 308)

½ cup coriander leaves

¼ cup Fried Shallots (page 310)

Ripe mango or other sweet-acid fruit, sliced

Place the rice and water in a heavy pot and bring to a boil. Let boil vigorously for several minutes, stirring frequently, then cover, lower the heat to medium, and cook for 10 minutes. Lower the heat to very low and let simmer, still covered, for about 30 minutes.

Just before the rice finishes cooking, place the coconut milk in a saucepan over medium heat and stir in the sugar and salt until completely dissolved. Heat just to a boil, then reduce to the lowest heat until the rice is cooked.

Add the coconut milk to the rice and stir well, then remove from the heat and set aside for 10 minutes, or as long as 2 hours.

Serve warm or at room temperature, in small bowls, with your choice of topping.

MAKES *about 4 cups; serves 4 to 8*

NOTE: *If you like, once the pudding has cooled (or if you have leftover pudding), transfer it to a small baking sheet or a baking pan and use a spatula to smooth the surface. Cover and place it in the refrigerator for several hours, or overnight, to firm up. Cut into strips and serve sprinkled, if you wish, with the sesame seeds, coriander, or fried shallots, or a combination, or topped with the fruit.*

Traditional Vietnamese straw hats offer shelter from sun and rain. Because they rest lightly on the head, they're remarkably cool.

OPPOSITE RIGHT: *Purplish slices of black rice pudding are set out for sale on banana leaves.*

TAPIOCA AND CORN PUDDING WITH COCONUT CREAM
[THAILAND, VIETNAM]

We've eaten versions of this thick-textured comfort food in the Mekong Delta and in Thailand. The corn is used here for its sweet taste, more like a fruit than a grain. It also gives an agreeable soft crunch to the smooth pudding. The combination of corn and tapioca is inspired, far from the bland gluey tapioca puddings of English tradition. The pudding is aromatic with rose water and enriched with a little coconut cream.

Tapioca is widely available, sold in clear plastic bags, in Asian groceries. Tapioca pearls come in large and small sizes, and the small ones, used here, are sometimes pale green, looking as if they've been soaked in pandanus leaf juice. (You can also buy pink ones and white ones.) If you can, use green tapioca for the pudding, because it's fun when combined with the yellow corn; but undyed tapioca is just fine too.

The tapioca sweetens and softens as it cooks. Sugar will make it tough, so don't add the sugar until the tapioca is cooked.

3¼ cups water

1 cup small Asian-style tapioca pearls

¼ teaspoon salt

1 teaspoon rose water

½ cup plus 1 tablespoon sugar

1½ cups fresh corn kernels (from 2 medium ears)

½ cup canned or fresh coconut cream (see Note)

Place the water in a heavy pot and bring to a boil. Add the tapioca and salt and stir as the water comes back to a boil. Lower the heat slightly to maintain a low boil and cook, stirring frequently to prevent sticking, until the tapioca is completely cooked and soft, 15 to 20 minutes.

Stir in the rose water and sugar until the sugar is thoroughly dissolved, then stir in the corn kernels and simmer over low heat for 5 minutes. The kernels should still have a slight fresh crunch.

Serve the pudding warm in small bowls, topped with a dollop (a generous heaped teaspoon) of coconut cream.

SERVES *8*

NOTE: *You can use fresh coconut cream (see page 315) or canned; canned coconut milk usually separates into a thick dense cream and a thin liquid. Use the cream in this recipe.*

SWEET CORN FRITTERS
[*taozhe yu mi* — Y U N N A N]

Fritters are a quick way to make a treat from simple ingredients. This is a version of the corn fritters sold by street vendors in Yunnan, usually in the morning. They're very easy to make at home if you have a large stable wok or a heavy pot. The fritters are tender as they come out and golden brown, with a slight sweet crunch of corn as you bite into them.

Make the fritters for a special breakfast or as a snack anytime, to accompany tea or coffee. You can also serve them for dessert, with sliced fruit or sorbet as a cool contrast.

1 medium egg
½ cup all-purpose flour
1 cup corn kernels (frozen or from 1 or 2 small ears)
½ cup water
¼ teaspoon salt
Peanut oil for deep-frying
Sugar for sprinkling

Break the egg into a medium bowl and whisk to blend the yolk and white. Stir in 2 tablespoons of the flour to make a smooth paste. Stir in the corn. Add the water, then stir in the salt and remaining flour. Transfer the batter to a blender or processor and blend or pulse for 30 seconds to 1 minute to break down the corn kernels. (See Notes below.) You should have about 1¼ cups batter. Transfer to a bowl and set aside. (*The batter can be made up to 2 hours ahead and set aside, covered, in the refrigerator. Bring back to room temperature and stir thoroughly before proceeding.*)

Place a large plate lined with several paper towels beside your stovetop. Place a large wok (make sure it is stable) or a wide heavy pot over medium-high to high heat. Add peanut oil to come to a depth of about 1 inch at the deepest point of the wok or in the pot and heat until hot. Test the temperature by dropping a blob of batter into the oil. It should sizzle as it drops down into the oil and should float back up immediately. If it blackens quickly, the oil is too hot and you should reduce the heat to medium-high. Or, if it doesn't rise back up to the surface, the oil is not yet hot enough; wait another minute or two before testing again.

Once the oil is at the correct temperature, scoop up just under 3 tablespoons of batter and drop it in a circle onto the hot oil. It will form a disk. After about 30 seconds, the underside should be brown. Use a slotted spoon or slotted spatula to turn the fritter over and cook for another 15 seconds or so on the second side until golden brown, then transfer it to the paper towel–lined plate. Sprinkle with sugar. Repeat with the remaining batter. If you have room in your pan, you can cook two or three at once. Serve hot.

M A K E S *about 8 fritters*

N O T E S : *The corn kernels must be coarsely pureed to eliminate all whole kernels. Whole kernels may pop while being deep-fried and spatter hot oil.*

We find that once the oil is hot, if we set our flame to medium-high, rather than high, it maintains the correct temperature.

COCONUT MILK STICKY RICE WITH MANGOES

[*khao neeo mamuang* — THAILAND]

Many people first encounter sticky rice in this classic Thai-Lao sweet. Most are astonished and delighted and immediately want to know how to make it at home. The recipe is very simple.

As with most of the sweets in Southeast Asia, you can eat Coconut Milk Sticky Rice as a snack or serve it as dessert.

3 cups sticky rice, soaked overnight in water or thin coconut milk and drained

2 cups canned or fresh coconut milk (see page 315)

¾ cup palm sugar, or substitute brown sugar

1 teaspoon salt

4 ripe mangoes, or substitute sliced ripe peaches or papayas

OPTIONAL GARNISH

Mint or Asian basil sprigs

Steam the sticky rice until tender, following the instructions on page 91 (about 30 minutes).

Meanwhile, place the coconut milk in a heavy pot and heat over medium heat until hot. Do not boil. Add the sugar and salt and stir to dissolve completely.

When the sticky rice is tender, turn it out into a bowl and pour 1 cup of the hot coconut milk over; reserve the rest. Stir to mix the liquid into the rice, then let stand for 20 minutes to an hour to allow the flavors to blend.

Meanwhile, peel the mangoes. The mango pit is flat and you want to slice the mango flesh off the pit as cleanly as possible. One at a time, lay the mangoes on a narrow side on a cutting board and slice lengthwise about ½ inch from the center—your knife should cut just along the flat side of the pit; if it strikes the pit, shift over a fraction of an inch more until you can slice downward. Repeat on the other side of the pit, giving you two hemispherical pieces of mango. (The cook gets to snack on the stray bits of mango still clinging to the pit.) Lay each mango half flat and slice thinly crosswise.

To serve individually, place an oval mound of sticky rice on each dessert plate and place a sliced half-mango decoratively beside it. Top with a sprig of mint or basil if you wish. Or, place the mango slices on a platter and pass it around, together with a serving bowl containing the rice, allowing guests to serve themselves. Stir the remaining sweetened coconut milk thoroughly, transfer to a small serving bowl or cruet, and pass it separately, with a spoon, so guests can spoon on extra as they wish.

SERVES *8*

NOTES: *You can substitute black Thai sticky rice (see Glossary) for half the white rice. Soak the two rices together; the white rice will turn a beautiful purple as it takes on color from the black rice. Cooking will take 10 minutes longer.*

Unlike plain sticky rice, Coconut Milk Sticky Rice has enough moisture and oils in it that it keeps well for 24 hours, in a covered container in the refrigerator, without drying out. Rewarm it the next day by steaming or in a microwave.

SILKY TOFU IN GINGER SYRUP

[THAILAND]

We don't know the true origin of this dish, except that the first and only place we've ever seen it served is by a street vendor who sets up at night on a sidewalk not far from the post office in Chiang Mai (see Chiang Mai, page 122). He's been there for years and years, and is there almost every night until very late. He doesn't seem to do a brisk business, but it's steady.

We have a feeling that this is somehow a "medicinal dessert," with the combination of tofu and ginger, but we've always loved it for its slippery texture, and because late in the evening, when we are walking back from the night bazaar and the air is cool, this sweet treat takes the nip from the night air.

1¼ cups water
½ cup sugar
1 heaping tablespoon minced ginger
1½ pounds silky tofu (4 small blocks or 2 large [12- to 14-ounce] blocks), chilled
Mint sprigs for garnish (optional)

Place the water in a small nonreactive pot and bring to a boil. Stir in the sugar until dissolved, then add the ginger. Lower the heat and simmer, uncovered, for about 20 minutes, stirring occasionally. (*The sauce can be made a day ahead and set aside, covered. Bring to a simmer before serving.*)

To serve, set out four shallow bowls. Use a large spoon to scoop up a smooth diagonal slice of tofu and place it in one of the bowls. Repeat, overlapping the slices and distributing the tofu slices among all the bowls. Spoon or pour the hot syrup over, then sprinkle the ginger from the bottom of the pot over each bowl. Garnish, if you wish, with mint sprigs.

SERVES *4 to 6*

NOTE: *If you want some crunch and color to contrast with the smooth white tofu, sprinkle on some finely chopped Dry-Roasted Peanuts (page 308) mixed with sugar, or some Dry-Roasted Sesame Seeds (page 308).*

BANANAS IN COCONUT CREAM

[*gluay bua chi* — CAMBODIA, THAILAND, VIETNAM]

This simple home-style pudding is often eaten as a snack at home or in the market, as most sweets are in Southeast Asia, rather than as dessert after a meal.

In Thailand and Cambodia, people sometimes make coconut milk by using scented water to extract the milk. You can achieve a similar effect by adding a little rose water to the coconut milk; be careful— it's very strong, so use restraint. The bananas simmer briefly in the slightly sweetened coconut milk, then are served in a small bowl, topped if you wish with a sprinkling of golden sesame seeds or chopped roasted peanuts.

1½ cups canned or fresh coconut milk (see page 315)
½ teaspoon rose water (optional)
¼ teaspoon salt
½ cup sugar, or more to taste
4 regular bananas or 10 small sweet Asian bananas
1 to 2 tablespoons Dry-Roasted Sesame Seeds (page 308) (optional)
1 to 2 tablespoons Dry-Roasted Peanuts (page 308), finely chopped (optional)

Place the coconut milk in a heavy pot over medium heat, add the rose water, if using, and the salt and sugar, and stir until completely dissolved. (*You can make the sauce ahead and let it stand for up to 1 hour before cooking the bananas. Reheat before proceeding.*)

Peel the bananas and cut into bite-sized pieces.

Add the bananas to the pot and cook until softened, 5 to 10 minutes, depending on the bananas you are using and on how firm or soft you like your bananas. Serve warm or at room temperature, in small bowls, topped with sprinkled sesame seeds or chopped roasted peanuts if you wish.

SERVES *8*

NOTE: *Leftovers, once cooled to room temperature, can be stored in a sealed container in the refrigerator for up to 24 hours.*

FRIED BANANAS

[*gluay khaek* — THAILAND]

For fried bananas, the bananas (you need firm regular North American–style bananas, not special small sweet ones) are sliced, then dipped in a sweetened batter just before they're fried. Sometimes the batter contains roasted sesame seeds; they're not necessary, they just give a little extra flavor and a slight change in texture before your teeth reach the soft hot sweetness of the bananas.

⅓ cup all-purpose flour
½ cup rice flour, or more if needed
½ teaspoon baking powder
2 tablespoons sugar
½ teaspoon salt
½ cup water or canned or fresh coconut milk (see page 315)
1 tablespoon Dry-Roasted Sesame Seeds (page 308) (optional)
4 to 5 firm ripe bananas
Peanut oil for deep-frying

In a large bowl, mix together the flours, baking powder, sugar, and salt. Add the water or coconut milk little by little, stirring until a smooth batter forms. The batter should be a smooth paste, not watery; add a little extra rice flour if it seems thin. Stir in the sesame seeds, if using. Let stand for 10 minutes.

Peel the bananas. Cut crosswise in half, then slice each lengthwise into 3 slices. Place a heavy pot or stable large wok over high heat. Add oil to a depth of about 1½ inches (in the deepest part of the wok) and heat until the oil just starts to smoke. To test for temperature, add a blob of batter to the oil: It should sink and then rise back up immediately, without turning black. If it blackens quickly, the oil is too hot and you should reduce the heat to medium-high. If it doesn't rise back up to the surface, the oil is not yet hot enough; wait another minute or two before testing again. Place a paper towel–lined plate by your cooking surface.

When the oil is at the right temperature, place a banana piece in the batter and turn to coat it, then slip it into the hot oil. Repeat with a second piece of banana. If the banana is very ripe and a little soft, the pieces may break into two smaller pieces; don't worry, it doesn't matter. Deep-fry, turning them over halfway through cooking, until golden brown, 1 to 2 minutes, depending on the size of your pot. Remove with a slotted spoon, pausing to allow excess oil to drain off, and place on the paper towel–lined plate. Repeat with the remaining bananas. Transfer the cooked bananas to a plate and cover or place in a 150°F oven to keep warm. Serve hot.

MAKES *24 to 30 pieces; serves 4 to 8, depending on the size of your bananas*

NOTE: *Vietnamese restaurants often serve a colonial fusion version of this, called* bananes flambées. *Long slices of banana are pressed flat, dipped in batter, and fried. Just before they go to the table, they're dusted with sugar and then a liqueur or high-alcohol rum is poured over and set alight. The bananas arrive glowing with quiet blue flames.*

DELTA ENCOUNTERS: Almost nine years after our first trip to the Mekong Delta, I went back, this time by myself, in rainy season. In Cantho (a large town at the heart of the Delta), I stayed in a cheap hotel by the market, situated between a twenty-four-hour restaurant run by a woman named Lulu and an old Chinese Buddhist temple.

Lulu is Chinese, smooth-skinned and plump. She and her husband work the evening shift, starting at about five in the afternoon; her sister works the opposite twelve-hour shift, seven days a week. The restaurant was closed for ten years after the end of the war in 1975, as private enterprise was discouraged by the Hanoi government. But things loosened up in the mid-eighties and now it's a bustling place, not just at lunch and supper, but all through the night, with boatmen and market people who come to eat after unloading produce at the dock across the road.

One day an alert young boatwoman named Vui and her friend Hanh sat down to chat with me while I was having lunch at Lulu's. They persuaded me to hire them for a morning's excursion along the small waterways not far from Cantho.

We got to a morning market just at dawn, a floating market. At floating markets, boats become market stalls, selling anything from household goods (pots and pans, plastic basins and buckets, metal spoons and cleavers) to dry goods and toiletries, to food of all kinds. Vendors hold weighing scales in the air because there's no level surface on which to place them. The buyer's and seller's boats lightly rock side by side, held together with a free hand while the buyer picks through the produce on offer. Food vendors have their cauldrons of broth, their piles of noodles and fresh herbs, all laid out in their narrow skiffs. We pulled up alongside one "stall," put in our orders, and soon were handed large, steaming white china bowls of noodle soup. We ate quickly with chopsticks and spoons, then handed the bowls back and pushed off.

Two days later we made our big expedition. In a powerful long boat driven by a friend of theirs named Tranh, we traveled across the southern branch of the Mekong and into Tra Vinh Province, a trip that even Tranh had never made. We left well before dawn, needing to be across the big river and into Tra Vinh before any police boats were out, for traveling by boat between provinces without a permit is against the rules. Once in new territory, a maze of straight canals and twisting smaller waterways, we had to stop several times and ask directions.

We traveled for miles and hours through low green swampy country. We passed a few villages and floating markets, we saw fishermen and farmers and children playing and women doing laundry. People looked at us oddly each time we pulled over and asked for directions, but we had no trouble and, eventually, pleased and relieved, we reached the town of Tra Vinh, the sleepy capital of Tra Vinh Province.

It was already midafternoon, so there was only time for a quick lunch and a visit to a Khmer temple before Vui and Hanh had to leave. As the boat roared back up the channel, heading for distant Cantho, they waved and waved. Then I went looking for a place to stay.

In many Delta towns, there's a small ferry crossing near the market. Women come and go all day, chatting as they wait for a boat across.

SWEET SATIN CUSTARD

[*sangkaya* — THAILAND, CAMBODIA, LAOS]

Sangkaya (the Thai name) is found in various versions from Vietnam (where it's called *banh gan*) to Cambodia (the Khmer call it *sankiah*) to Laos. It's a simple coconut milk–based custard, sweetened and flavored with palm sugar. In Vietnam, a little ground cinnamon, ginger, anise, and cloves may go into the custard, darkening it slightly and giving it a more complex flavor. Sometimes it comes topped with fried shallots and coriander leaves, a startling combination of savory and sweet. Coconut milk custard is sold by the slice in markets all over the region.

This is the basic Thai version of *sangkaya*. Serve it as a rich dessert, on its own or with sweetened sticky rice, as suggested below.

1½ cups canned or fresh thick coconut milk (see page 315)

⅔ cup palm sugar, or substitute brown sugar

⅛ teaspoon salt

4 large eggs

OPTIONAL ACCOMPANIMENT

2 cups Coconut Milk Sticky Rice (page 297) or Tashi's Favorite Black Rice Pudding (page 292)

Have ready six custard cups or small heatproof bowls that will fit in a steamer.

In a heavy pot, heat the coconut milk until lukewarm. Add the sugar and salt, stirring until the sugar has completely dissolved. Remove from the heat. Break the eggs into a bowl and whisk briefly, then stir into the coconut milk.

Pour the mixture through a muslin- or cheesecloth-lined sieve into the cups. Place in the steamer, cover, and steam over gently boiling water until the custard sets, about 15 minutes. (You can also use a roasting pan filled with 1 inch of water as an improvised steamer. Place one or more trivets in it to hold the cups of custard.) Remove from the steamer and let cool.

Serve at room temperature, or refrigerate and serve chilled, with the sticky rice or sticky rice pudding if you wish.

SERVES *6*

CLASSIC BANANA SHAKE
[THAILAND]

Banana shakes are foreigner food in Thailand, prepared for foreigners who crave a taste of home for one reason or another. Banana pancakes are another common foreigner food, and are even more ubiquitous, appearing on menus all the way from Indonesia to India.

Both have now been around so long that, like other dishes, they have their own culinary histories. We won't discuss banana pancakes (because we don't love them), but the shake is a different matter. The early shakes, the shakes of the late seventies and early eighties, were truly inspired. The vendor would put condensed milk, ripe or even overripe bananas, and lots of ice in a blender, then turn the blender on and, this is the important part, blend and blend and blend. The ice had to completely disappear, even the graininess of the blended ice had to disappear. The shake was thick and creamy, like ice cream.

Nowadays, banana shakes cost a lot more. The vendors put in ice cream or yogurt, trying to justify the cost, and they come out more like floats than shakes, kind of foamy and overrich. The old type can still be found, but it takes some looking.

The good news is that they, the old kind, are easy as pie to make (easier than pie . . .). We don't bother with condensed milk, just use regular milk, and the shakes are still plenty sweet. But be sure to blend them long enough; that's the secret.

2 to 3 ripe medium bananas, fresh or frozen,
   broken into pieces (see Notes)
2 cups ice cubes or crushed ice
1 cup milk
Sugar (optional)
Sweetened condensed milk (optional)

Place the bananas, ice, and a little of the milk in a blender and start blending on the lowest speed. As the machine starts to whiz, increase the speed. The blender will sound burdened and a little bumpy as it works on the ice cubes, and you may need to stop it and use a spatula to free a jammed ice cube or piece of frozen banana. Once the blender is going well, add the remaining milk, increase the speed, and blend for 20 to 30 seconds, until you no longer hear any bumping of large pieces against the sides of the blender. Taste and add a little sugar or sweetened condensed milk if you wish; we rarely find we need to supplement the bananas' natural sweetness.

Pour into tall glasses.

SERVES *2 to 4, depending on their capacity*

NOTES: *Whenever we have bananas that are ripening to overripe, we peel them, then put them in the freezer. This way we maintain a supply of very ripe and sweet bananas, so we're always prepared when the urge for a banana shake strikes.*

In Vietnam, in the Mekong Delta, we've had avocado shakes, made like a banana shake but with less ice and a whole large avocado. The shakes are sweetened with sugar and also salted lightly. They make a delicious and very beautiful pale green drink. The only problem is that they're so filling, we don't feel like eating for 24 hours.

ICED COFFEE WITH SWEETENED CONDENSED MILK

[*kafae yen* (Thai); *cafe suada* (Vietnamese)* — THAILAND, VIETNAM, LAOS, CAMBODIA]

Coffee is grown in the mountains of Vietnam, Cambodia, and southern Laos; it was introduced by the French in the colonial era. Throughout the region, except where instant coffee has made inroads, coffee is made strong and dark, by some version of the filter and drip method. Traditional Thai coffee has an almost mocha taste and is, we're told, grown in southern Thailand. If you find it in a Thai grocery store, buy some and try it.

In Laos and Cambodia and Vietnam, coffee is made in a little individual stacked metal filter, designed to let the boiling water filter slowly through the grounds into your cup; in Thailand, the ground coffee goes into a cloth bag and then boiling water is poured through it.

The coffee is bracing, hot, and thick and often smoky-tasting on its own. We confess that our favorite version of Southeast Asian coffee is over ice, flavored with sweetened condensed milk. You'll find it served in restaurants and also at street stalls. In Thailand, you can get it *sai tung* (meaning "in a bag"): It comes in a plastic bag tied at the top with an elastic band, with a straw stuck in one corner. You slip a loop of the elastic band over a finger, letting the bag hang down; as you walk along, you can take small sips, savoring each intensely flavored mouthful, trying to extend the pleasure as long as possible as the ice slowly melts. (If you're having Southeast Asian coffee first thing in the morning, you might want to drink it hot, with sweetened condensed milk and no ice. As the day warms up, the iced version becomes irresistible.)

This makes a dazzling treat to serve at the end of a Southeast Asian meal, even to guests who always drink their coffee black.

½ **cup sweetened condensed milk, at room temperature**
12 **to 16 ice cubes**
3 **cups hot strong coffee (Lao, Vietnamese, or Thai coffee, or espresso; see Note)**

Place 2 tablespoons sweetened condensed milk in the bottom of each of four small coffee cups before adding the hot coffee. Place 3 or 4 ice cubes in each of four tall glasses and put a long-handled spoon in each.

Serve each guest one cup of coffee with a small spoon, and one tall glass of ice cubes. Instruct your guests to stir the coffee thoroughly while still very hot in order to blend in the condensed milk, then to pour it into the tall glass. (The long-handled spoon prevents the hot coffee from shattering the glass.) Stir briskly with the long-handled spoon, making an agreeable clatter with the ice cubes, to cool down the coffee.

Sip the coffee slowly, as a treat on its own or to finish off a meal.

SERVES *4*

NOTE: *If making Lao, Vietnamese, or Thai coffee using metal filters, bring 4 or more cups of water to a boil. Place a Vietnamese metal filter over each cup and fill each with about 2 tablespoons ground coffee, depending on the coffee and your taste. Pour boiling water into the top of each filter and put on the lid. Or use a regular filter or drip pot or an espresso machine. If using espresso, make it just before you wish to serve, allowing ¾ cup per person; distribute it among the four cups, pouring carefully so as not to disturb the milk on the bottom.*

WINE AND SPIRITS: There is really only one rule in Southeast Asia about what to drink when, and that is that when you drink, you must also eat. It is extremely rare for someone to drink and not to eat; eating and drinking are intimately connected. But for wine, beer, and spirits, and what to drink with what, there are no rules.

Because of the French legacy in Southeast Asia, French wines are available in many cities in Vietnam, Cambodia, and Laos. Even in Thailand, in the last decade (with higher personal incomes), people have begun drinking imported wines. Now there is even a vineyard in northeastern Thailand near Loei, a vineyard producing some pretty good wine.

But, frankly, we find drinking wine with Southeast Asian food to be a bit crazy. For one thing, the food can be very chile-hot, in some cases extremely chile-hot. Why waste a good wine? Far better, we think, to borrow the Thai tradition of drinking a local whiskey or rum, served on ice and very diluted with soda water. At a well-heeled Thai meal, the whiskey or rum becomes an imported scotch, also served very diluted with soda. (It's not unheard of in Thailand to dilute red wine with soda water, so prevalent is the habit of diluting alcohol.) A traditional meal anywhere in the region, a festive meal, can last a very long time, with new courses coming to the table one after another after another. A diluted spirit holds up well in competing with all the big flavors, not to mention quenching thirst.

Beer is also commonly drunk. In each country there are several different local beers, as well as imported beer, and we like a number of these local beers a lot. In Yunnan, just as in the rest of China, each major city has its own locally produced beer, and that beer somehow miraculously finds its way into the smallest communities in the most remote regions. In 1989, we were in the Mekong Delta in Vietnam, all the way in the southern part of the country, drinking bottled Chinese beer at a time when the two countries were almost at war.

Yunnan also has a great many different spirits, many made from millet, sorghum, and rice. The ubiquitous *bai jiu*, or white liquor, is made from sorghum and has a taste we will never like; in fact, we find it absolutely foul. But many other spirits are just the opposite, and always worth at least an adventurous sip. Generally they are very strong, fifty to sixty percent alcohol. Occasionally we will see them in a big jar with a snake or some other creature inside. These are for medicinal reasons, impotence or better blood circulation or whatever. We can't vouch for their effectiveness, but they often taste fine, even fairly good.

Last but not least, there is something that we call wine, for lack of a better word. Known as *lao khao* in both Lao and Thai, it's made from ordinary rice or sticky rice, and is of a strength and taste not unlike sake. Rice alcohols can get very expensive and sought after in China or they can be common and very cheap. If we are out in the fields at harvest, or eating dinner in a little restaurant in a backwoodsy place, some version of this "wine" will often be served. We're always delighted, honored even, to be offered a homemade drink made from local rice, created for drinking right there, right then.

All kinds of drinks are sold sai tung *or "in a bag," from iced coffee to these cold drinks, at the Lao market in That Panom (see page 276).*

GLOSSARY OF FLAVORINGS

DRY-ROASTED FLAVORINGS Dry-roasting is a way of intensifying flavors (and, incidentally, perfuming your kitchen with wonderful aromas). It's a method widely used in Asia for peanuts and sesame seeds, which are then chopped or slightly ground and sprinkled on as a topping or flavoring for rice, noodles, salads. . . . Grated coconut, fresh or frozen, is also dry-roasted to bring out its flavor and make it less perishable. In Thailand, Laos, and Vietnam, sticky rice is not only a staple food, but also a condiment. It's dry-roasted, then ground to a powder and used as an aromatic ingredient in salads. All these prepared ingredients are easy and useful kitchen staples.

DRY-ROASTED PEANUTS

Start with whole skinless peanuts from an Asian grocery. They're white and fat. Sometimes they've been boiled, sometimes they're raw. If you can find only peanuts with the skins on, you'll need to rub the skins off after dry-roasting.

Place a heavy large skillet over medium heat. Add about 1 cup peanuts and use a wooden spoon to move them around the pan frequently to prevent sticking and burned spots as they roast. They will start to develop golden patches and become aromatic; if you notice any black patches on the nuts before they have turned light brown, remove the pan from the heat for a moment and lower the heat, then return the pan to the heat and continue. Once the peanuts are golden brown in large patches all over, transfer them to a large cutting board and coarsely chop. Or, let them cool, then transfer to a food processor and pulse briefly to coarsely chop; be careful not to overprocess—you do not want a paste.

Store, once completely cooled, in a well-sealed container in a cool place. In Vietnam and Cambodia, chopped dry-roasted peanuts are often mixed with sugar to make a sweetened topping for desserts or sticky rice.

DRY-ROASTED SESAME SEEDS

Like peanuts, these contain a lot of oil, so they can burn very quickly. Place a heavy skillet over medium-high heat and add about ½ cup sesame seeds (or whatever quantity you wish to roast). Use a wooden spoon to stir them continuously and keep them from burning. Once they are golden and aromatic, lower the heat slightly and continue to stir and turn until they are a rich golden brown. Transfer to a bowl and stir several times as they cool to help the steam escape. When they are completely cool and dry, store in a sealed glass container in a cool place.

If you want to crush or grind roasted sesame seeds, use a spice grinder or a mortar and pestle. The Japanese mortar known as a *suribachi* has ridges inside its bowl, ideal for grinding sesame seeds.

DRY-ROASTED GRATED COCONUT

To dry-roast fresh or frozen grated coconut, heat a heavy skillet over medium heat, add the coconut, and stir constantly. If you are using frozen grated coconut, it will give off some water as it heats, but this will quickly evaporate. After about 5 minutes for fresh coconut, 8 or more for frozen, the coconut will start to turn golden. Keep stirring and turning to ensure even cooking and prevent burning until the shreds are firm and dry, aromatic, and golden brown. Let cool completely before storing in a sealed glass or plastic container in the refrigerator. It will keep for about a week.

ROASTED RICE POWDER
[*khao kua* (Thai/Lao), *thinh* (Vietnamese)]

This handy condiment from northeast Thailand, Laos, and Vietnam is simple to prepare and adds good flavor as well as a slight and very pleasing texture to cooked salads. Make up a batch and keep handy for sprinkling on cooked vegetables and other soft foods as you please.

¼ cup Thai sticky rice or jasmine rice

Heat a heavy skillet over medium-high heat. Add the rice and dry-roast, stirring frequently to prevent sticking and burning, until it is an all-over golden brown. Transfer to a spice grinder, coffee grinder, or mortar and grind to a powder. Let cool completely. Store in a well-sealed glass jar.
MAKES *about ¼ cup powder*

AROMATIC ROASTED RICE POWDER

[*khao kua* — NORTHEAST THAILAND]

This variant on roasted rice powder is scented with lemongrass and wild lime leaf. The roasted rice holds the aroma of the herbs for a good long time, so it's a way of keeping some of that elusive wild lime leaf aroma alive in your kitchen. (We've kept the powder for as long as 4 months in a tightly sealed glass container, and at the end of all that time it was still pleasingly aromatic.) Use it as a condiment and flavoring in Thai-Lao salads and *laab* dishes.

½ stalk lemongrass
2 to 3 fresh or frozen wild lime leaves
¼ cup Thai or Lao sticky rice

Cut the tough root end and any grassy top off the lemongrass and discard. Peel off the tough outer layers. Use a cleaver or sharp knife to thinly slice, then mince enough to make 1 tablespoon. Fold each lime leaf in half and gently tear out the central vein. Stack the leaves, roll up tightly, and very thinly slice, then mince enough to make 1 tablespoon.

In a small bowl, mix together the rice, lemongrass, and lime leaf.

Place a heavy skillet over medium-high heat and add the rice mixture. Using a wooden spoon or spatula to keep the mixture moving to prevent burning, dry-roast until the rice has turned golden. Transfer to a spice grinder, coffee grinder, or large mortar and grind or pound to a coarse powder. (You may have to grind it in more than one batch.) Let cool completely, then transfer to a well-sealed glass or plastic container.

MAKES *about 6 tablespoons powder*

CHINESE PEPPER-SALT

[*jiaoyan* — CHINA]

This classic condiment and flavoring is widely used in China, especially in regions where the taste is for hot and spicy. Serve it as a dipping powder or use as a dry-rub or flavoring ingredient.

1 teaspoon Sichuan peppercorns
1 tablespoon kosher or sea salt

In a small heavy skillet, dry-roast the pepper and salt together until slightly aromatic. Transfer to a mortar or spice grinder or coffee grinder and pound or grind to a powder.

MAKES *about 1 tablespoon powder*

TWO PEPPER-SALT SPICE DIP

[*prik ji* — SOUTHERN YUNNAN]

This is the Dai version of classic Chinese pepper-salt. *Prik ji* in the Dai language means "dried red chiles." Serve this as a dipping powder or use as a dry-rub or flavoring ingredient.

3 Thai dried red chiles
2 tablespoons kosher or sea salt
1 teaspoon Sichuan peppercorns

In a small heavy skillet, dry-roast the chiles until soft. Remove from the skillet and tear into pieces, discarding the tough stems. Place in a mortar or a food processor and pound or grind to a powder.

Place the salt and Sichuan peppercorns in a heavy skillet over medium heat and dry-roast until slightly aromatic. Add to the mortar with the chiles and pound to a powder; or, grind to a powder in a spice grinder or coffee grinder, then mix together with the chile powder in a bowl. Store in a well-sealed container.

MAKES *less than ¼ cup powder*

FLAVORED OILS Flavored oils are simple condiments that can be drizzled on rice or noodles or soup to give them a little zip. You can also cook with the oil, then use the flavoring solids as a garnish for the finished dish if you wish. There's nothing like the crunch of fried garlic to brighten a steamed dumpling or a bowl of noodles.

Each of these oils is made the same way: The oil is heated, then the flavoring is dropped into the hot oil and the oil is left to steep and cool. Store flavored oils in the refrigerator; the oil will cloud in the cold, but this will not change its flavor.

HOT CHILE OIL

Chile oil is widely sold in Asian markets, but homemade is easy and better tasting. Be sure your chile flakes are bright red, hot, and very fresh. Use the oil as a condiment and flavoring, with or without a little of the chiles.

½ cup peanut or vegetable oil
3 tablespoons dried red chile flakes

Heat the oil in a wok or skillet. As soon as it starts to smoke, toss in the chile flakes, taking care not to splash yourself, and remove from the heat. Let stand until completely cool, then transfer to a clean dry glass jar and store in a cool place. If you wish, in several days you can strain out the chiles and store them separately or discard them, leaving you with just a gleaming orange hot oil.

MAKES *about ½ cup oil*

SCALLION OIL

This is a subtly perfumed oil with a cloud of pale green floating in it, very attractive served in a small glass dish. Use as a condiment for rice, noodles, and soups.

¼ cup peanut or vegetable oil
3 medium to large scallions, trimmed and finely chopped

Heat the oil in a wok or skillet over high heat. When it is very hot but not smoking, add the scallions, taking care not to splash yourself, and immediately remove from the heat. Let cool to room temperature, then transfer the oil and scallions to a clean dry glass container, cover, and store in a cool place. With the scallions in it, the oil will keep for only a few days; for longer keeping, strain out the scallions.

MAKES *about ¼ cup oil*

GARLIC OIL, FRIED GARLIC, AND VARIATIONS

Little bits of crunchy fried garlic or shallots make a great topping; the oil they are fried in is aromatic and another versatile flavoring. If you toss in dried red chiles, you have a chile-garlic oil . . . all easy variations on a theme.

¼ cup peanut or vegetable oil
2 to 3 tablespoons minced garlic

Heat the oil in a wok or skillet over high heat. When it is hot, toss in the garlic, taking care not to splash yourself, and use a spatula to stir and separate the garlic as it clumps in the hot oil. When the garlic begins to color, after 15 to 20 seconds, remove from the heat and let stand until the oil cools to room temperature. Transfer the oil and garlic to a clean dry container with a tight-fitting lid. The oil will keep for about 5 days; to keep it longer, strain out the garlic and discard. Store in the refrigerator or another cool place. Discard after 1 month.

MAKES *¼ cup oil*

VARIATIONS: *Use the same method to make* SHALLOT OIL *and* FRIED SHALLOTS, *substituting 3 tablespoons shallots for the garlic. Once the oil has cooled, scoop out the shallots, drain well on paper towels, and store separately in a well-sealed container in the refrigerator. You can also buy fried shallots in Asian markets, but, as always, homemade have a better flavor.*

TO MAKE SHAN-STYLE CHILE-GARLIC OIL, *dry-roast 4 dried red chiles, following the method in Two Pepper–Salt Spice Dip (page 309). Discard the stems, then pound or grind the chiles to a powder in a mortar or spice grinder or coffee grinder. Follow the recipe for Garlic Oil, and add the powdered chile just after you remove the oil from the heat. (This oil doesn't keep well in the tropical heat, so traditionally it is not made in large quantities.) Let cool, then transfer to a clean dry jar, seal tightly, and refrigerate. If you will be storing the oil for longer than 5 days, after a day or two, strain out the chiles and garlic, leaving you the fragrant oil.*

HOMEMADE PICKLES Pickling garlic, cabbage, and chiles is a way of keeping intense flavors alive well after the growing season is over. Pickles are handy to have around, to add extra flavor and crunch. Be sure that the jars you use are sterile and seal well. For a complete discussion of pickling and canning, including an explanation of health and safety issues and reliable sterilizing techniques, refer to *Preserving* by Oded Schwartz (*see* Bibliography).

THAI PICKLED GARLIC

[*kratiem dong* — THAILAND, LAOS]

Whole heads of unpeeled garlic are soaked in water to make them easier to peel, then bathed in a sweet-sour vinegar solution. In Thailand, the heads of garlic are smaller and are pickled whole. They're very beautiful in the jar, but we find the heads we get in North America are usually too large and tough, so we separate the garlic into (unpeeled) cloves before pickling. This also gives us a chance to discard any discolored or shriveled cloves.

Add slices of pickled garlic to Thai salads, serve as part of a fresh or cooked vegetable plate, or use as an ingredient for Mekong Subs (page 284).

8 large heads garlic (1 pound), preferably organic
1½ cups rice vinegar
1½ cups sugar
3 tablespoons kosher salt

Place the garlic heads in a bowl of water with a lid or other weight on top to keep them submerged. When they have soaked for an hour or more, drain, peel off the outer skin, and separate into cloves; do not peel the individual cloves.

Combine the remaining ingredients in a nonreactive saucepan and bring to a boil, stirring to dissolve the sugar. Once the sugar has completely dissolved, add the garlic cloves and simmer for 5 minutes. Remove from heat and let cool to room temperature.

Once the garlic cloves have cooled, sterilize one medium (1-pint) or two small (½-pint) canning jars and their lids.

Use sterile tongs or a sterile slotted spoon to lift the garlic cloves out of the vinegar mixture and place them into the jar(s), packing them tightly. Stir the vinegar mixture well with a clean dry spoon, then pour over the garlic, filling the jar(s) right to the top. Cover tightly and store in a dark place. You can use the garlic after a week, but the flavor improves with age. Refrigerate after opening.

MAKES *1 pint pickled garlic*

NOTE: *We've also made pickled garlic by peeling the cloves before pickling. The garlic absorbs the pickling solution more quickly, but without the protection of the peel, it also turns a slightly disturbing blue-green color (though it's nothing to worry about; in fact, it's the sulfur compounds in the garlic combining with some trace copper in the water). After pickling, unpeeled individual cloves will slide easily out of their skins.*

PICKLED CABBAGE, THAI STYLE

[*pak kat dong* — THAILAND]

Unlike many pickles, this slightly sweet, intense version of pickled cabbage doesn't make you wait for weeks. Two days after it goes into the jars, it's ready, still slightly crunchy and bursting with flavor. Over time, the cabbage softens and the flavors mellow. This makes a good addition to a vegetable plate or, finely chopped, a kind of chutney/pickle condiment to accompany any rice or noodle meal. Or stir-fry it as an accompaniment for a rice meal (see Note.)

1 medium Savoy cabbage (about 2½ pounds), or 2½ pounds
  Swatow mustard greens
2 cups rice vinegar
1 cup sugar
2 tablespoons kosher salt

Peel off and discard any discolored leaves, then cut the cabbage lengthwise in half. Cut out the core and discard. Cut the cabbage into thin wedges, then cut crosswise into approximately 2-inch pieces. (If using the greens, cut into roughly rectangular pieces about 1 by 2 inches.) Spread out on a tray or basket in a warm or sunny place, cover loosely with a white cotton cloth, and let wilt for 6 to 12 hours.

Place the remaining ingredients in a nonreactive pot and bring to a boil. Let cool to room temperature.

Meanwhile, sterilize two 1-pint glass canning jars and their lids. Stuff the cabbage into the sterile jars, using sterile tongs. Pour the vinegar mixture over to cover, then seal tightly. Let stand for 2 days at room temperature (or, if the weather is very hot, in a cool place) before using. Store in the refrigerator. Use within 3 weeks.

MAKES *2 pints pickled cabbage*

NOTE: *You can make a quick and easy stir-fry with pickled cabbage. Heat 2 tablespoons oil in a wok and toss in 3 dried red chiles and 1 tablespoon minced garlic. When the garlic begins to change color, toss in 2 cups drained, coarsely chopped cabbage. Stir-fry for about 2 minutes, until wilting, then season with 1 tablespoon Thai or Vietnamese fish sauce or 1 teaspoon salt. Stir briefly, turn out onto a plate, and serve. This makes an excellent foil for mild or rich dishes, such as coconut milk–based curries or soups. In Issaan it's called* pak som pad, *in Laos,* khoua pak.

PICKLED CHILES

[YUNNAN]

We came across this version of pickled chiles in Muslim restaurants in Yunnan. They are eaten as a condiment with meals, and also used as an ingredient in cooking. They're simple to make, but you could substitute the pickled chiles of Greek tradition, often sold in Mediterranean grocery stores alongside the olives, though they're generally not as hot as the chiles served in Yunnan.

Yunnanese pickled chiles are made with vinegar or with *bai jiu*, literally, "white liquor," a strong clear Chinese liquor. The recipe below calls for vinegar.

Serve these as a condiment/pickle to accompany a meal; set out on a salad plate, or use as an ingredient in stir-fries. Refrigerate after opening.

¼ **pound (about 2 cups) serrano chiles or other small hot**
  or medium-hot chiles
1 cup rice vinegar
½ **cup sugar**
2 tablespoons kosher salt
Pinch of Sichuan peppercorns (optional)
2 star anise, whole or in pieces

Wash and dry the chiles. Cut off the stems, leaving the chiles whole.

Heat the vinegar in a nonreactive saucepan, add the sugar and salt, and stir until completely dissolved. Add the Sichuan pepper, if using, and the star anise and simmer briefly, then let cool to room temperature.

Sterilize two ½-pint canning jars and their lids. Stuff the chiles into the jars and place 1 star anise in each jar. Stir the pickling solution, then pour over the chiles, filling the jars to the top. Put on the lids and seal tightly. Set aside in a cool place for 2 weeks before using.

MAKES *1 pint pickled chiles*

algae: *See* river weed.

anchovy fillets: Anchovies preserved in brine or olive oil.

anise: *See* star anise.

aromatic jasmine rice: Often called *Thai jasmine*, aromatic jasmine rice is long-grain aromatic rice that cooks to a tender, slightly clinging consistency. It is the staple rice in many parts of Thailand and Vietnam and in Cambodia. Similar rices are eaten in many parts of Burma. The highest-quality jasmine rice used to be grown in Cambodia. Now Thailand is the source of most top-quality Southeast Asian jasmine rice. Jasmine rice grown in Thailand is widely available in North America, in supermarkets as well as in Asian groceries. American-grown jasmine rices are similar, but often have less aroma. They are also widely available. *See* Index for recipes.

Asian basil: *See* basil.

Asian eggplant: *See* eggplant.

bac ha: This is eaten as a vegetable, especially in Vietnam, but is, in fact, the long, strong, bright green stem of a plant known in English as *giant taro*. It looks a little like a single giant smooth stalk of celery, but it is a brighter green color and has no thick fibers. To cook, boil until tender. Frequently used in Vietnamese sour soup, it is sold in Vietnamese grocery stores.

basil, Asian basil, holy basil: With purple flowers, medium to dark green pointed leaves, and a sharp anise taste that stands up better to heating than sweet Mediterranean basil, *Asian basil* (also known as *Thai basil*) is a tropical variety of sweet basil (*Occimum basilicum*) that has become a favorite with chefs and other cooks and eaters who like strong tastes. In Vietnamese, it's called *rau que*; in Khmer, *jii' liang vong*; in Thai and Lao, *bai horapa*; in the Luang Prabang region of Laos, *pak itoo*. You'll find it in Asian groceries and in many large supermarkets. *Holy basil* (*Occimum basilicum*) has narrower leaves than Asian basil, and the leaves are sometimes tinged with purple. Known as *bai gaprow* in Thai and *mareh preuw* in Khmer, it is often available in Southeast Asian grocery stores. It has little taste or aroma when raw; the flavor emerges strongly when it's cooked. In Thailand, there's another form of sweet basil, rarely available here, known as *bai menglak*. It has small bright green leaves, and it doesn't keep well.

bean curd: *See* tofu.

bean sprouts: Chinese and other East Asian cuisines make use of the sprouts of both mung beans and soybeans. Mung bean sprouts are widely available; they are about 2 inches long and white with a small green yellow pod (the bean) at one end. Soybean sprouts are yellow, thicker, and longer (4 inches or more), and the beans from which they sprout are big and yellow. Mung bean sprouts are the only sprouts called for in this book. Buy sprouts that are crisp and pale-colored. Rinse them well with cold water and store them in a well-sealed container or plastic bag in the refrigerator; they are best when they are very fresh. They can be eaten raw or briefly parboiled or stir-fried. *See* Index for recipes.

black sticky rice: The unpolished version of one variety of Thai sticky rice (*see* Sticky rice), black sticky rice is widely used in Southeast Asia, especially for sweet treats. Because it is an unmilled ("brown") rice, it takes longer to cook and is less sticky than white (milled) sticky rice. It is now widely available in Asian shops and large grocery stores. *See* Index for recipes.

black vinegar: *See* vinegar.

bok choi: Also sometimes spelled *bok choy*, this Chinese green and its close cousin *Shanghai bok choi* are increasingly available in large grocery stores as well as in Asian markets. Bok choi has wide dark green leaves and wide white stems; it grows in a small bunch or head, made up of several stems. Shanghai bok choi is shaped the same, but is bright green all over. Both are usually sold in bundles of two or three, bound with a rubber band. As with all these greens, the smaller the better in terms of tenderness and subtlety of flavor.

broccoli rabe: Also known as *rapini*, this member of the *brassica* family is now widely available in North America. It is a staple winter vegetable in Italy with dark green leaves and small heads of yellow flowers. Substitute regular broccoli.

canned coconut milk: *See* coconut.

carambola: *See* star fruit.

cassia (*Cinnamomum cassia*): Cassia bark has a strong cinnamonlike taste. It is sold in quills, long curved dried bits of bark, or powdered, and is usually labeled "cinnamon." Most of the cinnamon sticks and ground cinnamon sold in North America are in fact cassia, and that is the cinnamon we call for in this book, for in Southeast Asia it is cassia, not true cinnamon, that is used to give a cinnamon taste.

celery leaf, Chinese celery leaf: Used as a fresh herb in Chinese and Lao dishes (in the same way that coriander leaves are used), celery leaf is known in Laos as *tang sai*. Bundles of it are sold in Chinese and Southeast Asian groceries. It is long and pale green, like regular celery, but with thin green stalks and much stronger tasting leaves. You can substitute the Japanese herb mitsuba or leaves from regular celery (they'll be less strong tasting). Celery seeds are used in yellow curry.

cellophane noodles: *See* noodles.

chick-peas: Often known as *garbanzos*, these round golden yellow dried legumes are eaten in India, Central Asia, and the Mediterranean. They are available dried in most grocery stores and must be soaked overnight, then boiled for 2 to 3 hours until tender. Chick-pea flour, made from ground chick-peas, is known as *besan* in Hindi and is widely used in India.

chile pepper flakes: *See* chiles.

Chiles

Chiles are used both fresh and dried in the Mekong region. They vary greatly in chile heat, from mild to very hot. The general word for chiles in Thai and Lao is *prik*; in Khmer, *m'teh*; in Vietnamese, *ot*; and in Mandarin, *la jiao*. Use rubber gloves when cutting hot chiles, or wash your hands thoroughly with soapy water immediately afterward; do not touch your face or eyes with "chile hands." Wash all cutting surfaces thoroughly after chopping chiles, or you'll spread chile heat to other foods.

banana chiles, Cubanelles, Hungarian wax chiles: All these chiles are pale yellow to pale green, long, and 1½ to 2 inches wide at the top. They are mild to medium-hot, the heat varying even among chiles of the same type sold in the same bin at the produce stand. These are the closest approximation to the mild to medium chiles used in northern Thai and Lao cooking and known there as *prik num*; they are usually grilled, then pounded to a paste. They too vary in heat but are generally closest to banana chiles, in

our experience. Use whichever chiles you have available. If yours are very mild and you wish more heat, just add a little serrano or bird chile to the recipe.

bird chiles: These small, pointed very hot chiles come in small cellophane packages in Southeast Asian shops. They're known in Khmer as *m'teh k'mang*, in Vietnamese as *ot*, and in Thai and Lao as *prik kii noo*. They may be green or orange or red; most packages contain a mixture. You can substitute serrano chiles; you'll have less heat but a similar flavor.

cayenne chiles, red and green: Long narrow pointed chiles, shiny bright red or deep green, cayenne chiles are sold in large grocery stores and in Asian markets. They are hot, though less hot than bird chiles.

chile pepper flakes: Dried red chiles are ground to a coarse powder and sold as chile pepper flakes in Asian groceries. They come in small plastic packages. Buy the brightest-red ones you can find. Store well sealed; if they start to smell musty, discard them. You can substitute finely chopped dried red chiles or the red pepper flakes that are sold in supermarket spice sections.

dried red chiles, Thai dried red chiles: Called *prik haeng* in Thai, dried red chiles are sold in cellophane packages in Asian grocery stores and many supermarkets. Try to find those labeled "product of Thailand" and, if you have a choice, pick those that are brightest red. As they age, dried red chiles seem to darken, and they also break into pieces, so if the chiles in the package look fairly intact, it's a good sign. Store, once opened, in a well-sealed glass jar (this keeps them fresher and prevents moths and other infestations). Dried red chile flakes can usually be substituted.

chile oil: A bright-red flavored oil sold in most Asian grocery stores, in glass jars. Chile oil keeps almost indefinitely in a cool place. It's made by steeping chile flakes in canola, cottonseed, or soy oil. Making your own, better-tasting version is very easy (*see* Hot Chile Oil, page 310).

Chinese broccoli: Depending on who you're talking to, this name may refer to either of two

broccolilike Chinese greens, *gai laan*, with round stalks and small white flowers, or *choi sum*, also known as flowering Chinese cabbage, with ridged green stalks and small yellow flowers. Both are members of the mustard family (*Brassicaceae*), like broccoli; both are widely available in Asian markets; and both are delicious.

Chinese celery leaf: *See* celery leaf.

Chinese chives: Flat-bladed chives with a flavor that has some onion and some garlic in it. Widely available (sold in bundles) in Asian markets. Regular chives can be substituted, with a slight difference in flavor and texture.

Chinese mustard greens, Swatow mustard: Another group of Chinese greens from the *brassica* family, all of these are pale green, with leaves attached at the bottom of the stem, giving a loose or tight "head of lettuce" appearance. Traditionally in China, they are used fresh or salted and pickled.

Chinese pickled cabbage: Often known as *Tianjin* (or *Tientsin*) cabbage, this preserve has a salty vinegary taste, less sweet than Pickled Cabbage, Thai Style (page 311). Homemade or store-bought, pickled cabbage makes a great condiment, in small quantities, for congee-style rice soups and other soups. Tianjin pickled cabbage usually comes in small heavy plastic packages or in crocks, both sold at East Asian grocery stores. You can substitute other pickled vegetables, such as pickled lettuce (often sold in jars); it's fun to walk down the aisle of a Chinese or Vietnamese grocery and see all the pickled greens possibilities. Once opened, pickled vegetables should be stored in the refrigerator, well sealed.

Chinese rice wine: Known as *Shaoxing*, this pale brown cooking wine is available in Chinese grocery stores and some liquor stores. It gives a good depth of flavor to sauces and simmered dishes. It's similar in taste and smell to dry sherry, which can be substituted.

cilantro: *See* coriander.

cinnamon, cinnamon stick: True cinnamon has a milder flavor and more flaky, fragile bark than cassia, the spice that is usually sold as cinnamon and cinnamon sticks in North America. Cassia is the cinnamon used in Southeast Asia, and the one we mean when we call for cinnamon in this book. *See* cassia.

Coconut

Coconuts grow in tropical and subtropical climates, the fruit of the coconut palm. They are available, brown colored and hairy with fibers, at some markets in North America. Buy coconuts that are firm, not cracked. To tell if a coconut is ripe, pick it up and shake it; it should be heavy and have liquid sloshing around inside. To open, hit sharply with a hammer, or place the point of a large screwdriver on the coconut and tap the other end with a hammer. The inside of the coconut should be a gleaming fresh white with a slightly sweet smell.

grated coconut: This useful ingredient is produced by splitting open a ripe coconut and scraping the white meat from inside the fruit. To extract the meat, you need a coconut grater, a hand-held metal scraper attached to a board, available from Southeast Asian and Indian shops. You scrape the coconut against the grater to produce a pile of freshly grated coconut. (To improvise, for small quantities, you can use the sharp rippled edge of a large bottle cap to scrape out the coconut meat.) Use the meat immediately, fresh or to make Dry-Roasted Grated Coconut (page 308) or coconut milk, or freeze it. Grated coconut is also available *frozen* or *dried* in many Asian markets. For frozen, look in the freezer for 1-pound packages in heavyweight clear plastic; for dried, check the dried spices and flavorings section. *Note:* Be sure to read the package carefully. You do *not* want "young coconut"; you want *unsweetened* grated coconut, whether frozen or dried.

coconut cream and **coconut milk:** These are the thicker and thinner versions of the white liquid extracted from grated coconut. They are high in saturated fat (so that they solidify when refrigerated) and slightly sweet. *To make fresh-pressed coconut milk, using freshly grated coconut,* begin with 2 cups grated coconut. Place it in a large bowl and pour over 1½ cups warm (about 110°F) water. Stir with your hands, massaging and kneading the coconut for about a minute, or blend it briefly in a blender or food processor, then let it stand for a few minutes, if you have the time, before you squeeze the liquid out of it handful by handful, setting the meat aside in another bowl. Set this extracted first pressing milk aside; you should have just over 1½ cups. Repeat to extract a second (thinner) pressing, and discard the coconut meat. Use the milk immediately, or refrigerate in a glass container, well sealed, for no more than 24 hours. If you use less water, say about ¾ cup, the first pressing will be thicker and richer, "coconut cream." *To use frozen grated unsweetened coconut to produce coconut milk,* place 2 cups thawed grated coconut in a bowl with 1½ cups very warm water and follow the same method as above. The milk you extract will be a little less thick and tasty than that from freshly grated coconut, but still very acceptable.

　　If you are in a hurry or don't have access to good coconuts (we usually fall into both categories), then you'll want to keep a supply of **canned (unsweetened) coconut milk** in your pantry. It's available in most Asian groceries, in 14- and 20-ounce cans. Try any made-in-Thailand brand, such as Aroy or Mae Ploy. It usually separates in the can into a thick "cream" layer on top and thinner watery milk below. You can use these separately, or stir well to recombine. Once opened, canned coconut milk should be transferred to a glass container and stored, well sealed, in the refrigerator for no more than 36 hours. (*Note:* Su-Mei Yu, a Thai chef and writer of Chinese-Thai origin who is passionate about respecting culinary traditions, feels that canned coconut milk is an abomination, and she won't have it in her kitchen. Su-Mei lives in San Diego and manages to get good coconuts, from which she presses coconut milk. If your supply of coconut is unreliable, but you'd like to press your own milk, try pressing your own coconut milk from frozen grated unsweetened coconut [*see above*].)

cooking oils: For stir-frying Chinese and Southeast Asian food, we generally use cold-pressed Chinese **peanut oil**, sold in large tins in Asian grocery stores. It's less expensive and more flavorful than North American–style peanut oil. For an oil with very little taste, use Planter's peanut oil. Peanut oil can be heated to a very high temperature without breaking down, which also makes it ideal for deep-frying. You can substitute canola oil or corn oil if you wish; they are a little less stable at high temperatures. If preparing food for people with nut allergies, avoid peanut oil. In most of the Mekong region, **rendered pork fat (lard)** is the traditional cooking oil. It gives an incomparable flavor, but it is not in accord with current approaches to healthy eating. Pork fat is also something of a luxury for many people in the region, so that in fact many cooks in the Mekong area use a vegetable oil, such as cottonseed oil or soy oil, instead. Buy pork fat from your butcher or accumulate a supply over time by trimming fat from pork and storing it in a plastic bag in the freezer. *To render pork fat,* place pieces of pork fat in a heavy skillet over medium heat; the fat will gradually melt. When all the fat has melted, pour through a strainer, to catch any stray pieces of meat, into a container. Once cooled, store, covered, in the refrigerator or freezer.

coriander, coriander leaves, coriander roots: Known as *pakchi* in Thai, *pak hom pom* in Lao, and *rau ngo* in Vietnamese, coriander has now become widely available, even in small grocery stores. The leaves and roots of coriander, also known by its Mexican name, *cilantro,* are widely used in Southeast Asia. The roots are particularly important in Thai and Lao cuisines. Try to buy bunches of coriander with the roots still on. Stored in water (to the top of the roots) with a plastic bag placed loosely over the leaves, it will keep in the refrigerator for about a week. Because *coriander root* is so handy to have for preparing many classic Thai dishes, we try to stockpile it. We always buy coriander with the roots on; when we've finished with the leaves, we wash the roots, then wrap them in foil and freeze them. Defrost simply by running them under cold water.

cornstarch: Sold in any grocery store, cornstarch is used to thicken the sauce at the last minute in many Chinese stir-fry dishes. It's also an ingredient in Fresh Noodle Sheets (page 121). Store in a well-sealed jar.

curry pastes: Ready-made curry pastes from Thailand (red, green, yellow, mussamen, and sometimes others) are now widely sold in Southeast Asian groceries and large well-stocked grocery stores. You can also make your own (*see* Index). Curry pastes contain fresh and dried flavorings, usually including galangal, dried or fresh chiles, and shrimp paste, among other ingredients. They come in cans or jars or in foil packages. Once opened, stored in the refrigerator, well sealed, they will keep for a month or more. Most traditional Southeast Asian curries begin by heating the curry paste in oil or coconut milk to release the flavors; the remaining ingredients in the dish are then added and cooked in the curry-flavored oil.

daikon (*Raphanus sativus spp.*): A large white or pale green radish, also sometimes called *icicle radish* or *white radish*, this root vegetable is used sliced or grated in soups and salads and to make pickles. It is now widely available in large grocery stores as well as in Asian markets. Buy firm smooth-skinned daikon, and choose smaller ones over larger. Daikon keeps well in a plastic bag in the refrigerator. *Daikon* is the Japanese name; the Vietnamese is *cu cai tau;* the Thai, *hua pak had.*

dao jiao: *See* fermented soybean paste.

dill: Known in Thailand as *pak chi lao* and in Laos as *pak si,* fresh dill is used in the cooking of the Luang Pabang region, usually simmered in cooked dishes rather than raw. Fresh dill has soft frondlike leaves and long stems; the flowers are parasol-shaped and ripen into dill seed, used in Northern and Eastern European cooking.

doufu gan: *See* tofu.

dried mushrooms: *See* mushrooms.

dried red chile flakes: *See* chiles.

dried river weed: *See* river weed.

dried shrimp: These small orange-pink shrimp are salty and pungent-tasting, flavor-packed. They are widely used for giving flavor and depth to soups and curry pastes in many parts of Southeast Asia and in China. Known as *gung haeng* in Thai and *tngoi* in Khmer, they are easy to find, sold in clear cellophane packages in Chinese and Southeast Asian grocery stores. If you have a choice, choose larger over smaller shrimp and strong-colored over pale. Once you have opened the package, store in a tightly sealed plastic bag in the refrigerator for no longer than a month.

eggplant (*Solanum spp.*): Many different eggplants are used in Southeast Asian dishes, some cooked and some raw. Look for them in Asian shops and large well-stocked grocery stores. *Long eggplants*, also known as *Asian eggplants*, are pale or dark purple, white, or bright green in color and are stir-fried, grilled, or simmered; they are 5 to 12 inches long and fairly slender. Unlike Mediterranean eggplants, they do not need salting to draw out bitterness. Small round, firm, white or pale green *Thai eggplants* (*makheua khun* in Thai and Lao), also known as *round eggplants,* are the size of limes. They are often used in Thai and Lao curries, whole or halved. They may also come to the table uncooked, as part of the array of raw vegetables served to accompany cooked salsas and other dishes. Tiny green eggplants, known as *pea eggplants* (*makheua puong* in Thai and Lao), are used in curries to give an agreeable bitter taste. They are smaller than cherry tomatoes and bright green, usually sold on the stalk.

European cucumber: Long, tender-skinned European cucumbers (sometimes called English or seedless cucumbers) are mild-tasting, with small tender seeds, and ideal accompaniments to many Southeast Asian dishes. They are now widely available in grocery stores almost year-round. Substitute other cucumbers if you wish, but peel them and remove any tough seeds.

fagara: *See* Sichuan pepper.

fermented soybean cakes: Known in Shan as *tua nao,* these dark brown thin, almost crisp rounds are used in northern Thai and Shan cooking. In recipes, you can substitute fermented soybean paste (*see below*). These are the instructions we were given for making them: Boil soybeans in water until soft. Let sit for 3 days to ferment, then pound to flatten and shape into 3-inch disks. Flatten between two layers of cotton cloth. Dry in the sun. Grill lightly to dry out completely. To use, pound in a mortar with other flavorings such as dried red chile, sesame seeds, and peanuts (*see* Shan Chile Paste, page 37).

fermented soybean paste: Most readily available in Thai groceries and Vietnamese shops, this is the original fermented soybean product, the forerunner of soy sauce, miso, and other soy products. Fermented soybeans are a traditional ingredient in northern Thai and Shan cooking and in vegetarian Chinese and Vietnamese dishes. (Farther south, in central and southern Thailand, smoky fermented flavor comes instead from using shrimp paste and dried shrimp.) Soybean paste comes in glass jars; we keep it in the refrigerator once the jar has been opened. It traditionally contains only soybeans, salt, and water, but often there is also a little sugar as well as a preservative in it. The beans may be whole or already mashed; mash the beans before using it.

The Thai name is *dao jiao* and Thai versions are labeled "fermented soybeans"; the Vietnamese version (which contains a little sugar and is slightly darker) comes as a paste or sauce labeled *tuong cu da* or *tuong bac*. (*Note:* Read the label—if it contains ingredients other than soybeans, salt, water, sugar, and, perhaps, a preservative, it will have a different flavor, say, of garlic or hot chiles; look for a plain version.) You can also use Indonesian fermented soybeans (the brand we find most often is Yeo); again, it's a little sweet and the beans need to be mashed. A spoonful or two gives a distinctive and wonderful flavor to Thai rice noodles (*see*, for example, page 116), vegetable stir-fries, many Shan specialties, and vegetarian versions of many Thai and Vietnamese dishes.

fermented soybean sauce: *See* fermented soybean paste.

fiddleheads: The tender, edible tip of a kind of young fern, fiddleheads are available in the spring from well-stocked grocery stores and specialty produce markets. Fiddleheads from New England and the maritime provinces of Canada are the best known. They are best eaten very young and very fresh. To prepare, place in a large sink full of cool water. Gently rub off any remaining papery-like casing, trim off the tough stem ends, and wash thoroughly before cooking. Many ferns are poisonous, so don't go out into the woods to gather fiddleheads unless you know them well.

fish sauce: Known as *nam pla* in Thai, *nam pa* in Lao, *tuk trey* in Khmer, and *nuoc mam* in Vietnamese, fish sauce is the essential flavoring and condiment in much of Southeast Asia. The pale liquid released by heavily salted and pressed fish as they ferment, it is salty and the flavor varies from slightly smoky to very pungent. Thai and Cambodian fish sauces tend to be milder and less pungent than the Vietnamese. Fish sauce is sold in tall bottles, very inexpensively. (Some U.S.-based companies are now repackaging Thai fish sauce in small attractively labeled bottles with a much higher price.) You'll find it in Asian groceries and in many large supermarkets. Check the label for the list of ingredients: Avoid fish sauces that include sugar (many Vietnamese brands now being exported

are sweetened). Fish sauce keeps almost indefinitely in the cupboard; it does not need refrigeration. For salt equivalent, our rough rule of thumb is 1 tablespoon fish sauce equals 1 teaspoon salt. *See also* preserved fish.

five-spice powder: The ground version of the Chinese and Vietnamese "five spices" (often, in fact, six or seven), usually consisting of star anise, cassia, cloves, Sichuan pepper, licorice root, and fennel or anise seed, this strong-tasting, very aromatic spice powder is available in most Asian groceries. It makes an interesting rub for grilled meat.

fresh ham: *See* pork.

fresh-pressed coconut milk: *See* coconut.

freshwater algae: *See* river weed.

galangal (also sometimes spelled **galingale**): A close cousin of ginger, this rhizome has a sharp, more lemony pine-resin taste and a sharper but less pungent heat. It is widely used in Thai curry pastes and in some Mekong salsas (*see* Index). It was a common flavoring in the Middle Ages in Europe, then fell out of use. It is available in Southeast Asian groceries; look for a gingerlike rhizome with pink shoots or tips and a paler, thinner skin than ginger, marked with fine dark concentric rings. (Ask the shopkeeper for help.) The Thai and Lao name is *khaa*, the Khmer is *mtdaeng*, the Vietnamese is *rieng*, the Malay is *lengkuas*, and the Indonesian is *laos*. You may see Indonesian *laos* powder for sale, dried powdered galangal; avoid it, for it has little flavor.

ginger, young ginger: Often referred to as *gingerroot*, ginger is in fact a rhizome. Look for smooth, firm ginger with unwrinkled skin. Young ginger has thinner, paler beige skin than mature ginger and a milder, sweeter taste. Peel ginger before using (since the peel, except on very tender young ginger, is thick and tough), unless you're just adding slices to soup as a flavoring. Use the peels to make ginger tea.

glass noodles: *See* noodles.

glutinous rice: *See* sticky rice.

green mangoes: Small firm green, sometimes tinged with a little red, these unripe mangoes travel well and are now widely available. The flesh is pale green to pale yellow, firm, and tart-tasting. Slice or coarsely grate. Peel green mangoes just before using; store them in the vegetable drawer of the refrigerator. *See also* mangoes.

hog plum: Known as *makawk* in Thai and Lao, this small sour green fruit (*Selaeocarpus madopetalus*) is oval and about 3 inches long. It has a thin skin and large pit and is used, raw, in savory dishes as a sour flavoring. Mashed and simmered briefly in a little hot water, it also makes a very good Mekong salsa. It is sometimes available in Southeast Asian groceries. Tomatillos, with their tart green taste, make a good substitute.

holy basil: *See* basil.

jicama: Also sometimes known as *yam bean*, jicama is a roundish tuber with pale tan skin and a crisp white interior. Peel before using and use chopped in salads. It has a slightly sweet taste.

kabocha: Also known as *Japanese squash*, this small (8-inch-diameter) round squash has golden yellow firm flesh and dull green skin. It can be steamed, simmered, or braised. Use in place of pumpkin or other winter squash in savory recipes. It is widely available in Asian groceries.

kaffir limes, kaffir lime leaves: *See* wild lime leaves.

kaipen, khai pen: *See* river weed.

kosher salt: *See* salt.

krachai (Kaempferia panduratum): We use the Thai-Lao name for this rhizome because there seems to be no consistent English-language name. Some books refer to it as **rhizome** (and you'll see small packages of dried *krachai* sold as "rhizome powder"; it has little flavor, so avoid it). In others, it's called **lesser galangal**. *Krachai* looks like a small bundle of soft pale brown fingers. It's a rhizome, another in the ginger and galangal family, and is used in Khmer and Thai cooking, especially in fish curries and jungle curries.

lemongrass (*Cymbopogon citratus*): Long dry-looking pale green to beige stalks, sold in bundles of three or four in Southeast Asian and Chinese groceries and large produce markets, lemongrass is a wonderful, distinctive herb that keeps well in the refrigerator for 10 days or more, drying out over time. You can also freeze it, whole or minced. Avoid dried lemongrass powder; it has very little taste. Only the strongly aromatic 2 to 3 inches of the bulb end of the lemongrass stalk is used. To use, cut off the very tough root end and peel off the outermost layer of the stalk; discard both. Trim off and discard the top (grassy end), leaving you 2 to 3 inches of stalk. You can smash this flat with a cleaver and use it whole as a flavoring in soups and stews, or you can finely mince it before using it in a flavor paste or curry paste. Minced lemongrass freezes well; it makes a great rub for grilled meats. In Vietnamese, it's called *sa*; in Thai, *takrai*; in Lao, *sikai*; and in Khmer, *culs lakray*.

lime juice, limes: Lime juice freshly squeezed from the small juicy limes of Southeast Asia is a very important ingredient in the region, especially in Thai, Khmer, and Vietnamese cooking. Lime wedges are often served alongside fried rice so diners can squeeze on a little extra juice at their pleasure. Look for juicy limes, Key limes if you can find them. Try to keep several in your refrigerator at all times. If limes are absolutely unavailable, substitute lemons; avoid bottled lime juice, since it often has a metallic taste from the preservatives blended in.

lime leaves: *See* wild lime leaves.

long beans: *See* yard-long beans.

makawk: *See* hog plum.

mangoes: Ripe mangoes are sweet and juicy, wonderful tropical fruits. They originated in Asia but are now widely grown in Mexico, Central America, and the Caribbean, as well as in tropical Asia. The best mangoes have a smooth sweet golden yellow to orange flesh and no fibrous strands. All mangoes have a flat pit inside. *See* page 297 for instructions on peeling and slicing mangoes. *See also* green mangoes.

mint leaves: Mint leaves are used fresh throughout Southeast Asia. Try to find Vietnamese mint; it has fine, smooth tender leaves and a good flavor. Unfortunately, in most parts of North America, it is still hard to find in grocery stores. We substitute the fresh strong-tasting mint (spearmint) that grows widely in North America. It tends to be a little coarse, so we mince it rather than just tearing it as we do with other more tender green-leafed herbs.

monosodium glutamate (msg): This manufactured version of a naturally occurring substance is widely used in Southeast Asia to enhance flavor. It is sold as a crystalline powder, often labeled "flavor powder." Tasted on its own, it is not salty. Rather, it has a meaty taste, the flavor known by its Japanese name *umami*. We have not included msg in any recipes; most cooks in Southeast Asian towns and cities add msg to many savory dishes. They add it to taste when they add salt or fish sauce. To try it, generally add it in the same amount as you would salt (and if using fish sauce, use 1 teaspoon per tablespoon of fish sauce). Some people experience headaches or dizziness after eating foods overly seasoned with msg.

mung beans, split mung beans (*Phaseolus aureus*): Whole mung beans are dull green in color, small, and almost round dried peas. Split mung beans are sold in natural food stores and in Asian groceries. In Vietnamese, they're *dau xanh*. They may be hulled (yellow in color) or

unhulled (green on the outside and yellow on the split side). All the recipes in this book call for yellow (hulled) split mung beans. Hulled mung beans are a golden yellow color all over because the outer green skin of the bean has been removed. They cook quickly, like lentils, and are a delicious mainstay in our pantry. *See* Index for recipes.

Mushrooms

button mushrooms: The most commonly available mushroom in North America, these are also widely grown in Asia. Look for firm smooth mushrooms where the cap has not separated from the stem.

dried mushrooms: Also known as *black mushrooms* or as *dried shiitakes (hed hom* in Thai, *nam huong* in Vietnamese) these pantry staples may be beige to brown in color. Dried mushrooms have a very intense flavor and keep well if stored in a well-sealed plastic bag. They are widely available in Asian shops and in large grocery stores. They must be lightly rinsed, then soaked before using. The mushroom soaking water makes a good flavoring for soups and simmered dishes.

oyster mushrooms: Pale, almost luminous gray beige in color, these large flat-topped, asymmetrical, fragile-looking mushrooms are widely cultivated in Asia. They are now available in most large produce sections.

straw mushrooms: Widely cultivated in Asia, straw mushrooms are shaped like smooth pointed domes. They are pale beige when small, then turn a darker gray as they mature. Unfortunately, they don't keep well, so in North America they are available only in cans; drain and rinse before using. They have a mild, slightly earthy taste and an agreeable smooth texture.

tree ear mushrooms: Also known as *cloud ear fungus* or *wood fungus* (in Khmer and Thai, their name means *rat ear fungus*), these small dried black mushrooms are sold in Asian groceries. They are called *het hoonoo* in Thai and *mu-er* in Mandarin. Soak before using (they expand four to five times in volume once soaked) and cut off and discard any tough bits. They have a mild taste, a gelatinous surface texture, and a pleasing chewiness; they are believed to have a purifying effect on the blood.

white fungus (*Tremella fruciformis*): White to pale yellow, large dried pieces of white fungus look a little like dried-out sponges. White fungus is widely available in Asian groceries; it is sold in bulk or in boxes with a clear plastic window so you can see what you are buying. To use it, soak the large pieces, uncut, until tender and soft, then cut off and discard any tough parts. White fungus absorbs flavors very well and has a pleasant slightly crunchy texture, making it a good ingredient in Thai salads; *see* White Fungus Salad (page 79).

napa cabbage: Also known as *Peking cabbage* or *Chinese cabbage*, this green is pale green to white. It comes in heavy firm heads of tightly packed long, wide pale stems topped by crinkly edged leaves. Use raw or cooked; slice crosswise into chunks, or slice right through lengthwise if using the whole head, rather than using it leaf by leaf. Napa cabbage keeps well in the vegetable drawer of the refrigerator.

Noodles

cellophane noodles/bean threads/glass noodles: These noodles are made of processed mung beans. As sold, they're thin and white and tough, like tough plastic string; after soaking, they soften enough to be cut. If immersed in boiling water, they soften to transparent threads. Available in 1-pound cellophane-wrapped packages in Asian markets, they keep indefinitely in a cupboard, making them a handy staple.

Chinese egg noodles: Known as *bamee* in Thai, these pale yellow noodles are made from wheat flour and whole eggs or egg whites and come in various widths. They are sold in Chinese groceries, either dried or fresh. (Dried have a long shelf life; fresh should be used within a day or two.) Dried egg noodles are usually sold in small tangled bundles, meant to be dropped into hot soup. Fresh noodles, either round or flat, usually come in vacuum-packed 1-pound clear plastic packages; before cooking them, rinse off the oil they are usually coated with. If you come upon a source for fresh egg noodles, buy some and try them cooked in plenty of boiling salted water like pasta. They have a wonderful flavor and texture.

dried rice noodles, rice stick: Dried rice noodles, flat, long, brittle, and semitransparent, are the dried version of fresh rice noodles or rice ribbons (see below). They come in two widths, about 1/3 inch wide and less than 1/4 inch wide. They are often labeled "rice stick"; the narrower ones may be labeled "rice vermicelli." The wider dried rice noodles are known as *sen yai* in Thai and *banh pho* in Vietnamese; the narrower ones are called *sen lek* in Thai and *bun* in Vietnamese. They're sold in 1-pound clear plastic packages in many grocery stores and are a great pantry staple. They should be soaked for 15 minutes or so in warm water to become pliable, then stir-fried or briefly boiled in hot water or broth. When dried, they are almost transparent; they become opaque white when cooked.

fresh rice noodles, rice noodle sheets, rice noodle tubes, rice ribbon noodles, Sa-Ho noodles: Flat fresh rice noodles can be made at home (see Fresh Noodle Sheets, page 121). They are sold in 1-pound packages in Chinese and Vietnamese groceries (look in the refrigerated section, with the other noodles, and often near the tofu products). Fresh rice noodles come in many shapes, from wide and flat like very wide fettuccine to solid sheets (often labeled Sa-Ho noodles) to thick and round like fat spaghetti. They usually have a sell-by date and keep well until then if refrigerated and unopened. (They may harden slightly as the sell-by date approaches, but they soften when cooked.) Once opened, they should be used within 24 hours. To use, rinse off any oil (added to prevent the noodles from sticking to each other), slice if you wish, and then briefly heat in hot broth or water or stir-fry or steam until tender and heated through. The word for fresh rice ribbon noodles is the same in South Chinese languages as it is in Thai: *guaytio*.

mein/alimentary paste noodles: Plain flat Chinese noodles made of wheat flour, water, and salt, pale beige to white in color, come in several widths. You may find them fresh or dried, like pasta. They are more tender than pasta, though, and more fragile, since they are made of a softer wheat than the durum used for making pasta. If serving plain with toppings, cook in boiling salted water until just tender, then drain; if using for stir-fried noodles, rinse briefly in boiling water until tender, then stir-fry with vegetables, meat, and flavorings.

rice vermicelli: If we ever find a source for fresh rice vermicelli, we'll be very happy. It's one of the foods that people of Vietnam, and other parts of Southeast Asia, really miss when they live in North America. Dried rice vermicelli makes an acceptable substitute, excellent in fact, but without the soft, firm yet yielding texture of fresh rice vermicelli. Traditionally the noodles are made by soaking and grinding rice, then kneading it into a smooth batter. The batter is pushed through a perforated funnel into boiling water, making long thin round white strands, then drained. Fresh rice vermicelli, called *kanom jiin* in Thai and *kao poon* in northern Laos, is sold in village markets from Laos to Vietnam, usually in coiled bundles, known in Khmer as *chavai*. (See The Noodle Maker, page 142.) Thin dried rice vermicelli, like dried rice noodles, is sold in 1-pound clear plastic packages in many grocery stores, sometimes labeled "rice stick." The noodles are fine, round creamy white strands, very dry and brittle, like spaghettini. They should be soaked for 15 minutes in warm water before being either stir-fried with flavorings or briefly cooked in boiling water or broth. (Unless you're serving them in broth, drain the cooked noodles immediately.) If using them for deep-frying, add dried noodles directly to the hot oil, without soaking them first; when fried, they puff up to four or five times their size. Use fried rice vermicelli as a bed for stir-fried dishes or as a garnish.

okra: Okra pods, the fruit of a plant in the hibiscus family, are at their best about 1 to 1 1/2 inches long, bright green, and tender. They are widely available in the produce sections of well-stocked groceries. Larger pods (up to 4 inches long) take longer to cook and may be a little tough. If chopped before cooking, okra will thicken a soup or sauce, for it has a soft mucilaginous interior that okra-lovers love and that the rest of the world finds slimy. Fresh tender okra has a taste a little like tender green asparagus, but slightly sweeter. Okra is widely used in the cuisines of the eastern Mediterranean, India, West Africa, the American South, and the Caribbean.

oxtails: Widely available (and inexpensive) in Vietnamese groceries, oxtails are wonderful for making beef broths and soups (*see* Index for recipes). They are mostly bone, with some meat attached, and come in approximately 2-inch chunks. Rinse with hot water before using.

***padek*:** *See* preserved fish.

palm sugar: Palm sugar is made by boiling down the sap of the sugar palm. It has a pale golden color and a pleasing sweet and slightly smoky taste, very reminiscent of maple syrup. Brown sugar, Chinese rock sugar, or maple sugar blended half and half with white sugar can be substituted. Palm sugar is widely used in Southeast Asia, where sugar palms are common. It is sold in small round hard disks or as a paste in jars in Asian grocery stores. To use the blocks, use a cleaver or sharp knife to scrape off shavings, then add to hot liquid and stir well to melt them completely.

pandanus leaves: Sometimes shortened to "pandan" leaves, and also known in English as *screw-pine leaves*, these are the long (18 inches to 2 feet) sword-shaped green leaves of a Southeast Asian bush, *Pandanus odorus*, and, as the Latin name suggests, they are aromatic, with a mild floral scent. In Thai, they're called *bai toey hom*. They are used in Thailand, Vietnam, Malaysia, and Indonesia to dye sweets green, to flavor rice, and to wrap rice before grilling or steaming. They have a perfumy flavor and are available at

Southeast Asian groceries, fresh or frozen. To store, freeze, like banana leaves.

***pa raa, pla raa*:** *See* preserved fish.

peanut oil: *See* cooking oils.

peanuts: Peanuts are widely used as a snack, as a garnish and flavoring, and as the base for sauces throughout Southeast Asia. They are very handy to have in the pantry. Large pale raw or boiled peanuts are sold in cellophane packages in Chinese and Southeast Asian groceries. Look for ones without skins. Before using them as a garnish, dry-roast them in a dry skillet over medium heat until they are pale to dark brown all over. (See Dry-Roasted Peanuts, page 308.)

pea shoots, pea sprouts, pea tendrils: The tender growing tips of green pea plants have recently become more widely available in North America. They have a fresh, slightly sweet taste. They are often sold loose in bins, in a large green tangle, especially in spring and early summer. They are characteristic of Shan and northern Thai and Lao cooking and are also widely used in China. The Shan call them *pak tua noi*; the Thai and Lao, *yod tua lan tau*. Choose fresh firm shoots, wash well, and chop; stir-fry with garlic or cook in boiling salted water for a few minutes, until tender but still bright green. Use as a vegetable, simply dressed, or add to bowls of noodle soup (*see* Index for recipes).

pepper, black and white (*Piper nigrum*): Both black and white peppercorns begin as the berry of the pepper vine. Black peppercorns are green berries that are picked, fermented, and then dried; white peppercorns are the bleached seeds of the ripe berry. White pepper has a hotter, sharper taste than black pepper, which, when freshly ground, is more aromatic and complex-tasting.

pepper leaves: Heart-shaped dark green tender leaves from a tree of the *Piper* family, slightly pungent in flavor, these are known in Vietnamese as *la lot* and in Lao as *pak i leut*. They

are traditionally used to wrap *miang*, small wrapped foods (*see* Index for recipes), and are also the wrapping for betel nut chew, the mildly narcotic recreational drug that is chewed with pleasure by many people in India and Southeast Asia. Pepper leaves are sometimes available in Southeast Asian grocery stores, sold in small stacked bundles. Use as a salad green or for wrapping. Substitute salad greens.

pomelo: A larger-than-grapefruit-size thick-skinned citrus fruit, pomelo is occasionally available in Asian groceries. It is eaten as a snack in Southeast Asia or as an ingredient in savory salads. Grapefruit can be substituted.

poppy seeds: Gray-black poppy seeds are widely available, often used in European baking.

pork: This most widely used of meats in the Mekong region is very versatile. For most dishes, since the meat is cut into small pieces, the cut doesn't matter; use whatever is available to you that has good flavor (pork tenderloin can be less flavorful than less expensive cuts such as shoulder or butt). Meat is rarely trimmed of all fat in the Mekong region, for the fat gives flavor and succulence, so trim your meat to your taste. (Store any trimmed pork fat in a plastic bag in the freezer. Use it as a cooking oil [*see* cooking oils] or as an ingredient in sausages or paté.) Sometimes we call for *fresh ham*, a cut from the hind leg that also has good flavor. You can substitute any other boneless cut of pork. *Ground pork* is perishable. Buy it already ground, or use a cleaver to chop your own; that way, you'll know it's fresh.

pork fat, pork lard: *See* cooking oils.

pork skin, pork crackling, dried pork skin shreds: In most of the Mekong region, *deep-fried pork skin*, also known as *pork crackling*, is eaten as a snack or as an accompaniment to meals, usually used to scoop up *jaew* (salsalike dishes) (see page 238). In Lao, it's known as *khiep moo*. The skin is usually dried, then fried; as it fries, it puffs up and becomes a light, crispy golden brown. Fried pork skin is sold in Southeast Asian groceries, in small clear plastic packages (sometimes labeled with the Filipino name *sitsaron*); it's also available in Mexican groceries, where it is called *chicharrones*. In Laos and northern Thailand, water buffalo skin is also dried, cut into small strips that look like wide tough rubber bands, and then fried; when it is fried, it puffs up, hence its name, *nang bong*, which means "skin grows." Like fried pork skin, it's eaten with salsas. *Dried pork skin shreds* are sold in Asian groceries for use as an ingredient in various dishes. They give texture to Vietnamese pâtés and prepared meats. In Vietnamese, they're called *bi* or *bi heo kho*. To use, soak in warm water until softened, then chop into small pieces. Drop into boiling water for several minutes, then drain.

potato starch: Potato starch is very like cornstarch. It is used in some noodle doughs and as a thickener.

prahok: *See* preserved fish.

preserved fish, fermented fish: Along the middle and lower stretches of the Mekong river, and in central and southern Thailand, fermented fish, in the form of pieces of fish floating in a brine that often contains rice bran too, is used as a food and flavoring. The fish and the liquid are both used. In Khmer, the basic fermented fish sauce is called *prahok*; in Lao, *padek*; in Vietnamese, *mam*; in Thai, *pla raa*. Jars of preserved fish are sold in Vietnamese and other Southeast Asian groceries. They may be labeled "*poisson en saumure*" or "preserved gray featherback fish" or "preserved mudfish." Preserved fish has a stronger taste than fish sauce (*see* fish sauce), but it can be substituted for fish sauce in many recipes, to taste. (Go carefully.) *See also* Fermented Fish, page 220.

preserved radish shreds: *See* salted radish.

pressed tofu: *See* tofu.

pumpkin: Pumpkin, that useful native of North America, is eaten as a vegetable almost all over the world except in Europe and North America. It is sold here in Caribbean and Asian groceries, usually cut into wedges and wrapped in plastic wrap. Look for smooth-textured (less fibrous) pumpkin, and pick the piece with the richest-colored flesh; it will have the best flavor. Japanese kabocha squash can be used as a substitute. *See* Index for recipes.

red curry paste: *See* curry pastes.

rendered pork fat: *See* cooking oils.

rice flour, sweet rice flour, glutinous rice flour: Both plain rice and sticky rice are ground into flour and sold in Asian groceries and some specialty shops. *Rice flour* is used for making noodles and rice papers and some sweets; it can also be used as a thickener for sauces. The flour from sticky rice will be labeled "sweet rice flour" or "glutinous rice flour." It is softer and is used to make the dough for some sweets. In general, the flours are *not* interchangeable.

rice noodles: *See* noodles.

rice paddy herb: This Vietnamese herb, known as *ngo om* in Vietnamese and *ma om* in Khmer, has a sharp citrus taste and thick stems with small pale green leaves. It is used in Vietnamese sour soup and in some Khmer dishes. You'll find it in Vietnamese groceries, often sold together with sawtooth herb, and in some other Southeast Asian stores.

rice papers: Known in Vietnamese as *banh trang*, these dried semitransparent sheets are made from rice flour and water and sun-dried. They're a very useful and versatile pantry item, since they keep well and can be used for roll-your-own meals or for classic Vietnamese roll-ups. Rice papers come as rounds or as wedge shapes (a quarter of a round) and are sold in many grocery stores as well as in Asian markets. We prefer the thinner, finer ones, since they soften more quickly and are more tender. Rice papers carry the pattern of the bamboo mat on which they were dried. Since they're very brittle until moistened, plan on a few extra to allow for breakage. To use, moisten in lukewarm water until soft, then lay flat on a lettuce leaf or on a wet cloth placed on a work surface, and use to wrap other ingredients. *See* Index for recipes.

rice sticks: *See* dried rice noodles, under noodles.

rice vermicelli: *See* noodles.

rice vinegar: *See* vinegar.

river weed, dried river weed, dried algae, freshwater algae: In Laos and northern Thailand, fresh algae from the rivers is harvested in late November and December, then sun-dried. It is eaten stir-fried and flavored with hot oil, or it may be dried and pressed into crisp sheets. River weed is known as *khai* in Lao, *salai* in Thai, and *dao'* in Shan. The dried sheets of river weed, almost black and looking like Japanese *nori*, though a little thicker and flavored with sesame seeds, are called *khai pen*. They are now being imported into North America and sold as "kaipen." They can be cut up and toasted or fried, then used as a topping for rice or noodles. For more, *see* River Weed, page 164.

roasted sesame oil: *See* sesame oil.

round eggplant: *See* eggplant.

rose water: Available from Middle Eastern and Asian groceries, and sometimes in specialty shops, rose water is an aromatic flavoring liquid used for making sweets. A little goes a long way, so don't add more than the recipe calls for. It keeps indefinitely in the cupboard.

sakhan: The woody stem of a kind of *Piper* tree, *sakhan* is used in Luang Prabang cooking to give a bitter taste in stewed dishes, particularly in the class of dishes known as *oaw' lam*. Peel before using.

salt, kosher salt, sea salt: In Southeast Asia, salt may be extracted from the sea or from salt wells, so the type of salt used depends on what is available in the area. Salt is very important in Southeast Asia for brining and preserving vegetables and fish so they can be eaten year-round. We use sea salt or kosher salt for cooking and flavoring, kosher salt for pickles (when you want just straight salt with no extra flavors). For making pepper-salt, we usually use sea salt, for it has a more complex flavor. Compare the taste of different salts; you may be astonished at the range of flavors.

salted radish: Sometimes labeled "preserved turnip," salted radish is sold in small plastic packages in Southeast Asian and Chinese groceries. It is a pale beige-white clump of shreds, either dry or in a little liquid. Once it's open, store in a well-sealed plastic bag in the refrigerator. Salted radish is salty and intense-tasting; rinse it off or soak it briefly before using. It adds flavor and a little crunch to *pad thai* and other stir-fried dishes. In Thai, it's known as *hua pakkad kem.*

Savoy cabbage: This is the common pale green cabbage of Europe, round and firm, with a slightly frilled edge to its tightly packed leaves; substitute any head cabbage. Smaller heads tend to be sweeter and more tender.

sawtooth herb: This long fresh green leaf with serrated edges and a tender texture is widely used in Vietnamese cooking, especially as a last-minute flavoring for soups. (A close cousin is used in Mexican and Puerto Rican cooking and is known as Mexican or Puerto Rican coriander or, in some places, *culantro*.) It has a pleasing, corianderlike taste. In Vietnamese it's called *ngo gai* (*ngo* means "coriander," *gai* means "thorny") and you'll often be able to find it in Southeast Asian groceries; substitute coriander if you can't find it. In Khmer it's *jii banla'*. In Lao it's usually called *pakchi farang*; in the Luang Prabang area, it's known as *hom pen.*

scallions: Also known as *green onions*, or *spring onions*, these are widely available in supermarkets. Throughout Southeast Asia they are eaten both cooked and raw, and both the green leaves and the white bulb are used. In central Laos, the green leaves are frequently used as a garnish or topping, sometimes mixed with coriander leaves (the mixture is often referred to as *hom* or *pak hom*, meaning "aromatics"). Scallions are also part of the bundle of aromatics sold in markets in Cambodia and known as *chmoi*. Recipe instructions often call for smashing scallions. Use the flat side of a cleaver or a large knife to smash the scallions flat, then slice lengthwise or crosswise as called for. Smashing helps the scallions cook more quickly and evenly and also helps release flavors. In Khmer, scallions are *selak tum*; in Thai, *ton hom.*

sea salt: *See* salt.

sesame oil: *Roasted sesame oil* (the most reliable widely available brand is Kadoya) is used as a flavoring in many Chinese and Japanese dishes. It is sometimes referred to as *Asian sesame oil*. The sesame seeds are roasted before the oil is pressed, giving it a brown color and a distinctive and delicious nutty taste. Store in a cool place. *Do not* substitute plain (unroasted) sesame oil.

sesame seeds: Available hulled and unhulled, beige (white) or black, sesame seeds are rich in oil and so should be stored in the refrigerator, to prevent them from turning rancid. Sesame seeds are pressed for their oil. In cooking, they are most often dry-roasted in a hot skillet (*see* Dry-Roasted Sesame Seeds, page 308) before being used as a topping or garnish for both savory and sweet dishes.

shallots: Shallots are members of the same family as onions and garlic. They are an essential ingredient in Southeast Asian food, especially in Laos and northern Thailand. In Lao, they're called *mo hom daeng*; in Thai, *hom lek*. Shallots look like reddish bulbs, with a fine reddish-brown papery outer layer, under which the shallots themselves may be tinged with purple. They often come in a cluster of two or three. Peel before using. Asian shallots are generally smaller than European-style shallots. In grocery stores, you'll generally find the large ones, while the smaller Asian shallots are widely available in Asian markets. Some Asian shallots are really tiny, with a distinctive mauve tint on the bulb. In the recipes, we give quantities for both large and small shallots and also often give cup measurements.

Shanghai bok choi: *See* bok choi.

shrimp paste: Known in Thai and Khmer as *kapi* and in Vietnamese as *mam tom* or *mam ruoc*, shrimp paste is a concentrated flavoring made of fermented salted shrimp. The paste comes in many shades, from dull pink to gray, and is available in most Asian grocery stores. The most reliable brands we've found are those made in Thailand. Shrimp paste is a necessary ingredient in many curry pastes. It is also used in Malay cooking and is known in Malaysia and Indonesia as *trassi*. Shrimp paste must be cooked before using. Our usual method is to wrap a little in foil, then dry-roast it in a skillet or grill it over a flame. Though it gives off pungent fumes while it is being toasted (hence the wrapping in foil), once cooked, it adds a wonderful subtle salty, smoky taste. Wrap it well after opening and refrigerate.

Sichuan pepper (*Zanthoxylum piperitum*): The small berry of the prickly ash, Sichuan pepper is one of the oldest spices used in Chinese cooking. It gives a numbing warmth to the mouth and has a pleasing aromatic taste. In Japan, its close cousin, from the Japanese prickly ash, is called *sansho*; in English, Sichuan pepper is sometimes referred to as *fagara*. Sichuan pepper comes as small reddish-brown husks (dried berries), with some shiny black seeds inside. The flavor is in the husks; the seeds are very bitter. To use, dry-roast to bring out the flavor, then grind in a spice mill or mortar. If you are a perfectionist, you will want to take the trouble to pick out and discard the little black seeds; we usually don't bother. Sichuan pepper is used on its own during cooking, and is also used as part of the condiment known as "pepper-salt." *See* Index for recipes.

soybean paste/soybean sauce: *See* fermented soybean paste.

soy sauce: Soy sauce is the liquid produced when soybeans are brewed with wheat and salt. (Tamari is a kind of soy sauce that uses no wheat in the brewing process; we do not call for it in this book.) We use Kikkoman brand soy sauce, either regular or, for dipping sauces, the lighter, fresher-tasting reduced-sodium soy sauce. Pearl River soy sauce also has good flavor, though not quite as clear a taste. Avoid nonbrewed soy sauces, which are just harsh-tasting salty liquids. You can really taste the difference.

star anise (*Illicum verum*): This beautiful warm-brown star-shaped spice is sold in Asian markets and specialty shops. It tastes like licorice or aniseed and is used whole (in the same way as cinnamon sticks are) to flavor soups such as Hearty Vietnamese Beef Noodle Soup (*pho bo*, page 128) and some simmered beef dishes, such as Hui Beef Stew with Chick-peas and Anise (page 231).

star fruit: Also known as *carambola*, star fruit comes in tart and sweet versions. Both are pale green to yellow in color, with deep ridges that, when the fruit is sliced crosswise, make a star shape. Star fruit is used to give a tart or acid taste in a number of southern Vietnamese salads and savory dishes (*see* Index for recipes). The sweet variety, sliced, makes a decorative addition to sweet desserts.

sticky rice, glutinous rice, sweet rice: Medium- to long-grain sticky rice is a staple food in Laos and northern and northeastern Thailand. It is a different variety of rice, very low in amylose and high in amylopectin, that cooks to an agreeable sticky yet not mushy texture. It is usually eaten out of hand, rather than with utensils. Thai-Lao sticky rice must be soaked

before being steamed over (not in) boiling water. Sticky rice is available in Southeast Asian groceries, in well-stocked grocery stores, and by mail-order. Be sure you buy rice grown in Thailand or Laos, not short-grain Chinese or American sweet rices, for use in the recipes in this book (*see* Index).

Swatow mustard: *See* Chinese mustard greens.

sweetened condensed milk: Available in cans from most groceries, sweetened condensed milk is cooked-down milk that can be stored without refrigeration and is thus widely used in the tropics.

sweet rice: *See* sticky rice.

tamarind, tamarind pulp, tamarind paste: The *pulp* of the tamarind pod, dissolved in water, is used to give a sour taste in many Southeast Asian, Indian, and Georgian dishes. (It is also used to make wonderfully intense sour-sweet candies, especially in Vietnam.) Tamarind is called *mak kham* in Lao and Thai, *am peuhl* in Khmer, and *me chua* in Vietnamese. It is a dark brown, almost black, sticky fibrous mass of seeds and pulp and is sold in small cellophane-wrapped blocks in Asian grocery stores. It keeps almost indefinitely in the refrigerator, well wrapped in plastic to prevent it from drying out. Tamarind pulp must be dissolved in water and then strained through a sieve, as described in the recipes. If you can find only *tamarind paste* (sometimes labeled "tamarind concentrate"), reduce the quantity called for by half and dissolve in water as directed. We prefer the pulp because the flavor is more reliable; the concentrate often tastes metallic.

tapioca, tapioca pearls, tapioca starch/ tapioca flour: Tapioca is produced from the cassava plant, a starchy root vegetable that grows well even in poor soil. *Tapioca pearls* and *tapioca flour* are available in Southeast Asian markets. Tapioca pearls are small round granules made of tapioca starch; they come in small and larger

sizes, the small ones being most commonly used in Southeast Asian desserts, the larger being more commonly used in Europe. Small tapioca pearls are sold in Southeast Asian markets, either white or dyed pink or yellow or pale green. Tapioca pearls are first soaked in warm water, then boiled until tender; sugar must not be added until they are cooked, for it prevents them from softening. *Tapioca starch*, also sometimes known as *tapioca flour*, is finely ground and very powdery. It is used as a thickener and is also an ingredient in some rice noodles and rice wrappers.

Thai dried red chiles: *See* chiles.

Thai eggplant: *See* eggplant.

Thai jasmine rice: *See* aromatic jasmine rice.

Tofu

Many products are made from processed soybeans. The list below includes only those mentioned in this book. All are available in Chinese and Southeast Asian groceries, in the refrigerated section. All should be stored in the refrigerator, and none keeps for very long. You can also freeze tofu products; they change their texture but remain delicious and useful pantry staples.

fresh tofu/bean curd, firm tofu, silky tofu: White blocks of fresh tofu, or bean curd, are made by cooking soybeans, grinding them, pressing out the liquid, and then adding a coagulant (as is done in cheese making) to get the liquid to set into a dense block with a custard texture. Chinese fresh tofu is firm and smooth; blocks vary in size, but are usually about 3 inches square and 1½ inches thick and weigh about 6 ounces. A finer, more custardlike tofu is sold in Japanese stores; often referred to as *silky tofu*, it usually comes in smaller 2-inch square blocks. It's especially suited to desserts. *Doufu hua*, sometimes called bean jelly, is the Chinese name for soft tofu that has a more custardlike texture; it comes in loose curds, not in blocks. Fresh tofu is stored in water in the refrigerator; change the water every day. Freeze any that you can't use within 3 days.

pressed tofu/firm tofu/*doufu gan*: When fresh tofu is pressed under a weight, it firms up and compresses as the water drains out and then has the consistency of firm fresh cheese. Known as *doufu gan* ("dry tofu") in Mandarin, *dauhu leong* in Thai, and *dau hi ki* in Vietnamese, pressed tofu is available in Asian groceries. You can also make your own: Wrap several blocks of fresh tofu in cheesecloth, place on a flat surface, and top with a plate weighted with a 2- to 5-pound weight. Pour off the water as it drains out; after 8 to 12 hours, the tofu will be firm and fairly dry. It can be sliced and stir-fried, or eaten without cooking, just dressed with a little oyster sauce or dark soy and some chopped scallion greens. *See* Index for recipes.

tuong: The Vietnamese word for sauce/condiment (*tuong ot tuoi* is chile paste, for example), *tuong* is more specifically used to name fermented soybean sauce (*see above*).

turmeric: We all know the bright yellow orange of turmeric powder, but fresh turmeric has only recently become available here, in Southeast Asian groceries. Ask for *nghe* in Vietnamese, *khamin* in Thai. It is used in curry pastes and spice pastes. A member of the ginger family, turmeric is a small rhizome (about the size of a little finger) with a thin tawny-orange skin, bright orange flesh, and a hot gingery taste. The juice stains fingers and clothing.

vegetable oils: *See* cooking oils.

Vinegar

Vinegar is distilled from grains or fruit. Its acidity varies, with wine vinegars generally having a higher acidity (as much as 7 percent) than rice vinegars (which range from 3½ to 4½ percent acetic acid).

black rice vinegar: Almost black in color, manufactured in China, and sold here in tall bottles, black rice vinegar has a smoky, slightly sweet flavor; a mild balsamic vinegar can be substituted. Chinese black vinegars may also be made from wheat or sorghum or millet.

brown rice vinegar: A pale brown Japanese vinegar (called *genmai su* in Japanese) made from brown rice, this has a mild flavor with a little more depth than white rice vinegar.

cider vinegar: Widely available, made from fermented apples, this can be substituted for rice vinegar in a pinch.

white rice vinegar: Japanese white rice vinegars, mild-tasting and reliable, are a staple in our pantry. There are many good brands. Make sure you *don't* buy a vinegar that is marked "seasoned"; you don't want the salt and sugar already added to your vinegar.

Vietnamese coriander: Known as *pakchi wietnam* in Thai and Lao (or sometimes *pak payo* in Lao), as *rau ram* in Vietnamese, and *daun kesom* in Malay, this perennial herb is also known as *Polygonum* (its botanical name). It is one of our favorites, with a strong distinctive flavor (in the same way that both Asian basil and coriander are strong-tasting). It has narrow pointed tender leaves, medium to dark green, sometimes with a darker green marking in the center; the leaves alternate along the succulent stems. To use, tear the leaves off the stem, then use them whole or coarsely torn. Vietnamese coriander is particularly good with chicken or fish. It is now widely available in Vietnamese and other Southeast Asian groceries. If you put several stems in water, it will root quickly. Once the roots are well grown, you can plant it. We grow Vietnamese coriander in the house in a pot during the winter, then set it out in the garden during the warm summer weather; it needs plenty of water.

water spinach: Also known as *swamp cabbage*, *aquatic morning glory*, or *water convolvulus*, this green has long hollow stems and pointed arrowhead-shaped leaves. Its Latin name is *Ipomoea aquatica*. There are two similar versions, one that grows in damp soil and one that grows in water; the former is more widely available in North America. Known as *pak boong* in Thai, *pak*

bong in Lao, and *rau muang* in Vietnamese, water spinach is widely available in Asian markets. It is traditionally stir-fried with a little garlic in a very hot wok, tossed until the stems are limp, then seasoned with fish sauce or salt and served immediately.

white fungus: *See* mushrooms.

white radish: *See* daikon.

wild lime, wild lime leaves: Also known as *kaffir lime*, the wild lime (*Citrus hystrix*) has green fruit with a lumpy, wrinkled skin. (*Kaffir* is a derogatory term; we avoid the word.) The zest of the fruit is used in curry pastes; regular lime zest can be substituted. The leaves, double-lobed, dark green, and shiny, are aromatic and are used as a savory flavoring, much as bay leaves are used in Western cooking. Lime leaves freeze very well, so when you find them, buy plenty, then wrap in plastic wrap and freeze. Avoid dried lime leaves.

winged beans (*Psophocarpus tetrogonolobus*): Although these beans originated in southern Europe, they are now sold mostly in Asian grocery stores. They have long frilled edges running the length of the bean and are bright green in color. Tender and slightly sweet-tasting, winged beans are widely used in South Indian and Thai cooking. The Thai name is *tua plu*; in English, they are sometimes called *asparagus beans* (somewhat confusingly, since so are yard-longs!; *see below*).

yard-long beans/long beans/asparagus beans: These 18-inch-long slender green beans are the pods of the cow pea (*Vigna sesquipedelis*). They grow in temperate and tropical climates and are now widely available in Asian groceries, sold in bundles. There are two kinds, one pale green and the other a darker green. We like both kinds. Try to find firm, fresh-looking beans. In Southeast Asia, long beans are eaten raw or cooked. They are known in Thai as *tua fak yao*; in Vietnamese as *dau dua*; in Cantonese as *dau gok*; and in Khmer as *sangdek khoua*. *See* Index for recipes.

MAIL-ORDER SOURCES

Kalustyan's
123 Lexington Avenue
New York, NY 10016
(212) 685-3451
fax: (212) 683-8458
Web sites: www.kalustyans.com;
www.forspice.com; www.riceandbean.com
Catalog; wide range of rices and Southeast Asian
ingredients

Penzeys Spices
P.O. Box 933
Muskego, WI 53150
(414) 679-7207
fax: (414) 679-7878
Web site: www.penzeys.com
Catalog; dried chiles, whole and ground spices;
no curry pastes or fish sauce

The Spice Merchant
P.O. Box 524
Jackson Hole, WY 83001
(307) 733-7811; toll-free (48 states only):
(800) 551-5999
fax: (307) 733-6343
E-mail: stirfry@compuserve.com
Web site: www.email.com/spice (for orders and
for viewing what's available)
Catalog; condiments, spices, rices

Uwajimaya
519 Sixth Avenue South
Seattle, WA 98104
(206) 624-6248; toll-free (48 states only):
(800) 889-1928
fax: (206) 624-6915
Web site: www.uwajimaya.com
Catalog; wide range of Southeast Asian products

BIBLIOGRAPHY

Alford, Jeffrey, and Naomi Duguid. *Flatbreads and Flavors*. New York: Morrow, 1995.

———. *Seductions of Rice*. New York: Artisan, 1998.

An Englishman's Siamese Journals 1890–1893. 1895. Reprint, Bangkok: Siam Media International Books, n.d.

Aoyagi, Kenji. *Mekong: The Last River*. Tokyo: Cadence, 1995.

Bassenne, Marthe. *In Laos and Siam*. Translated by Walter Tips. 1912. Reprint, Bangkok: White Lotus, 1995.

Bhumichitr, Vatcharin. *Vatch's Thai Cookbook*. London: Pavilion, 1994.

Boun Thuy, Sovan, with Thiah Foster. *Cambodian Cooking: Authentic Recipes*. N.p., 1992.

Bremness, Lesley. *Herbs*. London: Dorling Kindersley, 1994.

Brydson, Sherry. *Thai Sensations*. Toronto: Macmillan, 1995.

Chang K. C., ed. *Food in Chinese Culture*. New Haven and London: Yale University Press, 1977.

Chunyang, An, and Liu Bohua. *Where the Dai People Live*. Beijing: Foreign Languages Press, 1977.

Cost, Bruce. *Foods from the Far East*. London: Century, 1990.

Dahlen, Martha. *A Cook's Guide to Chinese Vegetables*. 1992. Reprint, Hong Kong: The Guidebook Company, 1995.

Davidson, Alan. *Fish and Fish Dishes of Laos*. Rutland, VT: Charles Tuttle, 1975.

———. *A Kipper with My Tea: Selected Food Essays*. London: Macmillan, 1990.

De Monteiro, Longteine, and Katherine Neustadt. *The Elephant Walk Cookbook*. Boston: Houghton Mifflin, 1998.

Dodd, William Clifton. *The Tai Race*. 1923. Reprint, Bangkok: White Lotus, 1996.

Donovan, Holly Richardson, Peter W. Donovan, and Harvey Mole. *A Guide to the Chinese Cuisine and Restaurants of Taiwan*. Taipei: n.p., n.d.

Fraser-Lu, Sylvia. *Handwoven Textiles of South-East Asia*. New York: Oxford University Press, 1988.

Goodman, Jim. *Meet the Akhas*. Bangkok: White Lotus, 1996.

Grigson, Jane. *Charcuterie and French Pork Cookery*. London: Penguin, 1970.

———. *Jane Grigson's Fish Book*. London: Penguin, 1994.

Hallet, Holt S. *A Thousand Miles on an Elephant in the Shan States*. 1890. Reprint, Bangkok: White Lotus, 1988.

Harmand, Jules. *Laos and the Hilltribes of Indochina*. Translated by Walter E. J. Tips. 1878–79. Reprint, Bangkok: White Lotus, 1997.

Herklots, G.A.C. *Vegetables in South-East Asia*. London: Allen & Unwin, 1972.

Huang, Su-Huei. **Chinese Snacks, Revised.** Taipei: Huang Su-Huei Wei-Chuan's Cooking, 1985.

Hutton, Wendy. **Tropical Herbs & Spices of Thailand.** Bangkok: Asia Books, 1997.

———. **Tropical Vegetables of Thailand.** Bangkok: Asia Books, 1997.

Kahrs, Kurt. **Thai Cooking.** New York: Gallery Books, 1994.

Klausner, Walter J. **Reflections on Thai Culture.** Bangkok: The Siam Society, 1981.

Kongpan, Sisamon. **The Best of Thai Cuisine.** Bangkok: APA Villa, n.d.

Kritikara, M. L. Taw, and M. R. Pimsai Amranand. **Modern Thai Cooking.** Bangkok: Duong Kamol Books, 1977.

Lebar, Frank M. et al., eds. **Ethnic Groups of Mainland Southeast Asia.** New Haven: Human Relations Area Files Press, 1964.

Le Chant du riz pile: cent recettes Vietnamiennes. Paris: L'Harmatton, 1995.

Lefvre, E. **Travels in Laos: The Fate of the Sip Song Pana and Muong Sing (1894–1896).** Translated by Walter E. J.Tips. 1898. Reprint, Bangkok: White Lotus, 1995.

Le Roux, Pierre, and Jacques Ivanoff, eds. **Le Sel de la vie en Asie du Sud-est.** Thailand: Grand Sud, Prince of Songkla University and CNRS, 1993.

Lewis, Norman. **A Dragon Apparent: Travels in Cambodia, Laos, and Vietnam.** 1951. Reprint, London: Eland Books, 1982.

Lewis, Paul, and Elaine Lewis. **Peoples of the Golden Triangle.** London: Thames & Hudson, 1984.

Liangwen, Zhu. **The Dai: Or the Tai and Their Architecture and Customs in South China.** Bangkok: DD Books, 1992.

Livingston, Carol. **Gecko Tails: A Journey Through Cambodia.** London:Wiedenfield & Nicholson, 1996.

Lohitkun, Teeraparb. **Tai in Southeast Asia.** Bangkok: Manager Publishing, 1995.

Ly, Van Son. **Vietnamese Cookery Book.** Dong Nai: Dong Nai Publishing, 1995.

Mabbett, Ian, and David Chandler. **The Khmers.** Chiang Mai: Silkworm Books, 1996.

McCarthy, James. **Surveying and Exploring in Siam.** 1990. Reprint, Bangkok: White Lotus, 1994.

McDermott, Nancie. **Real Thai.** San Francisco: Chronicle, 1992.

Moura, J. **Le Royaume du Cambodge.** Paris: Ernest Leroup, 1883.

Ngo, Bich, and Gloria Zimmerman. **The Classic Cuisine of Vietnam.** 1979. Reprint, New York: New American Library, 1986.

Norman, Jill. **The Complete Book of Spices.** London: Dorling Kindersley, 1990.

Osborne, Milton. **River Road to China: The Search for the Source of the Mekong, 1866–73.** New York: Grove-Atlantic, 1999.

Passmore, Jackie. **The Encyclopedia of Asian Food and Cooking.** New York: Hearst, 1991.

Phia, Sing. **Traditional Recipes of Laos.** Edited by Alan Davidson and Jennifer Davidson. 1981. Reprint, Totnes: Prospect Books, 1995.

Routhier, Nicole. **The Foods of Vietnam.** New York: Stewart Tabori & Chang, 1989.

Sargent, Inge. **Twilight over Burma: My Life as a Shan Princess.** Chiang Mai: Silkworm Books, 1994.

Schwartz, Oded. **Preserving.** New York: DK Publishing, 1996.

Sepul, Rene, and Cici Olsson. **Laos.** Liège: Éditions Antoine Degive, 1997.

Simonds, Nina. **China's Food.** New York: HarperPerennial, 1991.

Sluiter, Liesbeth. **The Mekong Currency.** Bangkok: PER/TERRA, 1992.

Snacks of Thailand. Bangkok: The Color Books, n.d.

Sodsook, Victor, with Theresa Volpe Larsen and Byron Larsen. **True Thai.** New York: Morrow, 1995.

Sonakul, Sibpan. **Everyday Siamese Dishes.** 8th ed. Bangkok: Prachand Press, 1979.

Steinberg, David J. **Cambodia.** New Haven: Human Resource Area Files, 1959.

Swain, Jon. **River of Time.** London: Heinemann, 1995.

Trankell, Ing Britt. **On the Road in Laos: An Anthropological Study of Road Construction and Rural Communities.** Uppsala: Uppsala Research Reports in Cultural Anthropology, 1993.

———. **Cooking Care and Domestication, a Culinary Ethnography of the Tai Yong, Northern Thailand.** Uppsala: Acta Universitatis Upsaliensis, 1995.

Vincent, Frank. **The Land of the White Elephant.** 1873. Reprint, Bangkok: White Lotus, 1988.

Yee, Kenny, and Catherine Gordon. **Thai Hawker Food.** Bangkok: BPS Publications, n.d.

GUIDEBOOKS

Booz, Patrick R. *An Illustrated Guide to Yunnan*. Hong Kong: The Guidebook Company, 1989.

Buckley, Michael et al. *China*. Hawthorn: Lonely Planet, 1994.

Colet, John, and Joshua Eliot. *Cambodia Handbook*. Bath: Footprint, 1997.

Cummings, Joe. *Laos*. Hawthorn: Lonely Planet, 1998.

———. *Thailand*. Hawthorn: Lonely Planet, 1999.

Storey, Robert, and Daniel Robinson. *Vietnam*. Hawthorn: Lonely Planet, 1995.

ARTICLES

Evans, Grant. "Is Anyone Ever That *Roi* Percent? The Sinicised Tai." *Tai Culture*, June 1997.

Nathaloang, Siriporn. "Thai Creation Myths: Reflections of Tai Relations and Tai Cultures." *Tai Culture*, June 1997.

O'Neill, Thomas. "The Mekong: A Haunted River's Season of Peace." *National Geographic*, February 1993.

Peltier, Anatole-Roger. "Sujavanna, des Tai Khun." *Le Journal magazine des pays du Mekong*, March 1997.

ACKNOWLEDGMENTS

Our thanks to many people all over the Mekong region whose names we don't know, from market vendors to village cooks to fishermen and farmers. In addition, our heartfelt thanks and appreciation go out to all of the following people:

For information and help in Yunnan, and also in matters Chinese, in Menghan, Mae (Yu Jiao) and her husband, Ai Non, and their daughters and extended family; Hillary Buttrick and Ted Lo of Toronto; Barbara Tropp of San Francisco; and Catherine Bonnet. Special thanks to Oran Feild for sharing so much.

In the Shan State, and for information, advice, and help in matters Tai Koen, Tai Yai, and Burmese, we thank, first, the many people we cannot safely name in Yaunshwe, Kalaw, and Mandalay, and among the Karen on the Burmese border; thanks also to Shieng Wanpen Tanped and Chad and their extended family in Mae Sai; and to Joe Cummings.

In Laos, and for insights into the cuisine, culture, and history of Laos and of the tribal peoples in the region, special thanks to Sivone and Sousath Phenasy and their children, Melissa and Peter. Our thanks to Southiphone and Viradesa and family; Nupiit Sairaj and her friends; the staff at the Sisawad guest house in Vientiane; Dr. Leo von Geusau of SAEMP; Yann Guezel; Cas Besselink; Carol Cassidy of Lao Textiles in Vientiane, and her family and friends; Cici Olsson and Rene Sepul; Michael Hodgson of Raintree Books in Vientiane; Sarah Strawbridge; and the Leuang Thong family of the Vientiane grocery in Toronto.

In Thailand, and for help with matters Thai, Nupiit Sairaj and Yigal Kosziuk; Niyana in That Panom; John at Hollywood Film in Bangkok; Sujitra Pornprasit; Su-Mei Lu; Nancie McDermott; and Steve Martin. Special thanks to Oie and Supote Issarankura and their extended family; and special thanks also to Saratwadee Asasupakit of Chiang Mai.

In Cambodia, and for insights into Khmer cuisine, culture, and history, special thanks to Haeng Ly in Siam Reap, and Sao Pheha in Phnom Penh. Thanks also to the staff at the Hotel Indochine; Sandy DeCock; Paul Richard Fife; Nadsa Perry of Elephant Walk and Carambola restaurants in Boston.

In Vietnam, and for insights into Vietnamese cuisine, culture, and history, special thanks to Rocky Dang; and thanks also to Vui and Hanh in Cantho; Bich; Anh; Lulu; and all at the Pho Hung restaurant in Toronto.

In North America we have been helped and supported by friends in many places and with many different interests, including: Pat Adrian; Antonia Allegra; Wendy Baylor; Michael Buckley; Helen and Edith Buie; Greg Drescher at Greystone; Don Fry; Rajan Gill; Pat Holtz; Trisha Jackson; Nancy Jenkins; Cassandra Kobayashi; Deb Olson; Jim Poros; Ethan Poskanzer; Sandy Price and Jim Laxer; Bill Reynolds of the Culinary Institute of America; Tina Ujlaki; Kim Yorio. Thank you.

Many thanks to Cassandra Kobayashi and Wendy Baylor for thoughtful recipe testing and suggestions over several years; and to Dawn Woodward for test-driving our recipes at large dinner parties.

Special thanks to cherished friend and consultant in all matters food, Dina Fayerman, and to Liv Blumer, literary agent extraordinaire.

In transforming a ragged manuscript into a beautiful book, we are indebted to Judith Sutton for copyediting; Deborah Weiss Geline, Dania Davey, Nancy Murray, and Trish Boczkowski at Artisan; Rodica Prato who drew the map and language tree; designers Cliff Morgan and David Hughes at Level; photographer Richard Jung and assistant Sarah Kehoe; food stylist Sandra Cook and assistant Ann Tonai; and prop stylist Sara Slavin. In Canada, big thanks to Sarah Davies, Anne Collins, and Sharon Klein at Random House Canada.

At Artisan, editor and publisher Ann Bramson is the one person who from the beginning to the end worries over this book, *imagines* it a book, orchestrates work, lends clothes, shops for yo-yos. Once again, thanks, Ann.

INDEX

Numerals in italics indicate photographs.

A

Akha people, 9, *49*, *54*, *55*, *77*, *119*, *127*, *263*

alcoholic beverages, 307, 314

algae, dried (freshwater), *164*, 165, 321

alimentary paste noodles, *114*, 319

am peuhl, 323

anchovies

    fillets, 313

    Issaan Salsa with Anchovies, 38

Angkor Wat, *228*, 229

anise. *See* star anise

appetizers

    Beef and Lettuce Roll-ups, 268

    Chiang Mai Carpaccio, 230

    Classic Vietnamese Spring Rolls,
        274–275, *277*

    Dai Beef Tartare with Pepper-Salt, 230

    Green-Wrapped Flavor Bundles, *264*, *269*

    Grilled Eggplant Salad, 84

    Hot and Spicy Leaf Wraps, *264–265*, *266*

    Steamed Pork Dumplings, *270–271*

    Vietnamese Baked Cinnamon Pâté, 259

apples, Vietnamese Green Papaya Salad, *4*, 75

aquatic morning glory, 324

architecture

    Dai (Tai Lu), *140*

    of Vientiane, *178*

Aromatic Jasmine Rice, 90, *240*

aromatic jasmine rice. *See* jasmine rice;
    leftover jasmine rice

Aromatic Lemongrass Patties, 251

Aromatic Minced Pork, Shan Style, 250

Aromatic Roasted Rice Powder, 309

Aromatic Steamed Fish Curry, 180

Asian bananas, Bananas in
    Coconut Cream, 298

Asian basil, 313

    Cambodian Hot Pot, 222–223

    Duck in Green Curry Paste, 211–212

Jungle Curry, 246

    Quick Red Chicken Curry, 210

    Stir-fried Chicken with Holy Basil, 202

    Vietnamese Chicken Salad with
        Rau Ram, 197

    Vietnamese Herb and Salad Plate, 68

Asian eggplants, *163*, 316

    The Best Eggplant Dish Ever, 159

    Grilled Eggplant Salad, 84

    Jungle Curry, 246

    Khmer Chicken *Samla'* with Coconut Milk,
        204–205, *208*

    Quick Red Chicken Curry, 210

Asian sesame oil, 322

asparagus beans, 324. *See also* yard-long
    beans

avocado shakes, 303

B

babah, 94

bac ha, 313

bai gaprow, 313

bai horapa, 313

bai jiu, 307, 312

bai menglak, 313

Bai people, 9, *40*, *41*

bai toey hom, 320

Baked Bass with Spicy Rub, 184, *185*

bamboo steamers, 91, 98, *99*

bamee, 319

banana chiles, 314

    Chile-Vinegar Sauce, 117

    Grilled Chile Salsa, Shan Style, 45

banana leaf wrappers

    Aromatic Steamed Fish Curry, 180

    Baked Bass with Spicy Rub, 184, *185*

    Dai Grilled Stuffed Fish, 189

    steaming in, 180

    substitute for, 184

bananas

    Bananas in Coconut Cream, 298

    bananes flambées, 299

    Classic Banana Shake, 303

    Fried Bananas, 299

    overripe, storing, 303

Bananas in Coconut Cream, 298

bananes flambées, 299

banh gan, 302

banh mi, 287

banh pho, 319

banh trang, 321

banh xeo, 280–281

Basic Southeast Asian Broth, 50

Basic Sticky Rice, 91

basil. *See* Asian basil; holy basil; sweet basil

bass

    Baked Bass with Spicy Rub, 184, *185*

    Dai Grilled Stuffed Fish, 189

    Lao Hot and Sour Soup with Fish, 57

Bayon, *217*

bean curd. *See* pressed tofu; silky tofu; tofu

beans

    mung. *See* mung beans

    winged (asparagus), 324. *See also*
        yard-long beans

    yam, 317

    yard-long. *See* yard-long beans

bean sprouts, 313

    Ginger Chicken Noodle Soup, 130–131

    Morning Market Noodles, *119*, 138–139

    Pad Thai Classic Stir-fried Noodles,
        124–125, *126*

    Pickled Bean Sprout Salad, 85

    Rice Paper Roll-ups with Shrimp and
        Herbs, *176*, *177*

    Rice Soup, Khmer Style, 94

    soybean, 313

    Vietnamese Chicken Salad with
        Rau Ram, 197

    Vietnamese Herb and Salad Plate, 68

    Vietnamese Noodle Combos, 131

    Vietnamese Savory Crepes, 280–281

bean threads. *See* cellophane noodles

beef, 215–231

    Beef and Lettuce Roll-ups, 268

    Cambodian Hot Pot, 222–223